John Howard Yoder

John Howard Yoder

Radical Theologian

Edited by
J. Denny Weaver

with
Earl Zimmerman,
Zachary J. Walton,
Gerald J. Mast,
Ted Grimsrud,
and Glen Harold Stassen

Foreword by
Marva J. Dawn

Afterword by
Lisa Schirch

CASCADE Books • Eugene, Oregon

JOHN HOWARD YODER
Radical Theologian

Copyright © 2014 J. Denny Weaver. All rights reserved. Except for brief quotations in critical publications or reviews, no part of this book may be reproduced in any manner without prior written permission from the publisher. Write: Permissions, Wipf and Stock Publishers, 199 W. 8th Ave., Suite 3, Eugene, OR 97401.

Cascade Books
An Imprint of Wipf and Stock Publishers
199 W. 8th Ave., Suite 3
Eugene, OR 97401

www.wipfandstock.com

ISBN 13: 978-1-62564-585-2

Cataloging-in-Publication data:

John Howard Yoder : radical theologian / edited by J. Denny Weaver ; with Earl Zimmerman, Zachary J. Walton, Gerald J. Mast, Ted Grimsrud, and Glen Harold Stassen ; foreword by Marva J. Dawn ; afterword by Lisa Schirch.

xviii+ 420 p. ; 23 cm. Includes bibliographical references and index.

ISBN 13: 978-1-62564-585-2

1. Yoder, John Howard. I. Weaver, J. Denny, 1941–. II. Zimmerman, Earl, 1950–. III. Walton, Zachary J. IV. Mast, Gerald J, 1965–. V. Grimsrud, Ted, 1954–. VI. Stassen, Glen Harold, 1936–2014. VII. Dawn, Marva J. VIII. Schirch, Lisa. IX. Title.

BX8143.Y59 W44 2014

Manufactured in the U.S.A.

Revised Standard Version of the Bible, copyright 1952 [2nd ed., 1971] by the Division of Christian Education of the National Council of the Churches of Christ in the United States of America. Used by permission. All rights reserved.

New Revised Standard Version of the Bible, copyright 1989, Division of Christian Education of the National Council of the Churches of Christ in the United States of America. Used by permission. All rights reserved.

Scriptures quotations taken from the New English Bible, copyright © Cambridge University Press and Oxford University Press 1961, 1970. All rights reserved.

Last update: November 6, 2014

For our students
and all others
whose lives have been profoundly reoriented and shaped
by John Howard Yoder, radical theologian

Contents

List of Contributors | ix

Foreword—Marva J. Dawn | xi

Preface—J. Denny Weaver | xv

Introduction—*J. Denny Weaver* | 1

Part One: The Orientation of John Howard Yoder's Theology

1   Christology: From the Root—*J. Denny Weaver* | 27

Part Two: Sources of John Howard Yoder's Theology

2   Sixteenth-Century Anabaptist Roots
     —*Earl Zimmerman* | 89

3   Harold S. Bender, Anabaptist Vision, and the Goshen School—*Zachary J. Walton* | 117

4   Oscar Cullmann and Radical Discipleship
     —*Earl Zimmerman* | 145

5   Deconstructing Karl Barth—*Gerald J. Mast* | 167

Part Three: Extending John Howard Yoder's Theology

6   Jesus to Paul—*Ted Grimsrud* | 187

7   The Free Church as Body Politics
     —*Earl Zimmerman* | 207

Contents

8   Pacifism as a Way of Knowing—*Gerald J. Mast* | 226

9   A Nonviolent Public Ethic—*Glen Harold Stassen* | 244

10 Interfaith Conversations: Judaism to Islam to Hinduism
    —*J. Denny Weaver* and *Earl Zimmerman* | 268

11 A Model in Conversation with Black and Evangelical Theology
    —*J. Denny Weaver* and *Gerald J. Mast* | 294

12 Reflections from a Chagrined "Yoderian" in Face
    of His Sexual Violence—*Ted Grimsrud* | 334

13 Sin and Failure in Anabaptist Theology
    —*Gerald J. Mast* | 351

Conclusion—*J. Denny Weaver* | 371

Afterword: To the Next Generation of Pacifist Theologians
—*Lisa Schirch* | 377

Bibliography | 397

Index | 413

Contributors

MARVA J. DAWN, theologian, author, speaker, Christians Equipped for Ministry, Southwestern Washington State

TED GRIMSRUD, Professor of Theology and Peace Studies, Eastern Mennonite University, Harrisonburg, Virginia

GERALD J. MAST, Professor of Communication, Bluffton University, Bluffton, Ohio

LISA SCHIRCH, Director of Human Security, Alliance for Peacebuilding, Washington, DC, and Research Professor, Center for Justice and Peacebuilding, Eastern Mennonite University, Harrisonburg, Virginia

GLEN HAROLD STASSEN, Lewis B. Smedes Professor of Christian Education, Fuller Theological Seminary, Pasadena, California

ZACHARY J. WALTON, Assistant Professor of Communication, Bluffton University, Bluffton Ohio

J. DENNY WEAVER, Professor Emeritus of Religion, Bluffton University, Bluffton, Ohio

EARL ZIMMERMAN, pastor, Northern Virginia Mennonite Church, Fairfax, Virginia

Foreword

What a tremendous gift J. Denny Weaver and his friends have given the Christian community with this book! Though John Howard Yoder's many diverse interests and writings cannot be classified or forced into a unified whole, Weaver and colleagues have observed the fountainhead and central core of all Yoder's labor, a perception that is not found in any other study of Yoder's work. Weaver knew from his early participation in a class with Yoder and from his later analysis that the methodology of the latter's calling as an Anabaptist scholar was to take the narrative of Jesus into every new or different context and to use the language of that context to express or expand the narrative of Jesus.

Because of that fundamental insight, the authors of this book can more deeply understand in Part Two the sources of Yoder's theological growth in his formative, college, and graduate school years. Of special interest to me were the chapters in this section on Oscar Cullmann and Karl Barth because the authors of these analyses show how Yoder was able to learn from those European professors while going beyond them in many important ways. Accordingly, the story was frequently told, when I was a doctoral student under Yoder at Notre Dame, that Barth had said that John Yoder was the smartest man he had ever met. That was no surprise to us graduate apprentices because we were frequently overwhelmed by Yoder's brilliance.

Part Three of this book is equally intriguing because its authors demonstrate how Yoder could amplify his central focus on the narrative of Jesus to address many other topics of present theological, political, or social interest. Most importantly, not only was Yoder able to make this extension easily, but his clear methodology enabled him to teach many others to do the same kinds of expansion.

Foreword

As Yoder's graduate assistant, I was able to see this ability readily because he taught the R.O.T.C. students a course titled "The Legality and Morality of War." Just as with his book *When War Is Unjust*, Yoder, a committed pacifist, was able to assist those who did not share his passion to refrain as much as possible from unnecessary violence.

The importance of this third section of the book is illustrated by the fact that I disagree with Yoder's replacement of Trinitarian language for the sake of dialogue with Jews, Muslims, and Hindus. However, Yoder's imperative for discussion is so powerful that, if I want to maintain my use of the vocabulary, this chapter makes clear I must also fulfill the responsibility to find other means to make conversation with "the other" possible.

Finally, a word must be said about the necessity of dealing with John Howard Yoder's personal failures. Perhaps because I am physically handicapped, I did not have to deal with Yoder's "experiments" with friendship intimacy, except for one typically-Yoderian-clumsy attempt to console me once when I was deeply discouraged. I have three things to say in anticipation of these chapters. First of all, I write "clumsy" because Yoder was too brilliant to know how to relate to us "normal folk." Since I regularly welcomed members of the theology department at Notre Dame to my apartment for dinner, occasionally John would (falteringly) ask me to invite him and Annie over for dinner along with a new professor or a guest in town so that they could get to know each other. My point, first, is that part of John's problems was that he was, by personal deficiency, awkward.

Second, John abided by my firm "No" when he tried sympathetically to console me, even as I have been led to believe that he obeyed (a typical Yoderian response) when the Mennonite correction committee took him through the long process of dealing with his conviction on sexual charges. I know that this is no comfort to those who were hurt by his previous behavior, but at least it gives us a more positive basis not to let his sexual misconduct interfere with our appreciation of his theological contributions.

Third, I do have enormous compassion for those who were harmed by his "experiments" with intimacy. John was too respected a professor and theologian to reconcile his sinful behavior with his teaching and writing. I do pray that the chapters in this book will help to bring healing and forgiveness for John to those who were afflicted and some understanding to those puzzled by the depth of human sin in such a non-violent advocate as John Howard Yoder.

Marva J. Dawn
The day before "Reign of Christ" Sunday

Preface

This book joins what by now is a growing cottage industry of books on the work and the legacy of John Howard Yoder. As the Introduction explains in more detail, the book was stimulated by my growing uneasiness that the portrayal of Yoder's theology in the books and many articles that appeared in recent years did not reflect the understanding of his theology that I have had for more than a quarter century. My uneasiness grew to the point where I could not avoid acting on it. I developed a draft of the introduction, along with a suggested outline of chapters and contributors, and showed it to colleagues that I knew shared my uneasiness. The product, in approximately the form in hand, quickly gelled. Authors present in this volume all rapidly accepted an invitation to contribute to a book that put on display Yoder's understanding of Christology and the way that from there he could address any theological or ethical issue.

Although the authors of this volume have been profoundly influenced by Yoder's theology, they are not simply clones of Yoder. Several essays go farther than Yoder did, drawing out implications of his thought, or going through doors that he only opened.

The majority of writers in this volume had at least nodding acquaintance with John Howard Yoder in person. A few knew him rather well. Experiences with Yoder in person varied from warm affirmation to, at times, seeming indifference. Whatever those memories, all authors in this volume are profoundly grateful for Yoder's theological influence and welcomed the opportunity to contribute to this volume on his theology and its legacy.

The authors of this volume are also aware of Yoder's hurtful sexual conduct with numerous women. The final two chapters of the book deal specifically with that painful dimension of Yoder's story, which reminds us that Yoder was a fallible human being, even as this book acknowledges our great appreciation for his theological influence on our thinking, an influence already significant before we learned of his hurtful conduct.

Preface

I have done significant editing and shaping of each essay in this volume. Although multiple authors were involved, my goal was to edit all contributions into a parallel format and to shape them into a developing argument that would build throughout the book. The intent was to produce a book that was not just another collection of essays on John Howard Yoder but would be a unified and integrated book that was more than the sum of its parts. Readers will judge the success of this endeavor.

Given the way that this book was put together, I owe a great deal to the other authors who participated in this project. Thank you Ted Grimsrud, Gerald Mast, Glen Stassen, Zachary Walton, and Earl Zimmerman for our many email exchanges and for allowing me the privilege of editing and massaging your materials so that they contributed to a developing picture of John Howard Yoder's theological outlook. I am also grateful to Earl and Gerald for their wise council when I solicited advice during the conceptual stage of the project. I was well aware of Earl's book *Practicing the Politics of Jesus*, and he was interim pastor at my congregation of Madison Mennonite Church when I first raised the idea for this book over one of our frequent lunches. Gerald has been my frequent collaborator on many projects during our years as colleagues at Bluffton University and continuing unabated since my retirement from teaching. I am grateful to others who read parts of the manuscript and/or offered comments and encouragement—to Ron Adams for his helpful and supportive comments as well as his editing of the Introduction and chapter 1, to Fulco van Hulst for his continued interest and encouragement in my work on John Howard Yoder, to David W. Shenk for his insightful comments and contribution to chapter 10. I have had conversations too numerous to mention with people who asked what I was working on. When I have described the perspective that drives this book to colleagues, I was often greeted with responses of "it's about time," and "that's what I always thought." In other words, my interpretation of Yoder's theology vouchsafed their own reading of his work, and they are eager to see this book in print. I cannot adequately express my gratitude for the affirmation that comes from such conversations, as well as from other pieces of very useful advice that I have received. But theology is always in process. Thus I am grateful to Lisa Schirch for the Afterword, which introduces the next stage of developing peace theology in the wake of John Howard Yoder. As always I am eternally grateful to my wife Mary, who put up with a lot to allow me to focus on this manuscript.

Preface

Those who have written for this book have been or are professors, and some have pastoral experience as well. Through the years, our students and parishioners have often expressed thanks for being introduced to the work of John Howard Yoder. The book is dedicated to these students and to all others who, in spite of his acknowledged failures, have in many ways been profoundly shaped and reoriented by John Howard Yoder's radical, Jesus-centered theology and social ethics. May their numbers increase. May this legacy continue.

J. Denny Weaver, Fall 2013
Madison, Wisconsin

Introduction

J. Denny Weaver

The interest in John Howard Yoder's theology and ethics keeps growing. The book in hand joins an already swiftly flowing stream. The waters are also somewhat choppy and eddy-filled, with writers from several schools of thought and analytical perspectives promising to explain Yoder's theology better or to highlight a hitherto unexamined relationship or to fit Yoder's thought into one or more predefined boxes. This book promises no less. It too brings a new perspective to understanding Yoder's methodology and theology. But this book also promises a bit more. Its goal is not merely to provide one more interpretation to set alongside others, but actually to go beyond and supersede the existing interpretations with the most representative view to date of Yoder's approach to theology and ethics. That claim requires some explaining.

Yoder's publication of *The Politics of Jesus*[1] in 1972 "rearranged the landscape of theological ethics in the last third of the twentieth century."[2] When *Christianity Today* conducted a poll to identify influential books of the twentieth century, *The Politics of Jesus* came in at number five.[3] In a way that seemed new to theologians and ethicists but that Yoder considered an old view, his book argued that the life and teaching of Jesus were central and normative for Christian ethics. Since it concerned Jesus,

---

1. Yoder, *Politics of Jesus* (1972). The book was reprinted in 1994 with an epilogue to each chapter as Yoder, *Politics of Jesus* (1994). Citations in this book will follow the pagination of the second edition.
2. Zimmerman, *Practicing the Politics*, 23.
3. "Books of the Century," 92.

whom all Christians profess, the book was intrinsically ecumenical, that is, addressed to all Christians. And among Christians of all stripes—mainstream Protestants, Evangelicals, or Catholics—discussions about peace theology took on new dimensions. Whether we had previously identified with a peace church or not, Yoder taught us to think differently. How Yoder the seminal writer taught us to think differently is one particular focus of this book.

The chapters here display an understanding of John Howard Yoder that makes visible the christological outlook that underlies *The Politics of Jesus*, which he posed as a challenge to all Christians, and from which he could address any theological or ethical issue. Awareness of this underlying theological outlook is lacking in many treatments of Yoder's thought.

The distinct perspective presented here is a product of my own interaction with Yoder's thought in conversation with colleagues and scholars, a claim that every writer on Yoder can make. What distinguishes my perspective, however, is that I did not follow the most common, recent path to interaction with Yoder's thought. My route was and is uncommon, even rare.

My serious encounter with the thought of John Howard Yoder began in 1974 in my first year of teaching. That year I filled in for a professor on leave at Goshen College before moving to what is now Bluffton University, where I spent the remainder of my teaching career. My graduate school work was in church history, with a concentration in sixteenth-century reformation theology. But like most faculty in small, liberal arts colleges, I was asked to teach a course outside my area of study. It was a survey course in Christian theology, covering the standard topics such as Christology, Trinity, atonement, the church, and more.

The first question I asked my faculty colleagues was whether there was an Anabaptist or a Mennonite perspective on these issues and doctrines and their classic creedal formulations. In that epoch, it seemed as though one could conjure up an Anabaptist perspective on anything, and I expected to be referred to an article or two that would fill me in. To my surprise, the answers I received to my question were various versions of "I don't know."[4] In a sense, my career since then has been a long-running search for an answer to that original question. Not surprisingly, the

---

4. This was the epoch in which a humor book could joke that "the Academic Muppie," one of the varieties of Mennonite Urban Professionals, often tends to "work at writing an article or book on 'Anabaptism/Mennonites and Anything.'" Lesher, *Muppie Manual*, 26, 27.

formulation of the question itself has evolved considerably since I first posed it. That evolution is one of many understandings that I owe to John Howard Yoder.

I had no courses in systematic theology in graduate school. As a resource for my first experience in teaching theology, I turned to the one Mennonite theologian with whom I was most familiar, namely John Howard Yoder. In seminary some years earlier, I had encountered Yoder's theology in the course called "Preface to Theology." I retrieved my notes from that course and prepared my own lecture notes using material gleaned from Yoder's lectures, which traced theological developments from the New Testament through the Council of Chalcedon. Needless to say, when the informally published version of the *Preface* lectures became available,[5] I was delighted and immediately put it to use in my course preparations.

Among interesting learnings introduced to me by Yoder's lectures that became *Preface* were that the titles used for Jesus in the New Testament were more varied and had different meanings than when later used with reference to Nicea and Chalcedon; that theologizing about Jesus in the New Testament began with observations about the narrative of Jesus and was carried on with a wide variety of expressions; and that the doctrine of the Trinity was not taught per se in the New Testament but was developed later as an intellectual answer to questions raised but not answered in the New Testament. I soon came to realize that Yoder was allowing us to see that the classic creedal formulas were neither simply summaries of New Testament teaching nor transcendently true statements about Jesus. Rather he was pointing to the particular, historical character of the formulas and showing that they emerged from a particular context. A few short years later, I would learn to say that Yoder had "relativized" the classic formulas.

Thus my introduction to John Howard Yoder was first of all not to Yoder as ethicist but as *theologian*. And what was clear to me already in that early epoch was that Yoder as theologian was not merely repeating and explaining the standard or classic statements of Christology and Trinity. He was opening the possibility of using other language and categories to express the meaning of Jesus as depicted in the New Testament. He was putting on display his conviction that the basis for Christian belief and

---

5. Yoder, *Preface* (1981). This writing was edited posthumously and published as Yoder, *Preface* (2002).

practice was based, not primarily in the classic creeds and confessions of Christendom, but in the Jesus of the Gospel narratives. This Jesus was the basis for Yoder's theologizing and his ethics.

Meanwhile, observing Yoder's historical approach to Christology led me to ask whether there is a way to view Christology specific to the believers church. I was the primary organizer of a believers church conference at Bluffton University in October 1980 around the theme "Is there a Believers' Church Christology?" John Howard Yoder gave the keynote address, which was later published in expanded and revised form as the essay, "But We Do See Jesus."[6] This essay sketched an approach to a believers church Christology that began already in the New Testament and could bypass the classic categories while nonetheless addressing their concerns for a "high" Christology.

For the conference of October 1980, Yoder made copies of the address available. Following the conference, copies were distributed with a Postscript and a Postface. The Postface noted that the theme of the conference "was made important" by unresolved issues in Mennonite institutions and journals. One of these was his own "Preface to theology" lectures, which had taken "a narrative and relativizing approach" to the "development of early Christian dogma, with special reference to the development of christological creedal statements." Yoder also wrote that some "star performances" had dominated the conference, and the questions of the conference had not been "brought forward very far."[7]

Yoder's comment about his own "relativizing" of the context of the classic creedal statements displays clearly what I had observed in my use of the *Preface* lectures.[8] In the lectures, he showed that the creedal pro-

---

6. First published as Yoder, "But We Do," *Foundations*. Reprinted as Yoder, "But We Do," *Priestly Kingdom*. Most recently this essay was reprinted as Yoder, "But We Do," *Pacifist*. Citations in this book will refer to the versions in both Yoder's *Priestly Kingdom* and *Pacifist Way of Knowing*.

7. Yoder, "That Household We Are," 9. Since publication of the revised version in *Priestly Kingdom*, the version cited here is no longer available. A printout in my possession contains the postscript here quoted.

Yoder was correct that the conference did not really address the theme. I also recognized that lack. However, even though I was the organizer of the conference, I was still early in my career, and I lacked the courage to challenge presenters such as those Yoder called "star" performers to address the question specifically. In later years, I have often wished that I could replay that conference and vigorously push the theme!

8. The editors of the published version of the *Preface* lectures have this relativizing in mind when they write that Yoder had "deeply imbibed" "mid-twentieth-century prejudices against the 'mythological' character of Nicene Christianity." They believe

nouncements were a particular kind of philosophical answer within a particular, historical context, which raised the obvious question whether there might be different answers in another context. "But We Do See Jesus" did in fact set out a different kind of answer in the context of modern cultural relativism.

But equally important, I could read Yoder's other work from the perspective of what I had come to understand about Yoder as theologian. *The Politics of Jesus* was more than an independent statement of ethics based on the New Testament version of Jesus. Its idea of discipleship to Jesus, the assertion of the normativeness of Jesus for ethics, was a product of the same (non-creedal) theological understanding visible in *Preface*, which produced the relativizing of the classic creeds and put on display the ethical dimension they lacked.[9] *The Original Revolution*,[10] which appeared the year before *The Politics of Jesus*, was more than a display of the nonviolence of Jesus. It reflected Yoder's view of Jesus based on the New Testament rather than on the classic creeds, and exemplified Yoder's assumption that virtually any issue could be addressed from the perspective of Jesus from the New Testament. His christological essay, "But We Do See Jesus," was most certainly not a "provocative, and somewhat postmodern" statement of or link to "classic orthodox theology," as has been claimed.[11] In fact the essay used five New Testament models to demonstrate how to do Christology across cultural lines without simply repeating the classic formulations, and included a suggestion for using the narrative of Jesus in the recent, contemporary context of cultural relativism.

---

that had Yoder known about developments in patristic scholarship since he wrote the *Preface* lectures, "the text would undoubtedly have looked quite different." Yoder, *Preface* (2002), 26. I disagree with their assessment, which is in effect a defense of the classic formulas. Even if current patristic scholarship presents a different picture than the one current when Yoder wrote these lectures, patristic studies still describes a context that is not that of the New Testament. Yoder's point about recognizing historical particularity and context is still appropriate, and he would still have "relativized" the classic statements. A longer discussion of these comments appears in chapter 1, note 91.

9. For a confirmation by Yoder of this observation that *Politics of Jesus* was more than a statement of ethics and was in fact a theological statement that could address many issues, note his response when it was suggested that he should write a contemporary work on Anabaptist theology. Yoder replied that he had already done so. It was his book *The Politics of Jesus*. See Zimmerman, *Practicing the Politics*, 166 n. 10.

10. Yoder, *Original Revolution*.

11. For this designation, see Nation, "Politics Regarding," 39–40, 51 n. 9.

Alongside the christological essay, the other chapters in *Priestly Kingdom* had a coherency not visible to those who knew it only as Yoder's book that followed *The Politics of Jesus*. The well-known essay, "The Constantinian Sources of Western Social Ethics,"[12] was not a stand alone item. It was first printed in *Missionalia* in 1976. Along with "The Disavowal of Constantine,"[13] another major statement of the Constantinian theme also written in 1976, this essay would have been part of Yoder's thinking as he wrote the *Preface* lectures.[14] It seems clear that Yoder's understanding of what Constantine symbolized was a major dimension of the particular context for his historical treatment of Christology in *Preface*. One might even argue that a major but overlooked contribution of Yoder's discussion of Constantine was to raise awareness of the fact that theology always reflects a particular context. Similarly, statements in *Priestly Kingdom* about hermeneutics or the authority of tradition or the kingdom of God as social ethics would also all presuppose the christological, theological preparation available in the *Preface* lectures. In other words, the essays of a collection such as *Priestly Kingdom* or the later *For the Nations*[15] are not as fragmented as sometimes thought but reflect a theological coherency when they are read with awareness of the Jesus-centered, christocentric norm of Yoder the theologian gained from *Preface*.

The import of my journey with Yoder through *Preface* and *Priestly Kingdom* and eventually to *The Politics of Jesus* was to learn that the New Testament narrative of the life and work of Jesus was the basis for theological development and the criterion for evaluating ethics. Thus I observed that for Yoder, theology that used the narrative of Jesus as norm was in conversation with the classic christological categories but not beholden to them for answers in our contemporary context. This theology derived from the narrative was posed as an alternative to standard orthodoxy, an alternative that made living in the story an integral and

12. Yoder, "Constantinian Sources."

13. Reprinted from the 1975/1976 edition of *Tantur Yearbook* as Yoder, "Disavowal of Constantine."

14. That statement is far from a conjecture. Already in 1954 Yoder was writing about "the Constantinian heresy." "Peace without Eschatology: The Constantinian Heresy" was the title of a section of a 1954 lecture. The lecture was subsequently published in a pamphlet of the *Concern* series, and then as chapter 3, "If Christ Is Truly Lord," in Yoder, *Original Revolution*, 55–90, and with the original title as Yoder, "Peace without Eschatology?" 143–67.

15. Yoder, *For the Nations*.

inseparable dimension of theology about Jesus.[16] Yoder did not always stress the alternative nature of his theologizing, and he could also show how to reform orthodox theology from within.[17] But at the same time, the essay "But We Do See Jesus" among others makes clear the possibility of theology not beholden to the classic categories.

Few references to Yoder's *Preface* lectures appear in literature about him or his work. For example, Mark Thiessen Nation's biographical work on Yoder mentions *Preface* only twice, and those without analysis;[18] and the essays in recent collections barely acknowledge *Preface*. It is possible to develop reasonable conjectures why Yoder's *Preface* lectures have not figured prominently in analyses of his thought.[19] One reason is perhaps that scholars took him at his word that he was not doing systematic theology and he refused to write a systematic theology. "If you write a systematic theology," he once warned me, "you will end up defending your system rather than talking about Jesus." More significantly, *Preface*

---

16. A clarification from Chris Huebner's analysis of the way Yoder used narrative is important at this point. Huebner argued that while Yoder used narrative, he should not be called a narrative theologian. To privilege narrative in that way would make it a methodological given, a position that Yoder rejected. Huebner, *Precarious Peace*, 49–68.

17. For example, see A. Weaver, "Missionary Christology."

18. Nation, *John Howard Yoder*, 128, 175

19. There are some notable exceptions to this point. Among early treatments of Yoder, A. James Reimer quoted *Preface* when he rejected what he called Yoder's "historical-eschatological (horizontal)" approach in favor of an "ontological (vertical) understanding of the Christ event." Reimer, "Nature and Possibility," 33–55, quote 43. Contra Reimer, Craig Carter, whose work is critiqued in chapter 1, used the *Preface* lectures to argue that Yoder's thought did affirm classic Nicene-Chalcedonian orthodoxy. Carter, *Politics of the Cross*, 113–22, 246. Even as Reimer and Carter used *Preface*, it is interesting to note that both began the theological analysis of Yoder with his *Politics of Jesus* before moving to *Preface*. Alain Epp Weaver's treatment of Yoder and the classic creeds uses *Preface* as he points out that although Yoder posed something of an alternative to the classic creeds, it was certainly compatible with their high christological affirmations. A. Weaver, "Missionary Christology." Among the three recent collections of essays on Yoder referenced in this volume, only Phil Stoltzfus made use of *Preface* in his discussion of how Yoder dealt with the wars of Yahweh. See Stoltzfus, "Nonviolent Jesus." Two recent book-length treatments use *Preface*. Paul Martens' first chapter uses *Preface* in *Heterodox Yoder*. Branson Parler makes significant reference to *Preface* but limits the references primarily to Yoder's comments on Nicea, Trinity and Chalcedon. Since Parler does not follow Yoder's complete New Testament methodology described in chapter 1 to follow, his use of *Preface* misses the contextualizing element of Yoder's treatment. See Parler, *Things Hold Together*. Martens and Parler are both critiqued in chapter 1.

was likely viewed as class lectures and thus not as worthy academic writing, an impression fostered by the fact that Yoder did not seek formal publication. When the lectures did appear in print, it was in an informal format distributed by Associated Mennonite Biblical Seminary (now Anabaptist Mennonite Biblical Seminary) in Elkhart, Indiana, and later by the bookstore at Duke University. Neither the format nor this manner of distribution would garner wide distribution and attract attention to it as a major theological work by Yoder.

Such observations make it hardly surprising that *Preface* has not undergone widespread use among academic writers. Nonetheless, because of my early use of this writing, I have long observed that Yoder was doing theology in a way that reflected a peace church ecclesiology, and that this theology was presupposed if not always acknowledged specifically in his various statements of ethics. My particular path to understand Yoder has given me an element of interpretation that is missing from most of the current analyses and descriptions of his thought.

The book in hand makes clear the importance of understanding Yoder's thought via his methodology and Christology visible in the *Preface* lectures and the essay "But We Do See Jesus." This book contains the first treatment that presents Yoder's approach to theology and ethics in terms of his own methodology, namely to develop theology from the New Testament story of Jesus. With that starting point in view, it is evident that he did not reject the classic creedal statements but it is equally clear that he could envision ways to develop the meaning of Jesus that were not beholden to the classic statements. Chapter 1 describes how Yoder saw the development of Christology from its origins in the New Testament through to the emergence of the classic formulations of Nicea and Chalcedon. In this description, attention to the way christological images developed and to Yoder's methodology is as important as the images themselves. And with this complex of Yoder's methodology and images in plain view, it is apparent that the essay "But We Do See Jesus" is neither an aberration nor a statement of classic orthodoxy. This christological essay is a demonstration and a culmination of the methodology displayed throughout the *Preface* lectures.

Yoder's theology that used the narrative of Jesus as norm was not a narrow or sectarian approach. In fact, he considered it an ecumenical beginning point accessible to all Christians. This ecumenical dimension of a foundation in Jesus Christ appears in a 1964 lecture, in which Yoder noted that the original basis for membership in the World Council of Churches referred not to the Bible or the Trinity or other ancient doctrines but to Jesus Christ.

> The figure of Christ is crucial not only in the context of unity, as a more promising basis of common confession than the comparison of traditional creeds would be, and not only for mission, as one whose human ministry is explicable and can be communicated to man in every culture. Beyond this, the appeal to Christ represents a particular type of confession of truth, a criterion whereby to evaluate faithfulness (and unfaithfulness) within the Christian community.[20]

It is this appeal to the Christ of the New Testament narrative rather than to classic creeds and confessions that was visible to me in the *Preface* lectures.

These observations all make clear that John Howard Yoder's theology and ethics are christocentric, or Jesus-centered. This volume's designation of Yoder as a "radical theologian" is sparked by that description. He was radical in terms of the etymological meaning of the term, which indicates a relationship to the root or origin. Yoder is a radical theologian in that his theology and ethics stem from the root of Christian faith, namely, the Jesus depicted in the New Testament narrative.

Since Yoder eschewed labels for his work, it is hazardous to describe him with a label such as "radical." Even if Yoder might not have used it, an anecdote supports this descriptor. Early in my career I spoke to Yoder about my desire, following his lead, to write an "alternative theology," namely theology that would be an "alternative" to the mainstream theology of Christendom. Yoder cautioned me. Writing an "alternative theology," he said, is a "back-handed way" to establish what you disagree with as the norm. Rather than being an alternative to something, he said, our theology should be "specific to something." And with a faint smile, he suggested, "it should be specific to Jesus." Thus today I designate Yoder a radical theologian because his theology was specific to the New Testament narrative of Jesus, who is the root of Christian faith and practice.

The profound difference made by my distinct route to serious work with Yoder's thought crystallized for me recently, as I read another promise of newness in understanding him, namely the collection of essays

---

20. Yoder, *Original Revolution*, 133; reprinted Yoder, *Royal Priesthood*, 183.

in *The New Yoder*.²¹ In their introduction, editors Peter Dula and Chris Huebner describe an "old Yoder" and a "new Yoder" in Yoderian scholarship. Neither description quite captured my view of Yoder. A brief summary of their two Yoders and a number of other descriptions of Yoder's thought will clarify the significance of the view presented by the book in hand.

The designations by editors Dula and Huebner of "old" and "new" do not describe Yoder's work itself nor depict changes in his work. Rather these designations identify three changes the editors observed in the scholarly analysis and discussions about Yoder's thought. First, what Dula and Huebner call "old" Yoder essays, essays written before the 1990s, often concerned themselves with ethics. These authors worked primarily "within the parameters of the Christian ethics guild as set by Troeltsch, Rauschenbusch, and the Niebuhr brothers." These well-known writers posed the church-sect typology, with pacifism presumed to reside in the faithful but irrelevant sect types. Yoder's best known work, *The Politics of Jesus*, challenged the idea that pacifism was irrelevant, and old Yoder writers debated whether his articulation of peace was sectarian or "whether it is sufficiently realistic to have anything to say to the increasingly 'complex' world of contemporary politics."²² Second, most of the old Yoder discussions were carried on by Mennonites. And much of their concern was whether or not Yoder and Mennonite peace ethics were sectarian. And third, old Yoder essays concerned themselves "in a rather direct and narrow way with questions of peace and nonviolence." Thus as depicted by Dula and Huebner, for old Yoder writers, his thought was presumed to be focused primarily on peace and war issues, and for some writers, "peace tends to function as the tail that wags the theological dog."²³

The "new" Yoder scholarship described by Dula and Huebner poses a marked contrast to "old" Yoder writers. Where old Yoder writers often worried that Yoder was "too conservative" and did not fit within traditional liberal or orthodox categories, new Yoder essays "tend to see him as a radical" who challenged the categories rather than seeking a position within them. Old Yoder writers worried that Yoder's claims that there is no "scratch" from which to begin and that theology always begins with

21. Dula and Huebner, *New Yoder*.
22. Ibid., x–xi.
23. Ibid., xi–xii.

first-century texts left him unable to communicate with the wider world. In contrast, new Yoder writers assume that Yoder is correct about there being no "scratch," and thus they can read Yoder as a postmodern thinker in conversation with other postmodern writers. Further, new Yoder writers find him useful "in exposing the kinds of violence implicit in many of the old liberal orthodoxies." And new Yoder discussions "tend to be conversational or dialogical in their very form," which means that the essays are often part of a larger conversation rather than an exposition of Yoder per se.[24]

A number of other "Yoders" and descriptions of Yoder are also offered in recent scholarship, many of which fall in the "new Yoder" category. In a review of three essay collections referenced in this introduction,[25] David Cramer identified sixteen different Yoders or approaches to Yoder. Although many are compatible, Cramer identified three general approaches to appropriating Yoder. There is the dialogical approach of the essays in *The New Yoder*, which put Yoder in dialogue with other philosophers, ethicists, and theologians. Many of the writings in *Power and Practices* put Yoder in dialogue with himself, while *Radical Ecumenicity* features Yoder in dialogue with the Stone-Campbell denominational tradition.[26]

Other descriptions of Yoder evaluate him with respect to standard orthodoxy. There are claims by Mark Thiessen Nation and Craig Carter that Yoder was orthodox as defined by the classic creeds or that he based his ethics on standard Nicene orthodoxy. Most recently Branson Parler has put Yoder in the orthodox category by labeling him "trinitarian." Such designations have a counterpart, namely an earlier argument by A. James Reimer and the recent argument by Paul Martens that Yoder was heterodox vis-à-vis the classic creeds.[27]

---

24. Ibid., xii–xvi. A different summary of "new" Yoder is found in Huebner, "Work of Inheritance," 24–25. A book-length example of this "conversational or dialogical" form is Sider, *To See History Doxologically*.

25. *The New Yoder*, *Power and Practices*, and *Radical Ecumenicity*.

26. Cramer, "Inheriting Yoder Faithfully."

27. For the claim of orthodoxy, see Carter, *Politics of the Cross*, throughout, summary on 246, and Nation, "Politics Regarding," 39. For the claim of heterodoxy, see Martens, *Heterodox Yoder*, as well as Reimer, "Nature and Possibility." Branson Parler does not call Yoder "orthodox," but his description of Yoder as "trinitarian" and his stress on Yoder's compatibility with Nicea and Chalcedon is an effort to make Yoder acceptable to creedal-oriented Christians who would claim classic orthodoxy. See Parler, *Things Hold Together*.

Yet one more current designation belongs in the discussion, namely that of Yoder as "ad hoc" and "fragmentary" thinker. In his introduction to Yoder in *Power and Practices*, Chris Huebner described Yoder's approach to doing theology as "dialogical and ad hoc," and added that knowing this about Yoder's work can guide our understanding of it. Thus Huebner concludes, the ongoing relevance of Yoder's work across multiple generations perhaps "has something to do with the ad hoc, particular, nomadic, and fragmentary character of his theology."[28] This characterization carries forward the same observation that occurred multiple times in Huebner's earlier book of Yoder-shaped essays, *A Precarious Peace*.[29] Here Huebner suggests that the fragmentary character of Yoder's work "is firmly rooted in his understanding of Christian pacifism."[30]

The existence of these several Yoders and descriptors in the literature stems at least in part from the way that most readers have come to know the thought of John Howard Yoder. As indicated earlier, Yoder's notable influence dates from the publication of his *The Politics of Jesus* in 1972. The majority of scholars interested in Yoder have most often begun with that book and/or consider it his seminal work. For many readers, the next important Yoder volume for study may be his *Priestly Kingdom* followed perhaps by *Christian Witness to the State*[31] or *Original Revolution*, and then perhaps the more recent *Royal Priesthood* and *For the Nations*. *Preface to Theology* barely appears. Reading Yoder in this way may be particularly true for younger scholars. A quick perusal of footnotes in three recent collections—*The New Yoder*, *Power and Politics*, and *Radical Ecumenicity*—reveals that general approach to Yoder. Meanwhile, the posthumously published *Jewish-Christian Schism Revisited*[32] and *The War of the Lamb*,[33] both of which figure prominently in chapters of the book in hand, have yet to make major inroads into Yoder scholarship.

Beginning with *Politics of Jesus* to understand Yoder's work enables the various descriptions of Yoder to emerge. It can produce Yoder the peace ethicist, who was recognized as an articulate advocate of nonviolence in the wider world as well as by Mennonites excited finally to have

28. Huebner, "Work of Inheritance," 24, 25.
29. Huebner, *Precarious Peace*, 22, 101, 102, 118.
30. Ibid., 102.
31. Yoder, *Christian Witness*.
32. Yoder, *Jewish-Christian Schism*.
33. Yoder, *War of the Lamb*.

a widely-recognized and respected advocate for nonviolence. Those Dula and Huebner described as "new Yoder" writers have resonated with the anti-foundational perspective visible in *Priestly Kingdom, For the Nations*, and other writings. The peace ethicist who frequently employed remarkable Biblical exegesis and whose books of essays ranged across topics such as hermeneutics, social ethics, the authority of tradition, Christology, Anabaptism, ecclesiology, Emperor Constantine, political democracy, American civil religion, and more would seem to merit the designation ad hoc and fragmentary. Finally, seeing that Yoder could affirm that the classic christological formulas dealt with issues left open by the New Testament writers could allow Yoder to be aligned with traditional orthodoxy. At the same time, for those who accept the classic creeds as unquestioned givens, Yoder's historical critique of the creeds can earn him a designation such as "heterodox."

However, as chapter 1 will demonstrate, none of these characterizations account for the way Yoder actually did theology. The perspective on Yoder's theology presented in this book fits none of the current designations, neither old nor new, neither Nicene nor heterodox nor trinitarian nor ad hoc and fragmentary. Reading these numerous descriptions in recent scholarship focused sharply for me the significance of understanding John Howard Yoder's other writings through the lens of the *Preface* lectures, which display his theological methodology, and his view of christological images both classic and contemporary. The presentation in hand of Yoder as a radical theologian reflects Yoder the christocentric or Jesus-centered theologian visible in *Preface*, an orientation that is lacking or passed over in the several Yoders and descriptors of Yoder in recent scholarship.

It is not that the characterizations of Yoder in "new Yoder" analysis and labeling his writing as ad hoc and fragmentary are false. But they do not say enough. His theological and ethical analysis did range across a wide assortment of issues, and Yoder would address any topic that was requested of him. But the characterizations such as ad hoc or post modern thinker neglect the fact that he was not merely bringing a pacifist perspective to bear in scattered discussions and in a manner that was at home in a postmodern context. They neglect that Yoder's responses were shaped by the conviction that the particular story of Jesus in the New Testament was the basis from which to address any issue. His writings on scattered topics were efforts to take the narrative of Jesus into new territory and to apply its meaning in a new setting. *Preface* displays this technique of expressing the meaning of the story of Jesus in new contexts within the New Testament itself for the discussion of Christology. Sometimes the christological application in Yoder's essays is explicit; but often Yoder employed the methodology he described as using "the other guy's" language and frame of reference to move the discussion in a nonviolent or following-Jesus direction.[34] With the methodology put on display in *Preface*, these supposedly "scattered" discussions still have an amazing range, but an underlying coherency also comes into view. This coherency is often missed by those whose primary route to understanding Yoder is via *Politics of Jesus* and *Priestly Kingdom* and then other collections of his essays and sermons.

The claims of orthodoxy or trinitarian on one side and heterodoxy on the other are misleading but in different ways. The analysis of chapter 1 to follow will make clear that it is demonstrably false that Yoder based his ethics on Nicene orthodoxy, although the claim contains a kernel of truth. The claims about "heterodoxy" and "trinitarian" are misleading on different sides of the question. Again, although each contains a grain of truth, neither evaluates Yoder in terms of how he actually envisioned Christology.

Recently Gerald Mast described a different route to understanding John Howard Yoder that arrived at a location much like that one that I had identified.[35] Mast's story also introduces an additional element in identifying Yoder as theologian. This element is Anabaptism.

As Mast described his introduction to John Howard Yoder, he followed the common route sketched above of first encountering *The Politics of Jesus* and then moving on to *Priestly Kingdom*. And along the way he discovered that Yoder was relevant for discussions of the postmodern context, which was a major focus of Mast's graduate work in communication and rhetoric. Yoder did offer an interesting approach to methodology that addressed current debates about epistemology in the humanities.

However, Mast brought another interest as well to the reading of John Howard Yoder. Following an early interest in Anabaptist history, Mast's graduate study in communication dealt in a major way with

---

34. Yoder's mention of the "other guy's" language appears in the memo discussed at the end of chapter 1 to follow.

35. Mast summarized his path to understanding Yoder in an e-mail exchange with me on November 29, 2010. Most references in what follows come from this e-mail, but reflect other conversations as well.

Anabaptists. His dissertation was a rhetorical analysis of sixteenth-century Anabaptist texts.[36] His work in Anabaptist sources led Mast to study many of the same Anabaptist sources that had also occupied John Howard Yoder, such sources as those related to the origin of Anabaptism in Zurich and later the Schleitheim Articles. Mast realized that in Yoder's contemporary theologizing, he was picking up arguments that were not resolved in the sixteenth century and carrying them forward into our world in the twentieth century. These arguments that Yoder found in the Anabaptist sources dealt with the basic content of theology. With that impulse in mind, Mast saw that even a cursory reading of *Martyrs Mirror*, for example, reveals that Anabaptists did not accept the standard patristic or "orthodox" formulas as the final or definitive word. In other words, Mast discovered via Yoder's use of Anabaptist texts that Yoder was showing the way to a theology that was compatible with the high christological concerns of "orthodoxy" but could express those concerns in other ways. These new expressions gave visibility to the narrative of Jesus and his rejection of the sword, which are items lacking in the classic creedal formulations of "orthodoxy."

Mast then read *Priestly Kingdom* from this theological perspective and found that this book is not merely a methodological argument with scattered applications but has stated implications for Christian theology as a whole. For example, he points to Yoder's statement that a "radical reformation" stance is actually a "recurring paradigm" throughout church history and has a "defining agenda" that is "far broader" than any one of its particular instantiations. Or Yoder's declaration that "radical reformers" "changed not simply the definition of certain ministries or churchly practices, but also the entire understanding of what it means to be Christian," and the claim that "the humanity of Jesus of Nazareth" is the "substantial criterion of Christian ethical decisions" for the radical reformers. These emphases are encapsulated in Yoder's well-known statement, "the church precedes the world epistemologically. We know more fully from Jesus Christ and in that context of the confessed faith than we know in other ways."[37]

Thus via studying Anabaptism and reading *Priestly Kingdom*, Gerald Mast came to an understanding of John Howard Yoder's theology that

---

36. A book that drew on the dissertation but with significant additional sources analyzed is Biesecker-Mast, *Separation and the Sword*.

37. Quotes from Yoder, *Priestly Kingdom*, 5, 107, 116, 11.

is essentially the same as what I developed through *Preface to Theology* and *Priestly Kingdom*. As Mast explained, with the subtitle "Social Ethics as Gospel" Yoder put on display that the book concerned theological ethics. And for Yoder, ethics were not separate from theology. Thus one can see *Priestly Kingdom* as a summary of the methodology Yoder displayed in *Preface to Theology*, or that the ethical implications of *Preface* are instantiated in *Priestly Kingdom*. But the Anabaptist element in Mast's story means that alongside the identifier "radical," Yoder might also properly be called an Anabaptist theologian.

The identifier Anabaptist does need qualification, however. For one thing, Yoder was careful to state that the ecclesial motif he developed was visible in any number of traditions in addition to sixteenth-century Anabaptists. Thus in no way does the label Anabaptist mean that he was merely basing theology on sixteenth-century Anabaptist sources or writing confessional theology for Anabaptists or Mennonites. Further, and more significantly, Yoder's approach is a call to begin with Jesus Christ and his way and his life, and to hold all theology to the criterion of whether it helps Christians to a life that makes Jesus' way visible in the world. He saw historic Anabaptism as one historical instantiation of this impulse. Thus with references to Anabaptism or Radical Reformation, Yoder was pointing to one source (among several) that pointed back to the narrative of Jesus as the true norm of faith and practice, and the criterion by which to measure theological development. Since that call begins with Jesus Christ, Yoder's Anabaptist stance is thus also an ecumenical one that appeals to a confession made by all Christians. This understanding of Yoder as "Anabaptist theologian" is fully compatible with the designation of him as a "radical theologian."

That the paths to understanding John Howard Yoder's theology that I described for myself and for Mast end up at the same point is far from a conjecture or a coincidence. Earl Zimmerman's *Practicing the Politics of Jesus* lays bare that convergence in Yoder's legacy itself. Zimmerman explored the influences in Yoder's life that contributed to his development of *The Politics of Jesus*. Written after Yoder's death, Zimmerman's was the first book to make extensive use of Yoder's correspondence.

As used by Zimmerman, Yoder's correspondence makes clear both his intent to develop a theological perspective that was parallel to but also bypassed standard orthodoxy, and his belief that one root for that theology was found in Anabaptism. In a letter to Paul Peachey, Yoder wrote of his "growing conviction that there exists a consistent biblicism of discipleship, parallel to Anabaptism not only in ecclesiastical separateness from Calvinism, but in its entire rejection of medieval carryovers in doctrine as well as in life." He saw this happening with Conrad Grebel and Felix Mantz, who wanted to reject doctrine that stood between themselves and the Bible, and thus "we should be consistently *wissenschaftlich* [or scholarly], since the more the Bible talks for itself without Anselm or Augustine in the way, the more it talks [about] discipleship."[38]

Yoder's doctoral dissertation at the University of Basil was a historical study that analyzed the discussions and debates between Ulrich Zwingli and the radicals in Zurich who became the first Anabaptists. Yoder had originally sought to write a theological dissertation from within an Anabaptist perspective, a dissertation that would be "an Anabaptist *Vergegenwärtigung* (a contemporary, updated Anabaptist theology)."[39] However, as Yoder explained in letters to Harold Bender and Paul Peachey, he could not find a theologian in a European university who would allow him to work from an Anabaptist perspective. None, he wrote "were open-minded enough to let something they basically disagree with through." Thus he decided for historical work in Anabaptism as a way around the opposition of theologians, but he carefully chose a topic that would allow him to investigate the theological views of the earliest radicals who debated with Zwingli.[40]

Yoder believed that many of his theological views, including what went into *The Politics of Jesus*, had already surfaced in Anabaptism. The two prominent ideas from Anabaptism are the notion of following the way of Jesus, which is a Christian discipleship that is present in the world in the way that Jesus was in the world,[41] and the visible church as a voluntary community of discerning believers. When the idea of discipleship goes beyond the personal to include social ethics, the church appears, which is the beginning of the distinction or separation of church from civil society and civil authority. It is important to understand that in Yoder's view, this is an ecumenical stance. It is ecumenical because every Christian carries the name of Jesus Christ.[42]

38. Cited in Zimmerman, *Practicing the Politics*, 113.
39. Ibid., 143.
40. Ibid., 140–41, Yoder citation 141.
41. Ibid., 142, 161.
42. See ibid., 140–72, and Yoder, *Anabaptism and Reformation*, 285–99.

The book in hand is the first presentation of Yoder's theologizing that makes visible the impulses that truly empowered his thought. This theology was a radical—from the root—appropriation of the norm of Jesus Christ from the New Testament, and it carried forward his appropriation of Anabaptism as a movement that pointed back to the New Testament narrative of Jesus as norm of faith and practice. It is John Howard Yoder, radical and Anabaptist, that this book presents.

Of course one can plug Yoder's comments into mainstream or evangelical orthodoxy or a contemporary, postmodern philosophical framework. But that approach is to interpret Yoder via terms and norms that were not his own. Such approaches serve their own agendas, but they do not depict how Yoder actually worked nor do they truly define his theology. Understanding Yoder in terms of his own radical, Anabaptist assumptions (as these labels are defined here) changes the picture. He is neither "old" nor "new," not merely an "ad hoc" or postmodern thinker, neither truly orthodox nor trinitarian nor heterodox. The Yoder of the volume in hand is the theologian who wrote from a christocentric, bibliocentric effort to appropriate and apply the story of Jesus Christ as the Christian gospel in multiple contexts of the world in which he lived. This Yoder supersedes the other existing descriptors.

The description of Yoder's contextualizing approach to theology and the importance of the essay "But We Do See Jesus" to his theological outlook is validated from a different direction by Glen Stassen's account of his coming to value the work of John Howard Yoder.[43] Since Stassen dealt with Yoder's contextualizing of theology in person, his story suggests Yoder's own confirmation of the accounts here.

In graduate study at Union Theological Seminary and then at Duke University, Stassen focused mostly on historical theology, along with systematic and philosophical theology. He learned New Testament theology from W. D. Davies, who specialized in Jesus' Jewish context. An additional important learning came from work with visiting professor Henry J. Cadbury, whose skepticism on the historical Jesus project prodded Stassen to dig deeper. Finally Duke's Frederick Herzog led students into the history of German Protestant study of Jesus and to engage in dialogue with Günther Bornkamm. Stassen's dissertation focused on H. Richard Niebuhr's wrestling with historical relativism and its relation to Christology.[44] This wrestling with historical theology, historical

---

43. This account is summarized from e-mail conversation of July 18, 2012.

44. See Stassen, Yeager, and Yoder, *Authentic Transformation*; Stassen, *Thicker Jesus*.

relativism, and Jesus as historically contextualized allowed Stassen to appreciate Yoder's contextualizing of Jesus and the centrality of Jesus in his theology and ethics, as described above. Yoder recognized early that he and Stassen were headed in a similar direction, and initiated what became an enriching and life-long relationship.

Stassen values "But We Do See Jesus" both for its acknowledgement of the necessity of speaking in "pluralist/relativist terms" in our modern context but also that the focus on the message in that language is that Jesus is Lord.[45] From this stance Yoder addressed the problem of Gotthold Ephraim Lessing's supposed ditch between universal truth propositions that everyone could claim on one side and particular, relative truth on the other side. Yoder argues that in fact, all truth is relative, all truth is perceived from a particular perspective. Thus there is no other side of the ditch where truth is not perceived from a particular perspective. That there would be such solid ground on the supposed other side of the ditch was "an illusion laid on us by Greek ontology language,"[46] which, Stassen says, was itself a particular, relative perspective developed by people like Plato, who turned out to be advocating an authoritarian society in which the ruler claimed to possess universal truth. Thus Yoder's historical study enabled him to relativize Plato and Greek ontology, and then to interpret the creeds in their historical function but without rejecting them outright.

Thus Stassen came to value greatly the emphasis on the particular historical language about Jesus Christ as Lord as the basis of Yoder's theology. "Jesus participates in localizable, datable history, as many religious hero figures do not. Jesus intervenes in the liberation from violence and he identifies with the poor as many savior figures do not." Stassen emphasizes, with Yoder, that we do not need to try to overwhelm the pluralistic/relativistic culture in which we live. We have only "to stay within our bark, merely afloat and sometimes awash amidst those waves, yet neither dissolving into them nor being carried only where they want to push it."[47] We have an advantage in a culture that is historically and particularistically aware because our loyalty is to Jesus who is historical and particular. We can feel at home in our particular bark in this cultural pluralist/relativist stream.

---

45. Yoder, "But We Do," *Priestly Kingdom*, 56; Yoder, "But We Do," *Pacifist*, 32–33.
46. Yoder, "But We Do," *Priestly Kingdom*, 59; Yoder, "But We Do," *Pacifist*, 36.
47. Yoder, "But We Do," *Priestly Kingdom*, 57, 58; Yoder, "But We Do," *Pacifist*, 34.

The understanding of Yoder's thought that emerges from the stories from Mast, Zimmerman, Stassen, and myself is one that begins with the New Testament story of Jesus but is told in a way that has the capacity to address any issue. This christological outlook is a theology that is inseparable from its social and ethical dimensions. This theology is cognizant of the standard "orthodox" creeds and formulas and Yoder can advocate them on occasion.[48] At the same time, from early on Yoder was also convinced about the advisability of offering a theological parallel in conversation with but not beholden to the kind of orthodoxy that is based on doctrine but without much Jesus. In *Politics of Jesus*, he described this alternative as "more radically Nicene and Chalcedonian than other views."[49] He could make this claim because his approach actually used the humanity of Jesus and his life and word as an ethical norm in a way that was lacking in the classic formulas, while also affirming the Lordship of Christ, Jesus Christ as the revelation of God's character, God's self, as orthodoxy affirms. Thus when Yoder used the human life of Jesus as found in the Gospel narratives as criterion for the Christian life, it produced a new understanding of the church. Every theological and ethical assignment was in a sense new for Yoder, because it was always a new application of the life and work of Jesus; it was always a "looping back"[50] to discover again that foundational narrative and to use it as the criterion for judging the truthfulness of contemporary theology and practice.

This Yoder is the theologian that I have called radical and Anabaptist. This description has a wider scope and a more theological beginning point than is visible in the description of Yoder as theologian of nonviolence, and it is more theological than the views that see Yoder as postmodern interlocutor in conversation with others. Further, this description of a historical as well as theological Yoder rather clearly corrects those who would see Yoder's thought as based in a defense of classic

---

48. For example, in "A Theological Critique of Violence" (ch. 1 of *War of the Lamb*), Yoder based his critique on the Apostles' Creed.

49. Yoder, *Politics of Jesus* (1994), 102. This text has been quoted in efforts to argue that Yoder's Christology was linked to or depended on classic Nicene-Chalcedonian formulas. See Nation, *John Howard Yoder*, 128; Nation, "Politics Regarding," 39; Carter, "Liberal Reading," 88; Parler, *Things Hold Together*, 77. However, as the argument here demonstrates, as well as comments in some following chapters, rather than linking himself to the classic formulas, Yoder's intent was to put on display his differences with them and argue that he took their underlying assumptions and implications more seriously than did most proponents of these formulas.

50. Yoder, "Authority of Tradition," 69.

Nicene orthodoxy without sufficient attention to his insistence that theologizing begins with the New Testament story of Jesus.

Yoder is a radical in that his theology stems from the root or the origin of Christian faith, namely the Jesus of the New Testament. He is Anabaptist in that he recognized that sixteenth-century movement as one whose intent was to point to Jesus as the norm of faith and practice. Yoder's writing was an effort to bring Jesus—the root of Christian profession—into the faith and practice of contemporary Christians. As following chapters demonstrate, everything else was an extension or an application of that root. As a follower of Jesus, Yoder was thus a radical theologian.

Christology, both content and methodology, was the priority for Yoder's thought. The three Parts of the book display this orientation and its applications and implications in an interrelated and expanding fashion. The lengthy chapter 1 of Part One puts on display Yoder's methodology and multi-faceted view of Jesus and Christology as they become visible in *Preface to Theology* and the essay "But We Do See Jesus." This chapter concludes with references to a brief memo Yoder wrote on his methodology. These references verify the analysis of Yoder's thought and methodology described in chapter 1.

The four chapters of Part Two display Yoder's relationship to the important sources from which he developed the outlook described in chapter 1. In chapter 2, Earl Zimmerman describes the root of Yoder's thought in sixteenth-century Anabaptism. This chapter makes clear Yoder's intent to do theology that was compatible with but not beholden to classic orthodoxy. Three chapters then deal with contemporaries from whom Yoder borrowed or learned but whom he also modified or went beyond. The import of these chapters is to show that Yoder established his own independent voice vis-à-vis those from whom he learned. In chapter 3, Zachary Walton compares Yoder to Harold S. Bender and his "Anabaptist Vision," showing Bender's influence on Yoder but also how Yoder followed his own inclinations in ways that distinguished him from the Goshen School. In chapter 4, Earl Zimmerman describes Yoder's roots in biblical scholarship learned from Oscar Cullmann, but without Yoder being merely a Cullmann follower. In the final chapter of Part Two, Gerald Mast analyzes the extent to which Yoder was shaped by the theology of Karl Barth but was also somewhat uncomfortable with Barth as a mentor.

The chapters of Part Three extend or apply Yoder's Christology, as well as address a major lacuna in it. Chapter 6 by Ted Grimsrud leads this section by showing how Yoder understood Paul's ethics as a continuation of that of Jesus. In chapter 7, Earl Zimmerman displays how Yoder's Anabaptist thought becomes a way for the "body politics" of the church to be a witness in and to the world. Gerald Mast provides an analysis in chapter 8 of pacifism as patient witness and a way of knowing in Yoder's understanding. The next two chapters show that two posthumously published works by Yoder also reflect, are central to, and extend his application of the narrative of Jesus. In chapter 9, Glen Stassen describes Yoder's application of a theologically understood Jesus for a nonviolent public ethic of peacemaking, in dialogue with Catholic just war theorists and social scientific insights on just peacemaking. Stassen's essay makes major use of *The War of the Lamb*, a book that Yoder was working on at the time of his death. Chapter 10, coauthored by J. Denny Weaver and Earl Zimmerman, makes major use of *The Jewish-Christian Schism Revisited* in showing the implications of Yoder's christological analysis and understanding of the schism for Christian-Jewish dialogue. Then with reference to brief comments by Yoder on his website, this chapter extends the implications of Yoder's Christology to dialogue with Muslims and Hindus as well. Chapter 11, coauthored by J. Denny Weaver and Gerald Mast, uses Weaver's atonement theology to show that Yoder's approach can be extended as a new theological paradigm for the present time, but can also be appropriated to enter a discussion with evangelicalism and with what has been called a "new black theology." The chapter thus illustrates how Yoder's methodology can be extended through open doors into new territory, but can also become the basis for intervening in an ongoing discussion in "the other guy's" framework. These different possible extensions of Yoder's thought given visibility in these six chapters demonstrate why it is not possible to synthesize all of Yoder's writings into one coherent whole. Yoder opened doors but the results on the other side of those doors cannot be synthesized into a whole.

Chapters 1 through 11 deal with Yoder's intervention into theology and reflect the profound and wide-ranging impact it has had on many people, including the authors in this volume. Chapters 12 and 13 take Yoder into new territories, which have only begun to be explored. In chapter 12, Ted Grimsrud describes his own dilemma, his great appreciation for Yoder's theological insight that is confounded by Yoder's personal failure and the psychological harm caused by his sexual violence of inappropriate crossing of boundaries with numerous women. In the final chapter, Gerald Mast situates Yoder's failure in the longer history of Anabaptist efforts to live up to its ecclesiology and the need to develop addition understandings and resources to deal with our inevitable failings without loosing sight of the vision of Anabaptist discipleship.

The primary goal of this book is to show in widespread detail the view of Yoder just sketched for the three parts—the understanding of Yoder in which theology expands upon Christology, Anabaptist history is a historical marker of discipleship-based ecclesiology, and all resulting in an understanding of Jesus that poses a challenge to and for all Christians. The sketch includes Yoder's failure, which is treated in the last two chapters as well as the Afterword, and constitutes further stimulation to develop additional dimensions of this ecclesiology and our lives as fallible followers of Jesus Christ.

The chapters of this book expand pieces of this description of Yoder. Chapter 1 on Christology and methodology was written specifically for this volume. Chapters 3, 12, and 13 were also written new, specifically for this volume. But all remaining chapters were also produced specifically for this volume. Those who have read extensively in works about Yoder may recognize that parts of other chapters have appeared elsewhere in different contexts. However, any such material has been reshaped for the current discussion and in addition, much new material has been added to arrive at the chapters of this book. It would be impossible to reproduce this volume by assembling the paragraphs of previously published material, and nowhere else have these items been brought together in the present configuration. In other words, the dots connected in this volume draw a new picture of Yoder's approach to theology.

By this point in the Introduction, many readers will have noted that all writers of these chapters are male. The intent of this volume was to portray Yoder's christological methodology. Thus the chapters of this book are not a random collection of essays. They were solicited from Yoder scholars of a small, particular school of Yoderian thought, namely those who recognized Yoder the radical theologian, for whom Christology and practices of the church reach back to the biblical narrative of Jesus rather than standing on Nicene orthodoxy. Until this point, the circle of conversation represented by this book has not included women's participation. Given Yoder's abusive behavior, described in Chapters 12 and 13, Lisa Schirch's Afterword points to the obvious need to include female as well as male viewpoints in the ongoing discussion of Yoder's theology, as well as indicating the importance in general of seeing that pacifist theology and feminist theology should support each other. The Afterword points to *The Nonviolent Atonement* as one such linking of pacifist and feminist theology.

For the most part, conversation in this volume with other understandings of Yoder's thought occurs in the notes. The intent is that this second level discussion not detract from the goal of presenting the comprehensive theological vision of John Howard Yoder, but that the conversation be available in the notes for those who wish to pursue it.

The following chapter now turns to the task of displaying Yoder's methodology and his view of Jesus and Christology.

PART ONE

The Orientation of John Howard Yoder's Theology

Part One develops Yoder's view of Christology, both classic and contemporary, and his methodology for biblical interpretation and historical critique of Christology. Both content and methodology are important in this discussion.

1

Christology
From the Root

J. Denny Weaver

It is axiomatic that the story of the man Jesus was at the heart of John Howard Yoder's theology and ethics. As a result, it does not surprise that Christology, the church's words about Jesus and the meaning of Jesus, occupy priority of place—the root—in Yoder's thought, which makes him a "radical theologian." Other elements of his thought, in particular his advocacy of nonviolence and his development of a voluntary (or believers church) ecclesiology are derived from Christology. Chapters in Part Two describe several sources that Yoder drew on for his understanding of Christology, and the chapters of Part Three depict its expansion in such issues as nonviolence, ecclesiology, and interfaith dialogue.

Meanwhile, in anticipation of those discussions, the present chapter turns to an indepth analysis of how Yoder understood Christology. The chapter will survey Yoder's description of the development of Christology from the earliest statements in the New Testament through the first Christian centuries to formulation of the well-known formula that emerged from the Council of Chalcedon.

Fully comprehending Yoder's multifaceted approach to Christology begins with an analysis of the seminary lectures that he called *Preface to*

PART ONE—THE ORIENTATION OF JOHN HOWARD YODER'S THEOLOGY

Theology: Christology and Theological Method.[1] In this title, the indication of "theological method" has equal importance with the christological images themselves. Yoder's description of these developments is not, as has been claimed, an "in depth" statement of "the case for the ethical authority of the life and teachings of Jesus being based in orthodox Christology."[2] It is rather, as Yoder stated in the memo treated in the last section of this chapter, "the web" from within which one can discuss Christology. Yoder's point is that any theological conversation begins within a "web" of understanding. He presented the developments from the New Testament through Chalcedon as the web within which a discussion of Christology must begin before one can discuss alternative ways to state Christology in our contemporary context. *Preface* hints at such possible new statements, while the essay "But We Do See Jesus" opens the door wide to them.[3] Seeing the methodology of Yoder's approach to Christology will also explain why there has been so much disagreement about his view. He had no fixed Christology. It was always open to restatement in a different context when the narrative of Jesus, understood as gospel, was taken into new settings and contexts.

Key to Yoder's understanding of Christology is his focus on the variety of expressions—both in the New Testament and later—and on the fact or idea of change. Formulations change from one context to another and from one time period to the next. A one-sentence summary of Yoder's analysis of Christology in *Preface* is that he traces changes in the discussion of Christology from the earliest statements in the New Testament to the fifth-century councils and events that established an official view identified as "orthodoxy." His methodology asks, "Why does that thought follow from this one, and what would the alternatives be?" That process begins with samples from "a few sections of the New Testament," and then moves to deal with "post-biblical material along a narrative historical outline."[4] He chooses to follow discussions of Christology because it was a major concern of early Christians.[5]

1. Yoder, *Preface* (1981). These lectures were edited in a posthumous publication as Yoder, *Preface* (2002). Citations will follow the published version of 2002 unless otherwise indicated.
2. Carter, *Politics of the Cross*, 246.
3. Yoder, "But We Do," *Priestly*; Yoder, "But We Do," *Pacifist*.
4. Yoder, *Preface* (2002), 38.
5. It is important to recognize in the summary and analysis of Yoder's methodology to follow that Yoder did not intend to provide a comprehensive statement of New

In the course of the lectures that became *Preface*, Yoder said, the student will interact with ancient texts, observe "debates between competing positions," and develop an understanding of how tradition arises. These experiences lead to a very important conclusion, namely "that theology is a process more than it is a finished subject matter."[6] These references to "tradition" and to a never-finished "process" signal the possibility of multiple expressions that will eventually become visible in both the classic formulations and in the simultaneously opened door to alternatives.

First Statements: Sermons in Acts

Yoder's sample of what the New Testament says about Jesus begins with the sermons in the book of Acts. The presentation clearly reflects the class room, as he establishes a grid with New Testament texts in boxes across the top and a long list of statements about Jesus running down the sides. The first column of texts concerned the six sermons about Jesus contained in Acts: 2:14–20; 3:12–26; 4:8–12; 5:29–32; 10:34–43; 13:16–41. As the texts are read, checks in boxes would indicate which statements appeared in the sermons. Reading of other texts would then indicate differences and changes from these earliest statements in Acts.

Reading the texts and filling in the grid for these sermons reveal that two themes predominate—that "you killed Jesus" or "Jesus died" and that "God raised Jesus from the dead." Almost as prominent are three other themes—that these events are part of a promised age or constitute fulfillment of Scripture, that the speaker is a witness to the events, and lines that call hearers to repentance or offer forgiveness via this recitation.[7]

Yoder offered a series of "formal observations" about this outline. First, "the sermons . . . are just as important for what they do not say as for what they say." They concern Christology, but they say nothing about

Testament theology nor even a comprehensive statement of New Testament Christology. For the New Testament, he called his method "block-gap" in contrast to a "thorough survey," and wrote that he had "picked out from the story of the growth of the thought of the early Christians those elements best calculated to make a certain point visible." Yoder, *Preface* (2002), 137. For the New Testament, that point was to show how change and development occurred as expansion of the earliest story of the man Jesus who was killed and raised from the dead.

6. Yoder, *Preface* (2002), 39.

7. I was a student in Yoder's class when he drew the grid on the chalkboard, and the class read the texts with Yoder as he filled in the grid that brought these points to the foreground.

the "internal experiences of believers, . . . nothing about God as such; whether God exists, . . . is one, . . . is all powerful." God is mentioned as an actor, "the one who raised Jesus from the dead and exalted him and gave him a title." Further, the material of the sermons is "all narrative . . . rooted in the Old Testament story. . . . It is about a specific event in the work of Jesus, namely his resurrection." Third, "the narrative includes the speaker" who "claims to be a witness to those events." Furthermore, the event of the preaching "includes the listener." Listeners were participants in the event of killing Jesus and they are now invited to "be beneficiaries of the promised redemption" that is conveyed by the narrative. Finally, it is said that this series of events happened "according to the Scriptures." This places the event of Jesus in the line of the story from the Old Testament and in the history of God's acts for God's people.[8] Yoder also noted two other sermons in Acts, in chapters 14 and 17. His point was that in contrast to the other six sermons, these later two do begin with general statements about God—as creator and as controller of providence. Yoder explains this difference in terms of the context of the listeners. For the first six sermons, the hearers were Jews or God-fearing gentiles who assumed the Hebrew understanding of God. When the audience shifted to Gentiles, Paul began with more general statements about the nature and purpose of God before dealing with the message about Jesus. Yoder called this move "the first step toward talking about theology as such."[9] The reader will observe that already in this very first lesson on New Testament Christology, Yoder notes the impact of context, and he points to change in theological formulation.

"Primitive" Christology

By "primitive" Christology, Yoder meant the earliest references or descriptions of Jesus before the great theologians of the New Testament (Paul, the author of Hebrews, John) began more analytical reflection on Jesus. For this primitive Christology, Yoder described the titles for Jesus in the Gospels. The most important titles considered were Son of Man, Messiah or Christ, Son of God, and Lord. In each case, there is a development in the use of the term.

---

8. Yoder, *Preface* (2002), 56–57.
9. Ibid., 58.

Son of Man evolved from a title meaning human being to a form of address in Ezekiel. In Daniel it still refers to a human being, but not an ordinary one. Eventually one finds Jesus using it to refer to himself while carrying over earlier connotations of suffering. Thus it becomes a messianic title.[10]

In the Old Testament, messiah meant "anointed one" and referred to the one who would become king, a future authority figure. Translated into Greek, anointed one becomes Christ, a title eventually applied to Jesus. In later writers Christ becomes the personal name with which to refer to Jesus.

Usage of the term "son of God" evolves considerably. In the Old Testament, it refers to one "whose character is defined in relationship to God. It does not mean a little God." In Job, angels and the devil are called sons of God. In Psalms son of God refers to a righteous person, sometimes the king. Believers are also identified as "sons of God" (1 John 3:2). The term eventually becomes associated with Jesus. This association, however, does not mean "deity in the sense of metaphysically sharing in the nature of God." Rather, it has the meaning of "closeness to, or subordination to, God." Even when the term does come to identify "a unique, divine status" of Jesus, "the uniqueness of the Son of God is still a human uniqueness, still something that he has in common with us."[11]

Finally, Lord is probably the most important designation of Jesus. On the one hand, it was an ordinary form of address, such as "Sir" or "Mister," and implied the human authority of a boss. However, before Jesus' time, it was also being applied to Caesar, where it had connotations of deity for the emperor recognized as a god. Thus when the first Christians referred to Jesus as Lord, "they were using the language of deity about him." As shown in the hymn of Philippians 2, in which every tongue confesses Jesus as Lord, this title was the "center of the early Christian confession of faith, [and] was the strongest thing that the early church could say about Jesus."[12]

Following the survey of titles, Yoder stressed that "the early church lived without the New Testament." Much variety of thought and practice existed among these early believers, a variety that is covered over by modern efforts to harmonize all New Testament witnesses. "The New

10. Ibid., 63–67.
11. Ibid., 70–71.
12. Ibid., 72–73.

Testament is more diverse, when each text is read for itself, than most of us assume" and is even more true for "the total Christian movement."[13]

Pre-Paul Christology

These earliest christological statements, what Yoder called "primitive Christology," appeared in several other forms as well. One of these forms consisted of early material quoted by later New Testament writers. An important example treated by Yoder is the hymn text quoted by Paul in Philippians 2:5–11.

Philippians 2

Yoder described the most common interpretation of Philippians 2, in which the "image of God" in verse 6 gives Jesus an equality with God which he gave up—emptying himself—in order to become human. As a result of obedience, he was raised from the dead and returned to his former exalted state.

However, Yoder did not follow the common interpretation. Instead, he suggested that "image of God" makes Jesus parallel to Adam, who was created in the image of God. But from that status, Adam tried to grasp at equality with God. In contrast, Jesus continued as the "model of what Adam should have done, refusing to seize that which was not his." This later interpretation keeps in view the full humanity of Jesus, "even to the point of death."[14] Jesus is then given the title Lord because of this complete and perfect obedience. This title, Lord, depicts his status at the right hand of God where he is Lord of the universe.[15]

Yoder describes the movement from the Acts sermons, which focused on death and resurrection, to this hymn, where the focus is not on

13. Ibid., 77.
14. Ibid., 84.
15. Yoder adds that "the church is the people who call him Lord," but that he is Lord whether or not people recognize that. This distinction matters, Yoder says, "when we ask whether the Lordship of Christ applies in any way to the rest of the world." Yoder, *Preface* (2002), 86. This comment is parallel to Yoder's well-known statement that "those who bear crosses are working with the grain of the universe" ("Armaments and Eschatology," 58) and that in Jesus we see the kinds of "causation," "community building," and "conflict management" that "go with the grain of the cosmos" (*Politics of Jesus* [1994], 246).

death but on accepting full humanity and then beyond resurrection to exaltation as Lord. The hymn makes no particular reference to how Jesus' death might relate to forgiveness. Paul posed this description of Christ as the basis of church unity. Believers are called to imitate the humility of Jesus, Yoder said, and that humility becomes the basis for unity. Unity requires respect for the other person, which is based on following the example of Christ who humbled himself. The ultimate result will then be being raised with Christ.[16]

Other Pre-Paul Traditions

Yoder deals with a number of other texts that he treated as "the thought that went before Paul." These texts also point to a "two-phase structure," such as the "you killed him but God raised him" of the sermons in Acts or the humiliation and exaltation of Philippians 2. Ephesians 4:8–10 has a two-fold movement, descended and ascended, in order to "fill all things." Filling all things refers to the gifts of the Spirit given to the whole church. Romans 10:6–8 has another spatial displacement, descending and ascending.[17]

Romans 1:3–5 has a different duality, that of flesh and spirit—Jesus is "descended from David according to the flesh and was declared to be Son of God with power according to the spirit of holiness by resurrection from the dead." Second Timothy 2:8 has a similar duality in reverse order. Instead of death and resurrection, 1 Peter 3:18 has a duality of "death in the flesh, but made alive in the Spirit." When 1 Timothy 3:16 mentions "Manifest in the flesh, justified in the Spirit," Yoder notes that mention of justification is the beginning of an atonement concept. Romans 4:25 and "death for our trespasses and raised for our justification" is another beginning statement of atonement.[18]

Summary Thus Far

Yoder's summary of early Christology emphasized diversity around a prevalent pattern. "Thus we observe, with considerable variety but also considerable faithfulness, a recurrent pattern of seeing the work of Christ

16. Yoder, *Preface* (2002), 87–88.
17. Ibid., 88–89.
18. Ibid., 89–90.

as two-fold, with both its element of humiliation, condescension, becoming flesh, and its element of resurrection, Spirit. It seems that this was an easy way for the early church to preach, remember, or praise. Therefore, we can find traces of this two-fold pattern running all the way up and down the epistles."[19] Yoder thus observes significant diversity of expression among the New Testament's earliest statements about Jesus.

Theologians: Paul

As a counterpart to the "primitive" Christology of the early church, Yoder gives more extended treatment to the three New Testament "theologians," Paul, the author of Hebrews, and the author of the Gospel of John. He notes several things that characterize their writings. They are much longer than other theological statements, and they make more indepth arguments. Rather than simply passing on the earliest statements, they came up with original arguments and added something to or developed farther the original interpretations. This greater originality is the result of responding to three challenges. One was a desire to produce a coherent, consistent statement. Further, there was a desire to communicate, to say it in a way that is comprehensible in a new context. Finally, there was the desire to argue points, to prove something. Yoder added an important reminder to this description. The earliest Christians did not read these theologians. It was only with the passing of time that these theological writings came to occupy the central place in the New Testament that we accord them today.[20]

First Corinthians

Yoder used 1 Corinthians 15 to demonstrate the extension of the early Jesus narrative in an original way. In verses 3–5 appears the familiar narrative outline from the sermons in Acts. Paul made a point of positing this narrative as one that he received. It is therefore not original to him. However, Paul then extended this traditional formulation by appealing to the narrative to argue a point that it does not mention specifically. He argues that the resurrection of Jesus requires belief in a general resurrection of all of humankind. That argument works only with the

19. Ibid., 90.
20. Ibid., 92–93.

prior assumption of what Yoder called the "solidarity of Christ with all humankind." That solidarity means that what happens to Jesus will also happen to humankind. On the basis of that assumption, Paul argues that the resurrection of Jesus requires belief in a general resurrection and that denial of a general resurrection means denial of the resurrection of Jesus. That denial has a major impact, because without the resurrection of Jesus, people remain in their sins.[21] With these observations, Yoder is taking pains to show how theological statements begin to develop, and that such development occurs already within the New Testament.

In addition to the logic of solidarity, Yoder pointed to other elements of Paul's theologizing. With the linking of forgiveness of sins to resurrection, Paul has gone beyond the infrequent mention of death for sins in the sermon outline from Acts. Here Paul has taken a step in the direction of a "rudimentary" doctrine of atonement. Yoder also notes that Paul assumes the Old Testament story. Although Paul does not quote the Old Testament until the end of the chapter, his reference to Adam as representative of human solidarity in mortality assumes the Old Testament. With all these observations, Yoder was demonstrating how Paul's theologizing was extending and developing additional meanings from the earliest narrative about Jesus.[22]

With 1 Corinthians 12:2–3 Yoder made a point about Paul's methodology. Paul's key statement is that "No one speaking by the Spirit of God says 'Let Jesus be cursed!' and no one can say 'Jesus is Lord' except by the Holy Spirit." As Yoder explained the setting, Paul assumes that there are spirits working, including heathen spirits, and he also assumes that Christians expect revelation in Corinth to continue. The problem is how to determine when it is the Holy Spirit working in an utterance. Paul's criterion is that the Holy Spirit will say nothing contrary to Jesus. "Spirit working is not arbitrary as it is in paganism. It is not self-authenticating. It has a standard. . . . Paul reckons with the possibility that the Spirit will speak, lead, reveal. But let it be consistent." Yoder then points to 1 Corinthians 14:29 as an application of this process of weighing and authenticating. "Let two or three prophets speak, and let the others weigh what is said."[23]

21. Ibid., 95–97, quote 96.
22. Ibid., 97–98.
23. Ibid., 100.

Galatians

In Yoder's analysis, Galatians demonstrates several aspects of Paul's theologizing. He indicated points already observed, such as Paul's appeal to the story they have already heard and received, and Paul's continuity with that faith story.

Yoder points to a variety of ways Paul used to make a connection between Jesus and his readers. For one, he appealed to Abraham (Gal 3:6) to display the promise of grace prior to the law given by Moses. In another, an important point of connection between Jesus and humankind is the gift of "sonship." Whereas this link was simply assumed in 1 Corinthians 15, and was depicted in Philippians 2 via Jesus' willingness to accept servitude, this time Paul makes the link via Jesus' birth. He is "born of a woman . . . so that we might receive adoption as children" of God (Gal 4:4–5). Freedom from the law comes through humankind's identification with Jesus, so that via adoption, "we are made sons as he was Son."[24]

Galatians 6 expresses solidarity of humankind with Jesus in terms of the cross as a stance to the world. The cross has become more than a past event. It is not connected to forgiveness of sins; neither is resurrection mentioned. Rather it has become a stance. "May I never boast of anything except the cross of our Lord Jesus Christ, by which the world has been crucified to me, and I to the world" (Gal 6:14). As Yoder says, "the cross is the way the world and I have become dead to each other. . . . It is the model for the stance of the Christian in the world."[25]

Yoder's summary of comments from these major Pauline writings emphasizes the presence of a wide variety of ways to express and extend the meaning of Jesus. Paul displays "enormous liberty in finding many ways to make the connection between Jesus and me." Texts Yoder selected dealt with cross and resurrection, but a survey of the entire New Testament "would of course find lines that are drawn to his earthly career as well." Whatever the question, "somehow, a line can be drawn from Jesus." The important learning is, "this is very far from a rigid doctrinal approach, having only one right way to deal with every question." Drawing lines from Jesus to humankind "may well be done in different ways with different kinds of reasoning, but always something of this being

---

24. Ibid., 103–4, quote 104.
25. Ibid., 104–5, quote 105.

involved in the person of Jesus—something of the solidarity of Christ with all people."[26]

Pauline Texts: 1 Timothy 3

First Timothy 3 employs a different literary style and imagery from the writings of Paul considered thus far. Yoder's interest focuses on the hymn or poem quoted in verse 16:

> The mystery of our religion is great:
> > He was revealed in flesh,
> > > vindicated in spirit,
> > > > seen by angels,
> > > proclaimed among Gentiles,
> > > > believed in throughout the world,
> > > > > taken up in glory.

Yoder pointed out that where earlier confessions used a narrative, this hymn uses space, a "down and up" movement. The "mystery," the working of God in Christ, is now understood in terms of the relationship of the two realms: "the transcendent and the imminent, the Spirit realm and the flesh realm." This is now a picture of the gospel "working in the Hellenistic world." Jews had a sense of God working through history, the God of Abraham also worked through Moses and David and had promised another prophet. When speaking to Jews, the message was that the God of those events had now worked in Jesus as "the culmination of their history." However, the Hellenistic person had a different perception of the problem of sin, the alienation of humanity. It concerned the alienation of the upper, spiritual realm from the lower, fleshly realm. The text speaks to this context when it says that "Christ overcomes the alienation between these two realms; he manifests the reality of the Spirit and the angels in glory in the world of the nations and of the flesh." Yet, in spite of this difference in imagery, Yoder asserts, this statement from 1 Timothy shares commonality with the other statements. It is still about what happened in Jesus, and the important point is that "God did it."[27]

---

26. Ibid., 106.
27. Ibid., 107–8.

Second Corinthians 5

Second Corinthians 5 continues a theme found in Romans 6 and 8 and Colossians 2 and 3. For 2 Corinthians 5:15, Yoder described how Paul unfolded the solidarity idea with a circular argument between "Christ in our place and we in his." "And he died for all, so that those who live might live no longer for themselves, but for him who died and was raised for them" (2 Cor 5:15). As Yoder explains, by identifying with Christ, the believer shares in both "his dying and his life." With this statement, Yoder explains, Paul is no longer preaching in Jerusalem to Jews who killed Jesus, and crucifixion is no longer an event in which Jesus was killed. Nonetheless, Paul has kept the twofold movement of death and resurrection. "He makes of it a pattern of life and death in which the Christian is already living." The Christian shares in both Christ's death and his resurrection, and the solidarity concept "now provides the whole pattern of Paul's thought about the way Christ is relevant to us."[28]

Summary of Paul

Yoder selected texts that would illustrate Paul's methodology, "the way that he theologizes."[29] He made several points about Paul. For one, Paul's writings do not form a clear or systematic body of doctrine. Instead of an effort at coherence and consistence, in Paul "we find an enormous variety, a very creative flexibility." This flexibility appeared in the way that Paul could emphasize different aspects of the story of Jesus, mention cross without resurrection or vice versa, or in how he related cross and resurrection.[30]

Paul displayed a number of strategies for linking the story of Jesus to the present question. One was the use of the logic of solidarity, as in solidarity in sin with old Adam and with righteousness with the new Adam, the Son. Another dimension of solidarity was the logic of "fulfillment," the fact that the event of Jesus was part of an ongoing history. Paul expressed this point "by making all kinds of links between the Old Testament and the present." He used Old Testament imagery, or made use of a specific text in proof text fashion. He called believers "sons of Abraham." Paul did

---

28. Ibid., 108–9.
29. Ibid., 109.
30. Ibid., 110–11.

not follow correct exegesis by our contemporary standards. But what we need to observe, Yoder concluded, is the many ways that Paul conveyed continuity between Israel and the Old Testament and Jesus. Paul used the Old Testament to say that Jesus is the culmination of an ongoing story of Israel.[31] Thus in his analysis of theologizing by Paul, Yoder took pains to emphasize the variety of ways Paul used to express the meaning of Jesus. And Yoder emphasized that different contexts required different kinds of statements.

Theologians: Hebrews

Hebrews is written more as a systematic theology than are Paul's writings. In other words, Yoder said, Hebrews does not address a particular crisis or question in the way Paul did with his writings.

Hebrews opens with the book's theme, namely Christology. "Long ago God spoke to our ancestors in many and various ways by the prophets, but in these last days he has spoken to us by a Son" (Heb 1:1–2). This opening sentence of Hebrews points to the previously observed theme of fulfillment, the "awaited age," as God now speaks through a Son. Yoder indicates that the theme of fullment will become the central topic of the book of Hebrews.[32]

Hebrews "affirms the continuity of what God has done in Jesus with what God was doing before." That continuity, Yoder says, is visible in the imagery of priesthood and the sacrificial system as well as the expert exegetical use of the Old Testament by the author of Hebrews.[33]

Along with the ideas of continuity and fulfillment, however, is also the theme of newness. The new covenant has something added. Something has happened to bring an end to the practice of daily sacrifices. Putting Jesus in the image of sacrifice provides continuity with the old covenant. But there is also novelty in that Jesus is the last sacrifice. The statement that "Jesus Christ is the same yesterday and today and forever" (Heb 13:8) does not mean absence of change, Yoder says, but that "the change that took place at the point of incarnation stops the series." What

---

31. Yoder, *Preface* (2002), 111–12.
32. Ibid., 114–15.
33. Ibid., 115.

Hebrews does with "same yet different" in terms of sacrifice is similar to what Paul did on a number of occasions with the idea of law.[34]

The idea of continuity with change also appears in the use of the title "Son." In the Old Testament, the title "son of God" had applied to angels and the king, and in the New Testament it becomes Messiah. These are not identified with God by "nature," but through "dependence upon or subjection to God." Then in Hebrews, it is a case of divine Sonship that is more than and higher than angels. The Son is involved in creation, bears the "imprint of God's very being," sustains "all things," and is called Son by God the Father (Heb 1:2–7). Thus the Son is above the angels, and differs from angels through his identification with the Father.[35] This location above the angels in identification with the Father appears in the image of the seat at "the right hand of the Majesty on high" (Heb 1:3).

But the Son also differs from the angels in a second way. He is also lower than the angels; he is identified with humankind. This identity appears in his "suffering of death." He shared "flesh and blood" with those whom God sanctified, "For the one who sanctifies and those who are sanctified all have one Father" (Heb 2:10).[36]

In Philippians 2 we observed the twofold movement of humiliation and exaltation. Yoder pointed out that this movement also appears in Hebrews 2:7 and 2:10, where he is "perfected through suffering." In the earliest preaching, the movement was the concrete "you killed him, God raised" him. With Paul it had become more than this concrete meaning. Hebrews expands it even farther. Now the victory occurs in the suffering and death itself. One expression of this victory occurs in his location sitting "at the right hand of God." This symbolic location indicates governance. The one at the right hand of the sovereign "governs in the name of the king."[37]

The use in Hebrews of the image of priesthood provides another expression of fulfillment along with novelty. The image of sacrifice for purity is assumed from the life of Israel. Jesus is depicted as a better priest and as the last priest. The victim—the one who is sacrificed—has also changed. It is not an animal but a man, the unique man who is identical with God. But contrary to the common view of atonement, Jesus is not

---

34. Ibid., 116.
35. Ibid., 116–17.
36. Ibid., 117.
37. Ibid., 117–18.

a better victim because he is a divine victim. He is a better priest and the last high priest because "he gives himself." He is not making up to God what was missing by being more pure. "Rather he adds to this priestly process the gift of self and his total humanity, his identification with humanity." In his identification with us, with humanity, we participate in his death and thus in his victory and identification with God.[38]

The victory seems to come at the point of his obedience. In 2:9 he is crowned with glory and honor "because of the suffering of death." In contrast to the early message of "you killed him, God raised him," now "it is the suffering of death that is itself what he did. *It* is the victory." Christ's victory, Yoder says, is not only at the point of resurrection and exaltation. It is "already part of the quality with which he accepts humiliation." The suffering obedience that is his victory comes through his solidarity with humankind.[39]

Thus Yoder's treatment of Hebrews continues his emphasis on showing multiple ways to express the meaning of the life, death, and resurrection of Jesus.

Theologians: John

Yoder has brief comments on the Christology of John, focused primarily on the term Logos or the Word that appears in the Prologue to the Gospel of John. The writer of John is at home in the Greek language and imagery. Logos is the term from Greek philosophy that might be called "reason" or "the rationality of God that underlies the universe." The writer of the Gospel says that the Word was "preexistent" with God, and that it "became flesh."[40]

That the Word became flesh is, Yoder noted, not typical of the way Greek philosophy talked about divine rationality, nor is it typical of the Jewish mind, which considered God invisible. But that the Word became flesh and was therefore visible was important for John. In fact, in 1 John 4:2–3, that the Word was in flesh becomes a test of faith: "Every spirit that confesses that Jesus Christ has come in the flesh is from God, and every spirit that does not confess Jesus is not from God." That the Word came in the flesh—was seen and touched by the apostles (1 John 1:1–3)—was

---

38. Ibid., 118–19.
39. Ibid., 118–20; Yoder's italics.
40. Ibid., 120.

part of the apostolic witness. The Word in flesh, the incarnation, wrote Yoder "is a statement on the authority and the message of the church, and thereby the test whereby you know whether it is correct or not."[41]

Yoder also briefly identified a principle in John similar to the logic of solidarity. It is visible in John 15:4, "Abide in me as I abide in you." This logic also appears in the language of Sonship, which Yoder links to 1 John 3:1–2.[42] Through abiding in Jesus the Son, believers are also sons and daughters—children—of God. To see the link Yoder depicts between Jesus as Son and believers as children of God, one must read 1 John 2:24–25 about abiding in the Son along with 1 John 3:1–2 and the mention of being children of God.[43]

Summaries

Yoder summarized the theological method of the three theologians Paul, Hebrews, and John, and then provided a summary of theologizing as a whole in the New Testament.

The Three Theologians

The three theologians have clear differences, Yoder said. There are "major differences in style and in logic," and in the centrality of future eschatology or belief in an immediate return of Christ. For the later writings, the focus shifts away from expectation of an immediate return.[44]

These writings also share important similarities and themes. They all share a reference to "the Jesus history, whatever the theme being talked about." They all use the "logic of solidarity," which is expressed in different images—Sonship, "being in Christ," or simply expressed as a solidarity. Further, they all say that "salvation is a unity of status and a life." In other words, where later theologians might distinguish between "being saved and acting saved," or between "justification and sanctification," the New Testament assumed that "to be in God's purposes is the same as to be living in the light."[45]

41. Ibid., 121.
42. Ibid.
43. See ibid., 121 n. 3.
44. Ibid., 122–23.
45. Ibid., 123.

These theologians all have something of the concept that would later be called "preexistence." Expressions of this motif came in John's use of the eternal Word, Hebrews' use of Old Testament quotations to say that the "Son was working in the Old Testament story," the reference in Colossians to the Son's involvement in creation, and the "equality with God" of Philippians 2.[46]

Finally, these writers all move away from what later writers called "adoptionism," namely the idea that Jesus "became the Son," or was elevated to Sonship because of his obedience. This idea is there, but becomes increasingly "undergirded" or added to by the various themes of preexistence. That Jesus began life like all other people "is not enough to explain what he did," and from the perspective of monotheism, the idea of a man "being made God is unacceptable." The alternative, then, was that God had acted. God took the initiative and had "become a man among humans."[47]

New Testament Theologizing

This discussion of the New Testament, Yoder reminds readers, has not been a summary of Christian thought but rather "theology going on as thought—theologizing as a process." This thinking, this theologizing by the early church involved gathering "around a series of events," the events of the Jesus story, and ascribing meaning to those events. This developing meaning had three expanding circles of reference. The first was the confession "Christ is Lord," with focus on the resurrection which testified to the Lordship of Christ. Second, the story of Jesus is linked to the past history of Israel and thus links the listeners with Jesus into the future. The third level of reference involved statements about Sonship, mighty works, and more.[48]

Gathering around events indicates that there was "no radical distinction" between events and the meaning of those events. Where moderns would clearly distinguish the bare description of an event from its meaning, the New Testament did not. That lack of distinction appears in the claim that having witnessed the events of Jesus requires a response.

46. Ibid., 124.
47. Ibid.
48. Ibid., 125.

"We are witnesses to these things" indicates to the hearers, "You must repent."[49]

Further, these events are proclaimed as "the work of Jesus Christ." There is no independent discussion of a doctrine of God the Father or of the Holy Spirit. Statements about God or the Spirit concerned Jesus or related to Jesus. God was identified as the Father of Jesus and the Spirit was the Spirit of Jesus.[50]

The life of the early church is a continuation of this story of Jesus. An apostle was "one who was in continuity with that story." The early church gathered around the apostles because they were the ones "who could establish the continuity between the earthly ministry of Jesus and the resurrection." A further element of continuity occurred in the collection of sayings of Jesus. Paul referred to such sayings and eventually they were formed into the Gospels.[51]

There were different levels of theological sophistication in the primitive or early church. Contributing to the theology of the early church was

> the simple resurrection as the basis of Christ's Lordship, the testimony that the Old Testament is fulfilled in him, that a judgment is coming, and that we are called to a sober, suffering, and obedient life. This is the theology of the New Testament church, the church of the first century. Only on the shoulders of this church does theology develop that might be called a more "systematic," a more "self-conscious," or a more "abstract" theology on the part of Paul, Hebrews, and John.[52]

The language for this theologizing came from the key sermons whose outline was depicted in Acts. Snippets of hymns and liturgy, such as Philippians 2, also appear, along with oral reports of memories of Jesus.[53]

Yoder observed that changes occurring in the church required the development of theology. For one, early Christians faced the danger of false or improper doctrine. Spirits continued to speak. Thus development of theology was necessary in order to test whether the speech was of God. Further, they had a mandate to transmit the memory of the church to

---

49. Ibid., 125–26.
50. Ibid., 126.
51. Ibid.
52. Ibid., 127.
53. Ibid.

succeeding generations. Memory is what establishes their identity, what they have in common. Catechism developed to teach the community's story, its identity, to newcomers. This memory included the Old Testament. Acts pictures the early Christians reading this book together. However, catechism requires more than rote memory. It requires decisions about the priority of teachings and how teachings fit together. This requirement is the "mandate to think theologically."[54]

Theologizing took place through a variety of forms and offices. These included apostle, prophet, elder, and elder-teacher. Teaching occurred in worship meetings, in catechism classes, and in public debates.[55]

Another challenge to which theology responded came from paganism. The pagan religions and pagan worldviews focused on "ontology," which was concerned with the "essence" of things. Ontology had answers to questions about the origin of the world. And these religions contained mysteries, namely special ceremonies that enabled the worshiper to get beyond surface appearances in order to experience the essence of the world. The response of the first Christian preachers was to say that God is the origin of all things, and that this creator God was made known in Jesus Christ. "The God who made the earth and gave us a place to live has now spoken in the Son." And by the time of the major theological writings, there is a concept of "preexistence." Not only is Jesus accredited as the one whom God raised, but "the Word or the Son is involved in creation as well."[56] Thus the response to "ontology" as the invisible essence of the world was to say that God was the origin of all existence, and "preexistence" was the language for involving Jesus in that origin.

Yoder asks rhetorically whether the words about involvement of the Word in creation are "a statement about cosmology, . . . a piece of divinely revealed information." His answer is "no." This language is rather the normal way to speak about the meaning of Jesus in a pagan world that seeks to experience the essence behind what is visible. "Thus, at least in the immediate sense of the missionary experience of the church, these affirmations of preexistence and creation are not given as new information, revealed for their own sake, but they are the normal, appropriate missionary way to state the priority of Christ over the preoccupations of pagan faith."[57] Yoder's essay "But We Do See Jesus," considered in what

54. Yoder, *Preface* (2002), 127–28.
55. Ibid., 128–29.
56. Ibid., 130.
57. Ibid.

follows, makes this point even more forcefully. An application of this methodology of translating meaning rather than language also appears in Yoder's appropriation of the rubric of the Powers for such Pauline statements as "things visible and invisible" and "thrones or dominions or rulers": in Colossians 1:15 and the "elemental spirits" of Galatians 4:3, 9. Yoder's use of the Powers is treated in chapter 6 of this volume.

The strongly monotheist Jewish community constituted the other side of the church's missionary context. The Jewish community affirmed God above creation and the working of God in history, "but they denied the ultimacy of Jesus within this story." In response to efforts to contain the working of God within the cultural system of Judaism, the theologians proclaimed Jesus Christ as the fulfillment of the law. In his person, Jesus Christ has made present the working of the one God of monotheism. Thus in addition to the idea of "preexistence," which places Jesus above the pagan worship of creation, there was "a doctrine of fulfillment to place Christ above the Old Testament story," handled various ways in Paul, Hebrews, and John.[58]

Yet another challenge to the early church came from Gnosticism, which glorified philosophical and religious truth. Gnosticism valued the invisible, spiritual realm over the material world. Ultimate reality concerned the mind. No material events or person could be eternal. Thus Gnostics had a mystical system through which they hoped to save people from ignorance and put them in contact with ultimate reality. This view of reality meant that Gnostics denied the ultimacy of Jesus because he existed in time, in the flesh, in a particular place.[59] "The Gnostic depreciation of the material and the temporal is visible all the way through the New Testament." It is the backdrop for the many affirmations throughout the New Testament of the coming of Jesus in the flesh and the emphasis on the visible humanness of Jesus.[60]

Yoder brings these observations together with the assertion that theologians of the New Testament make "two sweeping affirmations," which are identified in contemporary technical language as "preexistence and incarnation." The claim that God raised Jesus was extended through discussion of the history of Jesus and calls for repentance. Eventually the wider claim

58. Ibid., 131.
59. Ibid.
60. Ibid., 131–32.

is extended in the affirmation of preexistence, which places it above pagan religions; it is extended in the affirmation of fulfillment, which places it above defensive Jewish religion; and it is extended in the affirmation of incarnation, which breaks through the Gnostic idea that it is only worthy of God to be working outside of matter.[61]

Yoder pointed out three questions not discussed explicitly in the New Testament. For one, there is no doctrine of atonement beyond the minimal statement that Jesus is Lord and that he died for sins. Further, there is no explanation of how the high claims about Jesus—he was involved in creation and existed with God from the beginning—correspond to Jewish monotheism. And it was not explained how Jesus was both identified fully with human kind but also more than human. These questions are all discussed extensively in the centuries following the New Testament.[62]

Yoder's description of theologizing in the New Testament focused on the factors of variety and change and development. He described development as "saying more." That is, writers assumed the original story, which said that Jesus was killed and God raised him. They then extracted additional meaning from the story and used different images and additional concepts to explain the meaning of the story in new contexts and to develop points not contained explicitly in that story. Together these developments added up to changes in both methodology and content for New Testament theologizing.[63] An important aspect of Yoder's analysis of these changes is the visibility he gave to multiple ways of expressing the additional meaning that addressed different contexts.

Yoder stressed that change in and of itself is neither good nor bad. It can be either a faithful or an unfaithful effort to carry forward the original story and its meaning. Thus the point is not to oppose change as the way to guarantee preservation of the original truth; in fact, change may be the faithful way to carry forward the original truth. And in any case change is inevitable. But the equally important point is that change should not always be supported as inherently good; change can also result in departure from the truth of the original story. Rather, Yoder said,

---

61. Ibid., 132.

62. Ibid., 132–34. The current chapter focuses on Christology. A discussion of atonement theology appears in chapter 11 of this volume.

63. Ibid., 134–35.

because change can be either faithful or unfaithful, faithfulness needs to be decided on an individual, case by case basis.[64]

In what he called a "Postscript" on Christology, Yoder made an important point for a proper understanding of his approach to Christology. In the postscript, he described a series of steps that led to the writing of the Gospels, from the collection of memories through to the approximate written form that we know today. The important point concerns the relationship of the Gospels to the theologians. The theologians wrote first. With "something like preexistence and cosmic lordship," they were unfolding the meaning of the story of "the earthly figure" of Jesus. The formulation of the Gospels followed later. They were written to fill out the minimal historical narrative recited by the theologians who had already made high claims about Jesus. Seeing this relationship undercuts the claims of an earlier epoch in scholarship in which it was argued that the Gospels had a simple Christology, "the religion *of* Jesus," which was then later made more complicated by the theologians with "the religions *about* Jesus." Rather, Yoder indicated, high Christology is not the prerogative of one or the other of the New Testament writings. "The Gospels were not written to give us a Christology less ambitious than that of the Epistles; they were rather written to clarify and hold fast the concrete human content of the faith in Jesus of whom the most exalted things were already being said."[65] The clear implication of Yoder's comment is that it is not necessary to access the later classic creedal formulas to defend a high Christology.

Historical Development (ca. 50–150 CE)

Yoder continued his emphasis on displaying multiple expressions or answers in the periods after the passing of the New Testament writers. The first such epoch was that of the Apostolic Fathers, the writers who knew the apostles.

Relevant for the focus of the current chapter on Yoder's approach to Christology are his brief comments on the development of the concept of Logos or Word. The Apostolic Fathers developed the meaning of Logos at greater length, and Gnostics used Logos as well as the churchly writers. Logos was a kind of divine energy, "not the same as Jesus but behind

---

64. Ibid., 135–37.
65. Ibid., 139–40; Yoder's italics.

him and active in creation." Philosophers conceived of many levels of intermediaries that stood between God and humanity and transmitted this divine energy down to the human level. On this ladder, Logos was the "rationality of creation." It helped the prophets, and it helped contemporary people. It was in Jesus, but also had an "identity behind Jesus." There were numbers of ways of conceiving of the impact of the Logos, including use by the Gnostics.[66] Yoder does not explain further at this point. However, it is important to have in mind his mention of multiple ways of referring to the Word when we later observe Yoder's analysis of the Jewish-Christian schism in chapter 10 of the book in hand.

The Christology of the Apostles' Creed

With his comments on the Apostles' Creed Yoder begins analysis of theology that has advanced beyond the formulations found in the New Testament.

The Apostles' Creed was likely an early baptismal formula. Yoder observed that the reference to the Father in the first article is little more than a prologue to the statements about the Son, and that the collection of phrases in the third article concerning the Holy Spirit have the appearance of an epilogue. Thus the second article, with its filled-out statements on the Son, is clearly central. Focusing on Christology thus aligns this creed with the emphasis on Jesus in earlier confessions, including the narrative character of the second article's statements on the conception, birth, death, and ascension of Jesus.[67]

But significant differences also exist between the Apostles' Creed and the earliest focus on the narrative of Jesus. For one, "There is no Old Testament story." Whereas apostolic preaching as well as John's Gospel and Hebrews used the Old Testament, this creed reaches back over that narrative to creation.[68]

A second significant change concerned the location of the call to forgiveness. In the early confessions, forgiveness was connected to hearing the story of Jesus, and it presumed the possibility of a real conversion—change—in one's way of life. In contrast, in the Apostles' Creed, forgiveness is a stand-alone item under the Holy Spirit—simply an entity

66. Ibid., 154.
67. Ibid., 160.
68. Ibid., 161.

to believe in. Further, the creed does not mention the life of Jesus, although his birth receives "proportionately more attention than in the Gospels." And from birth, it leaps to crucifixion under Pontius Pilate. This leap means that there is no mention of anything like "Jesus' call to repentance." Yoder attributes this absence to the fact that the creed functions during the time when it is assumed that everyone is already a believer. With the pagan world now coming under control of the church, the concept of the church as a minority in society, "calling people to listen, repent, believe, and receive forgiveness, does not quite fit."[69]

Third, "the 'fullness of time' theme is missing." That is, there is no mention of fulfillment of Old Testament prophecies. God the Father as creator substitutes for the Old Testament story, but it also creates a significant difference from Paul. Jesus spoke of "the Father" as the one to whom we pray, and for the early preachers such as Paul, God as Father was the Father of Jesus who had raised him. Thus, Yoder says, the creed's designation of the Father as Creator "deviates from the New Testament."[70]

These comments on the Apostles' Creed further display Yoder's awareness of choices made in theological expression and how they are reflected in theology

Nicea and Trinitarian Issues

Unresolved at the end of the New Testament was the issue of how to maintain the Jewish emphasis on monotheism while making high claims about Jesus. This question occupied much of the discussion of Christology into the fourth century, which Yoder follows until the formula from the council of Nicea is accepted as official doctrine. The debates around the issue involved "the phenomenon of getting off the track and getting called back." The idea of positions "off the track" means recognizing "the phenomenon of heresy—positions and doctrines held to be so wrong that they need to be explicitly condemned."[71] Until he discusses the meaning of these developments, Yoder's description differs little from the conventional story. Thus the account here presents only the briefest summaries of views as a lead up to his discussion of their meaning.

69. Ibid., 161–62.
70. Ibid., 162.
71. Ibid., 181.

Yoder gave general characteristics of the context for these ongoing conversations about Christology. For one, there was a gradual shift from Hebrew to Greek philosophical categories. Greek philosophy became the medium used to discuss how to retain high views of Jesus combined with monotheism.[72] In contrast to the earlier view of theologians such as Adolf von Harnack, Yoder is quite clear that this shift in categories is not intrinsically bad. As he said a few pages later, these words were the way that the Greeks discussed the issues in question. Nonetheless, as is described below, it was a shift that needs to be recognized.[73]

Yoder began the post New Testament discussion with the Word in John and its Old Testament parallel, Wisdom. In Proverbs 8, Wisdom speaks in the first person. In this voice, Wisdom describes roles parallel to those John depicts for the Word. Both are with God from the beginning and involved in creation. What John adds is that "The Word became flesh and lived among us." Yoder points out that John indicates no apparent problems in the chain of equations in which "the *Logos* is equal to God, and somehow becomes human, and in between is the order of creation." Thus at this point "Greek and Jewish traditions are nearly parallel."[74] Yoder notes that the heritage of this linking of Greek and Hebrew concepts was observed in his earlier lectures on New Testament texts and appears in the idea of "preexistence." What the New Testament does is bring this act of God in Wisdom and/or Word to earth. The newness is that "wisdom became flesh. Yet by becoming fully human, by living among us, the *Logos* did not become any less divine, because John also says the *Logos* was 'with God.'"[75]

The problem this sets up is how to maintain the unity of God in monotheism while taking seriously that Jesus was fully human. Yoder identified two lines of thought. "We can say strong things about Jesus, but then we have a potential threat to monotheism, or we can say strong things about the Father and then deal with the problems of how real Jesus could be and how necessary his work can be." He describes the development of doctrine to Nicea and Trinity as a study of the answers to these questions.[76]

---

72. Yoder, *Preface* (2002), 183.
73. See ibid., 202.
74. Ibid., 184–85.
75. Ibid., 186.
76. Ibid.

Yoder called this "an intellectual problem," a problem we have because of words. However, very significantly, he cautioned that merely using different words than those employed by the church of the second and third century will not resolve the problem. Even if we use different words, the problem still exists and must be faced.[77]

The answers Yoder described are well known in the history of doctrine. Since the important issue for this chapter is how Yoder evaluates the end result, brief summaries of positions here will suffice. He described two kinds of "Monarchianism," that is views that focus on preserving the unity of God. Ebionites preserved the unity of God by emphasizing the humanity of Jesus and denying his preexistence. Moving in the other direction was *patripassianism*. This likely pejorative name comes from words for "suffering" and "father," and stresses the unity of God in Jesus to the detriment of a true humanity of Jesus. Thus it has similarities with the various forms of Docetism. By the second and third centuries, docetic stress on the unity of God leads to the idea that distinctions in the way God acts, as in the Old Testament and in Jesus, are only appearances and do not reflect God in God's inner being. Thus in these docetic depictions of God and Jesus, Jesus' work is God's work and in Jesus God is really suffering. Yoder affirmed that none of these monarchian positions "fits the New Testament witness."[78]

Yoder described a new stage with Tertullian in the development of language. Tertullian was working at a system that keeps unity and distinction together—the unity of God together with the capacity of God in the Word to act differently. Within God's being are both the potential for incarnation and the actual incarnation. As part of this system, Tertullian started to talk of the Son rather than the Logos. This replacement is part of the desire to maintain unity within distinctness. From this effort, Tertullian may have been the first to use a threeness term, what later became Trinity, as a way to affirm distinctions within God that preserve the unity of God.[79]

In Yoder's description, Origen said that if it was good for God to have a Son, then God was always, forever having a Son and the Son was always being generated. However, this argument would also apply to creation of the world, which would then produce an eternal world along

77. Ibid.
78. Ibid., 187–88.
79. Ibid., 189–91.

with eternal God and Son. Thus Origen's view proved problematic.[80] Even more problematic was Sabellius. His view retained the oneness of God but considered the various ways in which God worked in the world as "modes," hence the name modalism. However, in Sabellius' understanding of the "mode" of a man, Jesus had only the appearance of a man and was not fully human.[81]

The discussion of Christology that has most impacted the church until the present time began in the fourth century with the response to Arius, a priest in the North African city of Alexandria. Arius came from the side of defending the uniqueness of God. In order to distinguish God from the Son, Arius purportedly said that there was a time when the Son was not; that is, God existed before time, and the Son was created in time. He also considered God to be the first cause, that God then created the Son, and then together they created the universe. In this way, Jesus was divine and similar to but not the same as God. Such views subordinated the Son to the Father. They produced a fire storm of reaction.[82]

In order to bring some unity to the theological situation within the church, Emperor Constantine called a council to attempt a resolution. This council met at Nicea in 325 CE. The solution that emerged from the council is well known. It used a statement like the Apostles' Creed, but expanded statements about the relationship of the Father and the Son. Father and Son are described with the same terms, with equality of being defined in terms of *ousia* or "substance." The phrase that symbolizes this equality is *homoousios*, which is translated "same substance" or "same being." It rejects the position of Arius, who would have accepted *homoiousios* or "of similar substance." The text that emerged from Nicea has become known as the Nicene Creed.[83]

The decision of Nicea was not immediately accepted as final. Debates on these issues continued for another half century. In 381 CE, the council of Constantinople restated the decision from Nicea. The form of the Nicene Creed still in use today follows the version that emerged from Constantinople. It finally attained official status after being cited by the council of Ephesus in 431 CE.[84]

80. Ibid., 191–92.
81. Ibid., 192–95.
82. Ibid., 195–97.
83. Ibid., 197–98.
84. Ibid., 198.

To this point, Yoder's description of the development of the Nicene Creed resembles the standard or conventional history of doctrine. His analysis becomes more interesting when he discusses the character and authority of this creed.

Yoder stated that doctrines, in particular one such as emerged from Nicea, are "basically a set of assumptions about how we should use words and rules about what certain words ought and ought not to be used to mean." He aligned the Greek, Latin, and English equivalents for the terms used to identity essence or substance of God and the Son, and the term *prosopon* or person to identify the different means of expression within the Godhead. In this case, Yoder explained, the discussion concerned the proper words to employ when naming the unity of God and in identifying its separate manifestations. "The doctrine of the Trinity," Yoder said, "in a very simple sense is just a set of rules about which of those words you use for what," that is, which word to use to assert the oneness of God and which word to use for the three distinct manifestations.[85]

The new answer, and the one still in use today, was developed in the late fourth century by the three Cappadocians, Gregory of Nyssa, Gregory Nazianzus, and Basil of Caesarea. It is from them that the convention developed to use what is translated in English as one "essence" or "substance" to speak of God the Father and the Son and the Holy Spirit as one, and to use the term "person" when designating the three distinctions or faces within the Godhead.[86] This usage then produces the familiar trinitarian formula, "One God in three Persons."

Yoder calls this a "merely verbal formality," but emphasizes that it also meets a need. "It safeguards the New Testament content with at least a degree of success in a quite different thought world." The specific New Testament content it protects is that "Jesus, the Word in Jesus, is genuinely of the character of deity and genuinely human, and that his is the work of God and yet the work of a man." Where the New Testament writers made these affirmations in a narrative, the theologians at Nicea said it in "ontological and philosophical language."[87]

Although Yoder called it "only" a verbal solution to a problem posed by the New Testament, he quickly adds that "only verbal" is not grounds for reproach. "Words are the only tools [we] have to deal with truth. The

---

85. Ibid., 199–200.
86. Ibid., 200–201.
87. Ibid., 201–2.

problem was verbal in the first place." Yoder also defended this formulation of the doctrine of the Trinity against the charge that it does not talk about God as love. Since Nicea affirms that God is actually present not only in the distant God of Arius but also in God's Son and in God's Spirit, "this is the way to say 'love' in the language of ontology."[88]

But following this defense, Yoder offered another qualification. Although these definitions are defending biblical ideas, it is equally clear "that *in form* we are moving farther and farther away from the Gospel story. The form of the confession is still used, but it has been so padded out with statements about the essence of Christ that one recognizes no narrative any more." The absence of narrative is significant, Yoder indicated. This statement without the narrative does not lead one to think that an action of God among humans at a distinct time and place is important.[89] In other words, focus on essences apart from narrative says nothing about ethics based on Jesus.

88. Ibid., 202. Much later, in an item on his website dated 1996, Yoder wrote that "there are good reasons . . . for favoring the special intellectual articulations we call 'trinitarian.' I have sought to give the trinitarian heritage a friendly interpretation, but it is an argument that needs to be made." His reference to "friendly interpretation" was to chapter 8 of *Preface*. He adds that "neither the imperial rubber stamp . . . nor liturgical repetition of the 'Nicene Creed' over the centuries can give those formulations more authority than what their intrinsic logic merits." Yoder, "Confessing Jesus in Mission," 2.

89. Yoder, *Preface* (2002), 202; Yoder's italics. A parallel statement, emphasizing obedience, appears in an essay rewritten from a 1964 lecture. Yoder wrote, "The concept of Incarnation, God's assuming manhood, has often made us direct our thought to metaphysics, asking how it can be that the human nature and the divine nature can be present together in one person. . . . But when, in the New Testament, we find the affirmation of the unity of Jesus with the Father, this is not discussed in terms of substance, but of will and deed. It is visible in Jesus' perfect *obedience* to the *will* of the Father. It is evident in Jesus that God takes the side of the poor. It is evident in Jesus that when God comes to be King He rejects the sword and the throne, taking up instead the whip of cords and the cross." Yoder, *Original Revolution*, 136, Yoder's italics; reprinted in Yoder, *Royal Priesthood*, 185.

Parler chastises me for neglecting a link in the fifth century between ontology and ethics and Chalcedon's link to Christian discipleship. See Parler, *Things Hold Together*, 95. In any such comment that I have made, I am thinking of a statement from Yoder such as the one just quoted, as well as comments from a number of scholars I have cited in other writings who also point to the absence of narrative and specifics of Jesus in the classic statements. And while Chalcedon should underscore Christian discipleship, as Yoder noted, history seems to demonstrate quite clearly that it has not, at least not the nonviolent discipleship that I have learned from Yoder. For a description of activity around Chalcedon not motivated by nonviolent discipleship, see Jenkins, *Jesus Wars*.

As Nicea moved away from the narrative form, Yoder observed, the subject matter also changed. The focus shifted away from resurrection and came to concern the eternal status of the one resurrected. And continuing cultural changes would require still more shifts. Earlier Yoder had pointed to the shifts that occurred when the New Testament theologians built upon the original narrative of Jesus. Each movement built upon another and "required a more involved inquiry to decide whether the new form expressed the same faith as the old." With that observation in mind, it becomes clear that "with Nicea we are still moving away from the biblical center in mode, in style, in content."[90]

90. Yoder, *Preface* (2002), 202. In their introduction to *Preface*, Hauerwas and Sider object to Yoder's description of differences in vocabulary and worldview between the New Testament and the classic formulas. In their view, in some of his efforts to draw contrasts, Yoder does not acknowledge the "extent that the Judaism of first-century Palestine had already been shaped by Hellenism." And thus Yoder's suggestion "that the fathers attempted to solve with the doctrine of the Trinity a problem created by the encounter between the gospel-bearing culture and the Greek philosophical tradition fails sufficiently to credit those Greek fathers' struggle with Scripture itself." They also suggest that scholarship of the "last fifteen or twenty years" displays in a way that Yoder did not know "the increasing realization that the ante- and post-Nicene fathers not only considered scripture their primary imaginative resource, but were also theologically motivated in the first place to produce coherent readings of Scripture, as opposed to coherent comprehensive worldviews." They suggested, however, that even where Yoder "gets it wrong," it is appropriate to publish this edition because it teaches students to reflect critically, and Yoder himself welcomed correction. Yoder, *Preface* (2002), 23, 25–26. Their comments reveal that Hauerwas and Sider actually agree with at least a part of my analysis of Yoder's relativizing of the classic formulas, but dispute Yoder's analysis. Further, their comment does not negate the fact that there was a shift in worldview from the assumption of narrative to the ontological, and that as the presentation of Yoder's thought in this chapter shows, he was careful to say specifically that the classic formulas were dealing with material from Scripture in the language of ontology. On this point see also the comment from Yoder in note 88. And finally, other recent scholarship on the politics of the early church would strengthen Yoder's argument that the classic formulas reflect a particular context but different than that of the New Testament. For examples, see Philip Jenkins' description of how political forces determined the assertion of orthodoxy; Virginia Burrus' argument that the Nicene formula supported patriarchy and raised the male above female, and that the idea of the Council of Nicea as the unified bulwark against Arius was a product of Athanasius' literary work more than two decades after the council; and Michel Barnes' conclusions that in the immediate aftermath of the council, the Nicene formula was suspected of being modalistic, and that "a careful reading of Athanasius' works reveals that it took him almost twenty years to come to [a normative] understanding of the significance of Nicaea, while he took almost another ten years to fasten upon *homoousios* as the *sine qua non* of Nicene theology." Jenkins, *Jesus Wars*; Burrus, *"Begotten Not Made"*, ch. 1; Barnes, "Fourth Century," quote 53. It appears that the critique of Hauerwas and

A further development that Yoder labeled a "deformation" concerns the meaning of the term "person" in the doctrine of the Trinity. In modern usage, "person" has come to mean "center of consciousness, a will distinct from other wills." That meaning would visualize three distinct personalities and seats of consciousness in the Trinity. Yoder rejects that development as "a new import into the doctrine of the Trinity." In Yoder's understanding, the earlier, proper understanding of "person" would be on the order of "three roles, three modes, three ways of acting." In this case, "mode" is not the shell that God moves in and out of for Sabellius, but rather a "way of being."[91]

In light of the recognition of Trinity as official doctrine, Yoder indicates another "point of deformation," namely to think that threeness in and of itself constitutes salvific knowledge. This deformation "arises if we think that God's self-revelation of threeness-in-oneness is itself something that saves us." An extreme form of this deformation appears, according to Yoder, in the medieval teaching that God existing in three persons "can only be known by revelation," that it is "a piece of information about deity" that we know "because it was given us by special supernatural revelation. As a matter of fact," he said, "it was not given us by revelation."[92] Popular versions of Yoder's concern might be the common practice of finding threeness in nature to bolster trinitarianism (such as the sun, its rays, its heat) and the claim that threeness is the unique attribute of the Christian view of God.

Yoder rejected the idea that threeness itself was a product of revelation. That there are three *hypostases* or persons and one *ousia* or essence "cannot be given by revelation. It is something the Cappadocians figured out in the fourth century." The Bible tells us, he said, that there is God the Father and the Son and the Spirit and that they are the same. However, how we relate them to each other while keeping in mind the differences "was worked out later. The doctrine of the Trinity is the solution to an intellectual difficulty that arises if we accept the statements of the Bible. It is not itself a revealed truth, but the solution[93] to the word problem

---

Sider is shaped in significant measure by their desire to protect the classic formulas as unquestioned givens, a givenness that is called into question by Yoder's relativizing of the classic creeds and formulas. For Yoder's own description of his methodology as "relativizing," see the discussion referenced by note 8 in the Introduction.

91. Yoder, *Preface* (2002), 202–3.

92. Ibid., 201, 203–4

93. Yoder's original version said "a solution," which became "the solution" in the edited version. For the original, see Yoder, *Preface* (1981), 140.

we get into when we accept revelation in Jesus, the continuance of that revelation in the Holy Spirit, and hold to monotheism at the same time."[94]

Yoder raised the question whether the doctrine of the Trinity is "valid in other cultures." He suggests that it may be possible not to use the "ancient Greek literary forms." However, merely avoiding those forms does not solve the problem. If Christians are to be Christian, they still have to deal with the problem that Trinity was trying to resolve, namely "the normativity of Jesus as he relates to the uniqueness of God." This doctrine is a test whether one's "commitments to Jesus and to God are biblical enough that you have the problem the doctrine of the Trinity solves. It may be that there will be other solutions, words, phrasings or ways to avoid tripping over the problem the way the Greeks did." But unless those solutions reflect a commitment to the man Jesus and to the unique God of Jesus, "we shall have left the Christian family."[95]

In an important point, whose significance will be developed later in chapter 10, Yoder wrote that the history of the ideas depicted in the post-New Testament period was complex and "enormously varied and enormously scattered." That means that the logical development of positions he described ought not be taken "as an actual description of what went on."[96]

Describing the doctrine of the Trinity as an intellectual problem brings Yoder to the question of the authority of the Nicene Creed. His statement reflects the two-fold comments on the doctrine of the Trinity.

---

94. Yoder, *Preface* (2002), 204.

95. Ibid. That Yoder could reject "threeness-in-oneness" as saving doctrine and as a product of revelation, and also raise the possibility that different language might be used in another culture, indicates why, in my view, it is inappropriate for Branson Parler to brand Yoder's approach to culture "trinitarian." Note the subtitle of Parler, *Things Hold Together: John Howard Yoder's Trinitarian Theology of Culture*, as well as his entire argument. Parler is of course correct that Yoder's theology affirmed both the presence of God in the work of Jesus and the unity of Father, Son, and Holy Spirit, which Yoder said was the intent behind the traditional doctrine. And the designation of trinitarian is certainly attractive to the creedal-oriented audience that Parler is most interested in addressing. Nonetheless, since Yoder indicated that threeness was not itself an intrinsic characteristic of God in Christ, and since Yoder implied that other language was appropriate, and since as is stated later in this essay Yoder mentioned giving a favorable analysis of the classic formulations "without being tied to the adequacy of these formulations in all other times and places," the designation "trinitarian" is a misleading descriptor of Yoder's theology. It is not a designation that he would have applied to himself.

96. Yoder, *Preface* (2002), 205.

On the one hand, he notes that it is "understandable" that the "high church tradition" would affirm Nicea and also later creeds "because the king was finally on that side." This political authority gives the Nicene Creed a "hermeneutical authority" that is "not theoretically above the Bible but practically above it in application."[97] But beyond this high church tradition, Yoder notes that many Christian groups and theologians, "who in principle refuse to grant the Catholic church any right to set up a normative interpretation of the Bible . . . , still give the Nicene Creed and its trinitarian statements equal authority with the Bible."[98]

Yoder listed two arguments that make it "dubious" to give this creed any authority. One argument concerns the politics between 325 and 431 from which the creed emerged, the motives and methods of the theologians involved, and "the personal quality of Constantine." The second argument against granting authority concerns the way that "Hellenistic thought forms" are "foreign" to the biblical way of thinking, and fit "neither the Hebrew mind nor, for that matter, with the modern mind."[99]

Thus Yoder rejects any authoritative claim for the creed based on the belief that it is "supernatural truth, supernaturally communicated for its information value." He rejects the idea that it might be "learning [that] the Holy Spirit gave to the Council Fathers at Nicea because there were bishops assembled from the whole world at the invitation from the Roman Emperor." Apart from adherents to a high church tradition, the "only claim" that fits with "the Believers' Church tradition, and for modern reading of the story" is that "it seems to have provided the best answer to an intellectual problem." The doctrine of Nicea "is not authoritative, but the claims of Jesus who creates the problem are." Nicea "is valid because it reflects the serious struggle of people, within their language and culture, with their commitment to an absolute God and to a normative Jesus."[100] As further comments from Yoder and analysis of his writing will reveal, that is not an endorsement of the Nicene Creed as a universal statement and it is certainly not the establishment of Nicene doctrine as the basis of Yoder's further theologizing and his ethics.[101]

97. Ibid.
98. Ibid., 204.
99. Ibid.
100. Ibid., 205.
101. See note 146, which discusses the claim that Yoder built on Nicea in the context of the analysis that displays his essay "But We Do See Jesus" as a continuation of his discussion from *Preface*.

Chalcedon and the Humanity of Jesus

Yoder began his discussion of the emergence of the formula of Chalcedon with the declaration that the more seriously one takes the deity of Jesus, as asserted by Nicea, the more acute become the questions concerning the human and divine natures of Jesus. "The more the doctrine of the Son as divine *hypostasis* is settled, the more difficult the relationship that he has to the man Jesus becomes."[102] Again, the general outline of these developments is well-known in the history of doctrine, and I supply only the briefest sketch for reference purposes.

The positions emerged from the differing emphases of the theological schools at Alexandria and Antioch. Alexandria was most concerned to preserve the unity of Jesus' person. In discussion of the incarnation, the Alexandrians used the language of the Word becoming flesh. The school of Antioch focused on the particular humanity of Jesus as a man. For them, the discussion of incarnation meant that Jesus became a man.

As Yoder told the story, both schools intended to be trinitarian and to affirm the statements from Nicea. However, their varying emphases lead to different concerns or fears. The Alexandrians feared Ebionitism, the idea that Jesus was a righteous man on whom deity may have descended. In contrast, the Antiochians were concerned to reject modalism, the idea that the visible form of a man was only a shell in which deity dwelled and not true humanity.

The most well-known deviant position in the Alexandrian line was articulated by Apollinarus. His effort at preserving both humanity and deity in a unified person produced the idea of a "divine mind," namely the "Logos of God," resident in Jesus' human body. Apollinarus' view thus is "docetic," a view in which Jesus is not fully human. He lacked a human mind. It "did not grow, did not make decisions, because it was the mind of God."[103]

The major controversy, which continued for several decades, concerned the supposed teaching of Nestorius, a member of the Antiochian school who became the patriarch of Constantinople in 428. In the following years he preached sermons against patripassianism and docetism, views that did not take Jesus' humanity seriously. As a part of his argument, Nestorius objected to the term Theotokos, or "mother of God."

---

102. Yoder, *Preface* (2002), 212.
103. Ibid., 214.

Because Jesus was the Son of God, Nestorius could accept the term, but he preferred the term "mother of Christ." With this term he sought to avoid the appearance of worshipping the mother as well as the Son. In order to embarrass the Antioch school, Cyril the bishop of Alexandria then accused Nestorius of teaching that Jesus was actually both a human son and a divine Son inhabiting one body. Politics had a great deal to do with the course of the argument, which went on for more than two decades. The details need not concern us here.

A council was called that met at Chalcedon in 451. The formula adopted by the council affirmed Nicea's declaration that Father and Son were of the same substance. Then it applied that language to Jesus and humanity as well. Mary was called Theotokos. And the person of Jesus was described in "two natures, without confusion, without change, without division, without separation." This answer presumed to speak to the concerns of both Alexandria and Antioch as it affirmed the unity of Jesus' person while also acknowledging both human and divine natures. Yoder called it a statement "of the distinctness of the natures in their unity." It was Nestorius' position, but he lost out in the politics and he was condemned personally.[104]

Yoder suggested several points for evaluation of the Chalcedonian formula. First and perhaps most important, it puts on display that the church took the declaration of Nicea seriously. There would have been no debate about the relationship of Jesus' humanity or human nature to his divine nature if there were not first a strong affirmation of Jesus' deity and unity with God the Father.[105]

Further Yoder raised some questions about the formula. He noted that a number of modern critics call it "verbal baloney,"[106] requiring Christians to accept "a bunch of verbal definitions that do not have to be accepted." Yoder does not deny this sharp critique, but nonetheless points out that the problem posed by the New Testament writing would still be there in a different culture and world view. The Chalcedonians "were solving a problem that came out of the encounter of different frames of reference and sets of definitions. They tried to safeguard what a Christian has to say to be faithful to Jesus and still say it in the terms of the cul-

104. Ibid., 217. On the politics around the condemnation of Nestorius, see Jenkins, *Jesus Wars*, 131–226.

105. Yoder, *Preface* (2002), 218.

106. Outside of conservative theological circles, it is not difficult at all to find skeptics, both Christian and non-Christian, who would echo Yoder's language.

ture in which they were speaking and as answering the questions that it raised." Even if we say that the Chalcedonian arguments were raising the wrong questions, Yoder said, it is not clear that we are raising the right questions.[107] Yoder's comments seem to acknowledge all the problems that modern scholars can raise, but nonetheless retain the idea that the Chalcedonians were struggling with a real problem even if we dislike their answer. These comments point to the particular context of the Chalcedonian formula and allow for the possibility of a different statement in another context.

Yoder noted that the meaning of Jesus' humanity "varies enormously from one theological scheme to another." For the Alexandrians, birth mattered most—salvation came through God's presence on earth. In contrast, the Roman tradition "sees Jesus Christ as exalted Lord and coming judge." For Protestants generally, and Yoder adds, "for the New Testament," the humanity of Jesus matters. "Humanity is in the image of God" and God has chosen to deal with humanity "in person." "The humanity of Jesus is the necessary prerequisite to whatever God wants to do with us." This focus on Jesus as a man is the place to see "the obedience that God wants of us."[108] Chalcedon is one way, then, to guard that humanity.

Yoder ended the discussion of Christology per se with a final comment on the authority of the classic creeds. It varies, he said. For Catholic tradition, "The creeds are the history of the church." This tradition holds

107. Yoder, *Preface* (2002), 219.

108. Ibid., 220. Yoder's best-known book, *The Politics of Jesus* (first published in 1972), expanded at length on the idea that the man Jesus reveals the will of God for the conduct of followers of Jesus. In an often quoted text from that book, Yoder wrote that "the view of Jesus being proposed here is more radically Nicene and Chalcedonian than other views. I do not here advocate an unheard-of modern understanding of Jesus. I ask rather that the implications of what the church has always said about Jesus as Word of the Father, as true God and true Human, be taken more seriously as relevant to our social problems, than ever before" (*Politics of Jesus* [1994], 102). As was indicated in note 49 of the Introduction, this text has been cited as evidence that Yoder's ethics depended on the classic Christology. See for example, Carter, *Politics of the Cross*, 133; Nation, "Politics of Yoder," 39; Parler, *Things Hold Together*, 77. This statement by Yoder demonstrates, as the chapter in hand has shown, that Yoder could make use of classic Christology and considered it a possible way of guarding and restating an important point from the New Testament. However, this quote is hardly a statement that demonstrates Yoder's dependence on the classic Christology as the basis of his ethics. It is rather a corrective, an explanation of why a different emphasis is needed and why it was insufficient to attempt to base ethics for Christians on the classic statements.

that the Holy Spirit has led the church to speak in Christ's name. Thus "when the church states dogma in a creedal document, it is authoritative."[109]

The classic Protestantism of Luther, Zwingli and Calvin has an ambiguous stance. The Protestant movement began with a debate about the authority of Scripture and proclaimed only the Scripture to be authoritative. Yet these reformers were products of the medieval church, and they assumed that the creed was "a handy summary of the Bible."[110]

Radical reformers—Servetus and Socinus—considered the Protestant view a problem. Since these radicals were biblicists, and since the doctrine of the Trinity and Chalcedon's form of two natures are not in the Bible, their stance was that such views cannot be required.[111]

Yoder depicted a position for Anabaptists between these radicals and the Reformation leaders. Anabaptists "assumed the Apostolic Creed, . . . But they did not give it any final authority." Anabaptists could accept this creed as a part of the tradition, "but they gave the creed no dogmatic quality. They gave no special importance to the fact that the church had made decisions about phrasing in the fourth or fifth century."[112]

Yoder used this description of an Anabaptist attitude to pose the question for the contemporary church, whether the Mennonite peace church or others, a question equally applicable to all who stand outside of the Catholic tradition:

> In what sense are we bound to doctrinal definitions of the fourth century, or the fifth, or the sixteenth? Is it only in the sense that they are useful documents of how the church struggled to keep the centrality of Jesus straight in the language of their time? Or do we, without thinking, take over from fundamentalism, which took it over without thinking from Calvinist Orthodoxy, which took it over without thinking from the Middle Ages, the idea that there is a certain amount of post-biblical dogmatic substance that all Christians have to believe?[113]

Yoder supplied the beginning of an answer to his question. "Probably, if we were to be fully honest, we would need to challenge more clearly the Catholic axiom that assumed the authority of the councils and

---

109. Yoder, *Preface* (2002), 222.
110. Ibid.
111. Ibid.
112. Ibid.
113. Ibid., 222–23.

therefore of the creeds." This challenge would mean refusing to grant the creeds "automatic authority, while being still quite interested in listening to that history, learning from it, sympathizing deeply with what it tried to say." At their best, the creeds "define the nature of the problem with which we are struggling. They are helpful as a fence, but not as a faith." Since they are helpful as a fence, Yoder suggests that partisans of a "radical Anabaptist faith" should probably not focus on fighting for the creeds. But yet even less should these Anabaptists fight against the creeds. These creeds are part of a "confused history" that includes "a lot of dirty politics,"[114] "but this is the history with which God has chosen to lead a confused people toward at least a degree of understanding of certain dangers and things not to say if we are to remain faithful."[115]

This journey through the development of Christology in *Preface to Theology* has covered a great deal of territory, both biblical and historical. Yoder identified the earliest narrative about Jesus in the New Testament. It was contained in the sermon outlines in the book of Acts. Then in earlier and later theological writings in the New Testament, he pointed to numerous ways that that story was expanded, and how new and additional meanings were extracted from it or based upon it. New Testament theologians emphasized different aspects of the story to address a variety of issues and concerns and expresses the meaning of the story in new contexts.

The New Testament theologians also left some questions unanswered. Most specifically, these unanswered questions concerned how their high claims about Jesus were to be reconciled with a firm commitment to Jewish monotheism, and how the high claims about Jesus could be held together with his life as a genuine human being. These were the questions that most concerned the theologians of the centuries after the first Christian century. In following the development of these arguments, Yoder showed the development of the classic positions in a context different from the New Testament, and also indicated positions that were unacceptable.

Yoder's last comments on Christology dealt with the authority of the classic creeds. As depicted, he wrote that they are the only history that the church has. On the other hand, he also questioned attributing

---

114. Yoder's language is more than justified by the description of these politics in Jenkins, *Jesus Wars*.

115. Yoder, *Preface* (2002), 223.

unlimited authority to these creedal statements. The clear implication of granting less than ultimate authority to the classic creeds is that there could be other ways of dealing with the unanswered questions from the New Testament. The caveat for those alternatives, Yoder emphasized, is that they must take as seriously the New Testament observations on high Christology and on the humanity of Jesus as did the debates that produced the classic statements.

That Yoder could affirm Nicene and trinitarian formulas as correct when answering the christological question within their frame of reference, but at the same time hold open the possibility of other answers in a different context ought not surprise. In terms of methodology, his discussion of post-New Testament Christology continues the approach he displayed for the New Testament. For the New Testament writers, he described multiple ways to express the truth of the narrative of Jesus, multiple ways to extend the meaning of that story, and theological statements that emphasized different aspects of the story and its meaning. His analysis of Nicea, Cappadocian trinitarian doctrines, and then Chalcedon follow that same pattern. Since he pointed to different worldviews in the New Testament, which required different answers, it ought not surprise that he both indicates the worldview of the classic statements and then holds open the possibility of other theological statements in other worldviews.[116]

Yoder carried his observations further and made even more explicit the possibility of alternative christological statements in his published essay "But We Do See Jesus."[117] It can be considered an example or even a culmination of the developments described in *Preface*.

---

116. Those who want to align Yoder's view with Nicene orthodoxy adopt several strategies—minimizing Yoder's view that these statements reflect a particular context, or using rather selective quoting, or stating that today he would make corrections. In some cases, Yoder's clearest statements are ignored. For specific conversation with those who would align Yoder with classic orthodoxy, see notes 90, 95, 108, 146, and 151.

117. Yoder, "But We Do," *Foundations*, reprinted as Yoder, "But We Do," *Priestly*; Yoder, "But We Do," *Pacifist*. Citations provide page numbers from both *Priestly Kingdom* and *Pacifist Way of Knowing*.

"But We Do See Jesus"

An earlier version of this essay was Yoder's keynote address to a Believers Church conference at Bluffton College (now Bluffton University) in October 1980. As noted in the Introduction to the book in hand, the conference asked the question, Is there a believers church Christology? I was the primary organizer of the conference, and the conference question was a direct outgrowth of my use of learnings from Yoder's lectures that were eventually published as *Preface to Theology*. In the lectures, as just described, Yoder opened the door to ways of discussing Christology that were true to the intent of the classic formulations but did not use their language or imagery. He had also posed an understanding of ecclesiology that emerged from following the narrative of Jesus and that differed from the ecclesiology of Christendom.[118] It was thus a logical step to organize the conference to ask whether this ecclesiology truly could pose a Christology that differed from the classic statements.

Yoder began his keynote address to the 1980 conference by commending the planners for posing the question whether an identifiable

---

118. One primary characteristic of this alternative or "believers church" was adult membership, which is characterized by adult baptism. Adult versus infant baptism then distinguishes the point at which the faith journey begins within the church. This difference was extremely important in the sixteenth-century Reformation, when Anabaptists rejected infant baptism and chose baptism again as adult believers. This act of baptism, which signaled the formation of a voluntary church, was a rejection of the state or established church that encompassed all of society and thus required baptism of infants. This rejection earned martyrdom for several thousand Anabaptists. The believers church continues the concept of a church of adult believers. A series of conferences beginning in the late 1960s worked at clarifying the concept of the believers church. Along with Donald Durnbaugh, John Howard Yoder was a prime mover of this series of conferences. Chapter 7 to follow has an extensive discussion of Yoder's ecclesiology in this tradition. The papers from the first believers church conference were published as Garrett, *Concept of Believers' Church*. For a history of believers church denominations, see Durnbaugh, *Believers' Church*. The idea of a church of voluntary membership in and of itself has little meaning in North America, where there is no established church. However, an important distinction still exists between the believers church as understood by Yoder, in which the church is distinct from the social order, and the idea of many Americans that the United States is a "Christian nation." This latter designation implies that Christian faith encompasses and shapes the social order. This difference between believers church and the assumption of Christian America requires conversation and clarification of particulars—some denominations that began as believers churches have embraced and now support the idea of a Christian nation, while some parts of denominations that began as established churches have now become more critical of the fusion of faith and social order.

ecclesiology could produce an identifiable Christology. He then specified that in his remarks he would not be working with "Christology as such." Rather than working with "*hypostaseis* and *physeis, personae,* and *ousiae,*" he would be dealing with "their socio-historical *Sitz im Leben*."[119] In the published version of the address, which the analysis here will follow, Yoder moved directly to that context.

The context Yoder sought to address is the apparent relativity of truth in the modern world. As a beginning point, he used the statement from Gotthold Ephraim Lessing that "Accidental truths of history can never become the proof of necessary truths of reason. . . . That . . . is the ugly, broad ditch which I cannot get across."[120] Yoder notes that the situation described by Lessing can be summarized as "pluralism/relativism," and that it poses a challenge "to a specifically Christian witness."[121] This then is the problem that he addresses in the essay, namely how to witness to the truth of Jesus Christ when there is no universally recognizable and accessible foundation from which to prove the truth of Jesus. In answering that question, Yoder also speaks to the question of a Christology specific to the believers church concept, or a Christology that does not use the classic formulas.

Yoder described several efforts to jump over Lessing's ditch or to find that firm, unmoveable foundation. What all of these efforts have in common, Yoder wrote, is the belief that truth resides in "the meaning system of the world claiming to be wider" than the one in which the observer is standing. But that wider world, Yoder argues, is still only one particular place. "Any given wider world is still just one more place." The mistake made "by the person emerging from the smaller world is thinking that the wider society is itself the universe," when in fact it is just one more particular place even if slightly wider or more prestigious. Thus Yoder states the question, "How can particular truths be proclaimed publicly?" In this case, the truth to be proclaimed is the particular truth of the gospel of Jesus.

Yoder began his answer with material from the New Testament, namely five different christological images. The material is easily recognizable as coming from the lectures that became *Preface to Theology*.[122]

119. Yoder, "That Household We Are," 1.
120. Yoder, "But We Do," *Priestly*, 46; Yoder, "But We Do," *Pacifist*, 22.
121. Yoder, "But We Do," *Priestly*, 46, 47; Yoder, "But We Do," *Pacifist*, 23, 24.
122. When Yoder drafted the keynote address for the conference in October 1980,

He cited the *logos* Christology of John 1, which was written against a Gnostic background. John identified Jesus with both the Word that was with God and described Jesus becoming flesh as a human being. Next came Hebrews, which pictured a hierarchy of angels and priests that mediated between God and humankind on earth. Against this backdrop, Jesus the Son was placed with God above the angels, but also depicted as a human being who was both priest and human victim. Colossians was written against the background of the network of heavenly powers and principalities that hold the world together. The writer situates Jesus as creator and lord of these powers but also able to be crushed by them. Since Jesus is risen, however, their power over him is broken. Yoder's fourth text was the image of the slain lamb in Revelation 4. Being able to open the scroll represented the Lamb as the key to the meaning of history, while having been slain qualifies the Lamb for the world's judgment and salvation. The final image is the new Adam from Philippians 2, who in contrast to the old Adam did not try to grab equality with God. Rather, Jesus accepted identification with humanity and remained obedient unto death, which qualified him for exaltation to the right hand of God.[123]

These texts contain five different christological images—logos, creator, high priest, lord of history, new Adam. Yoder explained that each image was the result of an apostolic writer confronting the challenge of explaining the meaning of Jesus in a new context, in "a previously formed cosmic vision." But in creating these different images, the five writers all made the same moves, which indicates "a syndrome or deep structure."[124]

Yoder identified six characteristics of this deep structure: 1) The writer is "at home in the new linguistic world, using its structure and facing its questions." 2) "Instead of fitting the Jesus message into the slots the cosmic vision has ready for it, the writer places Jesus above the cosmos, in charge of it." 3) In each case, there is strong emphasis on Jesus "being rejected and suffering in human form," which validates his lordship. 4) Instead of understanding salvation in terms defined by the host cosmos, "What we are called to enter into is the self-emptying and the death—and only by that path, and by grace, the resurrection—of the Son." 5) "Behind the cosmic victory, enabling it, there is affirmed (without parallel in the

---

that was also approximately the time that he would have edited his lectures into form for their informal publication as Yoder, *Preface* (1981).

123. Yoder, "But We Do," *Priestly*, 50–52; Yoder, "But We Do," *Pacifist*, 27–29.

124. Yoder, "But We Do," *Priestly*, 53; Yoder, "But We Do," *Pacifist*, 29.

synoptic Gospels) what later confession called preexistence, co-essentiality with the Father, possession of the image of God, and the participation of the Son in creation and providence." 6) "The writer and the readers of these messages share by faith in all that that victory means."[125]

Yoder described what the writers accomplished with the images that reflect this deep structure. For one, they challenged "the contemporary pagan mind, and they did it in terms familiar to that mind, from within its linguistic community." Further, they proclaimed their message from within Judaism. Rather than leaving it behind or requesting space for it as one view among many in the "Athenian marketplace of ideas," they made the claim that "the Hebrew story had widened out to include everyone; that, with the inbreaking of the messianic era, the Jewish hope in process of fulfillment was wide enough to receive all the nations and their riches." To accomplish this move, they took the categories of the majority cultures, "hammered them into other shapes, and turned the cosmology on its head, with Jesus both at the bottom, crucified as a common criminal, and at the top, preexistent Son and creator, and the church his instrument in today's battle." In other words, the categories of the world were not allowed to define the questions. Rather, it was the Rule of God that defined truth.

> The rebellious but already (in principle) defeated cosmos is being brought to its knees by the Lamb. The development of a high Christology is the natural cultural ricochet of a missionary ecclesiology when it collides as it must with whatever cosmology explains and governs the world it invades.[126]

This message about Jesus is good news. It is news about the way that the particular story of Jesus the Jewish messiah relates to the entire world. This message cannot remain in its small ghetto precisely because it is a message of good news for the world. And "because this news is only such when *received* as good, it can never be communicated coercively; nor can the message-bearer ever positively be assured that it will be received."[127] Although Yoder does not emphasize it here, the good news is intrinsically nonviolent, and there is no universally accessible point of appeal by which to coerce belief. But although the message is good news for the

125. Yoder, "But We Do," *Priestly*, 53; Yoder, "But We Do," *Pacifist*, 29–30.
126. Yoder, "But We Do," *Priestly*, 54; Yoder, "But We Do," *Pacifist*, 31.
127. Yoder, "But We Do," *Priestly*, 55, Yoder's italics; Yoder, "But We Do," *Pacifist*, 31.

hearers, the challenge of this good news "does not prove that people . . . in that other world view are bad. It simply brings them news."[128]

Clearly Yoder's description of the "deep structure" aligns itself with the classic christological categories.[129] That comment is particularly true for point six, which affirms "what later confession called preexistence, co-essentiality with the Father, possession of the image of God, and the participation of the Son in creation and providence." And in a point that needs to be emphasized, Yoder took pains to point out that the images, which expressed this deep structure, each used the language of the particular world view into which the narrative of Jesus was carried. Being aware of Yoder's stress on use of the local language and images is important for understanding his next step, which occurs in a section titled "How Not to Say It."[130]

Yoder writes that for the early Christians, it would have been the wrong question to ask if Jews should enter the Hellenistic world and adapt to its concepts, or if Paul should use Greek. Of course they should. Rather, the proper question is the strategy they should use in that new culture. It was "how to *be* there: how in the transition to render anew the genuine pertinence of the proclamation of Christ's Lordship, even in a context (*particularly* in a context) where even the notion of such sovereignty is questionable."[131]

Yoder then suggests that "we," that is, contemporary Christians, should follow the same strategy, which is to carry the good news of the story of Jesus into our context. That context is the "pluralism/relativism" identified at the beginning of his essay as Lessing's ditch. "We are now called to renew in the language world of pluralism/relativism an analogue to what those first transcultural recconceptualizers did; not to translate their results but to emulate their exercise." Thus, in a continuation of his

---

128. Yoder, "But We Do," *Priestly*, 54–55; Yoder, "But We Do," *Pacifist*, 31.

129. Point made by Hauerwas and Sider in their introduction to Yoder, *Preface* (2002), 17–18. At the same time, it bears pointing out that with high Christology present already in the New Testament, including in the earliest statements about Jesus, the classic formulas are not intrinsically necessary as the guardians of high Christology. Yoder would say that that guardianship role is fulfilled by the New Testament statements of high Christology.

130. Yoder, "But We Do," *Priestly*, 56–59; Yoder, "But We Do," *Pacifist*, 32–36.

131. Yoder, "But We Do," *Priestly*, 56, Yoder's italics; Yoder, "But We Do," *Pacifist*, 32.

comment from *Preface* quoted earlier concerning the concepts of "preexistence" and "participation in creation," Yoder continues,

> The last thing we should ask, then, would be whether we can translate into our time from theirs the notion of preexistence or of the participation of the Son in creation. That would be to contrast the rules of two language worlds instead of finding a message to express within both. That would be like asking whether with the bases loaded you should try for a field goal or use a number three iron. What we need to find is the interworld transformational grammar to help us to discern what will need to happen if the collision of the message of Jesus with our pluralist/relativist world is to lead to a reconception of the shape of the world, instead of rendering Jesus optional or innocuous.[132]

Since our context is that of pluralism/relativism, Yoder says, of course we should speak in those terms. Rather than asking whether to speak in those terms, the proper question is "What shall we say?" Yoder hastens to add that the answer is, "Jesus is Messiah and Lord," and our task is to figure out how to say that in pluralist/relativist language.[133]

Yoder gives further indications on how not to do Christology in this pluralist/relativist, contemporary context. For one, we should not attempt to claim that "Christianity, or Jesus, or anything, is absolute or unique or universal in some way that could be supported, kept dry above the ways of relativity."[134] In other words, we should not argue for a universal absolute that transcends relativity because, in fact, there is no such universally accessible and recognizable place from which to argue.

132. Yoder, "But We Do," *Priestly*, 56; Yoder, "But We Do," *Pacifist*, 33. In his assertion that Yoder "repeatedly emphasizes the biblical support for the . . . preexistence of the Son," Parler has missed or (ignored) the statement quoted here as well as the earlier quotation from *Preface* about not attempting to translate that language in our pluralist/relativist context. (See also *Priestly Kingdom*, 62, and *Pacifist Way of Knowing*, 38.) Of course Yoder noted the biblical view, but he also said that we should not try to translate that particular concept from a different worldview into our worldview. Thus Parler misuses what Yoder had said. But make no mistake at this point—Yoder does not need the language of preexistence to preserve his "high Christology" and the belief that the work of Jesus is the work of God. A high Christology was already vouchsafed in Yoder's frequently quoted statement that "a high Christology is the natural cultural ricochet of a missionary ecclesiology when it collides as it must with whatever cosmology explains and governs the world it invades." The high Christology of this statement is New Testament Christology.

133. Yoder, "But We Do," *Priestly*, 56; Yoder, "But We Do," *Pacifist*, 33.

134. Yoder, *Preface* (2002), 56–57.

Further, we should not adopt relativism/pluralism as a true worldview under the assumption that it is "wider" than the previous one, any more than the other wider views noted above were accorded priority. Rather we are seeking an "evangelical alternative," that is a witness about the truth of Jesus as Lord, which would follow the strategies of the New Testament writers in "the practical affirmation that the present world, the wider and the widest worlds of our day, is the arena with which it speaks; but one which would claim to have something more to say than to concede the sovereignty or the adequacy of the ideas currently dominating that wider arena."[135] In the first centuries, all the parties to the conversation "lived in cosmologies with the top open for transcendent validation." Obviously we no longer live in such a cosmology. Yoder described our context as "pluralism/relativism."[136] Our task, then, is to translate the meaning of "Christ is Lord" into our meaning frame of pluralism/relativism "in some continuity with what it meant in the first-century context."[137]

Witnessing to the claim that "Christ is Lord" in the pluralist/relativist context can have more than one answer, Yoder asserts. Answers might be fragmentary with partially overlapping meaning frames, but the fragments together might be the "functional equivalent of a proclamation of lordship." Since Jesus participated in datable, local history, it might be possible to make reference to Jesus at a point of partial overlap between such frames of meaning. For example, Jesus intervened in liberation from violence and in identifying with the poor and in constructing forgiving communities. Such actions might be the basis of conversation between other frames of meaning.[138] Of course these actions of Jesus are not

---

135. Ibid., 57.

136. Yoder, "But We Do," *Priestly*, 57; Yoder, "But We Do," *Pacifist*, 34. I would add a descriptor beyond Yoder's. The pluralist/relativist ethos he described occurs within a cosmology of an infinitely expanding universe consisting of finite pieces and objects. It poses a marked contrast to the cosmology he described as "top open for transcendent validation." It is also important to add that our current cosmology is also the particular view of our time; and in the long view, it is as subject to revision as the outmoded one Yoder described. For an example of the use of the "top open" cosmology, see comments throughout the *Paradiso* section of Dante, *Divine Comedy*. A description of the nine circles of heaven with heaven beyond as the location of God appears in Canto XXVIII of *Paradiso*.

137. Yoder, "But We Do," *Priestly*, 57; Yoder, "But We Do," *Pacifist*, 34.

138. In a lecture delivered in 1980, Yoder made a similar observation. After stating that we need to know what "Scripture and tradition" say on a given problem, he writes that we also need to know what other disciplines say "about human nature and the shape of society. We cannot discuss theology without interlocking with the human

unique and are "only relatively true," Yoder adds with a seeming wink. We are not seeking to overwhelm the sea of pluralism/relativism, but rather seeking "a way to stay within our bark, barely afloat and sometimes awash amidst those waves, yet neither dissolving into them nor being carried only where they want to push it."[139]

Returning to his introductory reference to Lessing's ditch, Yoder writes that we no longer need to build a bridge or figure out how to leap the ditch. In his analysis of relativism/pluralism, Yoder has explained that ground on the other side of the ditch is just as narrow and provincial. "Reality always was pluralistic and relativistic, that is, historical. The idea that it could be otherwise was itself an illusion laid on us by Greek ontology language, Roman sovereignty language, and other borrowings." Nonetheless, we still have a witness to make that Jesus is Lord. "Yet within this relativity and in the style of noncoerciveness, we can and must still proclaim a Lord and invite to repentance. We report an event that occurred in our listeners' own world and ask them to respond to it. What could be more universal than that?"[140]

This statement brings Yoder to a conclusion. His discussion has concerned context rather than message. The message remains "Jesus is Lord." The discussion has concerned the changing context in which that message is proclaimed.

In making a restatement of the meaning of Jesus, Yoder says, just as did the New Testament writers we should recognize that our context is a place to make peace and to witness. As they took the message of Jesus into a world not their own, we can as well. And we should even recognize that our pluralist/relativist world today, through a sequence of historical transformations, is the current product of their first venture of taking the gospel into a foreign worldview.

---

sciences that study the same phenomena from other perspectives. The believer says that faith in Jesus Christ makes love of the enemy imperative and possible. Could not a psychologist describe and measure this? If love leads one to go out and make peace with one's adversary, could not a sociologist describe this event? When a preacher claims 'Violence is self-defeating,' is that not a claim that a historian could verify or refute? As we flesh out the realism of the message of reconciliation, it is therefore appropriate, even imperative, that we attend to those other disciplines." Yoder, *War of the Lamb*, 125. For an example of the intersection of theology and psychology at the point of forgiveness, see Weaver, "Forgiveness and (Non)Violence."

139. Yoder, "But We Do," *Priestly*, 57–58; Yoder, "But We Do," *Pacifist*, 34.
140. Yoder, "But We Do," *Priestly*, 59; Yoder, "But We Do," *Pacifist*, 36.

With their venture into a foreign worldview, the New Testament writers of the messianic Jewish witness placed their Messiah both above and within the culture of the foreign worlds they entered. It was an affirmation that under the lordship of Jesus, the "cosmos will find its true coherence and meaning." Yoder supplied examples from Colossians, John, Hebrews, Philippians, and Revelation. It is this "evangelical Christology," which proclaims "Christ above the powers," that enables believers to live as though creation is being redeemed even before it is made whole in the second coming.[141]

This faith statement about the place of Jesus as Lord does not prove with historical certainty that the gospel about Jesus is true. It does not prove that creation is being redeemed by the work of God in Christ. "We still have not found a bridge or a way to leap from historical uncertainty to some other more solid basis that would oblige people to believe or make our own believing sure." However, certainty does not come from observing the world but from looking at the risen Christ. Yoder states this in words from Hebrews 2:8–9: "As it is, we do not see everything in subjection to him. *But we do see Jesus*, revealing the grace of God by tasting death for everyone."[142]

Although it may not be visible except to eyes of faith, this view of Jesus enables us to begin talking about God in our language, or as Yoder said, "to begin reconstructing God-language on this side of the ditch." Since this language works within our world, seeing Jesus in this way enables a number of tactical alliances, as long as the believer's true identity is remembered and retained. That is, we can make tactical allies as long as we do not allow the reference frame of the ally to become a new truth foundation. Yoder supplied a number of contemporary suggestions of such alliances. For example, there can be tactical alliances with those who critique the earlier "too-close identification of church and dominion." Another tactical alliance is one with the "pluralist/relativist deconstruction of deceptive orthodox claims to logically coercive certainty" as long as relativism is not allowed to become a "new monism" or unquestioned given. Other alliances include working with those who would "dismantle the alliance of church with privilege" but without allowing the promises of revolution to become a new ultimate. We might form "tactical alliances

---

141. Yoder, "But We Do," *Priestly*, 61; Yoder, "But We Do," *Pacifist*, 37–38.

142. Yoder, "But We Do," *Priestly*, 61, Yoder's italics; Yoder, "But We Do," *Pacifist*, 38.

with the Enlightenment, as did Quakers and Baptists in the century after their expulsion from the Puritan colonies, or with the Gandhian vision, as did Martin Luther King, Jr."[143]

For Yoder, it is the humanness of Jesus that is the basis for understanding his lordship. "For our world it will be in his ordinariness as villager, as rabbi, as king on a donkey, and as liberator on a cross that we shall be able to express the claims which the apostolic proclaimers to Hellenism expressed in the language of preexistence and condescension." This approach is in no way a "lowering of sights" about the significance of Jesus, Yoder asserts. It is rather "to renew the description of Christ crucified as the wisdom and the power of God. This is the low road to general validity." This low road that begins with Jesus working in the world is actually the result of a tactical alliance with relativism/pluralism. This alliance has "freed us, by suspecting all the remaining claims of any wider worlds, however accredited, to have the authority to pass judgment on the Lord." This low road "frees us to use any language, to enter any world in which people eat bread and pursue debtors, hope for power and execute subversives. The ordinariness of the humanness of Jesus is the warrant for the generalizability of his reconciliation."[144]

The universal meaning of Jesus in our relativist/pluralist world begins with his particularity. "The particularity of incarnation is the universality of the good." The only road is the low road. "The truth has come to our side of the ditch." It is the particular story of the man Jesus. Thus Yoder concludes, "The real issue is not whether Jesus can make sense in a world far from Galilee, but whether—when he meets us in our world, as he does in fact—we want to follow him. We don't have to, as they didn't then. That we don't have to is the profoundest proof of his condescension, and thereby of his glory."[145] In other words, in a pluralist/relativist world with no universally recognizable and accessible source of authority by which to coerce belief, we demonstrate our belief in the universal truth of the gospel about Jesus by living in his story when it is not required and even when it is costly. And with this conclusion, Yoder has stated the meaning of Jesus and how it is to be appropriated in our relativist/pluralist world, following the pattern set by the New Testament authors,

---

143. Yoder, "But We Do," *Priestly*, 61–62; Yoder, "But We Do," *Pacifist*, 38.
144. Yoder, "But We Do," *Priestly*, 62; Yoder, "But We Do," *Pacifist*, 38.
145. Yoder, "But We Do," *Priestly*, 62; Yoder, "But We Do," *Pacifist*, 39.

who restated the meaning of Jesus in the worldviews visible behind Colossians, John, Hebrews, Philippians, and Revelation.

Analysis and Comment

Just as Yoder promised, the lectures in *Preface to Theology* dealt with both content and methodology. The theological content consisted of Yoder's recitation of the development of Christology from the earliest statements in the New Testament through several centuries to the emergence of the classic formulas of Nicea, the Cappadocian definition of Trinity, and Chalcedon. That content follows the usual outline.

Equally important as content was Yoder's discussion—actually, a demonstration—of methodology, both that of the New Testament writers and his own that follows them. His analysis of the New Testament writers put on display their methodology. The earliest statements about Jesus recounted the narrative of his life as a man and expected a response from the hearers. Yoder then described the way that later writers—the theologians—drew additional meanings from the story or restated it with different emphases to extend the meaning of the story in new directions. In his description of the New Testament writers, Yoder made visible the fact that there were multiple ways to tell the story, and multiple ways to extract meaning from it with varying emphases and in different contexts. This description of multiple expressions continued in Yoder's analysis of the post-New Testament materials. The new part of the discussion for this period was taking notice that there were now also dead ends and incorrect efforts to develop meaning from the story of Jesus. And parallel to the way that he had pointed to different contexts and world views in which the New Testament writers took the story of Jesus, he also described the worldview in which the classic statements developed and showed how it differed from the worldviews visible in the New Testament.

With this brief summary of Yoder's treatment of Christology in *Preface to Theology*, it should be evident that the essay "But We Do See Jesus" was by no means a mere statement of standard orthodoxy in postmodern language. It stands as a kind of culmination—or perhaps better stated, a demonstration—of the methodology on display throughout Yoder's *Preface to Theology*. He pointed to different contexts and worldviews throughout *Preface*. Now in this essay he continued that methodology by pointing to five different worldviews in the New Testament and five different christological images produced within those worldviews. He cautioned that our task today was not to attempt to reproduce the answers produced within those worldviews, which are clearly not our worldviews. Rather than replicating those answers, we should identify our own worldview, which Yoder characterized as relativism/pluralism, and then figure out how to express the meaning of Jesus within that worldview in a way that both uses its language but places Jesus over it as Lord. The way to do that, Yoder suggested, was to work with the humanness of Jesus, and to make tactical alliances with others at the point where their concerns intersected with those visible in the story of the man Jesus. And it is by choosing to live in this story of Jesus, when it is not required and in the face of the challenge of relativism and its competing ideologies, that Christians today witness to the ultimate claims and the universal meaning of the story of Jesus as Lord.[146]

146. Those interpreters who argue that John Howard Yoder's thought was based on Nicene orthodoxy have either misunderstood the essay "But We Do See Jesus" or have ignored it. Mark Thiessen Nation wrote that Yoder connected his approach "to classic orthodox theology." In his description of "But We Do See Jesus," Nation does note that Yoder was asserting that the "canonical Jesus" was normative. But about the essay Nation writes, "By the early 1980s, Yoder was at times strategically employing post-modern terminology," which Nation then illustrates with Yoder's statement that "reality is always pluralistic and relativistic, that is, historical." However, Nation ignores entirely Yoder's comments about not translating notions of preexistence or the Son's participation in creation. Thus Nation also apparently missed the fact that Yoder's use of "postmodern terminology" was not a statement about Christology per se, but was a description of our contemporary context as distinguished from the early church context, which necessitates a new statement of the meaning of Jesus is Lord in this new context. See Nation, *John Howard Yoder*, 56–60, and Nation, "Politics of Yoder," 39–41, quote 39, 40. A similar mistreatment appears in the introduction by Hauerwas and Sider to the published edition of *Preface to Theology*. They speak of Yoder's "reclaiming of the dogmatic tradition," and their supposed proof, referring to the unpublished, keynote version of the essay, is to cite Yoder's description of the "deep syndrome" and his statement that culminates with the assertion that "the development of a high Christology is the natural cultural ricochet of a missionary ecclesiology." However, Hauerwas and Sider fail to recognize that the specific high Christology to which Yoder was referring was not Nicea but the high Christology of the New Testament images, which is then recognized in the deep structure that Yoder described. And since they chose to quote from Yoder's unpublished paper rather than the version revised for publication as "But We Do See Jesus," Hauerwas and Sider then miss or ignore the statement Yoder added about "How not to say it," and thus misread his concluding assertion that proclaiming the risen Lord was the way to assert high Christology in the context of relativism/pluralism, and was not simply a reassertion of the dogmatic tradition. See Yoder, *Preface* (2002), 17–19. In his own book, J. Alex Sider followed a similar strategy. He wrote that "one searches Yoder's texts in vain

As far as the question of the conference for which Yoder wrote the essay published as "But We Do See Jesus," Yoder did not explicitly identify any Christology past or present as a Christology specific to the believers church. What he did was to sketch a methodology for thinking about how to develop Christologies that would reflect believers church ecclesiology. Thus he implied strongly that the answer to the question of the conference was yes, there could be a believers church Christology, and even more than one. In the conclusion to the conference address, he noted that since the demise in the nineteenth-century of orthodoxy as self-evidently true, rather than fitting the Gospel under one of the prevailing Powers, we have again the possibility of "a renewal of the missionary arrogance (arrogance need not be a pejorative term) that dares to claim that Jesus, proclaimed as Messiah and Kyrios, transcends rather than being transcended by each new cosmos as well. When that happens, there is again a believers' church Christology."[147]

In his 1964 publication *The Christian Witness to the State*, Yoder suggested using "middle axioms" as a means of translating the impact of the reign of God into terms that the state could apprehend. Middle axioms "will translate into meaningful and concrete terms the general

---

for a decisive contemporary non-Constantinian refutation of pro-Nicene theology," but does acknowledge three ways that Yoder "did attempt to decenter Nicaea in the contemporary imagination." Sider, *To See History Doxologically*, quotes 107, 116. However, Sider does not acknowledge the ways that Yoder opened the door, particularly in "But We Do See Jesus," for expressions of Christology that bypass Nicea. In his book on Yoder's theology, Craig Carter uses *Preface to Theology* extensively, but quite selectively. In defending Yoder against a charge that he did not accept orthodox Christology, Carter asserts that Yoder's writing lacked an adequate balance, that is, "he did not emphasize orthodox Christology (or the work of the Holy Spirit or the resurrection of Christ) enough in his best-known writings." Nonetheless, Carter argues, "There is solid textual evidence in Yoder's writings for interpreting Yoder himself as holding to a solidly orthodox Christology," which is the foundation for "a constructive Christian theological ethics." Carter takes Yoder's statements that demonstrate how the classic categories reflected New Testament theology as Yoder's assertion of orthodoxy while neglecting Yoder's statements that show the possibility of alternative formulations. Further, although Carter deals extensively with Christology, he has only one, inconsequential reference to "But We Do See Jesus." Carter, *Politics of the Cross*, 116–36, quotes 135; see also 232, 233, 236, 239, and 246, where Carter says, "the case for the ethical authority of the life and teachings of Jesus being based in orthodox Christology is made in depth in *Preface*, which deals extensively with the relationship between the New Testament Christology and developments in the first five centuries." The analysis of the present book has demonstrated the error of Carter's description of *Preface*.

147. Yoder, "That Household We Are," 7.

relevance of the lordship of Christ for a given social ethical issue."[148] Examples were to use language available to governmental officials to oppose capital punishment, and to use just war logic to lessen violence or oppose war. Not long after the publication of this book, Yoder abandoned use of the term "middle axiom." However, he continued the practice in wide-ranging fashion of using the frame of reference of his interlocutor to move the conversation in the direction of the kingdom of God. He was demonstrating that practice already in the New Testament when he noted that the writers expressed the meaning of the narrative of Jesus in terms of the cosmology or worldview they were entering. It is visible in his willingness to appeal to the classic christological terminology (as in his statement that his view "is more radically Nicene and Chalcedonian than other views"[149]) while also opening the door to bypassing the classic language. In the memo considered in the next section, he described this methodology as embracing of cross-cultural communication "in the other guy's terms." The point to emphasize here is that this methodology presupposes and depends on the christological commitment displayed in *Preface* and the essay "But We Do See Jesus."[150]

148. Yoder, *Christian Witness*, 32. This book was reprinted as Yoder, *Christian Witness* (2002).

149. See note 108.

150. It is important to stress that the original need for middle axioms and then Yoder's continuation of the practice without so labeling it assumes the christological foundation described in this chapter. Thus I dispute the conclusion of Paul Martens that Yoder's "body politics" was in essence a substitution of the formula "church as paradigm" for the early "middle axioms," and results in a secular ethic and the designation of Yoder as "heterodox." According to Martens' analysis, when Yoder describes the practices of the church as a model for the world, Yoder has simply turned the lordship of Christ into "a form of secular social ethics," and faith into "just another idea" or "another form of ethics" in the line of theologians such as "Kant, Harnack, Ritschl, and Rauschenbusch." In Martens' view, these moves were related to Yoder's critical view of the classic doctrine of Christ. But this critique of the classic doctrines is insufficient of itself to earn the characterization of "heterodox," Martens said. That charge comes from a consideration of "the larger movements in Yoder's thought" that produced what Martens called secular ethics and which led to Yoder's "idiosyncratic assessment of the creeds." Since Yoder did not reject the creeds outright, he could not be called a heretic, but failure to embrace them eliminated orthodox as a descriptor—hence the designations "idiosyncratic" and "heterodox." See Martens, *Heterodox*, 26–27, 141–47, quotes 142, 144, 145, 146. The strong and clear christological foundation that is described in this chapter and is expressed in Yoder's ecclesiology reveals the misperceptions of Martens' conclusion. Chapter 7 to follow has an extensive discussion of Yoder's "body politics." While Yoder did relativize Nicea, "heterodox" does not properly identify him. This designation defines Yoder in terms of what he was *not*, namely beholden to

A major contributor to misreading Yoder's Christology stems from failure to recognize sufficiently this multifaceted approach. On the one hand, Yoder defended the orthodox formulations to the extent that he demonstrated how they developed as true answers within their context to questions posed by the New Testament. But on the other hand, he also pointed to the context of the classic formulas and the aspects that limited their ethical applicability, and explained how other expressions could be valid in different contexts. Thus he opened the door wide to formulas and answers that could bypass the classic formulas but would nonetheless be compatible with their concerns. The possibility of developing other formulations emerged from his demonstration of the variety of theological expressions visible already in the New Testament. Seeing this range of developments in the New Testament thus shows the way to using other language to convey the meaning of Jesus in contexts different from those of the classic formulas. The chapter in hand examines this multifaceted approach.[151]

Thus the implications are clear for one of the current points of discussion in the literature about the basis of Yoder's theology. Those who have argued that Yoder's theology is compatible with Nicene orthodoxy

---

standard orthodoxy, and it says little about what Yoder was actually attempting to do, which was to develop theology and ethics "specific to Jesus."

151. Those who would argue for Yoder's dependency on classic orthodoxy have used selective quotes or have failed to recognize or acknowledge the multiple facets of Yoder's methodology under the assumption that all of Yoder's christological statements could be fused into a single, orthodox view. They cannot. The analysis here displays the error of these efforts. Yoder has a consistent methodology of starting with Jesus, but statements made in different contexts and worldviews as expressions of that methodology cannot be synthesized into a single Christology.

Branson Parler makes a most recent effort to achieve such a synthesis. Parler even makes brief, oblique reference to the opening Yoder made to other formulations. However, his summary of Yoder's approach to the classic creeds lists five critiques Yoder made and five positive statements. Parler concludes that "in the end, [the positives] outweigh the negatives." Without labeling Yoder "orthodox," Parler consistently stresses the compatibility of Yoder's theology with these creedal statements. As previously indicated, this view is correct as far as it goes, but it ignores the door Yoder opened to other expressions. Parler's approach also contains an ambiguity. One is left to conclude that Yoder's compatibility with the classic creeds is the same as "depends on" or "extends." In my view, neither of those is a correct designation of Yoder. Since for Yoder every theological analysis is to begin anew with the Jesus of the New Testament, Yoder's own theology would not depend on or extend the classic creeds. Parler, *Things Hold Together*, 89–99; for "oblique" see 91, 99.

are partially correct.[152] Yoder did argue that Nicea and Chalcedon reflected genuine problems posed by the New Testament, and in their context were the best answers to those questions. However, the analysis here of Yoder's methodology shows why these attempts to define Yoder as orthodox Nicene are only partially correct. For one thing, when Yoder said that his view was more true to Nicea and Chalcedon than the Nicenes and Chalcedonians,[153] he was offering a corrective. His corrective was that he was saying more than Chalcedon. Chalcedon's affirmation of the full humanity of Jesus should include the particulars of his life as a human being, which would make his rejection of violence an integral dimension of affirmations about Jesus as fully God and fully human. The corrective is thus a suggestion on reforming the standard view from within rather than naming it as a foundation.

Thus those who have argued that Yoder did not stand on Nicene-Chalcedonian orthodoxy are also partially correct,[154] but defining Yoder in that negative way—what he did not espouse—is thus an inadequate and misleading designation as well. It neglects to understand Yoder in terms of what he did affirm, namely the priority of the New Testament's narrative of Jesus and the normativeness of the human Jesus for ethics and theology.

The analysis here addresses yet a third rather wide-spread conclusion on Yoder, namely that his ethics were ad hoc and that he was one postmodern thinker to be put in conversation with other postmodern philosophers and theologians. Again, as with the previous two disputed conclusions, there is partial truth in this one as well. He did discuss ethics on a wide range of topics and his anti-foundationalist stance does locate him in a postmodern mode. However, neither the ad hoc nor the postmodern descriptors fully account for the priority that he gave to the narrative of Jesus. His statements of ethics were wide-ranging, but they all reflect the priority of Jesus, sometimes expressed directly and sometimes in terms of the "other guy's" frame of reference. And the priority Yoder gave to the narrative of the Gospel identifies a beginning assumption not visible in the designation "postmodern."

---

152. See note 146.
153. See note 108 above.
154. For references, see note 150 above, as well as note 27 in the Introduction.

A Validating Memo

Yoder described his methodology in a memo written in late 1991, more than a decade after the completion of the primary sources analyzed above. He put the memo together from earlier sessions of "brainstorming" on the subject. It contains thirteen paragraphs that discuss methodology.[155] Comments from the memo support the description of Yoder's methodology and theologizing presented above.

The first and primary point of Yoder's memo, restated several ways, is that he rejects any foundationalism that would "impose on others the right language or the right place to start." He described his approach as "taking on issues in the categories of others, unfolding the critique of the other's view from their own structure rather than beginning with my own 'correct' position." His position is stronger, he wrote, "if/as/because it is not my own, not stated on the grounds of a basis I first lay out." "A foundationalist beginning is by definition sectarian. The only place to start a conversation is within the web." "I eschew foundationalism because it is a power move which seeks to win the game by decreeing the rules before the game, beginning somewhere else than in the midst of the story/web."

But on occasion it is still necessary to discuss where to start. In that case, Yoder says, since the only place to start is within the web, his procedure is "to discuss how and why one starts within the web, and then to lay out descriptively the shape of the web." The example given for this procedure is *Preface to Theology*. In other words, he applied his methodology of using "the other guy's language" in theology as well as in ethics. His description of the historical developments of Christology from the New Testament through several centuries to the emergence of the Chalcedonian formula was not the development of his supposed standard or orthodox christological foundation nor his establishment of this tradition as normative for all theology. It was rather his description of the web, the network within which theologizing can begin. As an example of this non-foundational approach, he wrote that in *Preface* he "can recount

---

155. The analysis in this chapter was written before the memo came into my hands. Thus Yoder's statements in the memo are truly a validation of this chapter's conclusions. The memo was addressed to Mark Thiessen Nation and finished on December 17, 1991. It is in Nation's Yoder Collection at Eastern Mennonite Seminary, Harrisonburg, Virginia. I obtained a copy of the memo from Earl Zimmerman, who discussed it in Zimmerman, *Practicing the Politics*, 180–82. In the following treatment of the memo, quotations not attributed to another source come from this memo. Typos in quotes from the memo are silently corrected.

supportively the development of early Christian dogma without being tied to the adequacy of those formulations in all other times and places." He wrote that "teaching of theology should be descriptive before it is normative. We watch it being done before it makes sense to discuss whether or why it can be done." As example, Yoder again referred to *Preface*. "The early history comes first; analyzing the place of the discipline arises out of seeing it going on."

The essay "But We Do See Jesus" occupied a prominent role in the earlier analysis of this chapter. Yoder refers to this essay twice in his 1991 memo. Once it was an example of what used to be called "induction," "the process of founding a generalization on a number of parallel observations." The second occurrence was one of his examples in a section in which he stated his appreciation for "symmetry [and] formal 'elegance,'" but only when the basis for it was clear.

This memo allows reinforcement of conclusions stated above. It is correct to see *Preface to Theology* as a central element of Yoder's theological writing. In the memo cited here, he referred to it five times, more than any other of his writings. He cited "But We Do See Jesus," twice, again indicating that it was important in his mind.[156] These references reveal that he considered them central to his thought, and they show clearly that he respected the historic Nicene and Chalcedonian Christology, but that he also specifically intended to keep the door open to alternative statements. It is clear that "But We Do See Jesus" was not a merely a strategic use of post-modern terminology to restate orthodoxy, and this essay is certainly much more than the basis for identifying Yoder as a postmodern thinker who could be put in conversation with other postmodern thinkers. It is rather an example of how to have a supportive view of the development of early Christology but without being tied to its adequacy in all other times and places. That example should be clear in his description of the deep "syndrome" that identified Jesus with both God at the top of the hierarchy and humanity at the bottom, and in his conclusion that the "high Christology" of the New Testament was the "cultural ricochet" that resulted when the missionary ecclesiology of the New Testament theologians was taken into another cosmology.[157] Naming and identify-

156. The only other of his writings cited more than once in this memo was "Sacrament as Social Practice," which he mentioned three times. Yoder, "Sacrament as Social Process," reprinted as Yoder, "Sacrament as Social Process," *Royal*. In revised and expanded form, this article became Yoder, *Body Politics*, which is discussed in chapter 7.

157. Yoder, "But We Do," *Priestly*, 53, 54; Yoder, "But We Do," *Pacifist*, 29–30, 31.

ing "high Christology," visible already in the New Testament, addresses the concerns of Nicea (and Chalcedon) but, as he said, is not tied to the adequacy of their terminology. Thus "But We Do See Jesus" is an example of his understanding of how the story of Jesus can be made to address any context, using language of that context, while being true to the New Testament's views, which are expressed in other ways by the classic creedal statements. Although one should never claim to know fully the mind of John Howard Yoder, it does appear that comments from his memo of 1991 support the description of Yoder's approach to Christology as outlined in this chapter.

One other noteworthy comment in the 1991 memo addresses christological issues. Yoder stated, "I do affirm the priority of the gospel but do not do it in dichotomized exclusive terms." As he understood his interlocutors, they heard his claims about affirming the gospel as a rejection of influence in the world, as an "against culture" stance. But Yoder claims that his stance is actually one of involvement in the world. He gave several examples—his belief that Christ transformed culture, his claim that Jesus was relevant to the real world, his embrace of the missionary task of cross-cultural communication "in the other guy's terms." It seems that this priority of the gospel and its application is reflected in Yoder's analysis of the story in the sermons in Acts, and the development of the meaning of that story in the five images of high Christology in "But We Do See Jesus."[158] This priority of the gospel means to be continually in a mode of asking what the gospel means and what it looks like in new contexts. This statement of priority recalls another statement of methodology. In the chapter, "The Authority of Tradition" in *Priestly Kingdom*, Yoder wrote of being always in the process of "looping back" or "reaching back" to the origins and the earliest memories.[159]

In other words, discussion of Christology always looks two ways. On the one hand, it has its orientation point in the story of Jesus in the New Testament. On the other hand, there is an understanding of the current context so as to carry the story into that context in a meaningful and transformative way. In this contemporary restatement, one can and will

---

158. In an article published in 1992 in *Faith and Philosophy*, Yoder again discussed taking the gospel into other cultures and using the language of those cultures to express the universal truth of the story of Jesus. He cited the five christological texts from "But We Do See Jesus" as examples. For a reprint of this article, see Yoder, "On Not Being Ashamed."

159. Yoder, "Authority of Tradition," 69–71.

learn from conversation with the received tradition but "without being tied to the adequacy of those formulations in all other times and places."

The following two parts of this book expand understandings of Yoder's christological orientation. Part Two explores sources that contributed to it. Part Three describes its most complete expression in the church, its expansion to include nonviolent engagement with the world, interfaith dialogue, and extension in additional theologizing.

Part Two

Sources of John Howard Yoder's Theology

Those who knew John Howard Yoder in person were sometimes awed by his powerful intellect, the breadth and depth of his knowledge, and his seemingly effortless ability to move between as well as to integrate the fields of theology, biblical studies, and ethics. But that wide grasp of data and issues did not just happen. It reflects the program that he followed in his graduate studies, an orientation that he continued to expand for the rest of his life. The chapters in this section display the important elements that oriented Yoder's scholarship for his life work, and thus also give visibility to the elements that shaped the theological orientation depicted in chapter 1.

Chapter 2 describes Yoder's roots in Anabaptist history. But as the chapter makes clear, Yoder's interest in Anabaptist origins was more theological than historical. When he could not pursue a dissertation in Anabaptist theology per se, he chose a historical topic that would allow him to approach theology from a different direction. He pursued research in historic Anabaptism as an example of a movement that returned its followers to the Jesus of the New Testament. By studying historic Anabaptist origins, he thus hoped to develop the basis of a theology that would be more true to the New Testament narrative of Jesus than the classic theology of the established churches of Christendom. Thus chapter 2 makes visible one root and impulse of the idea of a theology true to the narrative of Jesus that would be in conversation with but not beholden to the classic creeds of Christendom, the theological orientation that is clearly visible in chapter 1.

Another source of Anabaptist influence on Yoder was the "Anabaptist Vision" of Harold S. Bender, Yoder's mentor in Goshen. Some critics have displayed Yoder's Anabaptism as a near clone of Bender's. Yoder did learn from Bender, but Yoder's version of Anabaptism also challenged Bender. Chapter 3 uses rhetorical analysis to display Yoder's differences from as well as similarities to Bender.

Yoder was significantly impacted by the biblical scholarship of the postwar era in Europe as churchmen and scholars sought to understand how the churches had gone so wrong during the war just concluded. Chapter 4 displays important elements of Yoder's thought derived from those conversations. It includes his view on the kingdom of God and on a biblical approach to the state that he learned from Oscar Cullmann, as well as material from André Trocmé on Jubilee and the understanding of the Powers that he adopted from Hendrik Berkhof. Correspondence by Yoder cited in this chapter again displays his intent to develop theology with reference to the New Testament but not beholden to the received theological tradition.

Some scholars have identified Yoder as a Barthian, perhaps a pacifist version of Karl Barth. Chapter 5 describes ways that Yoder did indeed learn from Karl Barth. However, the use of deconstruction in this chapter also displays how Yoder "went beyond" or extended Barth to develop his own, unique approach to theology that expressed the presence of God in Jesus and used the story of Jesus as the basis from which to address any issue.

The chapters of Part Two fill out our understanding of the elements that shaped the theological perspective depicted in chapter 1. And noting the multiple ways in these chapters that Yoder's methodology pointed back to the root, namely the narrative of Jesus, displays why he is a radical theologian.

2

Sixteenth-Century Anabaptist Roots

EARL ZIMMERMAN

One root of John Howard Yoder's christological orientation takes nourishment from the sixteenth-century Anabaptist movement.[1] It seems important to emphasize that point in light of recently expressed skepticism about the task of developing and articulating a distinct and comprehensive theology shaped by Anabaptist convictions that can critically engage theologies rooted in classic Protestant or Catholic traditions.[2] Such skepticism is strange given Yoder's own considerable effort to develop that theology, which was demonstrated at length in the first chapter of this book. Since Yoder's theology was also a dialogical

---

1. Parts of this chapter draw on my discussion of John Howard Yoder's dissertation on the disputations between the Swiss Anabaptists and the Swiss Reformers in my book *Practicing the Politics*, 140–72. Used by permission of the publisher.

2. See Peter Dula's critical comments about J. Denny Weaver's lifelong commitment to articulating a distinctive theology shaped by Anabaptist or peace church assumptions. Dula, "For and Against Hauerwas," 379–80, 379 n. 15. Dula's article insightfully identifies the challenges posed to Anabaptist theology by Stanley Hauerwas, who affirms John Howard Yoder's pacifism but rejects his free church ecclesiology. Dula's theological commitments should parallel Weaver's more closely than his critical comments indicate, given his own expressed "confidence in the future of Anabaptism, of radical free church communities committed to lives of discipleship together." Ibid., 396.

pursuit, one can appreciate the recent comparative impulse to put Yoder in dialogue or conversation with various contemporary theologians or philosophers.³ However, this approach to Yoder's thought will become increasingly opaque and distant from the tradition that informed it unless it also actively engages the task of doing theology shaped by Anabaptist convictions rooted in the shared life and history of free church communities committed to following Jesus.

The description of Yoder's work as a fragmentary, ad hoc collage, which was noted in the Introduction, certainly misses the mark as well. This characterization too may lie in the failure to recognize or take seriously the fact that Yoder's theology is deeply rooted in Anabaptist convictions. This chapter therefore revisits Yoder's historical research on the Swiss Anabaptists in order to better understand his construction of such a theology.

Why Study Anabaptism?

In the 1950s, many young Mennonite scholars were doing historical research on the sixteenth-century Anabaptist movement, but few were working in theology. History was a safer endeavor. Most North American Mennonite churches held traditional or fundamentalist understandings of the Bible and distrusted theology. The anti-modernist volume, *Doctrines of the Bible*,⁴ which had borrowed heavily from Protestant fundamentalism, still functioned as a kind of catechism in many Mennonite communities.

That fundamentalist-shaped, cultural and religious ethos was slowly changing. Mennonite scholar John Christian Wenger had recently written *Introduction to Theology*.⁵ It moved away from the Bible doctrines

3. Various articles in recent, edited books on Yoder's thought, while erudite in other ways, certainly do not demonstrate a profound understanding of Anabaptist sources or the motivation to develop a contemporary theology shaped by Anabaptist assumptions that energized Yoder. For example, see the collected essays in Dula and Huebner, *The New Yoder*. Similarly, it is noteworthy that Craig Carter, whose book purports to be a comprehensive synthesis of Yoder's theology and ethics, lists none of Yoder's historical writings in the section on "A Beginner's Guide to Reading John Howard Yoder." Carter, *Politics of the Cross*, 243–47.

4. Kauffman, *Doctrines*. For an account of the doctrinal orientation of North American Mennonite communities in the first half of the twentieth century, see Juhnke, *Vision, Doctrine, War*, 112–19.

5. Wenger, *Introduction to Theology* (1954).

motif, but was still a conservative Protestant theology that incorporated various Anabaptist beliefs in its outline. It could be argued that it actually moved Mennonites closer to conventional Protestantism. Thus a real need existed for theological work from within the Anabaptist tradition. Given his talents and interests, it is understandable that John Howard Yoder wanted to undertake that task. It was also risky.

However, the initial resistance Yoder experienced did not come from his Mennonite community. When he began formulating a proposal for his doctoral dissertation at the University of Basel in Switzerland, Yoder discovered that it was impossible to find a theologian in a European university who would allow him to do theological work from an Anabaptist perspective. If he wanted to have an Anabaptist focus, he would need to do historical research. Yoder was in conversation with Fritz Blanke, a professor at the University of Zurich known for his work on the Anabaptists. In a letter to his friend Paul Peachey, who was also doing Anabaptist studies in Europe, Yoder wrote,

> The reason for not working with a theologian is that in Blanke's estimate they really aren't open-minded enough to let something they basically disagree with through, so the *Dogmengeschichte* lets you write on the same questions but with a broader-minded professor. If the thesis itself tried to be systematic the professor would be obliged to call in a systematiker, and none . . . would let Anabaptist stuff through.[6]

Consequently, Yoder decided to do historical work under the direction of Ernst Staehelin from the University of Basel. Blanke would serve as an outside consultant.[7] He divided the dissertation into two parts, a historical section that he submitted for his doctorial examination in 1957, and a historical theological section that reflected on his primary historical research.[8]

6. Yoder, letter to Paul Peachey, April 8. Peachey also added a question. According to Peachey, Fritz Blanke had a reputation as a *Sammler* (a collector) rather than a systematic thinker. That appears to be a derogatory assessment. Peachey suggested that working with a more systematic dissertation advisor would be better. See Peachey, letter to John Howard Yoder, April 4.

7. Yoder, letter to Paul Peachey, April 8. Some scholars have asked why Yoder disengaged from the world of sixteenth-century Anabaptist studies after the early 1970s. See Nation, *John Howard Yoder*, 39. Yoder's personal letters help answer that question. They demonstrate that he was always more interested in theology than in Anabaptist historical research.

8. Yoder published both in German. The historical section appeared as Yoder,

Yoder carefully chose the topic of his dissertation, focusing on the early conversations between the Anabaptists and the Protestant Reformers in Switzerland. That choice allowed Yoder to study the theology of the sixteenth-century Anabaptists as it emerged in those conversations. In this way, he was able at least partly to work around the barrier to his desire to do a theological dissertation. In addition, it allowed him to further the historical project of Anabaptist historian Harold Bender, who had been Yoder's undergraduate mentor at Goshen College. Bender had done his own doctoral work on the Swiss Anabaptists and his project led to a historical renaissance that would provide Mennonites with what historian Paul Toews calls a "usable past."[9]

Chapter 3 to follow depicts how Yoder both used and altered Bender's vision. Here it suffices to say that like Bender, Yoder was not interested in sixteenth-century historical research as an end in itself. His historical research and his theological examination of issues between Anabaptists and the Swiss reformers enabled him to develop the theological structure that informed his "politics of Jesus." That structure became central to his lifelong theological project.

Yoder believed that many of the central concerns he addressed in his "politics of Jesus" had already emerged in the sixteenth-century disputations between the Anabaptists and the Protestant Reformers. One set of issues came from Anabaptist ecclesiology, with its focus on the local congregation and its distinction between church and society. This focus informed his understanding of the church as a distinct community of discernment within society and his argument against the Constantinian synthesis of church and civil society. Accordingly, Yoder would argue that the very possibility of tolerance and religious freedom follows the Anabaptist understanding of the relationship between church and civil society.

Another set of issues emerged from Yoder's understanding that Christian social ethics should be based on following the "earthly way of Jesus." Yoder believed he had discovered this radical commitment to Christian discipleship in his Anabaptist research. Discipleship is not just a matter of imitating Jesus' actions but of being fully present in the world in the same way that Jesus had been. Such presence means being

---

Täufertum und Reformation: Schweiz. The second section, which he called a dogmatic examination, was later published as Yoder, *Täufertum und Reformation: Gespräch*. More recently these volumes appeared in English as Yoder, *Anabaptism and Reformation*.

9. Toews, *Mennonites in American Society*, 84.

willing to experience the same kind of persecution and suffering that Jesus experienced.

In this respect, interpreting Yoder as a Barthian theologian,[10] as a proponent or critic of creedal orthodoxy, or as a Mennonite apologist, easily become diversions for other theological agendas.[11] Such interpretations tend to obscure the central passion that gave life to Yoder's theology. In some ways, he was all these things, but none of them adequately defines his "politics of Jesus," which was rooted in his Anabaptist theological commitments and his passion to have the church take Jesus seriously in social ethics. His "politics of Jesus" needs to be understood as the creation of a contemporary theology shaped by Anabaptist convictions, with his doctoral dissertation on the Anabaptists a central part of that task.[12]

Yoder's primary theological convictions, and their formulation throughout his career, drew from his historical theological research on the Swiss Anabaptists.[13] His basic theological orientation, however, was formed before he began his doctoral research. It was already present in his desire to write what he called an Anabaptist *Vergegenwärtigung* (a contemporary, updated Anabaptist theology) as a young student.[14] While Yoder was committed to Bender's project of recovering a usable past for Mennonites, he was even more committed to articulating an Anabaptist social and political ethic in ecumenical circles. He believed that this theological ethic was not merely a Mennonite distinctive that other Christians

10. The fact that Yoder was not even able to have someone like Barth serve as a reader for his dissertation indicates that there was considerable theological distance between them. Chapter 8 to follow explores Yoder's relationship to Barth in detail.

11. A. James Reimer argued that Yoder's theology is incompatible with Trinitarian Christology. Contra Reimer, Craig Carter argued that Yoder had a deep commitment to creedal orthodoxy. As is apparent from J. Denny Weaver's argument in the first chapter of this book, neither Reimer nor Carter fully understood Yoder's approach. See Reimer, "Theological Orthodoxy," and Carter, *Politics of the Cross*, 113–36.

12. A comment Yoder made to Ray Gingerich, a former student of his, confirms the relationship between Yoder's Anabaptist research and his "politics of Jesus." Gingerich talked to Yoder about the need for a contemporary work on Anabaptist theology. Yoder's response was that he had already written it—it was his book *The Politics of Jesus*. Interview with Ray Gingerich, October 8, 2003.

13. Support for this statement includes Michael G. Cartwright in Yoder, *Royal Priesthood*, 5, and Nation, *John Howard Yoder*, 31.

14. A letter to Harold Bender expressed this interest. Yoder, letter to Harold Bender, January 12. For another comment from Yoder that expresses the desire to develop Anabaptist theology that bypassed the theology of Christendom, see the quote referenced by note 3 in chapter 4.

could easily dismiss. It was the gospel and belonged to the heritage of the ecumenical church.

From his historical research on the disputations between the Anabaptists and the Protestant Reformers, Yoder observed that it was the Anabaptists who almost always initiated the discussions. He was impressed with their non-defensive stance in those discussions and their willingness to change their position in light of new evidence. Even to enter into conversation with their powerful adversaries, who could rely on government religious sanctions, was a considerable risk that they were willing to take because of their commitment to share and proclaim the gospel.[15] The historical research on those conversations gave Yoder the ability to revisit the crucial issues they raised. There was an uncanny synergy between what Yoder was discovering in his sixteenth-century Anabaptist research and the heart-searching conversations about what had gone wrong with the Christendom paradigm that he was immersed in as a doctoral student in postwar Europe. This nexus enabled him to change the questions that had shaped the conversation in theological ethics for centuries.

Historical Anabaptist Research

Yoder's historical research focused in particular on the disputations between the Swiss reformer Ulrich Zwingli and emerging Anabaptist leaders, such as Conrad Grebel. He then traced the development of Anabaptism, especially through the influence of Michael Sattler, and the crystallization of the Anabaptist position in the articles of the *Brüderliche Vereinigung* or Brotherly Union, popularly known as the Schleitheim Confession.

Swiss Anabaptist Separation from Zwingli

Yoder made the historical argument that the Swiss Anabaptists emerged out of the Zwinglian reformation. Conrad Grebel, a key Swiss Anabaptist leader, had said that Zwingli had brought them into this matter.[16] Beginning from that premise, Yoder examined the conversations between the Swiss Anabaptists and the Swiss Reformers with the goal of clarifying

15. Yoder, *Anabaptism and Reformation*, 118–21.
16. Von Muralt and Schmid, *Zürich*, 89.

emerging Anabaptist theological and ethical commitments. He reconstructed the formal disputations and other conversations between the Anabaptists and the Reformers in order to identify the crucial issues that eventually caused them to go separate ways.[17] Yoder noticed that there are more recorded conversations between the Reformers and the Anabaptists than between other church groups in the sixteenth century and was impressed that the Anabaptists had generally initiated the conversations.[18] In turn, throughout his own career, Yoder emphasized the importance of ecumenical dialogue.

Yoder asked how it was that that the differences between the Swiss Anabaptists and the Zwinglians became so great that the Zwinglian party eventually banned the very existence of the Anabaptists. Yoder maintained that it was not the issues themselves that became intractable. There was initially a broad agreement as all parties worked together at the task of reforming the church, including matters such as the propriety of charging interest, the reformation of the Mass, and infant baptism. What eventually led to the parting of ways in 1525 was Zwingli's decision to involve the Zurich City Council in the implementation of the reforms. Yoder insisted that it was Zwingli's move from reform based on tolerance to mandatory reform applied to all citizens through government enforcement that created the intractable division between Zwingli and those who had been his followers. He wrote,

> By thus seeing the basic nature of Zwingli's shift in position we have at the same time found the crux of Grebel's clash with him. To place the unity of Zürich above the faithfulness of the church is not only to abandon the church; it is also the demonization of the state, for persecution becomes a theological necessity.[19]

---

17. In addition to Zwingli, the other Reformers included Wolfgang Capito and Martin Bucer in Strasbourg. The two most prominent Anabaptist leaders were Conrad Grebel, the son of a patrician Zurich family and a close confidant to Zwingli, and Michael Sattler, the former prior of the Benedictine monastery in the Black Forest. Yoder produced a separate book in which he translated and edited materials related to Sattler and the formative Anabaptist council at Schleitheim in 1527. See Yoder, *Legacy of Sattler*.

18. Yoder, *Legacy of Sattler*.

19. Yoder, "Turning Point," 140. This article, taken from his dissertation, demonstrates how much significance he placed on his argument about the basic difference between Zwingli and the Anabaptists.

As a consequence of their rejection of government authority in religious matters, the Anabaptists were beginning to rethink the role of government, including the use of force. In this struggle the Swiss Anabaptists were gradually developing their own congregationally based ecclesiology in opposition to the emerging Zwinglian Reformed ecclesiology, which made the civil authorities sovereign in matters of ecclesiastical discipline.

The Legacy of Schleitheim

The subsequent persecution by the Zwinglians threatened to destroy the budding Anabaptist movement. Internal dissensions also threatened the movement. In response to this crisis, a group of Anabaptist leaders met in the village of Schleitheim near the Swiss-German border in 1527. There they drew up the articles of faith often referred to as the Schleitheim Confession.[20]

According to Yoder, those articles of faith represented a further development in Anabaptist congregational ecclesiology. Baptism, communion, and church discipline were understood in relation to the distinction they made between the church and the civil society. All these practices now fit together as a whole. Their rejection of violence was not just a literal citation of New Testament passages but was underpinned theologically by this ecclesiology.[21] According to Yoder, Schleitheim "must be recognized as the coming of age of a distinct, visible fellowship taking long-range responsibility for its order and its faith."[22]

The influence of Michael Sattler, the former prior of St. Peter's Benedictine Monastery in the Black Forest, appears in the theological commitments of Schleitheim. Yoder notes that Sattler was recognized by both critics and admirers as the most significant first generation leader of the Anabaptists.[23] Sattler had not been involved in the disputations with Zwingli but, several years later, was in conversation with Martin Bucer and Wolfgang Capito, the leading Reformers in Strasbourg. As in Zurich,

20. The *Brüderliche Vereinigung* or Brotherly Union is not a full confession of faith. Its more limited purpose was to define the critical areas of agreement in the fledgling Anabaptist movement. For Yoder's historical overview of this period in the Swiss Anabaptist history, see "Persecution and Consolidation," in Dyck, *Introduction to Mennonite History*, 36–43.

21. Yoder, *Anabaptism and Reformation*, 130.

22. Yoder, *Legacy of Sattler*, 29.

23. Ibid., 10, 17 n. 5.

the fundamental disagreement concerned the Reformers' commitment to a uniform reform program enforced by government authority versus the Anabaptist congregationally based, voluntary reforms. Sattler opposed the use of force against religious dissidents and pleaded with the Strasbourg Reformers:

> Be mercifully considerate, I pray you, of those who are in prison and do not permit a merciful judgment to be superseded by a blind, spiteful, and cruel one. Those who are in error (if that they were) are not to be coerced but after a second admonition to be avoided. Christians admonish benevolently, out of sympathy and compassion for the sinful, and do not legalistically coerce persons this way or that.[24]

Bucer and Capito always spoke well of Sattler and considered him a Christian martyr when Austrian authorities burned him at the stake on May 20, 1527.[25]

The legacy of Schleitheim and Michael Sattler is significant for understanding Yoder's own theological commitments. He believed that Sattler and the Swiss Anabaptists were the most authentic representatives of the sixteenth-century Anabaptists. Their core beliefs, which he discovered in his historical research, became the building blocks of his constructive theology.

The Core of Anabaptist Beliefs

John Howard Yoder's historical theological examination of the discussions between the Swiss Anabaptists and the Reformers identified the central elements of sixteenth-century Anabaptist thought that he could use to construct his contemporary theology.[26] It was the "usable past" that he would use in his theological project.

Yoder wanted his theological project to have ecumenical significance. For that reason, it was necessary to explore the disagreements as well as the places of agreement between the Anabaptists and the Reformers. He thought the disagreements were actually more instructive and that they should not be covered over out of a shortsighted desire

---

24. Sattler, "Letter to Bucer and Capito," in Yoder, *Legacy of Sattler*, 23.

25. Capito, "Letter to Bürgmeister and Council at Horb," in Yoder, *Legacy of Sattler*, 87.

26. Yoder, letter to Harold Bender, January 12.

for church unity that ignored real differences.[27] The tragedy of Reformation history, Yoder thought, is not that there were differences, but that no constructive way was found to deal with them. When they could not be resolved theologically, the Reformers resorted to police action.[28]

The challenge, for Yoder, was to find the center that defined these differences. His problem was not only that insufficient resources were available on the Anabaptist position, but that the Anabaptists had no center of their own which held together by itself. Anabaptists understood the existence of their communities as a necessary consequence of the failure of the Reformers to bring about the needed changes they had initially embarked on. In Yoder's analysis, the Swiss Anabaptists were in basic agreement with the initial teachings and objectives of Zwingli and believed they were implementing those teachings in the life of their communities.[29]

In his work of reconstructing Anabaptist distinctives, Yoder followed earlier attempts to find deeper assumptions behind the confrontations over specific issues such as infant baptism. He was building on the work of Harold Bender, who had defined the Anabaptist vision in terms of discipleship, a voluntary church, and an ethic of love and nonresistance. Yoder said that trying to understand such Anabaptist distinctives systematically is made more difficult because the Anabaptists did not think in systematic categories.

According to Yoder, the opposition between the Anabaptists and the Reformers did not grow out of competing theologies but out of the implementation of a common body of belief associated with the Reformation in Switzerland. In discussions with their opponents, the Anabaptists kept insisting, rightly or wrongly, that the Bible alone should be the norm. Few of them were trained theologians, and they had neither the time nor the educational resources needed to develop a sophisticated theology.[30]

Because of those factors, Yoder believed that any theological reconstruction of their thought could only be an interpretation and a hypothesis. We need to ask, he said, if we are dealing with the legitimate possibility of a theology that is worthy of interpretation. The implied

---

27. The significance of difference in ecumenical conversations was a lifelong focus for Yoder. See, for example, his posthumously published article "On Christian Unity."

28. Yoder, *Anabaptism and Reformation*, 142.

29. Ibid., 142–43.

30. Ibid., 148–49.

answer was "yes," but only the expressed opinion and believability of the Anabaptists can provide that answer. In such a reconstruction, central Reformation issues such as justification by faith will not occupy the center of discussion. Instead, other issues will emerge. One should guard against too quickly deciding what is central. Yoder wrote,

> Things for whose sake the one side was ready to persecute, and for which the other side was ready to suffer persecution, are fundamentally important—even if they lie only on the periphery of systematic orthodoxy, they can become the center point of the test of obedience and witness.[31]

Dualism and Monism

One of the issues that divided the Reformed and Anabaptist positions, according to Yoder, was Zwingli's penchant toward a platonic, spiritual dualism, which the Anabaptists rejected. Zwingli's dualism allowed him to make a distinction between divine justice (which is ordained for heaven) and its implementation in sinful human society. Because of the reality of sin, divine justice can never be transferred to human society. Correspondingly, one cannot talk about Christian social ethics. Within a Christendom ecclesiology, Yoder explained, a Christian social ethic would mean applying those ethics to the whole society in a way that makes no distinction between church and society. Hence, the Reformers assumed it was impossible to apply the teaching of Jesus beyond private, personal ethics.[32]

Yoder noted that the general assumption is that it was the Lutherans, with their interest in justification for the individual, who left out social ethics, while the Reformed tradition drew political consequences from their striving for a holy community. He argued, however, that in the disputations he studied, it was the Reformed side that drew distinctions between the inner and the outer, while it was the Anabaptists who insisted that obedience to God's commandments and Christ's work was relevant for social ethics.[33]

---

31. Ibid., 150.
32. Ibid., 152.
33. Ibid., 162–63. An insight from Abraham Friesen's historical work on Erasmus and the Anabaptists supports Yoder's contention that such dualism undercuts Christian practice and social ethics. Erasmus, the sixteenth-century humanist and biblical

The other side of Zwingli's spiritual dualism, according to Yoder, was a covenantal monism that identified Christian baptism with Old Testament circumcision. The discussion soon went far beyond that of covenantal signs and raised the issue of the relationship between the Old Testament and the New Testament. Zwingli understood the unity of the two testaments to be based on God's covenant formation of the people of God. In this way, he could appropriate those parts of the Old Testament in which the community of faith was identified with a national community that had political backing.[34]

For Yoder, Zwingli's approach brought out a basic issue in Anabaptist biblical hermeneutics. The Anabaptists obviously could not agree with the way the Reformers associated Old Testament covenantal signs with baptism. As a consequence Anabaptists had to endure the charge that they had rejected the authority of the Old Testament. They denied that charge, arguing instead that they understood the relationship between the two testaments differently—as a relationship of promise and fulfillment. The Old Testament had to be interpreted through Christ, who was the fulfillment of God's promise.[35] Yoder appropriated this hermeneutic for his own interpretation of the Bible.

Yoder noted that the Reformed leaders wanted to interpret Christ through God's covenant with Abraham. In contrast, the Anabaptists insisted on interpreting Abraham through the new covenant with Christ. From a Reformed perspective, everything was essentially the same because God's inclination toward humanity always remained the same. For the Anabaptists, everything has become new because it is only in obedience to Christ that humanity can be in right relationship with God.[36]

From an Anabaptist perspective, in their relationship with Christ, the people of God are distinguished from the civil society. According to

---

scholar, noted in the *Annotations* to his Greek New Testament that the command to teach and make disciples precedes baptism (Matt 28:19). Friesen claims that the Anabaptists were the only Reformation-era group to put that insight into practice because they read Erasmus' work without the customary Platonic overlay that separates ideas and ideals from particular expressions in the world. See Friesen, *Erasmus, the Anabaptists*, 38, 44–48. The issue of abstract Platonic thought reemerges in Yoder's dispute with contemporary Protestant ethicists such as Reinhold Niebuhr, who claimed that God's law of absolute love could not be socially interpreted. See Niebuhr, *Moral Man and Immoral Society*, 76–82.

34. Yoder, *Anabaptism and Reformation*, 166–68.
35. Ibid., 168–72.
36. Ibid.

Yoder, the Anabaptist distinction between church and civil government became a source of misunderstanding with their Reformed interlocutors who assumed either that they wanted to impose a radical communitarian ethic on all of society or were anarchists. Instead, the Anabaptists were developing a free church or believers church ecclesiology. That ecclesiology is another core Anabaptist conviction that became central to Yoder's theology.[37]

The formal expression of the Anabaptist distinction between church and civil government is seen clearly in the Schleitheim Confession. It reads, "The sword is an ordering of God outside the perfection of Christ. . . . but within the perfection of Christ only the ban is used."[38] Accordingly, the ordering of God has two levels, but only the church is within the completeness of Christ, which is a new social and ethical reality for those who confess Christian faith.[39]

In summary, Yoder argued that both Zwingli and the Anabaptists attempted to grasp the duality of human existence. For Zwingli, this duality is platonic-ontological. It encompasses both an inner spiritual reality, in which Christ reigns, and the outer world, characterized by sin and compromise, in which we live. In this outer world no distinction exists between the national society and the people of God or between God's elect and the non-elect.[40]

The Anabaptist dualism, on the other hand, is historical-eschatological. The present age is embodied not only in individual sinfulness but also in authoritarian and violent social structures and the shortcomings of the old covenant with Abraham. The coming age is already being realized in the church through the new covenant with Christ. Baptism is the sign of entering into this community that was formed at Pentecost. It indicates our entrance into a new life described as the "completeness of Christ."[41]

---

37. Ibid., 172–73.

38. Yoder, *Legacy of Sattler*, 39. In this sixteenth-century Anabaptist parlance the word *sword* refers to coercive state power and the word *ban* refers to the simple avoidance of someone who has not responded to a process of church discipline and initiatives for dialogue. It was understood as a more humane approach to church order, in contrast to the Protestant and Catholic use of coercive government measures, including torture and execution, to discipline people charged with heresy.

39. Yoder, *Anabaptism and Reformation*, 172–73.

40. Ibid., 174–75.

41. Ibid.

These Anabaptist theological understandings of biblical hermeneutics and of the church in relation to Christ, the world, and eschatology became the driving force in Yoder's theology. Recognizing such Anabaptist motifs in his theological ethics underscores the importance of studying his historical research on the Anabaptists for an adequate understanding of the development of his thought.

Authority and Tradition

Another aspect of Yoder's thought is the careful way he worked with the authority of the whole Christian tradition from an Anabaptist perspective.[42] Such attention to tradition is evident in his Anabaptist historical research. He noted that, in their break with Catholicism, the Reformers had argued for the primacy of Scripture over that of church tradition. But almost immediately they found themselves in the position of protecting their young tradition from challenges by the Anabaptists, who appealed to the same grounds of biblical authority. The Reformers were in the uncomfortable position of arguing that the re-baptizers were schismatic and prone to cause uprisings because they did not respect the authority of church traditions.[43]

The irony of the situation was not lost on some of their Catholic opponents, who said that the heretics knew how to protect themselves against other heretics only by resorting to the authority of the church. One Protestant answer to this charge was that the "errors" that had caused their break with Catholicism (i.e., celibacy, papal authority, and monasticism) could be rejected because they were not part of the universal teaching of the church. Infant baptism, on the other hand, had been accepted by the whole church. The Anabaptists, in turn, argued that not even infant baptism had been universally accepted in church history.[44]

A complicating factor, according to Yoder, was that the three parties to these discussions had different perspectives on the church. Each claimed to be the one true church on the basis of their respective claims about the nature of the gathered community. The issues included episcopal hierarchy, historical continuity, biblical authority, and the work

---

42. As described in chapter 1, Yoder's respect for the theological tradition, without being totally dependent on it, is evident in his *Preface* (2002).
43. Yoder, *Preface* (2002), 56–58.
44. Ibid.

of the Holy Spirit. The Catholics emphasized historical continuity and episcopal authority. The Anabaptists emphasized biblical authority and the gathered community as a manifestation of the work of the Holy Spirit. The Protestant Reformers ended up in the uncomfortable position of arguing the one side of this debate against the Catholics and the other side against the Anabaptists.[45]

Yoder said that the Protestants did not necessarily represent a middle position between the Catholics and the Anabaptists. In some respects, such as an emphasis on concrete expressions of discipleship and on the role of government authorities in church matters, Catholics and Anabaptists were more in agreement with each other than with the Protestants. One instance is that when Zwingli referred reformation matters to the Zurich City Council, the Catholics had also protested that civil government officials were incompetent to decide on religious matters. Another instance is that both Catholics and Anabaptists thought that discipleship was undercut by the Protestant theological claim that justification was by faith alone. It was not an accident that the Reformers sometimes accused the Anabaptists of developing a new monasticism.[46]

The Anabaptists also made historical arguments. Yoder insisted that they were not merely biblicists who could not think historically. Their whole position actually depended on their historical argument about the development of the church. Like the Reformers, Anabaptists insisted that historically the church had gone terribly wrong and needed to be restored. The Reformers had located the place of deviation and error with the papacy and medieval developments. The Anabaptists located the problem much earlier, with the developments symbolized by Constantine that had made Christianity the religion of the Roman Empire. For Yoder, it was not only a question of reforming the medieval church, but of reestablishing the community of the New Testament before it had taken on the trappings of empire.[47]

The Anabaptist argument against the Constantinian shift that had taken place in church history became central to Yoder's theology. He discovered that the new postwar era (which many had begun to label the post-Christendom era of the church) had produced a new audience for the argument against Constantianism. It was not only a sectarian

---

45. Ibid., 65.
46. Ibid., 65–70.
47. Ibid.

argument, but a matter that concerned the whole church. It could even serve as the basis of interfaith dialogue about the nature of the church.[48]

The Church as a Community of Discernment

A crucial question for Yoder was why the Reformation failed in its central mission. It was not only the loss of the deepest views of the Reformation, which had become a wooden orthodoxy by the second generation, nor was it the splintering of the different Reformation groups. It was not even that the Reformers felt compelled to persecute dissidents. Nor was it that the Reformation churches became subservient to the emerging nation-states. These all constituted secondary problems. Yoder wrote,

> The deepest tragedy of the Reformation, from which all other problems arose, lies in the fact that what everyone believed did not show itself to be true. This was the belief that Scripture alone was sufficient to clearly decide *all* questions that arose concerning Christian teaching and Christian life.[49]

---

48. Yoder, "Disavowal of Constantine." As represented by Drake, *Constantine and the Bishops*, recent scholarship has altered considerably the picture of Constantine and his era since Yoder first analyzed what he called the Constantinian shift. Since Yoder used now somewhat dated secondary literature on Constantine, some scholars have challenged Yoder's credibility as a historian and his theological analysis of the shift; an example is Sider, "Constantinianism Before and After." Peter Leithart, who quotes Sider, published a book-length effort to defend Constantine and refute Yoder's analysis (*Defending Constantine*). Leithart says that there is little in the New Testament to indicate that Jesus rejected the sword. Thus Leithart can depict Constantine's wars and cruelty while claiming, contra Yoder, that no fundamental change occurred in the church's attitude toward the sword between the New Testament and Constantine. Along with the material in the current volume, for wide-ranging discussion of rejection of violence by Jesus and the New Testament, see Weaver, *Nonviolent God*. I would also argue that Yoder was concerned with the beginning and the end of the trajectory from the New Testament to Constantine. The recent developments in historiography change the details of how the shift occurred, but do not fundamentally impact Yoder's theological analysis of the significance of the change symbolized by Constantine. For detailed critique of Leithart's thesis, see Roth, *Constantine Revisited*, particularly the first three chapters, by John Nugent, Alan Kreider, and Mark Thiessen Nation.

49. Yoder, *Täufertum und Reformation: Gespräch*, 99–100 (author's translation). The translation in Yoder, *Anabaptism and Reformation*, 218, is cumbersome and confusing. The original German text reads as follows: "Das tiefste Verhängnis der Reformation, aus dem alle andere hervorging, liegt darin, das das sich nicht als wahr erwies, was alle glaubten, nämlich, das die Heilige Schrift genüge, alle auftretenden Fragen christlicher Lehre und christlichen Lebens eindeutig zu entscheiden."

It was not only that Zwingli and Luther could not talk with the Anabaptists, Yoder said. They were also unable to talk with each other. The basic problem was the heroic simplicity and the unquestioned and unquestionable trust they placed in the divine Word, believed to be authored and interpreted by the Holy Spirit, which they used to reject the teaching office of the Catholic Church. They failed to consider the further problems of theological knowledge; consequently they identified the Word as they understood it with the Word itself. In the practical application of the principle of *sola scriptura,* the place of theological knowledge was not the church but rather the thought of the individual theologian. Thus a theological opponent could not be seen as a brother or sister but only as an enemy of God.[50]

Yoder asked if *sola scriptura* inevitably leads to hopeless subjectivity. What would have been necessary for mutual understanding and a common confession? The answer, which he saw in the Anabaptist communities, was to see the local church as a community of discernment. The community stands under Scripture and over the theologian.[51]

In this model, the gathered congregation listens to the various arguments and decides which is in accordance with the teaching of Christ. Everyone, including the unordained, should have the right to speak. The community acts with the confidence that God's Spirit is guiding them in the discernment process. Consensus is reached when the silence of the community indicates that all objections have been answered. One need not be overly concerned that the many local communities, acting independently, will bring confusion, because the Word of God, interpreted through Christ, serves as an objective standard. It is the freedom of the local community that is a precondition to unity.[52] Rhetorical analysis in chapter 3 to follow shows that this dialogue within and from within the community is intrinsic to Yoder's ecclesiology, which was not true for the Goshen School of Anabaptism with which Yoder was in conversation.

50. Yoder, *Anabaptism and Reformation,* 219.

51. Ibid.

52. Ibid., 220–24. I add one caveat, namely that as part of the process of discernment, the local church will want to draw on all the hermeneutical resources available to it within the ecumenical body of Christ. In other words, the interpreting, discerning community needs to be bigger and wider than one local congregation. This is an affirmation of Yoder's congregational, free-church hermeneutic and ecclesiology, along with a desire to see it further developed and refined as a discernment practice in the gathered life of contemporary congregations. Chapter 13 expands this need of further development.

This Anabaptist understanding was an extension of Zwingli's early teaching. The first disputations in Zurich followed such a congregational model of decision-making. When Zwingli later began to refer decisions to the city council, the Anabaptists used the historical precedent of the first disputation in their arguments against Zwingli. This understanding of what constituted a correct process of discernment helps explain why the Anabaptists complained that they had not been heard in the Zurich disputations. Being heard was more than being allowed to speak. It meant that their concerns should be recognized in the decision-making process. If the Word and the Spirit agreed, there should be consensus. Instead, the Reformers forced agreement through coercion. According to Yoder, it was the inability of the Reformers to discuss differences that led to a theologically and historically distinct Anabaptist community.[53]

These congregational and ecumenical discernment processes, which Yoder discovered in his historical research, became central to his constructive theology. He was deeply committed to a discernment process in which consensus arises out of open conversation. He called such a process the "rule of Paul" (1 Cor 14:26–33). Closely related was his commitment to "ecumenical patience" and a willingness to be in conversation with one's theological opponents.[54]

Intolerance and Secularization

A central argument of Yoder's dissertation was that Zwingli's earlier emphasis on following Christ, human powerlessness, the omnipotence of God, and a suffering church gave way to an emphasis on the power of the preached Word, the doctrine of predestination, the invisibility of the church, and a reevaluation of the role of the civil government. At each step of the way, in the process of reform, the challenge for Zwingli was to initiate reforms without creating a backlash from those with Catholic sympathies while pacifying those who wanted to move more rapidly.

---

53. Ibid.

54. Yoder kept developing this Anabaptist hermeneutic and applying it to contemporary processes of discernment. He attributed the term "The Rule of Paul" to Zwingli, from whom the Anabaptists learned this process of discernment. See his article "Hermeneutics of the Anabaptists." Also see his chapters "Binding and Loosing" and "The Rule of Paul" in Yoder, *Body Politics*, 1–13, 61–70.

Grebel remained in basic agreement with Zwingli, as long as the Reformation proceeded on the basis of tolerance.[55]

The momentum of events in Zurich made Zwingli change his reform strategy. He had great faith in the power of the preached Word and confidence in his rhetorical gifts as a preacher. His initial confidence that this strategy alone would gradually weaken resistance became unrealistic. At the same time, his political clout was growing. This combination of factors made Zwingli decide not to move ahead with reforms until he had secured the backing of the city council and he had the political power to make them mandatory for all the citizens of Zurich. This meant that the Reformation had to become more authoritarian and would proceed on the basis of religious intolerance. That decision, according to Yoder, was the breaking point between Zwingli and Grebel.[56]

Grebel advocated proceeding on the basis of tolerance and beginning to implement reforms in those churches that were ready for them. According to Yoder, this approach made it impossible for Zwingli to understand the Anabaptists. Zwingli always considered the problems of the Reformation in terms of their implementation in the whole society. When the Anabaptists advocated a more rapid implementation, he thought they wanted to force reform on the Catholics. When they talked about more economic sharing, he thought they wanted to abolish private property in the civil arena. When they talked about nonviolence, he thought they wanted to abolish the civil government. Even though the Anabaptists kept insisting that they had no such intentions, he was convinced that they wanted to take civil power into their own hands.[57]

According to Yoder, Zwingli's decision to turn the implementation of the Reformation over to the Zurich City Council made intolerance mandatory. Using the civil authorities to force a unitary expression of the Christian faith had the added consequence of making the civil authorities the custodians of religious faith. Because it was so closely tied to the

55. Yoder, *Anabaptism and Reformation*, 246–47.

56. Ibid., 241–47. Yoder postulated that this change of direction involved an inner crisis for Zwingli. Zwingli later wrote that the Lord had revealed to him the necessity of waiting to abolish the Mass until he had the unequivocal support of the state to abolish it in all parishes. Otherwise, he would run the risk of having uncontrolled conventicles functioning independently. Yoder thought such an appeal to direct divine revelation indicated Zwingli's awareness of the fundamental shift in strategy he was making. It also indicated the personal struggle involved in making such a decision. See Yoder, "Turning Point," 139.

57. Yoder, *Anabaptism and Reformation*, 246–47.

implementation of the Reformation, their custodial role in suppressing Catholic and Anabaptist dissidents was inevitable. Zwingli may have wished that the authorities had used less violence in their suppression of Catholic and Anabaptist nonconformists, but nevertheless, he approved of suppression in principle. When there was tolerance in the course of the Reformation, it was often lenient statesmen who defended freedom of belief against the theologians.[58]

As a consequence of using civil authorities to enforce unity of faith within the Reformation territories, Yoder argued, the church as an independent sociological entity was removed and its authority was transferred to the emerging nation-state. The official churches became a branch of the organizational apparatus of the absolutist state to a degree not seen in medieval Europe. Even when a separate church administration existed within the Reformation, it was still a part of the state and not an independent entity. Church discipline became a function of civil authority.[59]

The further consequence of this policy was the secularization of Christendom. The Anabaptists have sometimes been hailed as the forerunners of democracy and modern religious pluralism. Yoder insisted that this is only true with reference to issues such as religious tolerance and the separation of church and state. It was the Reformers and not the Anabaptists who delivered the fatal blow to medieval Christendom. The Reformers had tied their project integrally into the various municipalities and city states that were called on to defend the Reformation. Consequently, only one choice remained. Either one waged religious war until the enemy was unconditionally defeated, or one made an agreement in which the matter of truth was put to the side. The latter is what happened in the peace of Westphalia, where it was agreed that each ruler would decide the religion in his territory. With that agreement, the emerging nation-states had become secular in order to put an end to the religious wars.[60]

Consequently, according to Yoder, the medieval religious and social synthesis collapsed. The nation-state had become autonomous along with the economy and the professions. The autonomous state had replaced the sacred realm of Christendom. The guidelines for Christian social conduct became patriotic and pragmatic. The concept of human justice

---

58. Ibid., 247–50.
59. Ibid., 252–53.
60. Ibid.

now served the concerns of the nation-state and the emerging capitalist economic order, even when it was justified in the name of God.[61]

Constructing an Anabaptist Theology

On the basis of these observations, John Howard Yoder could now begin to sketch the outline of a constructive theology from an Anabaptist perspective. It could not be a complete picture, but it could show the uniqueness of the answer the Anabaptists gave to the question of creating Christian communities in the sixteenth century. Yoder wrote that various factors make this a risky endeavor:

> It includes the working hypothesis that Anabaptism, as a form of justified theological thought, can be taken seriously, and that trains of thought can be developed further, for which the Anabaptists had neither the time, the freedom, or even the necessary conceptual material at their disposal. But if one is aware of how little reason or opportunity the Anabaptists had for thinking dogmatically, then the astonishing thing is not the lack of dogmatic material in the sources preserved for us, but rather the clarity and unity of the starting points that these sources offer for carrying these trains of thought further.[62]

As Yoder saw it, these Anabaptist avenues of thought raise two central issues for contemporary theology. The first is the relationship between the church and the world or the structures of human society. The second is the need to ground Christian ethics in a Christology that takes discipleship seriously. He began to draw out more fully some of the implications of these issues.

Church and Society

It is imperative, according to Yoder, to make some kind of distinction between the church and other social entities such as the nation-state. National structures are a part of the world and cannot be integrated into the church. Yoder argued that it was only in the cultural world of Europe in late Roman history that one could conceive of fusing church, state, and civil society. Even there, it was ambiguous and temporary. People who

61. Ibid., 254–55.
62. Ibid., 260.

find the Anabaptist way of formulating the relationship between church and society absurd stand in this European arena.[63] When the state is expressly non-Christian, there is logically no other way of thinking about the relationship than the way the Anabaptists did. That is true for the New Testament churches in their world as well as for the vast majority of Christians in our world.[64]

For the Anabaptists, it was not just a matter of turning back the clock to the pre-Constantinian world of the early church. They perceived that combining church and state was dysfunctional in their century. When the Reformers brought church and state together in a way that had not even been true in medieval Europe, it became destructive. They lost any sense of a world in relation to the church. In doing that, they lost the church as a viable theological and sociological entity.[65]

Yoder argued that the refusal of contemporary Christian social ethicists to consider the Anabaptist conception of church and society made it difficult to renew the church in the twentieth century. The twentieth-century world was much closer to the pre-Constantinian social world than to the sixteenth century. The problem is that most theologians are still caught up in such Reformation ways of thinking, even when the result has been so disastrous and has contributed to a post-Christian atheism. Yoder wrote,

> The church community did not want to separate itself from the world, so the world had to separate itself from the church community. The state had to establish itself against the church that had wanted to dominate it, by taking the form of *nation* and *reason*.[66]

63. Stanley Hauerwas, one of the most well-known interpreters of Yoder's thought, thinks he can affirm Yoder's pacifism while rejecting his ecclesiology. Hauerwas attributes this to his own "lingering longing for Christendom." Hauerwas, "Christian Difference," 50–51, 58 n. 40. See also the perceptive comments of Peter Dula, a former student of Hauerwas, concerning Hauerwas' rejection of Yoder's ecclesiology. Hauerwas can have it both ways only by failing to acknowledge the incipient violence embedded in all Christendom visions of church and society, which is the other side of failing to recognize that Yoder's pacifism needs the voluntary ecclesiology he described. Dula, "For and Against Hauerwas," 375–76. Peter Leithart is more perceptive when he sees Yoder's free church pacifism as the biggest challenge to his defense of Constantine and Christendom and his effort to apply Yoder's view of church to a contemporary mass church ecclesiology. See Leithart, *Defending Constantine*.

64. Yoder, *Anabaptism and Reformation*, 259–64.

65. Ibid.

66. Ibid., 264.

Yoder argued that whoever approves of the alliance between the Reformation and government authorities, with the pragmatic reasoning that it was a matter of survival, must also take account of what actually came of such an alliance. It tied the church to anti-church forces such as rationalism and nationalism, which led to the defensive situation of the church in later centuries. It is this situation that has made faith in Christ unbelievable for many people today.[67]

To understand the outlines of the church, Yoder claimed that we need to understand the world as a sociological fact. In the language of the New Testament, the world is understood as the fallen, disobedient, social entities of this age. Such disobedience is embodied in the state, in civil religion, in class economics, and in the demonic aspects of autonomous human culture. When the world as such became invisible to the Reformers, the church also became invisible.[68]

In contrast, Yoder noticed that the "world" and the "church" were very pregnant concepts for the Anabaptists. The tension between these two realms does not necessarily imply unrelenting animosity or public persecution. The world can decide that it is in its own best interest to have the church in its midst. It may even favor the church if this appears to be useful. But, such recognition and freedom does not give the church reason to baptize the world in a way that has happened since the fourth and fifth centuries.[69]

This refusal to baptize the world, Yoder claimed, does not mean that the Anabaptists were unconcerned about social and cultural matters. They saw the church as having an educational effect on the world, but this impact can be accomplished only with the kind of patience that God displays. Such patience allows the world to be the world and respects its prerogative not to accept the Christian message. It also refuses to equate society and culture with the nation-state and its coercive power, as many interpretations of human history do.[70]

---

67. Ibid. Yoder is concerned about the ever-tempting subordination of the Christian community's own distinct way of being in the world rooted in Jesus' politics of suffering love in order to serve the often violent politics of empire or the nation-state. This subordination undercuts the evangelical core of the gospel. Peter Leithart's defense of Constantine as a wise and honorable Christian emperor sidesteps the problem and does not negate Yoder's concern. Leithart, *Defending Constantine*. For a longer response to Leithart, see note 48 and Roth, *Constantine Revisited*.

68. Yoder, *Anabaptism and Reformation*, 265.

69. Ibid., 264–67.

70. Ibid., 268.

Yoder said that many are inclined to see the Anabaptist position as only dualism and withdrawal from the world. He argued, however, that nobody can get around such dualism. On the one hand, there is the Anabaptist model of a visible church living in tension with a visible world. On the other hand, there is the Zwinglian model of divine justice withdrawing into an inner spiritual realm, to make room for the state, allied with the church. Furthermore, the true church is understood to be invisible. One needs to ask, Yoder indicated, which model has the greater tendency to withdraw from history.[71]

Stated positively, the Anabaptist model, according to Yoder, sees worth in the world. It does not leave it to its own devices. The world, even in its non-belief, still stands under the lordship of Christ and the Christian can testify to the world about what that lordship means.[72] It means rejecting theocracy. The Anabaptists insisted that we should not impose our beliefs on others. The outlines of this Christian witness to the social order maintain a distinction between the church and the world, which contains an inherent dualism. Christian social ethics begin with the Christian community, but they have relevance for the rest of society.[73] Yoder would spend the rest of his life explicating the concrete implications of the Anabaptist model of church and society in the many different situations that arise out of the church's life in the world.[74]

Christian Social Ethics and the "Earthly Way of Jesus"

Yoder's study of the Swiss Anabaptists may appear to be a circuitous way to come to his notion of the "politics of Jesus." But there is logic to it. In a broad sense, one can even argue that his historical study of the

71. Ibid., 270–71. On the Anabaptist rejection of philosophical or theological dualism that distinguishes between the ideal of Christ and the imperfection of Christ's church, see also Biesecker-Mast, *Separation and the Sword*, 90–91.

72. Biesecker-Mast, *Separation and the Sword*, 281. Stating that the world is "under the lordship of Christ" indicates Yoder's indebtedness to Oscar Cullman's New Testament studies at least as much as to his sixteenth-century historical research. (See chapter 4 below.) While the difference is not necessarily contradictory, the Anabaptists did not formulate the relationship between church and world in this way. One way to see this difference is to compare it with the Schleitheim statement that "the sword is an ordering of God outside the perfection of Christ."

73. Yoder, *Anabaptism and Reformation*, 281–85.

74. Some of Yoder's books in which this explication is most evident are *Christian Witness*, *Priestly Kingdom*, and *Body Politics*.

Anabaptists prompted Yoder to research the social and political ethics of Jesus. In his sixteenth-century historical research, Yoder was impressed by the extent to which the Anabaptists insisted that "the earthly way of the person Jesus should be normative for the obedience of every Christian." He noticed that this conviction had been lost for the normal person in the medieval era but showed up again in the humanism of Erasmus.[75] Early in his career, Zwingli was drawn to Erasmus and consequently made following the way of the human Jesus central to his understanding of Christian faith. Grebel and other followers of Zwingli, who later became Anabaptists, brought this conviction to the Anabaptist movement.[76] Yoder found their emphasis on the earthly way of the human Jesus in his Anabaptist research. Using modern biblical research methods, he brought that same emphasis to his "politics of Jesus." It is this emphasis by Yoder on Jesus as the root of Anabaptism as well as of his contemporary ethics that earns for Yoder the title of "radical theologian" in this book.

Yoder argued that such discipleship only achieves its full radicalism when it goes beyond personal ethics. Following Jesus in personal ethics would not upset the status quo. It only becomes controversial when the Christian community chooses between the historically lived incarnation of Jesus and other criteria in social ethics. Such ultimate clarification is required in the relationship between the church and the state. Here, typically the appeal is to other standards such as human justice, natural law, or the order of creation. Consequently, it becomes imperative to demonstrate the difference between such ethical systems and Christ's revealed divine justice.[77]

For the Anabaptists it was not a simple matter of imitating Christ's actions but of being socially present in the world in the same way Christ was. For the state church, this option was excluded and discipleship became a secondary motive. That is why Zwingli, arguing against the Anabaptists, insisted that Christians should only follow Christ's example of humility and that the Old Testament kings should serve as the model for social ethics. Picking up the Anabaptist side of the argument, Yoder insisted that Zwingli's perspective undercut the ultimate ethical relevance of Jesus' earthly life, as well as the cross and the resurrection. In contrast,

---

75. Yoder, *Anabaptism and Reformation*, 285–86.

76. Ibid. This focus may also be indebted to the influence of the Benedictine tradition that Michael Sattler brought to the Anabaptist movement.

77. Ibid.

Yoder's notion of the "politics of Jesus" sought to demonstrate the relationship between Christ's incarnation and Christian discipleship.[78]

The meaning of suffering became especially poignant for the Anabaptists. For baptism candidates, this very act included a readiness to face certain persecution. In the most evident way possible, they recognized that following Christ meant taking up one's cross. Yoder claimed that the cross did not mean enduring natural calamities, nor did it refer to suffering that God brought to them to purify them. Instead, it had a hard ethical meaning. It was the result of their battle with the evil social structures of the world.[79]

This ethical commitment to "following Jesus" and the "way of the cross" powerfully shaped Yoder's thought. He committed his academic career to retrieving this Anabaptist social ethic and making that same argument again in the last half of the twentieth century, when the synthesis between church and state was increasingly being questioned.[80] Church leaders and scholars, Yoder believed, were now more ready to critique the legacy of Christendom that was inherited from the medieval world. Perhaps the Anabaptist argument for a consistent Christian social ethic, following the example of the human Jesus, would have a new opportunity to be heard.

Though that is still true, it has to be recognized that the motivation to use religion in the service of national politics is ever present. Politicians are always tempted to use religion for their own ends and religious leaders are always tempted by the perks that come from the cozy association with national political power. At the beginning of the twenty-first century, the so-called global war on terror has again raised the specter of a "Christian nation" fighting its enemies in the name of God.

Conclusion

It was out of a combination of both interest (a desire to work on a contemporary theology from an Anabaptist perspective) and necessity (the fact that European Protestants were unwilling to approve such a doctoral

---

78. Ibid., 287.
79. Ibid., 289–92.
80. This statement does not ignore the formal separation of church and state in the United States since its founding. Instead, it recognizes the cultural establishment of Protestantism that exists in the United States even in the twenty-first century.

project) that John Howard Yoder decided to do his doctoral work in historical theology by focusing his dissertation on the disputations between the Swiss Anabaptists and Protestant Reformers. That allowed him to do both historical and theological research. A central purpose of his historical work was to discern the avenues of Anabaptist thought that the disputations helped develop. With such concepts he built the theological structure of what he came to call the "politics of Jesus."

At one level this chapter has described one root of the approach to theology demonstrated in chapter 1. It has shown that one source for Yoder's insistence that Christian theology and ethics begins with the Jesus of history is found in the Anabaptist theological history that Yoder studied for his dissertation. In that sense this chapter is a complement to chapter 1. But more than displaying one source of Yoder's theology, this chapter has demonstrated that Yoder's Anabaptist convictions were integral to his entire theological and ethical program.

The two key concepts of Anabaptism, according to Yoder, were *community* and *discipleship*. Ethical commitments such as nonviolence, truth telling, servant leadership, and economic justice are integrally related as aspects of these two key concepts. If one views these concepts from the perspective of the breaking point between the Anabaptists and the Reformers, the concern for a visible community becomes dominant. But when one asks why such a community is necessary, it is a result of the central commitment to follow Jesus. Following the narrative of Jesus inevitably results in a visible community coming into existence. This community is more than an individual ethic of imitation. It is the body of Christ coming into existence as a distinct community in the world.[81] As valuable as was Yoder's articulation of this understanding of the visible community, his personal failure to live up to its insight points to the need to develop better ways to deal with individual failure so that such failure does not appear to challenge the validity of the theology of the community. Chapter 13 to follow makes suggestions along that line of inquiry.

The focus on community and discipleship, as extensions of the commitment to follow Jesus, were also the basis of Yoder's critique of classic Nicene Christology. As he noted, the formula did not model following the way of Jesus in the life of the church as the body of Christ. Such following requires reaching back to the narrative of Jesus in the Gospels,

---

81. Yoder, *Anabaptism and Reformation*, 299.

which Yoder said took Jesus' humanity more seriously than did Nicaea and Chalcedon.[82]

This distinct community in the world was the core of the "usable past" Yoder found in his sixteenth-century historical research. That work, along with his biblical scholarship, informed his theological articulation of "the politics of Jesus." There is no question about the quality of his historical scholarship and the contribution he made to sixteenth-century historical research on the Anabaptists. But his biggest contribution would come in theology. The avenues of thought Yoder developed from his findings in sixteenth-century Anabaptism had a far-reaching impact in academic circles as well as in the church and in various initiatives for social transformation. It spoke to concerns in the last half of the twentieth century in ways that he could not have imagined.

The following chapter develops a related component of Yoder's theological orientation, namely, his relationship to the so-called Goshen School of Anabaptist scholarship. The representatives of the Goshen School treated are Harold S. Bender, who wrote the seminal essay "The Anabaptist Vision," and Bender's confidant John Christian Wenger, a prominent advocate of "the Anabaptist Vision."

---

82. It is instructive to study Yoder's nuanced affirmation and his critique of the classic creeds in the construction of his Anabaptist-shaped theology as has been demonstrated in the first chapter of this book. Various interpreters of Yoder's theology take his claim that his view of Jesus in his *Politics of Jesus* is "more radically Nicene and Chalcedonian than other views" as an affirmation of classic creedal orthodoxy; see Nation, "Politics of Yoder," 39, and Nation, *John Howard Yoder*, 128–29. However, rather than affirming, Yoder was actually giving a subtle critique of the creedal formulations from the perspective of the scriptural narrative and confession of the person and work of Jesus. It is understandable that the high church tradition affirmed the Nicene formula, he says, "because the king was finally on that side." An especially troublesome matter from an Anabaptist or free church perspective is the undercurrent of coercion and violence contained in the claim that the creedal formulations are supernatural truth. See Yoder, *Preface* (2002), 205. This claim has been used to anathematize and persecute ecclesial opponents for political reasons and to forcibly undergird the establishment of Christendom. For an historical account of this coercive politics, see Jenkins, *Jesus Wars*.

3

Harold S. Bender, Anabaptist Vision, and the Goshen School

ZACHARY J. WALTON

Following the previous chapter's identification of the sixteenth-century roots of Yoder's theology, this chapter shifts to an assessment of Yoder's engagement with the twentieth-century renaissance in Anabaptist studies.[1] Yoder's theology developed in the midst of the new Anabaptist Vision school of thought identified with Goshen College and Harold S. Bender, Yoder's mentor. In his influential essay "The Anabaptist Vision," Bender challenged the centuries-long view that Anabaptists were descended from such revolutionaries as Thomas Müntzer and the violent radicals of Münster. Bender argued that true or evangelical Anabaptism was a nonviolent movement begun by Conrad Grebel in Zurich. It had three central characteristics: the essence of Christianity is discipleship to Jesus, a brotherhood concept of the church, and nonresistance to evil.[2]

1. Portions of this essay draw on Zachary J. Walton, "Achieving an Anabaptist Vision."

2. "The Anabaptist Vision" was Harold S. Bender's presidential address at the annual meeting in 1943 of the American Society of Church History. It was first published as Bender, "Anabaptist Vision" (*CH*), and then as Bender, "Anabaptist Vision" (*MQR*). It was also published as a stand-alone booklet, Bender, *Anabaptist Vision*, and reprinted in Hershberger, *Recovery*. Quotations in this chapter follow Bender, *Anabaptist Vision*.

Part Two—Sources of John Howard Yoder's Theology

Many scholars have argued that Yoder simply followed in Bender's historical footsteps and extended the Goshen School[3] project in the 1950s. According to this understanding, Yoder provided little original thinking in his presentation of Anabaptism. That is, he did not depart from the Goshen School consensus concerning Anabaptist origins and simply refined their conclusions.[4] Related to the claim that Yoder simply extended the Goshen school were those who marginalized Yoder's work as a simple repetition or defense of the Goshen School monogenesis idea, which fell out of favor soon after the publication of the article "From Monogenesis to Polygenesis" in 1975.[5] This article showed that contra Harold S. Bender's "Anabaptist Vision," which had posited that all true Anabaptism developed from a single point of departure in Zurich (thus monogenesis), there were actually several different Anabaptist movements that emerged independent of each other (thus polygenesis).[6]

---

3. This chapter refers to this movement interchangeably as Goshen School or Anabaptist Vision School or the Bender School of thought. For this chapter, the discussion of Goshen School scholars is limited to Harold S. Bender and Bender's confidant John Christian Wenger, who described the aim of his career as "to perpetuate the Anabaptist vision." See Wenger, "Sought and Found," 173. Others who might be included in a wider study of the Anabaptist Vision school include Guy F. Hershberger, Robert Friedmann, Melvin Gingerich, Donovan Smucker, and Cornelius Krahn.

4. For example, Ray Gingerich wrote that "Yoder was a product of the Mennonite community and . . . creatively expanded the theological paradigm of his mentors but never broke out of it." See Gingerich, "Theological Foundations," 431–32. Or, in a review of Yoder's *Anabaptism and Reformation in Switzerland*, Paul Doerksen commented that Yoder's work "aligned with Harold Bender et al. regarding belief in a 'true Anabaptism.'" Doerksen, "Review of Yoder," 81. C. Arnold Snyder denied any originality to Yoder's work; if anything, "his approach to the Anabaptist story and his work as a whole fit comfortably within the mid-century North American Mennonite historical project: rehabilitating the Anabaptists in the face of centuries of hostile Reformed, Lutheran, and Roman Catholic historiography." Snyder, "Doing History," 4.

5. Stayer, Packull, and Deppermann, "From Monogenesis."

6. For example, Mark Thiessen Nation argued that Yoder followed Bender by identifying a specific founder of Swiss Anabaptism; they differed only in their slight and negligible identification of the founder of Anabaptism, with Yoder opting for Sattler in contrast to Bender's choice of Grebel. Nation, *John Howard Yoder*, 38. In light of the demise of the "monogenesis" idea, Karl Koop went so far as to question both the validity and necessity of the long-delayed English publication of Yoder's dissertation. Koop wrote, "After all, Yoder's scholarship reflects the Anabaptist historiography of the mid-twentieth century and thus represents a somewhat outdated viewpoint of Swiss Anabaptist origins. This raises the question of whether this publication [of Yoder's doctoral dissertation] is truly an event to be celebrated, as the editor of the volume claims." Koop, "Review of Yoder," 277.

However, not all interpreters consider Yoder unoriginal nor conflated his work with Bender's. Earl Zimmerman's well-researched study of the origins of Yoder's theological ethics exposes some notable contrasts between Yoder and his Goshen School mentors. In particular, Zimmerman's work identifies a "bone of contention" which separated Bender and Yoder from the beginning. Bender borrowed significantly from American Protestant organizational models for denomination structures, whereas Yoder was sharply critical of this approach and instead argued that these larger structures, foreign to both the New Testament model and the ecclesiological organization of sixteenth-century Anabaptists, by their very nature "did not respect the integrity of local congregations."[7] As Zimmerman made clear in the previous chapter, the local congregation was central to the ecclesiology that Yoder found in sixteenth-century Anabaptism. Zimmerman is correct in identifying and stressing the significance of this contrast between Yoder and the Goshen School. In Yoder's understanding of Anabaptism, discernment and dialogue at the local congregational level are central to believers church ecclesiology.

This current chapter further explores the difference that Zimmerman identified between Yoder and the Goshen School. Using rhetorical analysis, I will demonstrated that Yoder revolutionized the foundational commitments of the Goshen School by locating the "essence" of sixteenth-century Anabaptism in the early Anabaptists' practice of communal dialogue and discernment. This ecclesiology flowed directly from Yoder's christological commitment identified in chapter 1 and he saw these same commitments embodied in sixteenth-century Anabaptism.

Rhetorical Historiography

Rhetoric plays a major role in historical inquiry. Thus a brief explanation of the contemporary discipline of rhetoric and the practice of rhetorical analysis will prepare us to contrast how the Goshen School and John Howard Yoder "saw" sixteenth-century Anabaptism.

Since the time of the ancient Greeks, rhetoric has been conceptually linked with persuasion. In the twentieth century, however, rhetorical theorists began to think of rhetoric as the power of communication to create networks of identification and identity. Influential rhetorical theorist Kenneth Burke argued that rhetoric is the process by which

7. Zimmerman, *Practicing the Politics*, 46.

individuals form a collective life.⁸ Burke also argued that rhetoric produces the categories of human experience and that communication helps individuals integrate themselves into collective groups. In other words, rhetoric provides the power to join biologically distinct individuals into a consubstantial relationship with others.⁹ Rhetoric, then, is not simply a tool for persuasion (although it certainly is that), but also shapes humans and their communities through identification.

Using this framework of rhetoric as identification, contemporary rhetorical theorists posit that all communication is ultimately rhetorical and have questioned the widespread assumption that historical inquiry involves "descriptive" statements about the past. Since all historians must make choices concerning what to include when telling the stories of historical communities, all historians are rhetoricians to some degree:

> The historian cannot recount *all* of "what happened," and the historian's view of "what happened" is influenced by his or her own perspective. Facts do not speak; they must be spoken for. Historical scholarship is an interaction between the scholar and the historical record. Necessarily, then, it is interpretive.¹⁰

Burke famously argued that "even if any given terminology is a reflection of reality, by its very nature as a terminology it must be a selection of reality; and to this extent it must function as a deflection of reality." For Burke, the sets of terms we use in the attempt to describe the world act like a color filter on a camera by allowing some concepts and identities to be foregrounded, while forcing others into the background. Specific sets of terms direct one's attention in particular ways. By selecting some elements of a situation over others, they deflect attention from unaddressed aspects of that situation. The terms that one uses direct attention in one way or another to such an extent that "much that we take as observations about 'reality' may be the spinning out of possibilities implicit in our particular choice of terms." By directing attention in different sorts of ways, particular terminologies lead to different "observations" or reality.¹¹ When it comes to doing history, in "the selection of some historical

---

8. Burke, *A Rhetoric*, 21.
9. Ibid.
10. Zarefsky, "Four Senses," 20.
11. Burke, *Language*, 45, 46, 49.

materials and not others, it is well to remember Burke's dictum that a reflection of reality is also a selection and a deflection."[12]

Historians also use rhetoric by imbuing meaning to particular categories of human experience in their historical narrations. The two most fundamental categories of human experience are space and time. The rhetorical critic analyzes how the discourse historians use positions audiences as closer or more distant to historical events. "Texts have the capacity to position their audiences in different ways, in some cases moving them 'closer' to an object or bringing the object into the 'presence' of the audience and in other instances moving them further 'away' from an object."[13] For example, a historian might narrate the past so that it becomes a source for inspiration and identification in their present moment (such as how the twentieth-century Mennonite historians used the heroic stories of sixteenth-century Anabaptists), or the past might be depicted in a way that the reader experiences as far distant or perhaps irrelevant.

The approach to rhetorical historiography used in this essay considers and analyzes how "the inventional and presentational practices of historians [create] a specialized discourse community." This type of rhetorical historiography focuses less on the primary historical materials themselves and instead analyzes "how historians talk and write *about* history." This approach also stresses that "historians not only argue about history; they argue *from* it, using historical premises to justify current actions and beliefs."[14] In this approach, the rhetorical analyst exposes how historians configure different historical narrations through their use of sets of terms and how these narrations are rhetorically generated. Here, the rhetorical critic focuses not on the "accuracy" of a historical account but on "stories and images as symbolic constructions of reality for their publics [which are] precisely the stuff of the rhetorical historian."[15]

In reading a text, audiences seek to identify with textual cues that suggest how they should think and relate to the world. To analyze the commitments of the resulting relationships, the rhetorical critic notes "stylistic tokens" contained in texts. These "tokens" appear as metaphoric terms or phrases and function as "cues that tell [auditors] how they are

---

12. Zarefsky, "Four Senses," 20–21.

13. Jasinski, "Constitutive Framework," 77.

14. Zarefsky, "Four Senses," 28. In addition to the methodology described here, Zarefsky also discusses three other approaches to rhetorical historiography.

15. Turner, "Introduction: Rhetorical History," 5.

to view the world, even beyond the expressed concerns, the overt propositional sense, of the discourse." These tokens, at first glance, may appear as marginal and disposable metaphors. However, from the perspective of the rhetorical critic, these stylistic tokens indicate the ideal hearer or reader implied by the text. Analysis of these stylistic tokens allows the critic to connect the discourse to the epistemological commitments toward which the rhetor—or, in our case, the historian—attempts to orient an audience.[16]

All texts address their audiences as particular sorts of individuals and thusly summon them into positions of identity and action. Even a text as mundane as a toothpaste advertisement attempts to call its audience members to adopt a specific identity position, namely, that of a consumer.[17] Historians also use stylistic tokens and we will find a number of stylistic tokens indicating epistemological commitments in the historical work of Goshen School scholars and in the early historiography of John Howard Yoder. I now turn to an examination of the primary stylistic tokens of Yoder and the Goshen School.

Visual Metaphors in the Goshen School

Bender and his Goshen School compatriots reiterated the Western proclivity to use sight as a ruling metaphor for knowledge and understanding. The metaphor of proper sight—which appears often in the historical discourse of Goshen School members and the historical work of Yoder—is more than a simple turn of phrase. In traditional Western historiography, "knowledge is gained through vision; vision is a direct apprehension of a world of transparent objects. In this conceptualization, the visible is privileged; writing is then put at its service. Seeing is the origin of knowing." Descriptive historical writing, then, rather than inventive or constitutive of knowledge, is conceptualized only as "reproduction [and] transmission—the communication of knowledge gained through (visual, visceral) experience." While they might deny their use of rhetoric and insist that theirs is simply a "descriptive" practice, "historian's rhetorical treatment of evidence and their use of it to falsify prevailing interpretations, depends on a referential notion of evidence which denies that it is anything but reflection of the real." This historiographic approach "takes

16. Black, "Second Persona," 112–13, quote 113.
17. Jasinski, *Sourcebook on Rhetoric*, 107.

meaning as transparent [and] reproduces rather than contests given ideological systems—those that assume that the facts of history speak for themselves."[18] As we will soon see, Goshen School members and, later, John Howard Yoder, used a number of visual metaphors that indicate their foundational epistemological commitments.

Harold S. Bender and "The Anabaptist Vision"

The primary "stylistic tokens" used by Harold S. Bender in "The Anabaptist Vision" were the metaphors of "vision" and "sight." Bender suggested that the "vision" caught by the sixteenth-century Anabaptists existed even if it was imperceptible at a specific historical moment. However, one had to have the "eyes to see" and this seeing took effort; it was only after becoming "intimately . . . acquainted with the [sixteenth-century Anabaptists] . . . [that] one [became] conscious of the great vision that shaped their course in history and for which they gladly gave their lives."[19]

For Bender, proper discernment of the "vision" that motivated sixteenth-century Anabaptists was difficult because of the distortions generated by centuries of hostile interpretations produced by Catholic and Protestant church historians. Indeed, Bender wrote that "there may be some excuse . . . for a failure on the part of the uninformed student *to see clearly* [emphasis added] what the Anabaptist vision was, because of the varying interpretations placed upon the movement even by those who mean to appreciate and approve it." In other words, the reader's view of the vision of the Anabaptists had been previously "obscured." But Bender was now undoing these historical distortions and recovering the historical outlines of authentic Anabaptism. He positioned the auditor of "The Anabaptist Vision" as one who could now see past the distracting, extraneous factors, and "aberrant" forms of Anabaptism to obtain a glimpse of the vision which inspired sixteenth-century Anabaptists.[20]

With this idea of a newly recovered vision, the text addressed and thereby treated the auditor as one who is involved in and invited to rediscover what was already present in Anabaptism, but left dormant and "obscured" over the centuries of prejudicial church history. This rhetorical positioning orients audience members to see a "non-rhetorical" history of

18. Scott, "Evidence of Experience," 775–76, 778.
19. Bender, *Anabaptist Vision*, 4–5.
20. Ibid., 11.

Anabaptism and acknowledge its "obviousness"; indeed, Bender claimed that there was "no longer any excuse" to question this new vision.[21]

Subsequent Mennonite discussions would extend, rather than depart from, Bender's metaphorical logic and attempt a "recovery" of the vision[22] or concentrate on "refocusing" it.[23] J. Denny Weaver recalled that, doing Mennonite history prior to the advent of polygenesis historiography in the 1970s, "we who stood in the line of Anabaptism were admonished to 'recover' its vision."[24] This metaphorical logic, rather than exterior or peripheral to Bender's propositional claims, instead is intrinsic to its epistemological foundations. Indeed, the eclipse of monogenesis and the rise of polygenesis brought about a potent dissolution of this metaphorical logic: "With the disintegration of a homogenous vision emanating from a single point of origin, not only are we [Mennonites] puzzled about what to recover, but the recovery motif itself is also discredited and abandoned by the wayside."[25]

John Christian Wenger

John Christian Wenger placed more emphasis than Bender did on evangelical winning of converts to the faith and witnessing to the wider world the truths of the gospel, and he used Bender's vision metaphor in order to make his case. For example, Wenger wrote that for the sixteenth-century believers, their "original Anabaptist vision [consisted] of bringing the gospel to all men [sic] and gathering the believers into God's kingdom, the church." By witnessing to and making converts of all people and all nations, the original Anabaptists were attempting to return to the pure example of the first century church, for "the reproduction of the apostolic church was the *vision* [emphasis added] which the Anabaptists earnestly sought to realize." Reformed churches in the sixteenth-century fell well short of achieving either of these two dimensions and "needless to say, this *vision*, if the state churchmen had it at all, was an empty dream for a people's (provincial) church."[26]

21. Ibid.
22. Hershberger, *Recovery*.
23. Roth, *Refocusing*.
24. Weaver, "Anabaptist Vision," 69.
25. Ibid.
26. Wenger, *Glimpses*, 186, 8, 170; my italics.

Wenger used the metaphor of a flame to describe the original Anabaptist vision, its weakening in the intervening gap between the sixteenth and twentieth centuries, and its subsequent "rediscovery" and "rekindling." Once the early Anabaptists earnestly read the Bible, they realized that

> God had to be obeyed at the cost of liberty, yea, of life itself. The Brethren saw the issues; they knew what the consequences of their decision would be; they did what they knew God required of them. And thus was Swiss Anabaptism born. *God Himself kindled the light that has shown*, though at times rather weakly, for more than four centuries. To Him be all the glory.[27]

Here, God was seen as solely responsible for the fire that enlightened the hearts of the faithful. For Wenger, God was the primary agent and cause in the development of Anabaptism.

Wenger described the original sixteenth-century leaders of Anabaptism, such as Conrad Grebel and Menno Simons, as heroic figures and highly competent leaders of their flocks. Under their guidance, the original Anabaptists' vision was like a fire that shone a spiritual light out into the darkness of the fallen world. Wenger also indicated that after the first generation of Anabaptist leaders, the movement gradually lost its passionate engagement and the fire began to die down, primarily due to violent suppression. After the executions of the early heroes of the faith, "the able leaders of the first years, some of them former priests and scholars, were in most cases succeeded by men of less ability." With the heroic leaders of Anabaptism undercut by persecution, "the missionary zeal of the Anabaptists was effectively dampened, if not extinguished altogether, during the dreadful persecution of the sixteenth century."[28] The fire that God had kindled with the founders of Anabaptism had spread, but began to wane with less competent tenders.

Without heroic leaders to guide the Anabaptist movement, it became complacent and withdrawn. As a result of the persecution, Mennonites physically withdrew from prophetic and missionary engagement with the world into closed communities where, according to Wenger, "they would henceforth seek only to perpetuate their faith in their families." This total withdrawal was a departure from the zealous traditions of their ancestors, and the flame which blazed in the sixteenth century

---

27. Ibid., 25; my italics.
28. Ibid., 185.

began to die down until "the fires of evangelism and missions had burned out."[29] However, Wenger could prayerfully thank God that "*although Thy church has fallen into grievous error throughout the centuries Thou hast not allowed the light of Thy work to be entirely blotted out.*"[30] The fire that appeared to have been visibly extinguished through unfaithfulness, was instead invisibly maintained by God. Once again, Wenger appealed to an ahistorical and invisible essential grounding—in this case God—in order rhetorically to make sense of the historical failings of Mennonites. When Mennonites were faithful to God, one could clearly see it in the historical record. When they were unfaithful, God sustained the essence of the people invisibly and ahistorically. In any case, Wenger argued, the Anabaptist people were never truly extinct, no matter how greatly they deviated from the patterns set by their original founders.

The metaphors of "vision" and the spiritual "flame" of Anabaptism indicate foundational epistemological commitments and provided a perfect fit for the narrative logic promoted by Goshen School Anabaptism. Both metaphors expressed an epistemological understanding that narratively preserved the essence of Anabaptism even when the view of it was "obscured" or the fire had died down.

In addition, these visual metaphors provided a flexibility for the rhetors to artistically fit the historical data into their normative narrative. Where the historical record indicated harmony with the Goshen School ideology, such as "evidence" of the heroic faith of (particular) sixteenth-century Anabaptists, the rhetors could argue that, at this time, the "vision" was clear because the "fire" burned bright. But when, according to the historical records, future Mennonite behavior did not fit the normative narrative of the Goshen School, the rhetors reconfigured the metaphors to express invisibility or concealment. Poor history from hostile church historians had "obscured" vision and, in the case of the fire metaphor, unfaithfulness meant that the flame burned low and was nearly extinguished, but was not utterly snuffed out. These metaphors also permitted a narration of a contemporary "recovery" of that which was nearly lost: the lies and historical distortions that "obscured" the proper apprehension of the Anabaptist vision were removed, and in the case of the fire metaphor, if Mennonites began acting like their Anabaptist forbearers, the flame would burn brightly, with God's help.

29. Ibid., 186.
30. Wenger, *Separated Unto God*, 87; Wenger's italics.

The Rhetorical Metaphors of John Howard Yoder

Like his Goshen School mentors, Yoder's early historiography utilized a number of directional, spatial, and visual metaphors—"stylistic tokens." Much as in the case of Bender and Wenger, these "tokens" denote significant epistemological commitments.

Recall that the rhetorical and metaphorical use of the categories of time and space are not merely empirical givens. Rather, as many contemporary theorists and critics observe, they constitute symbolic frameworks through which we understand historical narratives. Some might be tempted to argue that Yoder's "stylistic tokens" aligned him with the Goshen School. However, they instead indicate a number of epistemological commitments that were a bit more complex than those of the Goshen School writers.

Like the members of the Goshen School, Yoder followed the Western tradition of using visual metaphors to stand in for knowledge, which denotes epistemological assumptions. Yoder's historiographic discourse positions the auditor as one who "sees" or "observes" certain historical events. When noting a change in Zwingli's theological commitments, Yoder wrote that it can be "observed" that Zwingli held two different positions concerning the church's relation to the state and that "later there is one clearly visible difference of posture."[31] In his dissertation, Yoder commented in much the same way, saying "we have previously observed among the Anabaptists, namely that Zwingli was still in agreement with them inwardly, but remained silent only out of fear of the authorities."[32] In seeking to analyze Zwingli's change, Yoder prompts us to see whether or not "a turning in the position of Zwingli can be observed."[33] This, of course, is the language of empirical observation, which assumes ideas standing in a visual field can be "seen."

These visual metaphors abound in Yoder's historiography. He often likened the creation of historical narratives to painting a particular sort of picture. When Yoder added other data to support his conclusions, he wrote the evidence "fills in the picture in some ways."[34] Indeed, by analyzing "different eyewitness testimonies, we must attempt to recon-

---

31. Yoder, "Evolution of Zwinglian Reformation," 95.
32. Yoder, *Anabaptism and Reformation*, 53.
33. Yoder, "Evolution of Zwinglian Reformation," 95.
34. Ibid., 113.

struct a picture of the events." History is like an incomplete puzzle, to which the historian and reader collaborate in order to "see" the gaps and the pieces. However, not all can be known and tracing "out a positive depiction of the Anabaptist solution . . . can in no way be a complete picture."[35] Zwingli's involvement in social reforms in Swiss society, Yoder wrote, "could understandably have an effect upon his picture of history and his understanding of the church."[36] Zwingli's use of the "rule of love," for example, or the Reformers' reluctance to respond to calls for dialogue, cannot adequately sum up the essential nature of the conflict. Instead these are only "the fruits, and not the roots of the separation. . . . One cannot proceed from them to sketch a believable total picture of what the Reformers wanted, let alone draw a proper picture of Anabaptism."[37]

Like his Goshen School mentors, Yoder thought that the main contribution of Goshen School historians was their clearing away obstructions or distractions from the core understanding of Anabaptism. He commented, a "major portion of the clarification in our generation comes from establishing clear distinctions among the dissenters of the Reformation Age."[38] In this, Yoder and Bender shared an appreciation that the removal of historical distortions had been the primary innovations of twentieth-century Mennonite historical scholars. When surveying earlier historical work, Yoder described Bender's generation as "rediscovering" historical truths of the early Anabaptists.[39] The job of the historian was to clear away the obstacles which impaired the clear "seeing" of essential nature of Anabaptism.

While Yoder appreciated the challenging of poor and biased church history achieved by Bender and other Goshen School members, he also recognized a greater difficulty than they did in distinguishing the earliest Anabaptists from other Reforming groups. It is here that a difference between the Bender school and Yoder becomes apparent. For Yoder, there were no clearly identifiable "marks" which distinguished the early sixteenth-century Anabaptists from their contemporaries apart from their distinctive practice of community dialogue. To delineate these relationships, Yoder used spatial rhetorical figures, such as "paths," "lines,"

35. Yoder, *Anabaptism and Reformation*, 29, 260.
36. Yoder, "Evolution of Zwinglian Reformation," 119.
37. Yoder, *Anabaptism and Reformation*, 217.
38. Yoder, "Recovery of the Anabaptist Vision," 8.
39. Ibid., 7.

"directions," and "locations" which, for him, denoted the gradual unfolding of different theological notions in the larger dialogue. This is especially apparent in Yoder's description of his methodological assumptions in his doctoral dissertation:

> If it is the case that both opposing groups, Anabaptism and the Reformation, grew from one and the same root, then it would be an error to want to consider Anabaptism as an independent development. But in addition, it would be improper to begin from the moment of visible separation or from the closest disputed *loci* (for example, infant baptism). . . . The difference in the respective paths can only be understood as coming from the place where the two groups were in agreement, or at least believed that they were. Only from here can it be seen what fundamental decisions led to the separation.[40]

Yoder compares Zwingli and Anabaptism on the number of steps in a direction that one group took with the other and progressing along a path. The true essential core of Anabaptism—those attributes of the movement that constituted uniqueness and defined its differences from other Reformation groups—was not, for Yoder, readily apparent to the historical eye, as Bender and his Goshen School compatriots assumed. Rather than a simple overthrowing centuries of biased church history, it required a laborious tracing out of the dialogues of the time.

> If we look back over the path we have traveled thus far, we must conclude that the clearly asked questions we have extracted from the discussion material still have not provided us with the key that completely opens up our understanding of the Anabaptism—Reformation opposition. Certainly we have found points of opposition, and indeed, some important ones. Still the impression remains that the centre of the dispute lies elsewhere, and the core of the controversy remains hidden. The differences dealt with in the discussions appear to be secondary ones, derived from that hidden core.[41]

Yoder's historical method did not assume Bender's "obvious" conclusion that Anabaptism was the logical climax of the Reformation. In his doctoral dissertation, he took great pains to trace the emergence of a distinct and "genuine" Anabaptist alternative to Zwinglisim. According

---

40. Yoder, *Anabaptism and Reformation*, 143.
41. Ibid., 204–5.

to Yoder, "history is interested not only in knowing when we can see the first hints of a later difficulty; it is just as important to know when the actors in the drama themselves became aware of the problem."[42] This suggests that the job of the historian is to make visible distinctions that are less than obvious and that the true "question is when [problems became] discernible to the participants, or to the historian." Indeed, it is the case that the historical eye, with the benefit of hindsight, could "see" the situation more clearly than the original historical participants. Thus Yoder notes that one should not be shocked that Zwingli could not see important developments in his theological positions because "the perception of such a quality in one's own thought, and of the point where one strand gets a definite edge over the other, is linked with one's social power."[43] Contrast this admission of the difficulty of "observing" the historical genesis of early Anabaptism with Bender's complaint that Anabaptism was "obscured" simply by centuries of biased church history.

Like the Goshen School historians, Yoder described the Anabaptists as motivated by the desire to overcome centuries of unfaithfulness that "obscured" the vision of faithful Christianity. Anabaptists wanted to restore the church "only because [the] apostolic order was no longer visible." For Yoder, the Anabaptists experienced knowing as an occurrence in a visual field. When they were certain of their theological commitments, "on the side of the Anabaptists, things were just as clear."[44] The Anabaptists possessed great faith that "the Spirit of God actually did work in a unique and historical way so as to make clear truths which had for centuries been hidden."[45] Again, truth for Yoder possessed a visual component; the original Anabaptists would have submitted themselves in a "humble manner in the face of a newly seen truth."[46]

Yoder concluded that Anabaptism took root in the fertile soil of Zwinglism. Anabaptism, for Yoder, was not the result of a radical break from other reforming movements, but rather it was Zwingli whose development of thought led him to depart from the original intention of the Reformation. He described this change by Zwingli as a "shift," although he did not think that Zwingli "veered" from a free church orientation to a

42. Yoder, "Turning Point," 129.
43. Yoder, "Evolution of Zwinglian Reformation," 109, 112.
44. Yoder, *Anabaptism and Reformation*, 193, 123.
45. Yoder, "Hermeneutics," 303.
46. Yoder, *Anabaptism and Reformation*, 121.

state-sponsored one. However one rhetorically characterizes the changes in Zwingli's thought, Yoder hypothesizes that he was able to conceal or otherwise "obscure" the shifts in his thought so that tensions were not addressed for some time. Yoder claimed that "it is now visible that Zwingli did shift his ground. . . . but his concession could still remain hidden under the ambiguities which had been present from the beginning."[47]

A critique from Robert Walton[48] would later prompt Yoder to temper the metaphor of Zwingli's "shifts." Instead, Yoder wrote that Zwingli "drifted" from a congregationally focused ecclesiology to one that adapted to the state church. The drift "did not take place in a striking turnabout but gradually, with every gradation almost imperceptible when taken alone." Indeed, the development of Zwingli's thought gradually emerged and became clear over time, "but," Yoder insisted, "we cannot speak of it as a change in direction." Here, Yoder exchanged metaphors so that the "impression we get is one of not a sudden shift but an almost unconscious drift."[49] While modifying the language of Zwingli's transformation of thought from a "shift" to a "drift" implies less of a dramatic change, the directional epistemological expressions of the metaphor remain unquestioned.[50]

Meanwhile, Anabaptism continued in the same trajectory and did not "shift" or "veer" in any significant way. The progress of the movement involved disclosing theological commitments present but unseen from the beginning. Since there was no "shift" for Anabaptism, it developed in a liner direction, according to Yoder, and "continued to take shape in a straight line." While Zwingli changed his conception of the nature of the church community, the Anabaptists took the original concept and "carried it further, made it more precise . . . and [brought] forth an alternative to the state church."[51] Thus Anabaptism did not shift or deviate from its original theological impetus, but rather came into its own and

47. Yoder, "Evolution of Zwinglian Reformation," 105.
48. Walton, "Was There a Turning Point of the Zwinglian Reformation?"
49. Yoder, "Evolution of Zwinglian Reformation," 113.
50. While Craig Carter is correct in stating that the conflict between Walton and Yoder certainly consisted of more than a disagreement over the proper use of historical facts, he understates the case by suggesting that the conflict was instead a matter of clashing "interpretative frameworks." This chapter demonstrates that the metaphors deployed in historical texts indicate differing foundational epistemological commitments, rather than being simple interpretive approaches to historical material. See Carter, *Politics of the Cross*, 37.
51. Yoder, *Anabaptism and Reformation*, 221, 125.

defined itself in and through continual struggles with civil authority. In contrast, Zwingli's thought gradually transformed in order to accommodate governmental authority. Thus, while Zwingli may have "shifted," the Anabaptists stayed true to directional momentum present in the earliest Reformation movements.

Yoder used directional metaphors to describe Anabaptism's relationship with both the past and the church's future restoration. He insisted that the early Anabaptists, rather than ignoring or being ignorant of history, instead took history quite seriously because their "right to exist stood or fell on whether their understanding of the historical development of the church was correct or not." For them, the church had fallen into unfaithfulness from its original founding. Thus reforming the Roman Catholic church would not be efficacious "but rather the New Testament community needed to be re-established, and thus begin again, because the entire train had derailed."[52] This metaphor of a train expressed a deep epistemological perspective in which travel is carried out in a straight line with a determined beginning and end point. In addition, this linear metaphor was future oriented and involved forward motion. The Anabaptists rejected the notion of "leaping back into the first century or of repeating in some childish way the exact patterns of the primitive church. The concern was for faithful restoration and moving forward, not for an impossible reversal of the course of history."[53]

As we will soon see, the only way that differences from Zwingli and others came to the fore, and therefore provided antithetical "lines" for Anabaptism to define itself against, was through the activity of community dialogue and disputation. For Yoder, the practice of communal dialogue exposed disagreements and provided opportunities for Anabaptism to "emerge" as a distinct theological alternative.

The Bender School Rhetoric on Protestantism and the Reformation

Bender's primary claim in "The Anabaptist Vision" was that the Anabaptist movement represented the high mark of the Reformation, rather than a derivative and marginal movement as previous church historians had insisted. Sixteenth-century Anabaptism was, according to Bender, "the

52. Ibid., 194.
53. Yoder, "Hermeneutics," 302.

cumulation of the Reformation, the fulfillment of the original vision of Luther and Zwingli, and thus . . . a consistent evangelical Protestantism seeking to re-create without compromise the original New Testament church, the vision of Christ and the apostles."[54] In his interpretation, Anabaptism was not a derivation from Protestantism, but rather the logical zenith of the Reformation.

Bender argued that the Reformers had attempted to revive the ethos of the first century church in their era and that "the original goal sought by Luther and Zwingli was 'an earnest Christianity' for all . . . [but] the level of Christian living among the Protestant population was frequently lower than it had been before under Catholicism." While both Luther and Zwingli had originally envisioned a church constituted by true and fervent believers set apart from the mass of nominal "Christians," they had given up this lofty vision and "both reformers decided that it was better to include the masses within the fold of the church than to form a fellowship of true Christians only." The leaders of the Reformation gradually came to believe that "they reckoned with a permanently large and indifferent mass" and that the sacraments, distributed to all, would have a minimal effect in improving this mass.[55]

While some might see these more as adaptations and less as "compromises," in Bender's interpretation, "in taking this course, said the Anabaptists, the reformers *surrendered* their original purpose, and *abandoned* the divine intention [emphases added]." Provocatively, Bender posed the rhetorical question "may it not be said that the decision of Luther and Zwingli to surrender their original vision was the tragic turning point of the Reformation?" Bender certainly believed so. The Anabaptists, however, refused the compromises made by Luther and Zwingli and strove to set themselves apart from "the world." They refused to compromise the will of God for political or pragmatic reasons: "The Anabaptists . . . retained the original vision of Luther and Zwingli, enlarged it, gave it body and form, and set out to achieve it in actual experience."[56]

Wenger, following Bender, demonstrated that the results of the reforms of Luther and Zwingli did not lead to higher standards of living for their followers and fell well short of the achievements of the Anabaptists to reform the daily lifestyles of believers. Luther's and Zwingli's followers

---

54. Bender, *Anabaptist Vision*, 13.
55. Ibid., 17–18.
56. Ibid., 19, 18.

realized a lower level of Christian living than the Anabaptists and "large numbers of them did not take the matter of religion very seriously, as the reformers themselves lamented."[57] For Wenger, this turn of events was "tragic [because] the Reformation did not result in the reestablishment of Christian congregations patterned after those of the New Testament."[58] He speculated that the original "Swiss Brethren must have been bitterly disappointed in Luther . . . and in the fruits of his reformation."[59] Whether due to timidity or outright political expediency, Wenger argued that Reformation leaders betrayed the radical implications of their own Reformation.

Rather than outright compromise, as in Luther's "tragic" case, Wenger stated that the original Anabaptists broke from Zwingli because he showed timidity and slowness in carrying out, with prompt "earnestness," necessary radical reforms. Although Grebel was originally part of Zwingli's movement, Wenger claimed that over time "disappointment began to color the attitude of Grebel and his colleagues toward Zwingli." Grebel believed that "Zwingli was going too slowly and too mildly in his reformation. Greater earnestness was required, [Anabaptist leaders] thought, than Zwingli was manifesting." Zwingli's delays left remnants of Catholic practice in worship and doctrine; therefore the Anabaptists were forced to "set up their church because Zwingli did not go far enough in his deviation from Catholicism." In contrast to the timidity of Zwingli, Grebel manifested true biblical bravery, which motivated all his efforts; according to Wenger "once Grebel began to read God's Word with an earnest determination to follow God in everything, he simply had to come to a break with the Roman priest, Zwingli."[60] A simple and earnest reading of the Bible on the part of the original Anabaptists exposed the fault lines of Zwingli's compromises.

In Bender's narrative, Anabaptism was not part of the historical continuity of reforming groups but rather was a deliberate departure from all of Christendom and prior history. For Bender, Anabaptism was the attempt to make manifest, in the purest way ever attempted and without any compromise, the first-century church; the Anabaptists "preferred to make a radical break with the fifteen hundred years of history and culture

---

57. Wenger, *Doctrines*, 52.
58. Wenger, *Separated Unto God*, 200.
59. Wenger, *Glimpses*, 15.
60. Ibid., 19, 8, 25.

if necessary rather than to break with the New Testament."[61] This rhetorical maneuver collapsed the distance between the sixteenth-century Anabaptists and twentieth-century Mennonites because "by describing Anabaptism as a recovery of the church of the New Testament, Bender's formulation separated Anabaptism conceptually from the rest of church history."[62] Other Goshen School scholars would follow Bender's logic and imply that "Anabaptism in its genus essentially had no history . . . it simply emerged from an unfettered reading of the Scriptures."[63]

While committed to the modernist historiographical assumptions of his day, Bender attempted to articulate the "essence" of Anabaptism rather than simply its exterior "form." Indeed, for Bender, "the content was more important than the form. Thus, by opposing form to content and by associating religious liberty with mere form, Bender constituted his own vision as an essence that could fill out the purely 'formal' concept of religious liberty."[64] For Bender, the confusion—taking the outer forms of Anabaptism rather than considering its inner "essence"—had been one of the primary historical mistakes of previous historians and he sought to amend those errors. He argued that the true "essence" of sixteenth-century Anabaptism could be found in three distinct marks—voluntary discipleship, the praxis of the church as brotherhood, and an ethic of absolute nonresistance. According to him, these marks constituted the "central teachings" and "major points of emphasis" of "genuine Anabaptism."[65]

When Anabaptism is perceived as the culmination of the Reformation and the necessity of separation understood in terms of ecclesiological practices and ethics—discipleship, brotherhood, nonresistance—both Bender and Wenger could then claim that the Anabaptists shared a theological foundation with the Reformers. J. Denny Weaver has identified this shared theological foundation as a trend in Mennonite theology to posit two major sections or "lists" of theological commitments. The first list is often dedicated to the doctrinal similarities between Anabaptists and evangelical Protestantism, while the second addresses Mennonite "distinctives," such as nonresistance.[66]

61. Bender, *Anabaptist Vision*, 19.
62. Weaver, "Anabaptist Vision," 74.
63. Sawatsky, *History and Ideology*, 129.
64. Biesecker-Mast, "Towards a Radical Postmodern Anabaptist Vision," 60.
65. Bender, *Anabaptist Vision*, 20.
66. Weaver, *Keeping Salvation Ethical*, 24.

The existence of these two theological "lists" is assumed in "The Anabaptist Vision," where Bender called Anabaptism "consistent evangelicalism Protestantism."[67] Other comments from Bender fill out the theological content of "evangelical Protestantism." His "two lists" assumptions come into view when he writes,

> All the American Mennonite groups without exception stand upon a platform of conservative evangelicalism in theology, being thoroughly orthodox in the great fundamental doctrines of the Christian faith such as the unity of the Godhead, the true deity of Christ, the atonement by the shedding of blood, the plenary inspiration and divine authority of the Holy Scriptures as the word of God.[68]

Bender insisted that the Anabaptists were in agreement with Reformed theologians on the central doctrines, such as "the sole authority of the Scriptures, grace, and justification by faith, [and] in the classic Christian loci of doctrine" and in fact "they had much in common with the Reformers."[69]

Like Bender, Wenger also perceived that few scholars had considered how closely original Anabaptism clove to core fundamentals of the Protestant Reformation. The closeness on fundamentals is clearly evident in writings by Wenger, especially in his perhaps most influential book, *Introduction to Theology*.[70] This book is primarily a statement of the theological "first list": Mennonite alignment with Protestant orthodoxy. He articulated what is essentially evangelical theology with little mention of the unique contours of Mennonite history and even less attention to Goshen Circle style historiography. Both lists appear in Wenger's *Glimpses of Mennonite History and Doctrine*; notably the chapter on theology has two major sections, "Major Doctrines" and "Mennonite Emphases."[71] He writes, "Since Anabaptism was simply a radical form of Protestantism, on the so-called fundamental doctrines the Anabaptists were in agreement with the Lutherans and the Reformed. This basic unity on the major doc-

---

67. Bender, *Anabaptist Vision*, 13.
68. Bender, "Mennonites," 79.
69. Bender, "Walking," 102.
70. Wenger, *Introduction to Theology* (1954). This book was later reprinted with subtitle revised to "A Brief Introduction to the Doctrinal Content of Scripture Written in the Anabaptist-Mennonite Tradition."
71. Wenger, *Glimpses*, 137–79. For additional examples of this two-list approach to theology, see Weaver, *Anabaptist Theology*, 51–65.

trines of the Christian faith has often been overlooked by writers on the Anabaptists."[72] In contrast, as the following section demonstrates, Yoder rejected the foundational disjuncture between the performative form of Anabaptism and its content, placing emphasis on ethics and ecclesiology over and against doctrinal orthodoxy. Yoder's linking of theology and ethics and his willingness to bypass the terms of standard orthodoxy were described in different categories in chapter 1.

John Howard Yoder on Protestantism and the Reformation

At first blush, Yoder's historiography, like Bender and his Goshen compatriots, seems to align Anabaptism as realizing the highest hopes of the Reformation, and thus orthodox as defined by the dominant Protestant reformation. In his historical work, Yoder seems to indicate this relationship in his use of a directional metaphor: "the Anabaptist stood not only geographically, but also theologically in close proximity to the Reformation." Indeed, Yoder wrote that "in relation to justification and other fundamental Protestant truths, the Anabaptists remained in thorough agreement with the Reformers." Also, like Bender, Yoder critiqued the Mennonite search for "pre-history" of Anabaptism by writing "we certainly can bring into question the sympathetic-sounding attempt in Mennonite circles and among some researchers to derive the Anabaptists from the Waldensians in the sense of a kind of apostolic succession of dissidents."[73]

Like his Goshen school mentors, Yoder hypothesized that the Anabaptists eventually came to a low opinion of Zwingli and were disenchanted with the sluggishness and reticence on his part to carry out necessary reforms. In using phrasing reminiscent of Wenger's narration of the split between early Anabaptists and Zwingli, Yoder wrote, "Even if Zwingli gave other reasons for his decision, in the Anabaptist view these could only be attempts at covering up his fear." This discourse parallels the Goshen School's reading of the Anabaptist evaluation of both Luther and Zwingli. In this narrative, once Zwingli claimed extra-biblical revelation for this reforming program, "Anabaptism necessarily became the entity that would unrestrictedly carry the Reformation impulse forward

72. Wenger, *Glimpses*, 137.
73. Yoder, *Anabaptism and Reformation*, 115, 142, 121–22.

and would hold firmly to the unconditional validity of the Word of God."[74] In another discussion, Yoder evoked Bender's "vision" discourse to insist on Anabaptism's alignment with fundamental Reformation impulses: "The Anabaptists demonstrate[d] a continuity with the best *vision* of the medieval church, and it [was] Luther who . . . [took] a radical new position."[75] Here, Luther, like Zwingli, departed from the linear trajectory of faithfulness followed by the Anabaptists.

Unlike the Goshen School, however, Yoder did not attempt to posit an essential ahistorical nature of Anabaptism outside of the communal process of dialogue and discernment. He noted that the original Anabaptists had no desire to found a separate movement and that "Anabaptism did not wish to have a centre that it held 'for itself.'" The only reason, Yoder argued, that Anabaptists separated into distinct communities was based simply on the "the failure of the official Reformation churches. They never wanted to be anything other than the church community the Reformation had initially wanted, but then did not bring about." Anabaptism, according to Yoder, was then to be defined in its negation of numerous other options which threatened its restorationist momentum. Anabaptist identity, Yoder wrote, developed by standing in opposition to deviations and "in drawing the boundaries on the right and the left, above and below, and in the elaboration of its own line of thought, the Anabaptist understanding of the church community now took on a form of its own." It was only through the insistence of dialogue, by discursively drawing lines of agreement and opposition, that "the Anabaptists . . . show themselves to be a unified group with definite boundaries."[76]

Yoder described the sixteenth-century Anabaptists as much more concerned with conducting open dialogue within the church than with the community's alignment with any external orthodox standards. For example, he noted that the early Anabaptists treated the Apostolic Creed as part of the historical tradition of Christianity without imbuing the creed with any final dogmatic authority over Christian life and belief.[77] In contrast to both Catholic and Protestant theology, which—in different but related ways—assumed that the creeds were equivalent with the Bible, the Anabaptists placed the community of believers as central to

---

74. Ibid., 290, 154.
75. Yoder, "Hermeneutics," 296.
76. Yoder, *Anabaptism and Reformation*, 142, 130, 135–36.
77. Yoder, *Preface* (2002), 222.

Christian discipleship and therefore regulated the creeds to peripheral and contingent elements of their historical situation. According to Yoder, the early Anabaptists thought "the fact that one is a member of the church community and is therefore a participant in the communal process of theological discernment is more important than the orthodoxy of previously-gained knowledge." Rather than alignment with orthodox claims and creedal statements that appeared "outside" of communal dialogue, the Anabaptists' basis for truth was communal participation in dialogue on the basis of the biblical texts. For Yoder, this becomes most evident in disputations where "we find no attempt to lead the opposition . . . back to basic systematic lines. In the dialogues, the Anabaptists demanded of their opponents always, simply that the Scriptures should count as the norm."[78]

The sixteenth-century Anabaptists called for dialogue because it was the necessary precondition of their ecclesiology, which was an outgrowth of their radical christological convictions. Yoder wrote that "the Anabaptists repeatedly called for dialogue . . . [this call] arose out of a fully-developed theological epistemology, yes, an ecclesiology." The basis of the Anabaptist communities was not an external set of creeds or orthodox statements, but rather the communal practice and praxis of discernment, disputation, and dialogue. This trust in dialogue as a defining practice took "seriously the promise that the Spirit would be granted to those who assembled in the name of Christ. . . . the dialogue that they demanded was not called a discussion, but rather, a community." Yoder states that the Anabaptists believed that belonging to a community of faith was a necessary precondition for valid knowledge of God. The participation in the dialogue at the level of the local faith community constituted a necessary epistemological basis for the Christian life. Even with their most bitter opponents, the Anabaptists demanded to be heard and "their right to be heard really stems from their inexhaustible will to dialogue."[79]

---

78. Yoder, *Anabaptism and Reformation*, 272, 149. An example of this relationship of the community to classic creedal statements appears in a story about Yoder told to me by J. Denny Weaver. Weaver asked Yoder about Menno's nonstandard Christology. In Weaver's account, Yoder said that rather than using Menno's Christology to show that he was a bad theologian and an example of why we should stick to the classic creedal formulations, we should rather give Menno credit for attempting to articulate a Christology shaped by the new Anabaptist ecclesiology of discipleship to Jesus. Gerald Mast explored this idea in Menno at significant length; see Mast, "Jesus' Flesh."

79. Yoder, *Anabaptism and Reformation*, 223, 219, 136.

The Anabaptists, therefore, took strong objection to Reformers and others who extinguished dialogue through violence or coercion. Persons or institutions who would preempt or otherwise constrain dialogue became especially questionable for Anabaptists and indicated to them divisions between themselves and others. It was the "inability to dialogue that finally made the Reformation churches questionable for the Anabaptists and led them, both theologically and concretely-historically, to form communities." While the Anabaptists believed that every person who claimed to be a Christian should be addressed as such, refusal to dialogue raised the most suspicion of one's authentic faith so that "only one's refusal to enter into dialogue allowed the confessing community to consider someone a nonbeliever (Mark 18:18)." Dialogue opponents who identified themselves as Christian did not have to be persuaded to change, but it was only "until they show[ed] by way of a refusal to 'listen' that they [were] unwilling to be spoken to. Only this conviction explains why the Anabaptists always called for dialogues."[80]

Within the community, the Anabaptists trusted that dialogue would expose difference and clarify positions, which accounted for their reluctance to pass judgment on their friends and even their enemies. For these believers, "even regarding those excluded from their communities the Anabaptists did not venture a final judgment." With such a trust, the Anabaptists did not see recantations as a blow to the community, but rather a clarification of where individuals stood. Indeed, Yoder suggests, "it is not as paradoxical as it might seem at first glance, to see the 'recantation' of some Anabaptists as final evidence for their readiness for discussion." Success in dialogue was not necessarily winning over the other, but coming to a new understanding of where the participants stood and, for these Anabaptists, "life under the 'rule of Christ' saw to it that immature confessions would mature, and that incorrect confessions would reveal themselves as such."[81]

In addition to potentially winning over others, the goal of disputations was to clearly define "lines" or positions, and Anabaptists disputations achieved their goals when showing that "the lines were clear" between those inside and outside of the community. Community dialogue did not always lead to consensus, but for Yoder, this did not make them any less valuable or necessary. Occasionally, the primary advantage

---

80. Ibid., 224, 275, 274.
81. Ibid., 273, 100, 121, 273.

of dialogues and disputation was the exposure of deep and previously unknown differences to which communities struggled to respond. Through dialogue, especially disputations, the "hidden" divergences in thought become apparent. An example was the first Zurich disputation in January 1523, during which, "despite the appearance of agreement and victory, real problems [became] visible for the first time."[82]

Yoder argued that by observing shifts in dialogues and disputations, one could see previously hidden or unobserved dimensions of ideas rise "to the surface." For example, when teasing out contradictions in Zwingli's theology, "we . . . observ[e] how an inner contradiction between two strands of Zwingli's theological personality gradually comes to the surface."[83] When reflecting on how contemporary historical and theological questions differ greatly from those that were active or even on the horizon of imagination for the sixteenth-century Anabaptists, Yoder observes, "These questions could not really come to the surface in the sixteenth century. . . . the intellectual tools which we currently use for dealing with such questions were not available, and they could hardly have come to the surface in this particular form."[84] It was only through continual dialogue, in the form of disputations, that these differences came to the surface and were exposed.

In the rhetoric of Bender and other Goshen School members, Anabaptism was the "cumulation" of the Reformation and an "inevitable" outgrowth of faithfulness and the movement of God's Spirit, whereas in Yoder, this came about by continual dialogue and disputation within the specific body of believers called the church. Thus, the true mark of Anabaptism was not simply their refusal to use state resources as at least one interpreter of Yoder has concluded,[85] but rather that Anabaptists refused to use state resources to silence critics or to preemptively interrupt the process of dialogue. Yoder wrote,

> If one seeks to find the breaking point on which the Anabaptists separated themselves from the Reformation, then the first concern is for the community, its visibility, and its capacity for action. But if one asks why the community should be visible and capable of action, and one finds this answer: It has to do with the

---

82. Ibid., 56, 128, 7.
83. Yoder, "Evolution of Zwinglian Reformation," 109.
84. Yoder, "Hermeneutics," 294.
85. Snyder, "Doing History," 7.

light of Christ in his members. Both are ultimately inseparable simply because discipleship is not a Franciscan ethic of imitation for the individual, but rather a work of the body of Christ.[86]

For Yoder, the "hermeneutical community was always before, the setting for, and the final arbiter of any system of argumentation. The process of discernment includes what he called the 'walk' or socially engaged praxis of the community."[87] Ultimately, this communal ecclesiology was rooted in a radical Christology that Yoder saw operative in the sixteenth-century Anabaptists. Thus, unlike Goshen School scholars, Yoder eschewed a "fruits, not roots" metaphorical logic in describing the early Anabaptists. He refused to conceptualize the Anabaptists' performance of suffering and patient love, as embodied in non-coercive dialogue, as a secondary "distinctive" practice somehow subordinate to an orthodox "core." This refusal also characterizes the overall content of Yoder's later theology, which considered the practice of nonviolent suffering love made visible in the Christian life and ministry as the essence of Christian discipleship. At the same time, as indicated by Yoder's hurtful sexual behavior dealt with in chapters 12 and 13, additional elements need to be added to this discipleship ecclesiology.

Conclusion

Like all historians, Goshen School writers utilized metaphors, or rather "stylistic tokens," which expressed deep epistemological convictions. Bender's use of the metaphor of "vision" accounted for both the historians' and the Mennonites' unawareness of their own illustrious past, in spite of the fact that Mennonites were "clearly" and "obviously" the direct heirs of the Anabaptist's vision. Wenger's use of a fire metaphor communicated a clear message: the essence of the people existed and was passed on through time. In those intervening dark centuries, the fire had simply burned low, but was being rebuilt by Wenger's Mennonites, so that they could once again "see" clearly the evangelistic and radical vision of Anabaptism. This dialectic, implicit in their metaphors between visibility/invisibility and concealing/revealing, expressed an epistemology that tempered the search for the "exterior" and "visible" marks not fully reducible to the "essence" of Anabaptism.

86. Yoder, *Anabaptism and Reformation*, 299.
87. Zimmerman, *Practicing the Politics*, 178.

In a similar fashion, Yoder equated proper historical knowledge with having a clear "vision" that shared a number of rhetorical sensibilities with his Goshen School mentors. He conferred meaning on not only the propositional arguments of "The Anabaptist Vision," but also the metaphorical conception regarding the "visibility" of any historical "picture," and the notion that the Anabaptists unswervingly held to original Reformation impetuses. Yoder, however, departed from the Goshen School by stressing communal dialogue, discernment, and disputation as constitutive factors that distinguished the Anabaptist community and to such a degree that even alignment with orthodox Christian claims was of secondary concern when compared with the process of defenseless dialogue with the other. Certainly this stress on the necessity of communal dialogue would later find expression in Yoder's most important theological works and become a constitutive element of his broader theological edifice. To the extent that the dialogic process of the community took precedence over orthodox commitments and with the Christ-centered community investing great trust in God's participation in communal discernment, Yoder argued that the "shape" of Anabaptism was determined by communal praxis and constituted its primary "mark."

By using the tools of rhetorical analysis to understand and compare the historiographical work of Bender and Wenger to that of Yoder, I have shown the error of reducing of Yoder's historiographic program and epistemological assumptions to simply another reiteration of the Goshen School consensus. A rhetorical, rather than historical, analysis of the Anabaptist historiographies generated by the Goshen School members and John Howard Yoder offers a deeper, or at least different, perspective on their similarities and Yoder's departures. This rhetorical analysis has demonstrated the centrality of the metaphors in the articulation of Anabaptist history and the degree to which Goshen School scholars' metaphors of "vision" and the spiritual "flame" of Anabaptism are not exchangeable or reducible to more essential meanings. Rather their metaphorical character provides the basis for their ideological functioning. Likewise, Yoder's insistence that that true outline of the Anabaptist program "surfaced" or "emerged" so that the reader and historian could "see" it and "fill in a picture," while also tracing the "lines" of the dialogues, constitutes a central aspect of his historical discourse.

By understanding the ethic of dialogue that Yoder observed in the sixteenth-century Anabaptists, one discerns a consistent communicative ethic that embodied theological principles of respect, patience, and vulnerable enemy love that ultimately drew from a deep source of radical defenseless Christology. As Earl Zimmerman has observed, Yoder's epistemology was "indebted to his historical work on the congregational process of discernment among the Swiss Anabaptists, where the silence of the community indicated that all objections had been met."[88] Yoder also saw historical work as a method of deepening and enabling ecumenical dialogue that allowed participants to discern the commonalities of their origins and expose differences.[89] So, for Yoder, the primary task was that of listening and, in his words, "instead of the question of who is right, we would rather take as our standard the openness to dialogue itself. The question of who is ultimately right is not decided by dogmatic history in any case."[90]

Thus rhetorical analysis has also underscored the dialectical aspect of Yoder's thought. Chapter 1 dealt with Yoder's approach to Christology, with the narrative of Jesus serving as the basis of his theology and ethics. Chapter 2 identified sixteenth-century Anabaptism as one historical root of this christological orientation, and argued that Yoder saw the Anabaptists' ecclesiology emerging from living out of the narrative of Jesus. In chapter 3 we have now observed the way that ecclesiological dialogue is an intrinsic element of Yoder's ecclesiology. These findings concerning the inseparable elements of Christology, ecclesiology and dialogue in Yoder's thought thus challenge some contemporary applications of Yoder. In particular, these findings challenge those who affirm Yoder's pacifism apart from his ecclesiology,[91] and render questionable any effort to apply Yoder's ecclesiology without pacifism to a contemporary mass church ecclesiology.[92]

---

88. Ibid.
89. Blough, "Introduction," xli–xlii.
90. Yoder, *Anabaptism and Reformation*, 146.
91. Hauerwas "cannot have both Yoder and nostalgia for the papacy." Dula, "For and Against Hauerwas," 375–96, quote 394.
92. Leithart, *Defending Constantine*, esp. 333–42.

4

Oscar Cullmann and Radical Discipleship[1]

EARL ZIMMERMAN

The real issue is not whether Jesus can make sense in a world
far from Galilee, but whether—when he meets us in our world,
as he does in fact—we want to follow him.[2]

Building Interdisciplinary Bridges

One part of the genius of Yoder's work is the way he engaged in interdisciplinary discussions, what he would later call an attempt "to throw a cable across the chasm" that separated biblical studies from theology and social ethics.[3] Chapter 1 described Yoder's approach to the

---

1. Parts of this chapter draw on my work in *Practicing the Politics*, 114–30. Used by permission of the publisher.

2. Yoder, "But We Do," *Priestly*, 62; Yoder, "But We Do," *Pacifist*, 39.

3. Yoder, *Politics* (1994), 2–3, quote 3. His interdisciplinary concerns extended further, as reflected in his mention of "tactical allies" (see "But We Do," *Priestly*, 61; "But We Do," *Pacifist*, 38) and the disciplines of psychology, sociology, and history (*War of the Lamb*, 125).

New Testament understanding of Jesus that resulted in the discipleship-oriented Christology reflected in the epigraph of this chapter. One could describe it as a cable or a bridge between theology and ethics. The focus of the discussion to follow sketches the contribution of New Testament scholars, primarily Oscar Cullmann, to Yoder's development of the discipleship-shaped Christology made visible in *Preface to Theology*, *The Politics of Jesus*, and the essay "But We Do See Jesus."

Alongside his intent described in chapter 2 to develop a contemporary Anabaptist theology, Yoder's desire to bridge biblical studies, theology, and ethics constitutes yet one more indicator that he was beginning to chart a new theological direction. This desire was reflected already in a letter he wrote while a doctoral student at the University of Basel to his friend Paul Peachey:

> It is my growing conviction that there exists a consistent biblicism of discipleship, parallel to Anabaptism not only in ecclesiastical separateness from Calvinism, but in its entire rejection of medieval carryovers in doctrine as well as in life. . . . Since the more the Bible talks for itself without Anselm or Augustine in the way, the more it talks [about] discipleship. . . . There is a widening gulf between the exegetes (Cullmann) and the systematikers (Barth), for while the exegetes, digging deeper and deeper into the text, are discovering discipleship, the systematikers, swinging back fad-wise to conservatism, have less and less to do with man's real need, and the professional ethikers who reject discipleship (Niebuhr) have less and less vital Gospel.[4]

What immediately stands out in this letter is Yoder's assessment of what needs to be deconstructed. The first is orthodoxy as a religious pillar of empire and the second is abstract Troeltschian or Niebuhrian social ethics as a pillar of Western civilization or the secular nation-state. Neither takes Jesus seriously. Conversely, Anabaptism and a consistent biblicism could be used to construct a theology of radical discipleship—of following the way of Jesus in the world. In light of such convictions, it is to be expected that Yoder would focus his energy on developing a biblically based, constructive theology as seen in *The Politics of Jesus*. His theology of radical discipleship rooted in the gospel narratives and the epistles of Paul serves as a bookend to his non-creedal Christology seen in chapter 1 of this volume. The previous two chapters explored the

---

4. Yoder, Letter to Paul Peachey, 15 June.

Anabaptist history and convictions that shaped Yoder's theology. The current chapter and the following one explore its biblical and theological roots.

The European Postwar Context

In the aftermath of World War II, many European Christians had a pervasive sense that they had allowed themselves to be sucked into that violent nationalistic conflagration in a way that had undercut their faith. They were mortified that their churches had been so poorly prepared to resist the two world wars that had enveloped their continent in the first half of the twentieth century. What had gone wrong? They were also alarmed by the emerging Cold War conflict between the United States and the Soviet Union, two nuclear armed adversaries, who had divided Europe into competing economies and an armed standoff along the geographical line of control. Karl Barth, John Howard Yoder's theology professor at the University of Basel, was on record that Christians should not be party to this conflict.[5]

This situation drove the quest for a more robust and radical discipleship—of following Jesus, the Jewish prophet from Galilee—in a world of human suffering, competing ideologies, and a new global power struggle. What did it mean to claim that the man Jesus was Messiah and Lord? What would be the shape of faithful communities of disciples formed on that premise and how would these communities prophetically engage their postwar world? John Howard Yoder was actively involved in this intense debate as a graduate student at the University of Basel and in discussions with various European church leaders who had survived the war.

Much of the debate involved questions about Christology, the historical Jesus, and the relationship between church and state. An especially live topic was discerning what had gone wrong in classic Christology that allowed most Christians to relegate the life and teaching of Jesus to relative insignificance for contemporary discipleship and social ethics.[6]

---

5. Barth, "Church between East and West," 127–31

6. Later, Yoder would say that the classic creeds can serve as fences for what we can say about the human Jesus and his relationship to God but they can hardly nurture an active faith. For the latter one has to turn to the gospel accounts of the life and teaching of Jesus. Yoder, *Preface* (2002), 223. In his historical analysis, J. Alexander Sider says that one searches "in vain" to find a "non-Constantinian refutation of pro-Nicene

Yoder brought his pacifist, non-creedal Mennonite perspective[7] to the European discussion of Christology but he was not alone in seeing the problem and trying to find an adequate response. Thus his theology also became deeply indebted to his European interlocutors. Among them are two of his professors at the University of Basel: Oscar Cullmann in biblical studies, the primary focus of this chapter, and Karl Barth in theology, whom Yoder considered a problematic mentor and whose influence is treated in the following chapter.

Others include Jean Lasserre, Hendrik Berkhof, and André Trocmé. Lasserre was a former colleague of Dietrich Bonheoffer. Yoder had extensive conversations with Lasserre concerning Oscar Cullmann's concept of the "reign of Christ." From Berkhof Yoder learned to apply his groundbreaking work on the biblical language of "principalities and powers" to political structures of domination and their ideological justifications. Yoder incorporated much of Berkhof's thought into the chapter "Christ and Power" in *The Politics of Jesus*, and he also translated Berkhof's book *Christ and the Powers* into English.[8] French pastor Trocmé had led a nonviolent, congregationally-based resistance movement during the war and helped to rescue many Jews from the Vichy government during the Nazi occupation.[9] He and Yoder became good friends. As a capable biblical scholar, Trocmé recognized that Jesus' proclamation of the reign of God was deeply immersed in the Jewish tradition of Jubilee and economic

---

theology" in Yoder's writing. He does acknowledge, however, that Yoder did "decenter Nicaea" in the "contemporary imagination," although that decentering is strongly influenced by theologians such as Barth and Berkhof, "for whom the accommodation of the *Deutsche Christen* to Nazism was a major issue." See Sider, *To See History Doxologically*, 106–22, quotes 107, 116, 114. The import of such observations by Sider appears to be to call into question Yoder's relativizing of classic orthodoxy, as depicted in chapter 1, and is thus an implied defense of the classic creedal statements by separating them further from the political intrigue of their time. Sider's argument ignores the extent to which Yoder not only contextualized the classic terminology but also opened the door to Christology not beholden to it, as displayed in chapter 1.

7. Mennonite congregations such as the one that Yoder grew up in rarely, if ever, recite the historic creeds as part of their worship. Confessions of faith have been produced regularly as adapted responses to changing historical contexts. They serve not as unchanging, dogmatic creedal statements but as teaching tools for catechism and for discernment of what Mennonites can affirm in common at a given time.

8. Berkhof, *Christ and the Powers*. Extensive discussion of Yoder's use of Berkhof and the powers occurs in chapters 6 and 7 to follow.

9. For an account of Trocmé's nonviolent resistance, see Hallie, *Lest Innocent Blood*.

redistribution. Yoder incorporated this insight into his own constructive theology and freely adapted parts of Trocmé's work in the chapter "The Implications of the Jubilee" in *The Politics of Jesus*.[10]

Oscar Cullmann and Biblical Studies[11]

Yoder was convinced that biblical research on the life of Jesus and the early church was vital to recapturing the meaning of discipleship. The biblical exegesis of people like Oscar Cullmann was opening up promising new possibilities. Such biblical scholars were studying the social and political situation in first-century Palestine, and were asking how Jesus and the early Christian communities related to their world. Yoder wanted to put such biblical exegesis into conversation with contemporary theological ethics.

Yoder appropriated several significant things from Cullmann. One was the work Cullmann did on the relationship of Jesus and the early Christian communities to the Roman Empire. To do this, Cullmann examined the teaching of Jesus in the Gospels, the teaching of the apostle Paul, and the perspective of the Johannine Apocalypse. There was intense interest in this topic in the conversation between the historic peace churches and the established European Protestant churches at the Puidoux Theological Conference held in Switzerland in 1955. The theme of the conference was "The Lordship of Christ over Church and State."[12]

One of Cullmann's papers discussed at the conference was "The Kingship of Christ in the Church in the New Testament."[13] It was an exegetical study of the concept of the "reign of Christ" and the confession among the early Christians that "Jesus Christ is Lord." The other paper was titled "The State in the New Testament."[14] It was an abbreviated version of material later published in a book with the same name. The time and energy the conference put into discussing Cullmann's biblical

10. Yoder, *Politics* (1994), 60–71. For a recent republication of his classic work, see Trocmé, *Jesus and the Nonviolent Revolution*.

11. This section on Oscar Cullmann's influence uses material from Zimmerman, *Practicing the Politics*, 114–30. Other material in this chapter draws on material in chapter 4 of *Practicing the Politics*.

12. MCC Peace Section—Conferences, MCC Peace Section.

13. Cullmann, "Kingship of Christ." This paper was later published with the same title as a chapter in Cullmann, *Early Church*.

14. Cullmann, "State in the NT."

exegesis indicates how important they believed such research was for the difficult task of rethinking the role of the church and the state in the aftermath of the war.

Wrestling with Traditional Two-Kingdom Theologies

The European Protestants were especially interested in overcoming the deficiencies of traditional two-kingdom theologies that made a clear distinction between the spiritual, eternal realm of the church and the temporal, political realm of the state. According to this conceptualization, the church served as the earthly custodian of the spiritual realm and the state served as the earthly custodian of the temporal realm. It was built on an ethical dualism in which the clergy and religious followed a counsel of perfection involving a commitment to a life of poverty, nonviolence, and celibacy. The laity or ordinary Christians, on the other hand, needed to participate in mundane affairs and were not expected to follow such a strict ethic.

According to this doctrine, God had charged the church with preaching the gospel and the state with ensuring the political order. Such traditional two-kingdom theologies have their roots in the Constantinian era. Pope Gelasius I had formulated the thesis in 495. It is instructive to follow this formulation of the relationship between distinctive spiritual and temporal realms through subsequent church history. During the medieval era, there was an assumption of the primacy of the spiritual realm. This primacy provided the basis by which the church could intrude into the affairs of the temporal realm while resisting state intrusion into church affairs.[15]

This way of conceptualizing the relationship between church and state changed during the Protestant reformation. Luther rejected the dual morality of the medieval two-kingdom theology but tragically introduced another dualism by transferring it to the life of each individual. According to Luther, we all live with the tension between being a Christian and a citizen of a given state. As a Christian one follows the example and teaching of Christ, while as a citizen one follows the natural law, which God has implanted in our hearts.[16] It was such ethical dualisms that had helped undermine Christian resistance to the secular totalitarian state

15. Sturzo, *Church and State*, 37–43.
16. Bainton, *Christian Attitudes*, 136–38.

in the modern world. That undermining had become painfully apparent to European theologians and church leaders in the postwar era as they reflected on German Christian responses to the Nazis.

It had become evident that such theological formulations, at their worst, had divinized the state and left the church impotent in the face of totalitarian schemes. As a result, the conversation at Puidoux in 1955 turned to the limits of Christian obedience to the state. Oscar Cullmann recognized that the state, within its own sphere, sometimes ceases to be founded on law and actually reverses any criterion of justice in the civil order. He was very cautious, however, when it came to making judgments about when a state had crossed this line and no longer remained within God's plan. He said that, from the perspective of the New Testament, one clear criterion of such demonic folly was the imposition of emperor worship.[17]

Jean Lasserre, a French Reformed pastor and scholar, was frustrated by such caution. The issue that French Christians faced under the Vichy government during the war was not overt emperor worship. Surely, Lasserre argued, theologians and ethicists should be able to draw up some criteria for determining when the state has exceeded its bounds. He gave several examples of situations where the state obviously asked people to do things that were unjust. Must a German woman obey the Nazis who required her to divorce her non-Aryan husband? Must a policeman obey when he is ordered to interrogate a woman by stripping her and burning her breasts with cigarettes? Lasserre exclaimed, "So the church of Jesus Christ has absolutely nothing to tell believers faced with problems of conscience such as I have evoked, but leaves them entirely to their own resources: this seems to be yet another sign of a church which is no longer faithful and has given up the struggle."[18]

The Reign of Christ

While Cullmann was reluctant to challenge government authority, he was a gifted biblical scholar. It was here that he made his contribution

17. Cullmann, *State in the New Testament*, 78.

18. Lasserre, *War and the Gospel*, 120–21. Jean Lasserre was a friend of Dietrich Bonhoeffer and a longtime French IFOR leader. See Durnbaugh, *On Earth Peace*, 22. John Howard Yoder worked closely with Lasserre in the Puidoux conferences and wrote the preface to the English translation of his book, *War and the Gospel*. Yoder always demonstrated a deep respect for him and his work.

to the discussion. He claimed that the problem of church and state was rooted in the very nature of Christianity from its beginning. The New Testament referred to the *reign of Christ,* which Cullmann insisted was distinct from the church or the future kingdom of God. He built his argument on the apostle Paul's discussion of the reign of Christ (1 Cor 15:23 ff.), which was the basis upon which the early Christians proclaimed that Jesus Christ is Lord (Rom 10:9). Christ's kingship extends to all creation (Phil 2:10). Cullmann claimed:

> It is, therefore not true that Christ now exercises his kingship only in heaven or the invisible world. Christ also rules on earth and over the state as well as the Church. Admittedly, he does not rule over the states of this world directly, but only through the mediation of the "powers and authorities" which he has subjected and which are provisionally attached to him. These invisible powers are active on earth.[19]

The New Testament uses various terms for such invisible powers, which were believed to be behind the state authorities who executed Jesus. Herod and Pilate were merely the human functionaries they used for their purposes. If these powers had known God's plan of salvation, they would not have crucified Jesus because this led to their own defeat (1 Cor 2:7–8). Though they have been conquered, their power still persists through the terrible power of the *sarx* (body or unregenerate human nature) and the *last enemy,* which is death. Even though the divine Spirit is already at work, it will only transform these enemies at the end (1 Cor 15:35ff.). Even so, it is a mistake to think that these powers can escape the rule of Christ. In other places, Paul uses the image of *head* to describe Christ's rule over the invisible and visible creation, including every *ruler and authority* (Col 2:10).[20]

Accordingly, Cullmann insisted that the reign of Christ must not be identified with the church. Nevertheless, the New Testament concentration on the church as a definite point within creation signifies that it is the heart and center of the reign of Christ. What happens in the church has a decisive influence for all of creation. The church itself, however, must resist any theocratic aspirations, because such aspirations belong to the future in heaven (Phil 3:20).[21]

19. Cullmann, *Early Church,* 120.
20. Ibid., 122.
21. Ibid., 126–28.

On the other hand, Cullmann argued that the state does not have any independent right of its own. Governments function as God's servants within the reign of Christ (Rom 13:6). As such they are entitled to our obedience and active support. But, when they become disengaged from the reign of Christ, they are extremely questionable and become demonic. In this sense, Cullmann claimed that the earthly state, though not ultimate and divine in itself, is nevertheless a member of the reign of Christ by the will of God. But there is a crucial difference between church and state within the reign of Christ. Cullmann wrote,

> The fact that the members of the church are conscious of all this, they know that Christ rules, and are therefore members of the kingdom of Christ consciously, is what distinguishes them as a Church from all the other members of the *Regnum Christi* [or reign of Christ] who may be its servants unconsciously.[22]

Even though Lasserre criticized Cullmann's cautious reluctance to say when the state had overstepped its limits, he accepted Cullman's premise that government officials were God's servants within the reign of Christ. In his own presentation at the Puidoux Theological Conference, he had this to say about the role of such people:

> Their function, as God sees it, is in no way placed outside the Revelation as though they enjoyed some kind of autonomy that they had to themselves. Very much to the contrary, they carry out a ministry—extra-ecclesiastical, to be sure—which is integral to the framework of Redemption. I think that the picture of Cullmann, who speaks of two concentric circles representing the Church and the *Regnum Christi*, is right. In the plan of God, the magistrates are placed, not in the circle of the Church, but in the larger circle of the "Reign of Christ." But they are always under the control of Revelation.[23]

There was general agreement on this way of formulating the relationship between church and state among the theologians and church leaders at Puidoux. On this basis they could argue that Christ was Lord of both church and state while still maintaining a distinction between the two. On this basis the church could witness to the state about the will of God as understood in Christ. It enabled the church to maintain its own freedom in relation to the state. They could insist on a certain primacy of

---

22. Ibid., 128.
23. Lasserre, "The 'Good' of Rom. 13:4," 133.

the church in God's economy. Christian social and political ethics should always begin from the premise of the reign of Christ.

John Howard Yoder on Biblical Studies and Social Policy

Church and State

Such a conceptualization of the relationship between the church, the state, and the "powers" under the reign of Christ became central to the way Yoder worked at social and political issues. We cannot understand his theological ethics apart from this conceptualization.[24] It became the basis on which he would prod Mennonites out of their separatism and toward a more engaged witness to the larger society. It was also the basis on which to prod American Protestant proponents of "social responsibility" toward taking the church seriously in their ethics.

Like Lasserre, Yoder criticized Cullmann's reluctance to define the limits of the state's authority, short of emperor worship or self-deification. He argued that it was more than the vagueness of the criterion that makes it suspect. Most German Christians had not even seen such extreme self-deification in Hitler. There is no evident reason why violating the first commandment of the law should be understood as more grievous than violating any of the other commandments. Idolatry need not become cultic to make it rebellion against God. The problem with making the extreme case of self-deification the criterion for such rebellion is the implication that there can be an exercise of violent domination that is not intrinsically self-glorifying that there can be a nationalism that is not prone to idolatry, or a total war that is not indicative of the state's self-aggrandizement.[25]

An early contribution to the discussion was Yoder's paper "The Theological Basis of the Christian Witness to the State," which he presented at the Puidoux Theological Conference. Here Yoder argued that Christianization of the world is possible in the sense that there is a Christian influence on what happens in the world. The important question, however, is *how* one exercises that influence. His paper makes various references to the work of Jean Lasserre, who presented an earlier paper at

---

24. For two examples of the way Yoder conceptualized the relationship between the church, the state, and the "powers," see Yoder, *Christian Witness* (1964) and Yoder, *Politics* (1994), 134–61.

25. Yoder, *Christian Witness* (1964), 37–38.

the conference. It is also deeply indebted to Cullmann's exegetical work on the reign of Christ.[26]

Yoder addressed the relationship between church and state and the problem of traditional two-kingdom theologies. He defined the difference between the church and the world on the basis of their respective responses to the invitation of God in Jesus Christ. The church says *yes* to God while the world says *no*. God respects the world's freedom to say *no*. Therefore, in the world, which includes the state, God's requirements are adapted to that *no*. Accordingly, all that can be counted on is a basic ethical minimum that is valid despite humanity's *no*. His paper was a heuristic attempt to formulate and test the duality that results from humanity's *no* to God, while recognizing that there is ultimately only one ethic established in the reign of Christ.[27] The church is where humanity's *no* is overcome through God's grace. Consequently, Yoder argues, "In speaking of the Church, we must say that the meaning of history and the significance of everything that happens in the world is not the fate of Western culture, of civilization, of the human community of justice, or of the world, but the formation and building of the body of Christ."[28]

Such distinctions, grounded in his understanding of the reign of Christ, became the basis of Yoder's argument against an ethic of responsibility rooted in the life of a given nation-state. It is not the nation but the church that carries the meaning of history. That is why the Christian must, at some point, make a break with human continuity rooted in family, ethnic identity, social identity, and national identity to place her or his faith in the church, which is the resurrection body of Christ.

While the church has an immediate relationship to God through Christ, the world, including the state, has a mediate relationship through the "powers" (*exousiai*). These "powers," though originally part of God's good creation, are fallen in the sense that they resist God. In this sense, pragmatically speaking, the state is also fallen because it is always less than submissive to God. Since it is never as submissive as it could be, it is with reference to relative degrees of submission that we can say that a given state is Christianized. Hence, we could say that a relatively democratic and nonviolent state is more Christian than a brutal totalitarian

---

26. Yoder, "Theological Basis."
27. Ibid., 136–39.
28. Ibid., 140.

state. But, a state is never so submitted to God's rule that we can do anything but make such relative comparisons.²⁹

Finally, according to Yoder, the reign of Christ over the "powers" and over the states is conservative rather than redemptive. The purpose is not to bring in the kingdom of God but to keep things from falling apart so that the church can do its redemptive kingdom work. For that reason, Yoder said, "There is always this distinction between these two areas, or orders, and the duality is defined in that one is redemptive and the other conservative."³⁰

Having laid this theological groundwork, Yoder tackled the question of the church's witness to the state. It is not true that Christians who follow Christ's way of self-giving and nonviolent love have nothing to say to the state. If they recognize that the state is not an abstraction but various people doing different tasks, they will address them as individuals. The first message to these people is an invitation to become Christian, which means being a disciple who follows Christ's way of nonviolent love. Government officials who are Christians should be reminded that it is not a government office but being a disciple of Jesus that defines their actions.³¹

Even if the statesperson does not accept the challenge to become a Christian, Yoder insisted, it does not free the officeholder from responsibility before God. If these persons choose to say *no* to this invitation of God, they are still under the *yes* of God that reaches out to them. They are still under the reign of Christ, and God still has claims upon them. For those who say *yes* to God in Christ, the demand is to bear the cross, and those who say *no* to this invitation are still called to do justice. Correspondingly, the concept of a just war has some value in defining the demands of justice for such people, even though it becomes less and less useful as governments keep building more and more sophisticated weapons of mass destruction.³²

Yoder insisted that the state is not autonomous nor an authority to itself. But even if it functions as an autonomous authority, we can always challenge it to make a particular choice with reference to justice. Because of its frame of reference, we cannot ask the state to be perfectly just, but

---

29. Ibid., 141.
30. Ibid.
31. Ibid., 142.
32. Ibid., 142–43.

we can ask it to be more just. We can ask the state to live up to its own concept of justice. For example, we can ask France to take seriously its commitment to liberty, equality, and fraternity. Because each state is already committed to some understanding of order, Yoder said, we can appeal to it to live up to its own principles.[33]

Jesus and the Jewish Religious Parties

John Howard Yoder's theology also owes a debt to Cullmann's insights from biblical research on the relationship between Jesus and the various Jewish religious parties in first-century Palestine. Biblical scholars during that time were researching the relationship between Jesus and the Zealots.[34] The Zealots were a loosely defined group of Jewish revolutionaries committed to the violent overthrow of the Roman occupation of Palestine. Cullmann identified at least five of Jesus' disciples as Zealots and said that Jesus had to continually come to terms with the Zealot question throughout his ministry.[35] Yoder was less interested in the immediate question of Jesus' relationship to the Zealots than he was in the broader question of Jesus' political stance in relation to the various options available to him in first-century Palestine.

Cullmann was clearly Yoder's mentor in such research, even though Yoder pursued the question farther than Cullmann had. Cullmann set the question of Jesus' relationship to the state in the context of the Jewish theocratic ideal as espoused by the Maccabees. Such theocratic aspirations were a significant source of political unrest in Palestine under the imperial occupation of the Romans. The Zealots, a potent revolutionary force, espoused such a theocratic ideal. Cullmann, however, argued that

---

33. Ibid., 143.

34. Scholars were already working on the subject in the 1950s and various books appeared in the 1960s. Cullmann included a brief chapter on the Zealots in Cullmann, *State in the New Testament*. He later wrote *Jesus and the Revolutionaries*. Other scholars working on this were Hengel, *Die Zealoten*, and Brandon, *Jesus and Zealots*.

35. Cullmann, *State in the New Testament*, 17. Some more recent scholars, including Raymond Brown, Richard Horsley, and John P. Meier, have questioned the belief that there was a smoldering Zealot insurgency during Jesus' lifetime. See Brown, *Death of the Messiah*, 679; Horsley, "Death of Jesus"; Meier, *Marginal Jew*, 2:1040. Others, including N. T. Wright and Ben F. Meyer, depict a more turbulent social situation during Jesus' lifetime, creating periodic surges in the number of poor people, emigrants, revolutionaries, bandits, and beggars. See Wright, *Jesus and the Victory*, 150–51. See also Meyer, "Jesus Christ," 777.

Jesus and the early Christians rejected theocratic aspirations as demonic. He tied the struggle to Jesus' temptation in the wilderness, where he rejected Satan's offer of world domination (Luke 4:5–8). In doing so, Jesus rejected the state in any sense as a final or divine institution. Cullmann thought the temptation account demonstrates that Jesus accepted the state and rejected any revolutionary attempt to overthrow it.[36] According to Cullmann, the Romans had not understood Jesus when they crucified him as a revolutionary. However, Cullmann did not consider that Jesus might nevertheless have posed a real threat to the established social order in Palestine, even though he rejected violent revolution.[37]

The Original Revolution

In his own interpretation of Jesus' political involvements in first-century Palestine, Yoder followed the general outline of Cullmann's work. Like Cullmann, Yoder made the temptation story central to the interpretation of Jesus' political stance. Like Cullmann, Yoder focused on Jesus' relationship with the Zealots, but he also went beyond Cullmann to look at the other political options available to Jesus. Like Cullmann, Yoder understood Jesus' execution by the Romans as definitive for our understanding of who Jesus was. But, unlike Cullmann, Yoder did not think the crucifixion involved a misunderstanding of Jesus by the Romans. He saw Jesus as a real threat to the political powers in first-century Palestine. Yoder wrote:

> Both Jewish and Roman authorities were defending themselves against a real threat. That the threat was not one of *armed,* violent revolt, and that it nonetheless bothered them to the point of their resorting to illegal procedures to counter it, is a proof of the political relevance of nonviolent tactics, not a proof that Pilate and Caiaphas were exceptionally dull or dishonorable men.[38]

36. Cullmann, *State in the New Testament*, 8–23.

37. Ibid., 41ff.

38. Yoder, *Politics* (1994), 49. Italics Yoder's. N. T. Wright agrees with Yoder's understanding of the politics of Jesus in first-century Palestine. Wright argues, "Anyone announcing the kingdom of YHWH was engaged in serious political action. Anyone announcing the kingdom *but explicitly opposing armed resistance* was engaged in doubly serious political action: not only the occupying forces, but all those who gave allegiance to the resistance movement would be enraged" (*Jesus and the Victory*, 296). Italics Wright's.

Yoder's portrait of the historical Jesus was more socially and politically involved and considerably more radical than that of Cullmann. Yoder's more popular book on Jesus and the early church that preceded *The Politics of Jesus* was titled *The Original Revolution*. Here he wrote, "If we are ever to rescue God's good news from all the justifiable but secondary meanings it has taken on, perhaps the best way to do it is to say that the root meaning of the term *euangelion* would today best be translated 'revolution.'"[39] He insisted that Jesus' message involves real social and political choices that are revolutionary in nature if we take them seriously. He was convinced that Jesus is "the bearer of a new possibility of human, social, and therefore political relationships."[40] It is this political Jesus, found in the gospel narratives by biblical exegetes, whom Yoder placed in conversation with contemporary theology and theological ethics. And again one sees the focus on Jesus as the root of theology and ethics that earns for Yoder the title of "radical theologian."

The Politics of Paul and the Early Church

Additionally, one needs to ask how the revolutionary nature of Jesus' life and message formed the life of the early churches. It can be argued that there is a radical break between Jesus' proclamation of the reign of God and the worship of the heavenly Christ in the Gentile churches during the following decades. To counter such an interpretation, Yoder drew on the themes of discipleship and imitation found in the epistles. Through a careful study of these themes, he was able to argue that the way of the cross should not be understood as literally following Jesus' lifestyle or an existential identification with suffering in itself. Instead, the cross points to the concrete social meaning of Jesus' political stance in relation to dominant structures of power in our world.[41]

The big question for this argument was whether the apostle Paul's stance toward the Roman Empire differed significantly from that of Jesus. Cullmann worked on this question as it related to Paul's counsel to Christians to submit to the governing authorities because they have been ordained by God (Rom 13:1–7). Various two-kingdom paradigms have

---

39. Yoder, *Original Revolution*, 15.
40. Yoder, *Politics* (1994), 52.
41. Ibid., 129–31.

claimed this passage as the central basis for the argument that God has ordained government to function as a distinct authority rooted in natural law rather than in the gospel of Jesus Christ. Christians should obey governing authorities in matters pertaining to national citizenship such as waging war.[42]

Cullmann insisted that such interpretations misunderstand this Scripture passage and Paul's stance toward the Roman Empire. The only way Romans 13:1–7 could be interpreted as unequivocal support for the state is by taking it out of context. Both in chapter 12 and in the rest of chapter 13, Paul is speaking directly to Christians about their responsibility to act out of love, not to resist evil with evil but to do good to one's enemies. The Roman state, as Paul knew it, often did the exact opposite. Nevertheless, Christians are to accept the state as an institution despite that reality. But Paul is not suggesting, Cullmann argued, that Christians should participate in the retributive aspects of state vengeance against evildoers. Instead, he calls for a positive expression of the Christian love ethic in relation to the state. While he does not explicitly explain how that is possible, Paul argues that the state is also a servant of God as long as it does not exceed its bounds.[43]

According to Cullmann, one needs to recognize that Paul is talking about Nero's regime. Christians had reason to feel animosity toward this tyrannical government. Paul is encouraging them not to reject the validity of the state as a matter of principle. Paul needs to be explicit about that point because the retributive nature of the state makes it less than self-evident. Nevertheless, they are to subordinate themselves to the state as long as it functions within its proper sphere and does not demand that which belongs God. Even when it demands more than it rightfully should, the Christian response should still be guided by the love ethic. It is the same stance toward the state that Jesus had.[44]

This stance becomes even more evident when we examine other passages where Paul addresses Christian relationships to the state. He chastises the Christians in Corinth for filing lawsuits against each other in Roman courts of law (1 Cor 6:1ff.). They should settle their quarrels within a congregational discernment process, rather than relying on

42. This way of stating the problem especially reflects traditional Lutheran theology. Roman Catholic and Reformed theologies have their own variations of this two-kingdom theological formulation.

43. Cullmann, *State in the New Testament*, 57.

44. Ibid., 58–59.

punitive government institutions. When Paul tells the Corinthians that they will someday judge the world, it is clear that he understands the state to be a temporary institution whose scope is limited.[45]

Finally, Cullmann emphasizes Paul's recognition of a demonic element in the state. Paul tells the Corinthians, "None of the rulers of this world understood the wisdom of God; for if they had understood it they would not have crucified the Lord of glory" (1 Cor 2:8). The phrase "rulers of this world," like the expression "authorities" or "powers" (*exousiai*) in Romans 13:1, refers not only to political figures but also to invisible spiritual powers that stood behind them—a common understanding of power within the first-century Jewish worldview. References to authorities and powers have a double meaning, referring to both the state and such invisible spiritual powers. Jesus conquered these powers through his death and resurrection (Col 2:15). Cullmann wrote,

> Against the background of this belief in the vanquished powers at work behind earthly happenings it becomes especially clear that the State is now a temporary institution not of divine nature but nevertheless willed by God; that we must remain critical toward every State; that we must nonetheless obey the State as far as it remains within its bounds.[46]

Accordingly, Cullmann sought to make a distinction between a state that lived within the bounds of Romans 13 and a state that moved outside these bounds (the demonic state of Rev 13). Christians had an obligation to obey the state that stayed within its bounds, but not the state that moves outside these bounds by becoming totalitarian and self-deifying.[47]

Yoder followed the general argument of Cullmann's exegetical work. Cullmann sought to harmonize a vast and disparate body of New Testament material dealing with the question of church and state. This material ranges from the Gospels, though the Pauline Epistles, to the book of Revelation. Yoder began by recognizing that the New Testament contains different strands of thought concerning the state, but then followed Cullmann in the effort to demonstrate that Paul's argument in Romans 13:1–7 is consistent with these other materials.

Cullmann and Yoder try to harmonize too much difference. Other biblical scholars have even suggested that Romans 13:1–7 may be a later

45. Ibid., 60–62.
46. Ibid., 69–70.
47. Ibid., 73ff.

interpolation because it demonstrates a much more positive assessment of government than the rest of the New Testament and even the rest of the Pauline material (e.g., 1 Cor 2:6–8). The New Testament did not have a univocal understanding of how Christians should relate to the state. Even Paul apparently was not completely consistent in his attitudes toward imperial Roman government.[48]

There is a crucial difference between Cullmann's and Yoder's understanding of the threat that Jesus' ministry and community organizing posed to Roman rule. As seen earlier, Cullmann begins with the belief that Jesus had not posed a threat to the Roman Empire. He writes, "Jesus was in no sense an enemy of the State on principle, but rather a loyal citizen who offered no threat to the State's existence."[49] Yoder had a considerably more radical and revolutionary Jesus. Jesus' nonviolent community organizing in Palestine did pose a real threat to the ruling authorities. In its own way it was an even greater threat than violent insurrection.[50]

The most important common agenda of Cullmann and Yoder is that both sought to discredit the two-kingdom theologies that had been prevalent until the postwar era. Yoder said that the basic premises of such theologies (built on Rom 13:1–7) had not been questioned until the crisis of Nazism made it necessary to re-examine them. Before this crisis, these verses had served as a sort of capsule, guiding the Christian statesperson (punishing evil and rewarding good) and the Christian citizen (obeying state authorities). Within such a theological construct, the government that wields the sword by divine decree was exempted from the general prohibition against killing. All that remained were some borderline questions concerning things such as determining what constituted a just war.[51] Yoder made it clear that he was challenging the tradition of two-kingdom theology at its very core:

> Let me then put most precisely the challengeable claim of the tradition we intend to challenge; it is that by virtue of the divine institution of government as a part of God's good creation, its mandate to wield the sword and the Christian's duty to obey the state combine to place upon the Christian a moral obligation to

---

48. A recent study that fits the general interpretation of Cullmann and Yoder but is more mindful of the tension between this passage and other New Testament materials is Elliott, "Romans 13 in the Context of Imperial Propaganda."

49. Cullmann, *State in the New Testament*, 54.

50. Yoder, *Politics* (1994), 49.

51. Ibid., 193–94.

support and participate in the state's legal killing (death penalty, war), despite contrary duties which otherwise would seem to follow from Jesus' teaching or example.[52]

The first part of Yoder's argument was that Romans 13:1–7 is not the center of New Testament teaching about the state. The New Testament speaks in many ways about the problem of the state. A strong strand of teaching in the Gospels even sees the state as demonic. Following Cullmann, Yoder argued that Romans 12 and 13 constitute a complete literary unit. Therefore Romans 13:1–7 should not be understood by itself. It becomes a static or conservative underpinning of the present social order only by refusing to take its larger literary context seriously.[53]

Revolutionary Subordination

Next, Yoder tackled the question of Christian submission or subordination to the state. Such subordination, he said, merely recognizes whatever power exists or whatever structure of sovereignty happens to prevail. This subordination does not imply recognition of a particular government as divinely instituted. Yoder rejected Cullmann's argument that governments living within the bounds of Romans 13:1–7 are instituted of God in a way that other governments are not.[54] This point is significant for understanding Yoder's basic stance toward government authority. With reference to Romans 13:1–7, he wrote,

> God is not said to *create* or *institute* or *ordain* the powers that be, but only to *order* them, to put them in order, sovereignly to tell them where they belong, what is their place. It is not as if there was a time when there was no government and then God made government through a new creative intervention; there has been hierarchy and authority and power since human society existed. Its exercise has involved domination, disrespect for human dignity, and real or potential violence ever since sin has existed. Nor is it that in his ordering of it he specifically, morally approves of what government does. . . . God does not take responsibility for the existence of the rebellious "powers that be" or for their shape or identity; they already are. What the text says is that he orders

---

52. Ibid., 194.
53. Ibid., 194–98.
54. Ibid., 201 n. 11. Yoder is also arguing against Karl Barth, who takes a position similar to that of Cullmann.

them, brings them into line, that by his permissive government he lines them up with his purpose.[55]

Another central aspect of Yoder's position involves his understanding of what it means for Christians to be subordinate to government authorities. Paul was calling the early Christians away from any notion of violent revolution or insubordination. Instead, he was asking them to take a position of nonresistant love toward tyrannical Roman rule. Yoder explained that subordination does not mean compliance or acquiescence in evil, but rather the suffering renunciation of retaliation in kind. It does not rule out other kinds of resistance to evil.[56] In this sense, Christians should be subordinate to but also rebel against all forms of government. Yoder argued that such subordination is actually a Christian form of rebellion because, in doing so, we share God's patience with a system we have basically rejected.[57]

Yoder shared Cullmann's understanding of the limited scope of appropriate government authority. Accordingly Yoder said that the appropriate government functions, to which Paul calls Christians to be subject, are the juridical and police functions of the state. These functions cannot include such things as the death penalty or war. It certainly cannot mean that Christians need to participate in the military or even in police service.

Accordingly, Yoder argued that Paul does not believe governments are self-justifying or that whatever they ask of their citizens is automatically good. Paul is not asking citizens to mindlessly obey government authorities but to be subject to them. Christians who accept their subordination to government nevertheless retain their moral independence. Yoder followed Cullmann in seeing an allusion to the words of Jesus (Matt 22:21) in Romans 13:7 where Paul instructs the Roman Christians to "pay to all what is due them." This change means giving to Caesar what

---

55. Ibid., 201–2. Italics Yoder's. Yoder does not refer to the opinion of any other biblical scholar to help substantiate his interpretation of God "ordering" the powers. Neither does he examine the possible range of meanings of the Greek word *tasso*, which he translates as "order" instead of "ordain." Instead, Yoder makes a logical historical argument about the formation of governments. He also makes the argument from the Old Testament that God did not approve morally of the brutality with which Assyria chastised Israel (202). He apparently assumes that these arguments in themselves substantiate his interpretation.

56. Ibid., 202 n. 14.

57. Ibid., 200 n. 10.

is his (taxes and a certain amount of respect and honor), but giving their primary allegiance to God. This stance follows the example of Jesus, who accepted subordination and humiliation from the hands of government authorities.[58]

Subordination is one of the most misunderstood parts of Yoder's theology.[59] He claimed that subordination was not simply a calculated recognition of the strength of the powers that are operative in our world. It is not a passive acceptance of one's lot nor is it a willingness to suffer passively. It is actually a strategy of engagement and resistance. He wrote:

> The willingness to suffer is then not merely a test of our patience or a dead space of waiting; it is itself a participation in the character of God's victorious patience with the rebellious powers of creation. We subject ourselves to government because it was in so doing that Jesus revealed and achieved God's victory.[60]

That is, acknowledging the authority of the government—being subject to it—while living in the reality of the reign of God can be an active protest. Biblical examples that Yoder later used for such resistant subordination are the stories of Joseph, Esther, and the Hebrew captives reported in Daniel.[61]

Conclusion

As seen in this chapter, John Howard Yoder's constructive biblical theology, which he called the "politics of Jesus," responds to the agonizing questions about why Christian efforts failed to resist the violent nationalist conflagration that led to World War II. His European mentors and colleagues, who contributed much to his thought, were equally concerned that Christians would not now be similarly drawn into the superpower rivalry between the United States and the Soviet Union. Cullmann especially contributed to Yoder's political understanding of Jesus. Barth provided the theological tools that Yoder used to such great effect. The

---

58. Ibid., 205–9.

59. Complete agreement is lacking on what Yoder intended with "revolutionary subordination." Additional discussion of nuances and applications of Yoder's view of subordination occurs in chapters 6 and 8 to follow. Chapter 13 includes a suggestion for using less easily misunderstood terms for reciprocity and power sharing.

60. Yoder, *Politics* (1994), 209.

61. See Yoder, *For the Nations*, 57; Yoder, *Jewish-Christian Schism*, 71, 86, 244.

next chapter assesses Barth's influence. Lasserre was his colleague in the struggle against two-kingdom theologies. Trocmé gave Yoder insights into the function of the Jubilee year in Jesus' social agenda. Berkhof gave him the language of "powers" in reference to social structures. These pieces become the building blocks in Yoder's articulation of what radical discipleship looks like—discipleship whose reference point is the root of Christian faith and practice, namely the story of Jesus. As a "radical theologian," Yoder is inviting us to follow Jesus when we meet him in our world, the Jesus of the Christology made visible in chapter 1.

5

Deconstructing Karl Barth

GERALD J. MAST

It is by now widely accepted that Karl Barth played a significant role in the development of John Howard Yoder's theological ethics, even if there remain disagreements about the extent of that influence. Despite some confusion among scholars about how much study Yoder did with Barth, it has been established that Yoder took five courses and five colloquia with Barth during his doctoral studies at the University of Basel in the early 1950s, even though theology was not the focus of his doctoral research.[1]

Earl Zimmerman provides a convincing list of ideas that Yoder got from Barth: "(1) reading the Bible as a narrative centered in Jesus Christ; (2) making the particular story of Jesus decisive for discipleship and ethics; (3) rejecting natural theology as a source independent of the story of Jesus; and (4) drawing a distinction between the church and the world for all social and ethical reflection."[2] Other scholars, such as Craig Carter, insist that Yoder received an appreciation for orthodox creedal convictions from Barth.[3]

1. Nation, *John Howard Yoder*, 18.
2. Zimmerman, *Practicing the Politics*, 104.
3. Carter, *Politics of the Cross*, 66. Or as Carter states in a summary section titled "Barthian, Anabaptist Social Ethics," "By creatively uniting aspects of his own

Rather than offer another entry aimed at the ongoing debate about Barthian influence on Yoder, I will instead offer a reading of Yoder's engagement with Karl Barth's theological ethics, showing how he exhibited hospitality to a trajectory in Barth's argumentation that exceeded Barth's own intention or purpose. The contemporary, although by now somewhat tired, name for such hospitality to the Other within a text, is deconstruction. Although the Barthian influence is not the focus of the chapter, the resulting deconstructive analysis does eventually provide an answer in the debate about Barth's influence on Yoder.

In one of his more lucid descriptions of his approach to reading the texts of the canonical philosophers, Jacques Derrida described deconstruction as "an analysis which tries to find out how their thinking works or does not work, to find the tensions, the contradictions, the heterogeneity within their own corpus."[4] Derrida points out in this discussion that such an analysis seeks neither to repeat nor to attack a text, but rather to exhibit "love and respect" toward the "functioning and dysfunctioning" happening in the text.

In my view, it is exactly this posture of loving and respectful fidelity to the functioning and dysfunctioning of Karl Barth's theological arguments that accurately characterizes John Howard Yoder's regard for the work of his theological mentor. Moreover, it is apparent that he learned this kind of respectful and affirmative deconstructive exploration from Karl Barth himself. For example, in the first chapter of *Karl Barth and the Problem of War*, Yoder remarks that readers who might feel that his book is too "uninhibited" in his questioning of Barth's theological ethics might "compare its tone" with Barth's criticisms of Emil Brunner and Lorraine Boettner.[5] More to the point, in a chapter Yoder wrote for a collection of essays by numerous authors gathered into a book entitled *How Karl Barth Changed My Mind*, Yoder noted the "playfulness and elegance" that he thought characterized Barth's *Church Dogmatics*, insisting that "from the outset, Barth was clear about being on the move."[6] Although

---

Anabaptist-Mennonite theological heritage with the method and major themes of Karl Barth's theology, Yoder was able to build on and to develop social ethics in the tradition of Barth" (226).

4. Caputo, *Deconstruction in a Nutshell*, 9.
5. Yoder, *Karl Barth*, 10.
6. Yoder, "Karl Barth: Kept Changing," 167–68. This essay was reprinted with the same title in Yoder, *Karl Barth*, quote, 170–71. This comment about Barth being on the move is consistent with Graham Ward's observation that "theology for Barth takes

Yoder does not cite a specific passage from Barth here, it may be that he was referring to Barth's critique of theological methodologies that merely repeat achieved conclusions rather than seek to apprehend the ways in which God's revelation exceeds any particular historical concepts and words. As Barth put it: "The success of our undertaking stands or falls with the fact that we are on the way; that therefore any goal that is attained becomes the point of departure for a new journey on this way, on which the revelation of God and its veracity are always future to us."[7] By contrast, "a repetition of our work can mean that we want to master God, that we are therefore no longer obedient to His grace."[8]

Whether Yoder had this passage in mind or not, it is clear that he did not wish to simply repeat Barth's project: "It is more important to seek to characterize Karl Barth strategically not by the way in which he did and did not continue the lines set by his heritage, but by where he was going, even though—by the nature of the case—such a reading of the implicit trajectory must be based on an unfinished story."[9] In other words, Yoder's reading of Barth is concerned with the unfulfilled promise of Barth's theological writing, with what was left unsaid as well as with what was actually stated.

In this chapter I illustrate the deconstructive reading strategy that Yoder employed in his interpretation of Barth—and arguably learned from him—by focusing on Yoder's attention to the direction Barth's work pointed in three areas of inquiry: Christology, ecclesiology, and cosmology. My argument is not that Yoder or Barth were practitioners of Derridean deconstruction. The differences and similarities between deconstruction as Derrida practiced it and the openness to a non-repetitive revelation in the manner of Barth has been considered more thoroughly elsewhere.[10] For the purposes of this chapter, the primary similarity I want to highlight between Derrida and Yoder/Barth is the suspicion of system and the hospitality to that which transcends any orderly system of meaning, a suspicion that results in a patient and affirmative reading of a valued text in a way that makes visible what the text cannot contain.[11] This

---

place as a continual negotiation and renegotiation of a problematic that cannot be, cannot be allowed to be, resolved." Ward, *Barth, Derrida*, 239.

7. Barth, *Church Dogmatics* II.1, 214.
8. Ibid.
9. Yoder, "Karl Barth: Kept Changing," 168–69; Yoder, *Karl Barth*, 171.
10. Ward, *Barth, Derrida*; Blum, "Yoder's Patience."
11. Blum, "Yoder's Patience," 109–10.

suspicion of abstract systems leads Barth toward stressing the hiddenness of the Word of God and its irreducibility to any human scheme or invention, whereas for Yoder this suspicion of abstraction leads toward an affirmation of the concrete historical reality of God's Word made visible in the life of Jesus Christ and in the existence of the church as Christ's body.

Concrete Christology

Yoder reads a robust and biblical yet practical and concrete Christology in Karl Barth's theological ethics. In his most extended engagement with Barth's work—the book that critiques Barth's position on war—Yoder asks the following question: "Why should it not be possible for a general statement in Christian ethics to have the same validity as a general statement within some other realm of Christian dogmatics?"[12] Yoder's equation of ethics with dogmatics here relies on a number of moves that Barth makes in *Church Dogmatics*, while arriving at a conclusion that Barth was unable to reach himself, namely, that an ethical practice such as pacifism can have the same epistemological status as a doctrinal belief about atonement.

First, Yoder follows Barth's critique of a purely abstract dogmatic confession, in which Barth rejects the idea that theology is primarily concerned with "timeless truths" and instead points to the concreteness of the life of Jesus Christ as it is presented to us in the Bible.[13] Throughout *Church Dogmatics*, Barth asserts that dogmatics should be understood as Christology and that Christology should be seen as the revelation of God in the life of Jesus Christ. This means that theological inquiry must begin with the "Easter story" of "the life and passion of Jesus Christ" which for Barth is the defining event that relativizes all other sources of knowledge, including those deriving from what is sometimes called "natural theology."[14] Moreover, the command of God that comes to us in this Easter story lays an authoritative claim on our lives: "God calls us and orders us and claims us by being gracious to us in Jesus Christ."[15] Barth goes so far as to say that we must seek the command of God "only in what

12. Yoder, *Karl Barth*, 43.
13. Ibid., 84.
14. Barth, *Church Dogmatics* I.2, 122–24.
15. Barth, *Church Dogmatics* II.2, 560.

happened at Bethlehem, at Capernaum and Tiberius, Gethsemane and on Golgotha, and in the garden of Joseph of Arimathea."[16]

Next, picking up on this insistence by Barth on the definitive stature of the story of Jesus Christ in Christian epistemology, Yoder explains that the concrete obedience called forth by such a discovery of God's command as it comes to us exclusively in the life of Jesus Christ is not somehow less truthful or real or binding because of its situated particularity. Just as Jesus Christ appeared in a specific time and place in human history, visited by shepherds and sages, followed by tax collectors and fishermen, crucified for heresy and treason and raised from death to life, so God's will for the world appears in the actual and visible practices of the faithful church—the body of Christ in the world throughout history and today.[17]

In an essay that begins as a "gloss" on a lengthy passage from *Church Dogmatics* IV.2, Yoder explains that the gospel is in its essence not merely abstract but social, and therefore a historically situated experience of grace and obedience.[18] The text he cites from Barth makes the claim that "the Christian church, as the body of Jesus Christ and therefore the earthly-historical form of His existence, is the provisional representation of humanity sanctified in Him."[19] I discuss the ecclesial implications of this claim in the section on ecclesiology below; for now, I want to attend to how Yoder used this assertion by Barth as a jumping off point for radicalizing Barth's christological convictions.

Yoder highlights the way in which Barth's depiction of the church as the "earthly-historical form" of Jesus Christ's existence leads us to acknowledge that Jesus was an "exemplar" for us, both in his ministry as a human person and in the extension of that ministry in the life of the church—hence Yoder's claim that we can understand "social ethics as gospel."[20] In other words, the gospel is "connected with a particular name and place and time, with Jesus and the Jews and Jerusalem," and it comes to us as a story about events that took place in that time and place. This particularity has troubled Christian thinkers throughout the church's

---

16. Barth, *Church Dogmatics* II.2, 599.
17. Yoder, *Royal Priesthood*, 112–14.
18. Ibid., 104–5.
19. Barth, *Church Dogmatics* IV.2, 719.
20. Yoder, *Royal Priesthood*, 103–4.

history insofar as they worry that such a specific narrative will not be seen as applicable for ethics "in general" or for a "mainstream" audience.

Yoder notes that Barth himself can both embrace this particularity and also at times be inclined to regard it as a basis for restricting the application today of specific obedience to God's action in the world exemplified by Jesus. The particular restriction comes at the question of war. Barth refers to the notion of a *Grenzfall* when discussing the question of whether a Christian can participate in armed violence. A *Grenzfall* is a limit experience or borderline case in which an exception to the rule is necessary. Barth stresses that because God's command is not an ahistorical rule that exceeds time and space, Christians should be prepared to take up arms in defense of homeland under some circumstances, even though this contradicts the apparent command of God in Jesus Christ as revealed in Scripture. Barth writes, for example, that in the case of an emergency, such as when a nation is unjustly attacked, "Christian ethics can no longer be absolutely pacifist."[21]

In response, Yoder insists that according to Barth's own criterion of gospel faithfulness (the command of God as it appears in the grace that God offers us in the life of Jesus Christ), God cannot will an action that contradicts what has been made visible in the historical life of Jesus Christ: "If dogmatics—or for that matter any Christian communication—is possible, we cannot count on situations ever arising in which God would take back what he said in Christ, or give us commands which are not concordant with his revelation of himself in Jesus Christ."[22]

This response by Yoder should not be understood as an absolutist imposition by Yoder of a timeless creedal claim about the wrongness of participation in armed conflict. Rather, Yoder is taking seriously Barth's own view that Christian ethics must remain within a realm of possibility shaped by the life, death, and resurrection of Jesus Christ, rather than by some other set of rules or contingencies that can be imposed as a prior authority. Yoder accuses Barth of invoking exactly such a non-biblical realm of contingencies and criteria by imagining circumstances under which obedience to Jesus Christ as revealed in the New Testament is not possible—the *Grenzfall*. Barth, in other words, has ruled out in advance that the command of God as manifested in the concrete historical nonresistance of Jesus Christ, as well as in his teachings about enemy love,

21. Barth, *Church Dogmatics* III.4, 462.
22. Yoder, *Karl Barth*, 48.

could ever be always followed even in extreme circumstances. Yoder effectively undermines Barth's violence-justifying conclusion by following more rigorously Barth's own development of a concrete christological framework for ethics that rests exclusively on the command of God as found in the life, teachings, death, and resurrection of Jesus Christ recorded in scripture and embodied by the church when it is faithful. In other words, by pushing Barth's commitment to the radical particularity of the command of God, Yoder shows how Barth's invocation of the *Grenzfall* is less driven by the particularity of concrete obedience and more oriented by an abstract "rule book" than is Yoder's commitment to the nonviolence of Jesus. So, Yoder can conclude that what Barth began "by labeling the freedom of God has turned out to be the autonomy of pragmatic political judgment."[23] In other words, Barth is more guilty of limiting God's command than are the pacifists.

Yoder's deconstruction of Barth's theological ethics demonstrates that Barth is unable to arrest the momentum in his own writing toward an ethics derived entirely from the defenseless life, death, and resurrection of Jesus Christ. By critiquing a crucial departure in Barth from such a thoroughly concrete Christology, Yoder pushes for a more consistent relationship between the content and form of Christology, which are unified in the appearance of the event of Jesus Christ that displayed God's loving and defenseless grace. Like Barth, Yoder understood the command of God not as an abstract principle that can be leveraged against the contingencies of human experience and history, but rather a concrete event that takes place in history and to which we respond in history: "the Word which God speaks to every time and at every place is always Jesus Christ."[24]

Yoder explicitly follows Barth on this point before extending Barth's argument. For example, Barth explicitly denies that the command of God is a general rule to which we provide specific historical content in the existential challenges of our own human contexts. Challenging the distinction between theory and practice in Christian ethics, Barth insists that "we cannot deal evasively with Jesus Christ as one does with an idea" and that "God's decision as it is really embodied in Him is a sovereign decision" that "characterizes not only our conduct but our asking what

---

23. Ibid., 87.
24. Ibid., 16.

we ought to do as responsible decision."²⁵ Such a collapse of theory and practice "forces us out into the open, exposing us to the divine claim and the radical questioning of our whole being which it involves."²⁶ It is for this reason that Barth acknowledges both that the historic confessions of the church should be respected as responses by the church to God's command and at the same time that we should not claim for such confessions more than the status of "partial and temporary" agreements that are relativized by the Word of God, by Jesus Christ himself.²⁷ Yoder accepts all this.

But while Yoder is aligned with Barth here, Yoder also demonstrates more fully than Barth what it might mean to unite theory and practice in a process of discernment that exposes us to the graceful and whole command of God, which is to say, to a command that can, like Jesus Christ, be rejected.²⁸ This possibility of rejection is manifested not only in a suffering servant who was "despised and rejected by others" (Isaiah 53:3) but also in the defenselessness of Jesus' body in the world today—the church that does not seek to impose itself on the world, either by political force or by creedal and sacramental traditions that seek to speak on behalf of everyone—the free church. In other words, Yoder highlights the intricate relationship between the pacifism that Barth cannot help but affirm and the uncoerced confession of faith that the command of God in Jesus Christ invites.²⁹

Real Church

Just as Yoder pushed Barth's theological argument toward the unavoidable affirmation of a pacifist social ethics framed in uncoerced confession, Barth's own reservations to the contrary, so Yoder also demonstrates that the logical outcome of Barth's ecclesiology is a church that offers rather than imposes its witness—a free church or a believers church—what I will call here a "real church." Yoder develops this argument in a number

25. Barth, *Church Dogmatics* II.2, 660.
26. Ibid.
27. Barth, *Church Dogmatics* I.2, 592.
28. Yoder, "On Not Being Ashamed," 43.
29. My observations about Yoder's radicalization of Barth here are indebted to Chris Huebner's evaluation of the command of God described by Barth as a "gift" that can be rejected. See Huebner, *Precarious Peace*, 86–88.

of places, perhaps most thoroughly in his essay "Why Ecclesiology is Social Ethics." The title states Yoder's thesis succinctly: Christian social ethics should be properly understood as an inquiry into the life and witness of the church, not primarily a matter of how individuals conduct themselves on the basis of independently determined rational norms.[30]

One way Yoder arrives at this conclusion is to interpret Barth's ecclesiology in free church terms.[31] He does this first by highlighting Barth's acknowledgement in *Church Dogmatics* that the task of the church in the world is primarily a matter of conducting its own life according to the "law of the kingdom of God" as a witness to the world that God's kingdom has already arrived and is being made visible in an actual human society.[32] This is by contrast with the temptation for the church to impose its law on the world or to assume that its own mission is identical with that of civil society—the logic of Christendom.[33]

Yoder then depicts Barth's description of the relationship between the church and the world as a free church vision, based on distinctions between church and world made in Barth's earlier essay on "Christian Community and Civil Community." Yoder notes that Barth acknowledges the civil community should not be understood as "Christian" in the way that the prevailing assumptions about Christendom suggest. Rather Barth stresses that the civil community is a community based not

---

30. Chapter 2 above explores sixteenth-century Anabaptism as one root of this ecclesiology, which grows out of a commitment to discipleship to Jesus Christ.

31. By free church, I mean a believers church that consists of members who have voluntarily confessed faith in Jesus Christ and on that basis have received baptism. I am aware of Stanley Hauerwas's critique of "voluntary" Christianity because of the emphasis this idea places on personal choice, which can easily turn the church into a matter of preference or consumer decision. I would argue that in the real church, the bondage associated with consumer culture's meaningless choices (between Corn Flakes and Cheerios, say, or Nike and Converse) is decisively broken. In other words, the church, when it refuses to coerce baptism or social conformity to the command it has received from God, actually makes a real choice possible for the first time. The choice for baptism, when made as an act of voluntary confession, is a response of freely chosen obedience that renders all future decisions also truly free, when they are made according to the rule of Christ and the power of the Holy Spirit. For Hauerwas's critique of voluntary Christianity, see Hauerwas, *Sanctify Them*, 164–67.

32. Barth, *Church Dogmatics* IV.2, 721. Yoder cites a long section from this page of *Church Dogmatics* in Yoder, *Royal Priesthood*, 105.

33. Yoder, *Royal Priesthood*, 106.

on Christian commitment but on citizenship whereas the church is made up of people who have in common a confession of faith in Jesus Christ.[34]

Insofar as Barth, like Yoder, rejects the vision of a civil society in which "the name of Christ was invoked over a global cultural/social/political phenomenon without regard for whether all the participants in that process were invoking that name as their own confessional identity," so Barth can be understood as advocating a free church ecclesiology in which the church is understood as an alternative community to that of civil society.[35] Yoder attributes this view to Barth by noting that Barth recognizes "for the first time in mainstream Protestant theology since Constantine" that members of the wider society long identified as "Christendom" should not be assumed to confess Christianity and are thus not properly addressed on the grounds of Christian faith.[36] By contrast, those who do confess faith in Christ should be addressed from the standpoint of this confession in the context of the church; that is what distinguishes the church from civil society and that is also what distinguishes Christian ethics from other kinds of ethics.[37]

Yoder stresses that the difference between the church and civil society to which Barth attends is not a difference of "levels" or "realms," nor is it a distinction between vocations or sociological types, whereby it is assumed that the church has a particular, limited role in society and when one enters a different arena, say the government, then one simply needs to abide by a different set of ethical criteria. Instead, what Yoder claims Barth is opening up in his distinction between the church and civil society is a difference between the community of those whose decisions about every area of life—social or political or institutional—are subject to the Lordship of Jesus Christ and the community that includes those who have not yet accepted such a subjection in every arena of life.[38] When posed this way, the difference between the church and civil society is a difference that matters because the difference between confessing Jesus Christ and not confessing Jesus Christ takes on a signficance that it cannot when everyone in civil society is assumed to be Christian, whether

---

34. Ibid., 107. For Barth's discussion of civil society versus the church, see Barth, *Community, State, and Church*, 151.

35. Yoder, *Royal Priesthood*, 151.

36. Ibid., 108.

37. Ibid., 109.

38. Ibid., 108–9.

or not they have made such a confessional decision.[39] Yoder claims that Barth has correctly identified the "the most important error" of the Christendom vision, which is "the ascription of a Christian loyalty or duty to those who have made no confession and, thereby, denying to the non-confessing creation the freedom of unbelief that the nonresistance of God in creation gave to a rebellious humanity."[40]

The church that no longer ascribes Christian identity to everyone is now liberated (and commanded) to proclaim in its life together the whole gospel that it has received. In other words, the church that has been liberated from its Constantinian captivity is now able to say more, rather than less, about God's command as it was given in the life of Jesus Christ. The church can speak and act with the confidence that the way of life given to it in the proclamation of the gospel is the life that God intends for the whole world, even when the world continues to reject it.[41] It is a real community, not a sideshow in support of the nation or the empire.

Yoder makes it clear that this kind of church that does not require validation by the terms of civil society is the free church or believers church, whether or not Barth is willing to call it that and even if Barth is unwilling to go so far as to accept rebaptism as a valid correction of a mistaken attribution of faith. Yoder points out that even though Barth did not start out with this ecclesial vision, it is where he ends up, even to the point of accepting the critique of infant baptism in *Church Dogmatics IV*.[42] Moreover, Yoder insists, this free church vision of Barth's is "not rehabilitating orthodoxy or establishment."[43]

39. Ibid., 109.
40. Ibid.
41. Yoder, "Karl Barth: Kept Changing," 170–71; Yoder, *Karl Barth*, 173.
42. Yoder, "Karl Barth: Kept Changing," 170; Yoder, *Karl Barth*, 173. For Karl Barth's qualified repudiation of infant baptism, see Barth, *Church Dogmatics* IV.4, 193–94.
43. Yoder, "Karl Barth: Kept Changing," 171; Yoder, *Karl Barth*, 174. It seems to me that a statement like this by Yoder quite clearly challenges those, such as Craig Carter, who want to insist that Yoder learned orthodoxy from Karl Barth. Carter, *Politics of the Cross*, 61–90. At the same time, it should be clear from the argument laid out thus far that Yoder is not simply "heterodox" either, as Paul Martens would have it. Martens, *Heterodox Yoder*, 144–45. "Not rehabilitating orthodoxy" is not to be equated with repudiating or even dissenting from orthodoxy. Rather, Yoder is following Karl Barth by insisting that the command of God is not reducible to an abstract formula of any kind, which is not the same thing as saying that an abstract formula that establishes guidelines in a given setting for determining what is true does not ever have some limited value, even if it should not be used as a basis for determining for all times and

Perhaps even more significantly, Yoder questions the logic of analogy that Barth uses to describe the free church's witness to the world. Yoder argues that the church is not merely a communication vehicle by which the command of God can be heard by the world, say insofar as it provides a model or an example of what God wills or is simply a channel for a prior message.[44] Rather, the life of the church "is itself the beginning of what is to come," the actual existence in the world of the way of Jesus Christ.[45] The church, when it is faithful, is the real beginning of the coming kingdom. Such a church is a real church right here and right now, not a virtual representation of some other more real presence, whether Jesus in the heart or Jesus in the next dispensation.

This argument about the church's existence as the new world on the way is most fully developed in Yoder's *Body Politics* where he explains how it is that the church is called to be today what the world is called to be ultimately.[46] Unfortunately, this turn by Yoder toward the church's practices as its witness to the world is often interpreted as a reductionist move in which the church's life is politicized and evacuated of specific theological content.[47] However, from this reading of Yoder's appropriation and extension of Barthian theology, it is at least as plausible to

---

places what it is that God is or is not saying in the life, death, and resurrection of Jesus Christ. Or as Yoder said with reference to Barth's use of the Bible, "Creeds and compendia are respected but made relative." Barth's appeal to the Bible "eschews any claim to 'higher ground' or general validity from which truth claims could be 'validated' . . . In this respect Barth is not precritical but postmodern." Yoder, "Karl Barth: Kept Changing," 169; Yoder, *Karl Barth*, 172. To say that Yoder is "heterodox" is already to accept the criteria of orthodoxy rather than the event of Jesus Christ as the criterion for meaningful evaluation. A parallel critique of Martens appears in note 150 of chapter 1. Rather than say that Yoder is orthodox or heterodox, it would be more accurate to say that Yoder is biblical, insofar as he accepts the canonical scriptures as authoritative for theological and ethical discernment in a way that perhaps relativizes the authority of creedal statements that are deemed "orthodox." In this context we can also recall the conversation with Yoder that J. Denny Weaver recalled in the Introduction, in which Yoder suggested that rather than defining our theology in relation to standard orthodoxy, we should do theology that was "specific to Jesus."

44. Yoder, *Royal Priesthood*, 125.

45. Ibid., 126.

46. Yoder, *Body Politics*, ix. Chapter 7 below has extensive discussion of Yoder's ecclesiology as body politics as expression of discipleship to Jesus Christ.

47. See, for example, Paul Martens, who argues that Yoder "reduces the sacraments to social processes." Martens, *HeterodoxYoder*, 138. In my view, Yoder expands the sacraments when he describes them as social processes. For an additional critique of this charge, see note 41 in chapter 7.

understand Yoder to be enlarging the material of the church's witness to include not just the specific doctrinal content of the gospel message (such as that which is often associated with historic orthodoxy) but also the social and ethical form in which that message was once delivered to the saints and by which it is made visible in the life of the church today.[48] This enlargement is what makes the church not merely a vehicle for true knowledge but an instance of real saved life. In the following section I argue why Yoder's framing of the church's witness in terms of concrete social practices should be seen as such an expression of a fuller, rather than a reduced, gospel witness.

Reconciled World

Barth clearly understood the church's mission in terms of the redemption and reconciliation that God had accomplished for the world, indeed for the whole creation. In *Church Dogmatics IV.2*, for example, in the same section glossed by Yoder in his essay "Why Ecclesiology is Social Ethics" as discussed above, Barth writes that "If the community were to imagine that the reach of the sanctification of humanity accomplished in Jesus Christ were restricted to itself and the ingathering of believers . . . it would be in flat contradiction of its own confession of its Lord."[49] While the sanctification of the world is the sanctification of Jesus Christ, this sanctification is a "game-changer" for the whole world, a liberation and reconciliation of creation that is on offer everywhere, even as it is most clearly and definitively offered in the context of the faithful church—the community that participates in the sanctifying work of Jesus Christ.[50]

Following this line of argument in Barth, Yoder acknowledges that through Jesus Christ, God has sanctified the world by sending it in a different, reconciling direction than the destructive one it blindly continues to affirm. By acknowledging this salvation and sanctification that God has accomplished for the world, Yoder is not conceding that the apparent or "natural" world is by itself now a ground of authority for our lives.

---

48. It is often assumed that by shifting the focus of the church's witness to social processes, Yoder has stripped the gospel of its particular content so as to make it more accessible to the surrounding culture. However, it appears that Yoder actually makes the gospel more, rather than less, particular by acknowledging that something as specific as the decision-making process of the church is a feature of its witness.

49. Barth, *Church Dogmatics* IV.2, 723.

50. Ibid., 516–17.

Instead, this recognition that God has sanctified the world and its history through Jesus Christ makes it possible for us to receive this world and its history with gratitude—to "see history doxologically" which is to "describe the cosmos in terms dictated by the knowledge that a once slaughtered Lamb is now living."[51] Alex Sider points out seeing history doxologically (or reading it christologically) led Yoder to place an even higher value than Barth on the life of the church in heralding God's sanctification of the creation. This is because for Yoder in the life and worship of the church the self-emptying of this slain Lamb is vindicated and the creation itself renewed.[52]

Perhaps Barth granted less significance to the church's visible sanctification than did Yoder because of his conviction that the sanctification of the world remains hidden in Christ and thus the ethical actions associated with such sanctification cannot be described independently of the life of Jesus Christ.[53] Thus, in Barth's argument, insofar as this goodness is hidden in Christ, it remains free from captivity to moral orders based on human will and power alone that lead ultimately to death and destruction, as do all human projects of self-assertion and independence against the Word of God.[54] Barth was responding here to the assimilation of Christian theology and ethics to the autonomy of Enlightenment reason in the modern era, as well as to his perception that Catholic moral theology had granted too much authority to natural theology.

By contrast, Yoder emphasizes that what has been hidden in Jesus Christ is made visible in the church and therefore throughout the world.[55] Moreover the precise and defining form of that sanctification has taken shape in the church's actual participation in the self-emptying service of Jesus Christ to his enemies. It is because of this defining feature of the church's reality, when it is faithful, that the sanctification of the world can be received with gratitude, without the worry that such gratitude will end up simply celebrating the triumph of secular reason.[56]

---

51. Yoder, *Royal Priesthood*, 128.

52. Sider, *To See History Doxologically*, 48.

53. Barth, *Church Dogmatics* I.2, 782–83.

54. See Gerald McKenny's thoughtful explanation of how Barth invoked the hiddenness of sanctification in order to deflect naturalistic accounts of ethics. McKenny, *Analogy of Grace*, 140–43.

55. This is the thrust of Yoder's *Body Politics* in which he argues that the church makes visible in its life the calling of the world. See Yoder, *Body Politics*, vi–xi.

56. Yoder's essay "To Serve Our God and Rule the World" makes clear the

Some of Yoder's interpreters, most notably Stanley Hauerwas, have highlighted the extent to which the church's witness makes visible the worldliness of the world, its dividedness and its lack of a future.[57] But there is in Yoder's writing a notable extension of the Barthian affirmation of the world's sanctification, a curiosity about the ways in which the world is already reflecting in its witting or unwitting discoveries and actions the reality of the slain Lamb's sanctification and reconciliation of all things.[58]

Indeed, Hauerwas has convincingly demonstrated that the witness of Barth stands behind Yoder's well-known apocalyptic statement that "People who bear crosses are working with the grain of the universe."[59] This statement, perhaps more than any other, captures the decisive qualification of Barth's insistence on the world's sanctification in the life of Jesus Christ by making the self-emptying and reconciling practices of

relationship between the kenotic and doxological form of the church's life and the anxiety-free embrace of those evidences of reconciliation that appear in the world's history. Because the church sees history doxologically, it can, for example, "claim for the Gospel its share of those democratizing thrusts which have created in North Atlantic societies more space for political dialogue than ever or anywhere before" (135).

57. Hauerwas, *Community of Character*, 91–94.

58. The presence of the church in the world makes it possible to recognize those practices in the world that witness to the truth of Christ's lordship in service, his triumph in weakness, and his justice in peace. This is why not every Christian celebration or advocacy of nonviolence or restorative justice requires an accompanying theological narrative that situates the event properly in a christological framework, even though that is an important gift that Christian theologians and ethicists contribute to the witness of the church. The more important framework for recognizing the world's sanctification is already here in the life of the church. So, for example, it is possible to advocate for nonviolent solutions to human conflict in terms that acknowledge the connection of these solutions with a reality that "works" in the most truthful and eternal sense that anything can work, without always accompanying such advocacy with a gospel tract or theological treatise. Yoder describes such a witness as an employment of "middle axioms," which in my view does not contradict and is not superseded by his emphasis on practices in *Body Politics*. See Yoder, *Christian Witness* (2002), 32–35. Chapter 9 to follow has extensive discussion of Yoder's support of initiatives that "work" to extend peace in the real world. For an account of ways that the nonviolence of Jesus Christ can be recognized in the liberal arts curriculum, when it attends to the ways that nonviolence really works in a variety of human contexts, see Weaver and Biesecker-Mast, *Teaching Peace*. For a critique of accounts like *Teaching Peace* on the grounds that they are not christologically specific enough, see Derksen, "Milbank and Nonviolence," 44–49.

59. Hauerwas, *With the Grain*, 215–25. The well-known quote from Yoder about the relationship between cross-bearing and the universe's grain is from Yoder, "Armaments and Eschatology," 58. With the same application Yoder wrote of the "grain of the cosmos" in Yoder, *Politics of Jesus* (1994), 246.

those who participate in the body of Christ definitive of the salvation that has been accomplished by God in Christ for the whole world. Cross-bearing gives meaning to all of those practices by which God's salvation is made visible in the world and it is itself part of the momentum associated with the cosmos's subjection to the rule of Jesus Christ. That subjection includes the power of nonresistance and the refusal to force a subjection that is not freely chosen, a refusal that continues to be visible in the defenselessness of the church and therefore in the peace that the world discovers.

For Yoder, more than for Barth, it is the life and obedience of the church (not only the proper narration of that life by its theologians and scholars) that animates the hidden truth of the world's sanctification and that attributes the nonviolence that is really practiced in the world to the Lordship of the Prince of Peace. This redemption-defining life of the body of Christ may include the theologians who write about such things as "atonement" and "sanctification" but more importantly it is the real church gathered for worship and discernment, sharing bread and wine, binding and loosing in the power of the Holy Spirit, and caring for the world that God has entrusted to it.[60]

This church is distinguished from the world, separated from it, not only so that the world can know that it is the world, as Hauerwas emphasizes, but so that the world can come to know its own sanctity as the deepest and largest reality of existence. If the church is simply collapsed into the world, the sanctity of the world is lost because of the disappearance of the church's witness, including its freedom to proclaim in word and deed the new world, the coming kingdom, and the actual realization of this kingdom on the shores of the present. That is why the church is necessary for the world's salvation, even though that salvation is not limited to the church. That is also why the "common grace" sometimes spoken about in Reformed theology should not be understood as something different from the grace of Jesus Christ that is offered to all.[61]

---

60. Yoder, *Body Politics*, 26–27.

61. In his meditation on common grace from a Calvinist perspective, Richard Mouw correctly writes that "the Spirit of the reigning Lamb is indeed active in our world, not only in gathering the company of the redeemed from the tribes and nations of the earth, but also in working mysteriously to restrain sin in the lives of those who continue in their rebellion, and even in stimulating works of righteousness in surprising places." See Mouw, *He Shines*, 86–87.

This sanctification and reconciliation already present in the world is dramatically visible in the story of three American members of Christian Peacemaker Teams who were in Iraq when the United States attacked that country in March 2003 with cluster bombs and guided missiles during the "schock and awe" of that war's beginning. As they careened out of Baghdad crammed in a small car, Shane Claiborne, Cliff Kindy, and Weldon Nisly found themselves injured and stranded in a war torn landscape after losing control of their car, following an explosion. In the hours and days that followed, these American Christians were rescued and cared for by Sunni Muslims from the city of Rutba, where American bombs and missiles had just destroyed their hospital and brutally killed many of the city's inhabitants. Shaine Claiborne eloquently states the sanctification of the world he and his two American friends discovered among the Muslims of Rutba: "Even though the people of Rutba have suffered some of the most horrific stuff human beings can do to one another, there is this constant, steady, almost instinctive witness of goodness and grace."[62] For Claiborne, the hospitality of enemies he experienced in Rutba strengthened his Christian faith: "even though many of my friends in Iraq are Muslim, I feel like I am a better Christian for knowing them."[63]

In *The Politics of Jesus*, Yoder declares that "it is the Good News that my enemy and I are united, through no merit or work of our own, in a new humanity that forbids henceforth my ever taking his or her life in my hands."[64] Surely it is this Good News that those three Christian Peacemaker Teams members witnessed in their experience of being loved by their enemies. It is also this Good News that Yoder read in the works of Karl Barth—the conviction that the merciful and enemy-loving grace of God as exhibited in the life of Jesus Christ and offered to the world is also the command of God: to love our enemies as God has loved us and so to make visible in the real church God's concrete reconciliation of the world in Jesus Christ. Yoder's deconstruction of Barth reveals a Jesus Christ more concrete, a church more real, and a world more reconciled than Barth's theology at first suggests. Because the sanctification of the world in Jesus Christ is an actual event, not only a theological narrative, it is possible for a cup of water to be offered to Jesus Christ, without anyone saying "Lord," for enemies to be reconciled without someone speaking

62. Barrett, *Gospel of Rutba*, 140.
63. Ibid., 141.
64. Yoder, *Politics of Jesus* (1994), 226.

first of the cross. This is so, not because the world now stands on its own, but because the church exists, because the real body of Jesus Christ gathers, worships, and obeys.

Conclusion

In conclusion, Yoder's interaction with Karl Barth's teaching and writing display a similar posture to that found in his interaction with other important sources for his theology, from sixteenth-century Anabaptism to Bender's Anabaptist Vision to Oscar Cullmann. Yoder learned much from Barth and also pushed beyond the limits of Barth's theology in the areas of Christology, ecclesiology, and cosmology.[65] Thus Yoder should not be identified simply as a Barthian, but rather as a Christian theologian concerned most of all in expressing discipleship of Jesus Christ, using whatever sources are helpful in strengthening attachment to Jesus Christ, and putting aside all that detracts from such a radical theological and practical attachment. It is this attachment to Jesus Christ, the root of Christian faith and practice, that makes Yoder a radical theologian.

---

65. In the conclusion to his essay on how Barth's mind kept changing, Yoder called "unfinished" Barth's "path from mainline to radical churchmanshcip" and the *Church Dogmatics* a "torso." But the real reason they are unfinished, he said, is that the free church position toward which Barth was moving is itself "intrinsically unfinished." "The freedom of the church is a command and a hope." Yoder, "Karl Barth: Kept Changing," 171; Yoder, *Karl Barth*, 174.

PART THREE

Extending John Howard Yoder's Theology

The chapters of Part Three are not a random collection of items that just happen to concern John Howard Yoder. Each chapter makes an extension or application of the view of Yoder's Christology that was sketched in chapter 1. In contrast to earlier thinking that would separate the religion of Jesus from the theology of Paul, in chapter 6 Ted Grimsrud demonstrates that for Yoder, Paul continued the story of Jesus, and that Paul's theology was derived from that narrative. Earl Zimmerman's chapter 7 displays the way that for Yoder, living out of the narrative of Jesus produces the visible church that poses a nonviolent witness to the world. Yoder's *Body Politics*, for example, is an extension of his understanding of sixteenth-century Anabaptism. In chapter 8, Gerald Mast develops and extends Yoder's understanding that patient suffering is indeed a witness that confronts evil with the power to change it. Glen Stassen develops the activist, even interventionist dimension of Yoder's nonviolent ethic in chapter 9. This element of Yoder's peace ethic is less well known, but Stassen's chapter reflects the book Yoder was working on at the time of his death. Chapter 10 deals with one of the most important applications of Yoder's Christology, namely its potential to change the nature of interfaith dialogue. J. Denny Weaver and Earl Zimmerman summarize Yoder's approach to the Jewish-Christian schism along with the parallel analysis of Jewish scholar Daniel Boyarin, and then use comments from Yoder's website to extend the interfaith discussion to Islam and Hinduism. Chapter 11 by J. Denny Weaver and Gerald Mast illustrates three ways to appropriate

Yoder's approach. First, the authors sketch a theological model that is a result of going through the doors Yoder opened to developing new theological imagery in our modern context. Then it displays two other theological matrices and indicates how Yoder and Yoder-oriented theology can enter into these ongoing conversations. What these seemingly different chapters have in common is their roots in Yoder's approach to Christology. Following these discussions stimulated by Yoder's theology proper, the final two chapters deal with the major dilemma posed by the fact that Yoder's hurtful, personal behavior with numerous women was in sharp contrast to his peace theology. In chapter 12, Ted Grimsrud describes the dilemma, along with a statement of learnings from Yoder and a suggestion that nothing in Yoder's theology reflects this misconduct. In chapter 13, Gerald Mast situates the enigma of Yoder's conduct vis-à-vis his peace theology in the context of the expectations for a changed life that exists in Anabaptist theology from the sixteenth-century to the present, and suggests that the outrage at Yoder's behavior actually reflects the way that Yoder's theology has contributed to this expectation. While he does not argue that Yoder's theology allowed for his behavior, Mast does offer suggestions for further theological development so that transgressions by individuals do not appear to threaten the entire edifice of Anabaptist theology.

6

Jesus to Paul

TED GRIMSRUD

A somewhat overlooked element of John Howard Yoder's argument about the normativity of the "politics of Jesus" for present-day Christians has been his effort to show that, contrary to traditional assumptions, the thought of the Apostle Paul actually reinforces Jesus' social-ethical message.[1] In fact, Yoder uses quite a bit more space in *The Politics of Jesus* making the case for Paul's support for Jesus' agenda than he does in outlining the content of that agenda in the Gospels. Earl Zimmerman's earlier chapter pointed to the influence of Oscar Cullmann's research on Yoder's theology, including his understanding of Paul. This chapter will sketch Yoder's argument that Paul supported and extended the nonviolent social message of Jesus.[2]

As a prelude to seeing Yoder's rather extensive use of Paul in *The Politics of Jesus*, we do well to appropriate for the purpose of the present chapter Yoder's comments on Paul's methodology from chapter 1. The analysis of that chapter dealt with Yoder's approach to Christology in *Preface to Theology*, a writing that existed in some form before he wrote

---

1. An exception is Harink, *Paul among the Postliberals*.

2. With significant revisions and additions, this chapter draws on material that appeared in another form in Grimsrud, "Against Empire."

The Politics of Jesus. These lectures display Yoder's clear assumption that Paul's thought was an extension and reinforcement of the narrative of Jesus as gospel.

After pointing to six sermons in Acts as the early church's first statements about Jesus, Yoder wrote that in 1 Corinthians 15, Paul was using the same narrative outline. Thus Paul's theologizing was a continuation of the theologizing of the early church. Yoder described the concept of "solidarity," which lay behind Paul's linking of Jesus' resurrection to belief in a general resurrection and the salvation of believers. And Yoder noted that Paul assumed the Old Testament story of Israel, with Adam as the representative of human solidarity. Thus as chapter 1 said, "Yoder was demonstrating how Paul's theologizing was extending and developing additional meanings from the earliest narrative about Jesus." The point that Paul was extending the meaning of Jesus is underscored by Paul's argument that one judges the truth of the message of the spirits by whether or not their message is contrary to Jesus.

From Galatians, Yoder pointed out that Paul used a variety of ways to make a connection between Jesus and his readers. Paul appealed to Abraham to demonstrate "grace" prior to the law of Moses. He called believers sons of Abraham. In Galatians 6 Paul expressed the idea of solidarity in terms of the cross of Christ as a stance to the world in which the believer shares.

In other words, in the *Preface* lectures, Yoder pointed to multiple ways that Paul's writings appealed to or assumed the narrative of Jesus. Paul linked his thought to Jesus and to the history of Israel that had produced Jesus and which Jesus was fulfilling. With this material in view from chapter 1 of the volume in hand, it should not surprise that significant parts of *The Politics of Jesus* can emphasize the continuity of Paul with the social-ethical message that Yoder found in Jesus.

Yoder makes two central arguments in *The Politics of Jesus*. The first is to show that it is possible to read the story of Jesus (in fact, it is the best reading of this story) to teach that he is "of direct significance for social ethics."[3] The second argument is that what Jesus actually said and did in relation to social ethics remains normative for our present day. In making this second argument, Yoder turns to the writings of the Apostle Paul since these writings have so often been interpreted in ways that marginalize Jesus' own message.

---

3. Yoder, *Politics of Jesus* (1994), 11.

Rather than seeing Jesus and Paul as representing two more or less mutually exclusive approaches to ethical life, Yoder suggests that we should see Paul as a faithful and accurate interpreter of Jesus' message. Jesus and Paul are not stage one and stage two of the development of Christian ethics that leads inevitably to Constantinianism. Rather, whatever we understand to be central to Jesus' message we should also expect to find in Paul's message as well.

Yoder spelled out his affirmation of the close link between Jesus and Paul—and the latter's central relevance for our appropriation of the messianic ethic—in a series of chapters in *The Politics of Jesus* on four key elements of Paul's thought. These include discussions of Paul's portrayal of the social character of justification, Paul's challenge to the hegemony of the Powers, Paul's call to revolutionary subordination, and Paul's political perspective according to Romans 13.

The Social Character of Justification

One central way that the majority Christian tradition has created a tension between Jesus' life and Paul's theology is in its understanding of Paul's concept of "justification."[4] In the tradition, the words and deeds of Jesus end up on the margins of theological and ethical development as a result of the belief that Paul had narrowed down the core of the gospel to justification by faith alone.

In this reading, Paul opposed any approach to salvation that could be focused in piety, religious practices, or ethical behavior in ways that would turn the believer's attention toward human good works rather than toward salvation as a free gift from God. As Yoder put it in his summary of the traditional reading, "Does not the insistence that justification is by faith alone and through grace alone, apart from any correlation with works of any kind, undercut any radical ethical and social concern by implication?"[5] Even if Jesus himself taught and practiced a countercultural social ethics, it was argued in the mainstream theological tradition, this part of his message had no long-term relevance. Paul understood that well and zeroed in on what matters most—justification by faith alone apart from "works righteousness."

---

4. Ibid., 212.
5. Ibid., 213.

But according to Yoder, this is not an accurate reading of Paul's actual teaching. Yoder asserted that for Paul "justification" has at its heart ethical, *social* concerns. According to Yoder, Paul's central concerns were with the social character of the messianic community. Depending on a well-known article by Krister Stendahl,[6] Yoder wrote that for Paul, faith was not primarily a subjective experience. "Paul was not preoccupied with his guilt and seeking the assurance of a gracious God." For Paul, faith was "not a particular spiritual exercise of moving from self-trust through despair to confidence in the paradoxical goodness of the judgment of God." Rather, faith concerned what separated Jewish Christians from other Jews, namely the belief "that in Jesus of Nazareth the Messiah had come." Paul was not really struggling with whether Jewish Christians had to keep the law, Yoder said. Paul's concern rather was that Jewish Christians had failed to recognize that with the Messiah, "the covenant of God had been broken open to include the Gentiles." Thus Paul's concern was with the social form of the church. And Yoder could ask concerning this community, "Was it to be a new and inexplicable kind of community of both Jews and Gentiles, or was it going to be a confederation of a Jewish Christian sect and a Gentile one? Or would all the Gentiles have first to become Jews according to the conditions of pre-messianic proselytism?"[7]

Paul's statement in Galatians 3:24 reflects this new, social reality. "Gentiles do not need to pass by way of the law, but can be incorporated directly into the new community." This incorporation of Gentiles into the community was a recognition of Paul's own sin. Before he recognized that the Messiah had come in Jesus, "he had persecuted the church and fought the opening of God's covenant to the Gentiles." Paul was now setting things right. But this setting right was not that "he has overcome inner resistances" and has come "to trust God for his right status before God." Rather, the change is now that "Paul has become the agent of the action of God for the right cause." Before meeting Jesus, Paul himself had *violently* persecuted followers of Jesus in the name of strict and exclusionary boundary markers that would keep Gentile Christians out. Thus Paul's theology of justification by faith in Galatians and Romans emerges directly from his own experience as the perpetrator of social injustice—and speaks to how important he now saw it to be that the churches embody the new social reality of reconciled enemies that Jesus inaugurated.[8]

6. Stendahl, "Apostle Paul."
7. Yoder, *Politics of Jesus* (1994), 215–16.
8. Ibid., 216–17.

When Paul proclaimed the "righteousness" (or justice) of God—the message of justification—he emphasized that the message goes forth "to both Jew and Gentile." That is, the message goes out to *both*, together, whether or not they have come by way of the law, with the intent that they join in one new community devoted to embodying the way of Jesus. This reconciliation of these former human enemies reflects the reconciliation that is most central for Paul. He was less concerned with the end of "hostility" between God and human beings (as a good Jew, he understood God to be merciful) as the end of the hostility between Jew and Gentile.[9]

Paul argued in Galatians (see especially 2:14–21) that Jews and Gentiles must be joined together in *one* fellowship. "To be 'justified' is to be set right in and for that [new social] relationship." The term "justification" in Galatians hence links with the later language in Ephesians about "making peace" and "breaking down the wall" that previously alienated Jews and Gentiles.[10]

Paul's most detailed theological statement, his letter to the Romans, also picks up this sense of the social nature of justification, that is, reconciliation of former enemies. Citing another author, Yoder points out,

> The issue of the polarity of Jew and Gentile is present at major turning points throughout the argument of the book, as well as in the introduction and conclusion. The foreground meaning of the issue of the place of the law was not systematic theological speculation about how human beings are to made acceptable to God.

Yoder thus emphasized that the problem of Romans was not about a subjective experience of becoming acceptable to God, "but rather the very concrete situation in which Jew and Greek, legalistic Christian and pagan Christian need to accept one another."[11]

In his summary of Paul, Yoder emphasized that for Paul, reconciliation was "a real experience," (that is, not limited to an inner or subjective experience), and the message Paul proclaimed was the same message that Jesus had given early in his ministry. Paul "says that the triumph of God's love in his own sustaining of his creation is that he blesses equally insider and outsider, friend and enemy in such manner that the genuineness (Jesus said, 'perfection') of our love is also made real at the point

9. Ibid., 217, 218–19.
10. Ibid., 220.
11. Ibid., 223–24.

of its application to the enemy, the Gentile, the sinner." This reconciliation produces a "new humanity." The demonstration "par excellence" of this new, reconciled humanity concerns its inclusion of "enmity between peoples, the extension of neighbor love to the enemy, and the renunciation of violence even in the most righteous cause. . . . It is the Good News that my enemy and I are united, through no merit or work of our own, in a new humanity that forbids henceforth my ever taking his or her life in my hands."[12]

Yoder's discussion of justification by faith showed that for Paul, justification envisioned a social entity, namely the church, in which former enemies, that is Jews and Gentiles, were reconciled. This social entity of reconciled former enemies is a continuation of the social ethic of Jesus. Yoder is thus very clear that no disjuncture exists between Jesus and Paul on the matter of justification.

Paul's Social Analysis: The Powers That Be

Another important way that Jesus' messianic ethic has been marginalized in the history of Christianity is the assumption that he did not give us a social philosophy but spoke rather primarily to the personal realm. "One of the strands in the argument against the normative claims made by or for Jesus has always been that his radical personalism is not relevant to problems of power and structure."[13] Even less has Paul been understood as providing a way of applying Jesus' ethical directives to our social lives.[14] Yoder suggests, however, that we have in Paul's writings insights that do speak directly to social ethics. And these insights help us make sense of Jesus' message and strengthen both the link between the social ethics of Jesus and Paul and between theirs and ours.

Using insights gained from Hendrik Berkhof,[15] Yoder teases out Paul's social thought under the rubric of "the Powers." The language of

12. Ibid., 225–26.
13. Ibid., 134.
14. Ibid., 135–36.
15. See Berkhof, *Christ and the Powers*. Chapter 7 below also deals with Yoder's use of Berkhof. In the years since the publication of *The Politics of Jesus* in 1972, what Yoder called "the most thorough review of the theme" of the Powers is the work of Walter Wink: Wink, Naming *Naming the Powers*; Wink, *Unmasking the Powers*; Wink, *Engaging the Powers*. Yoder's description of Wink's trilogy is Yoder, *Politics of Jesus* (1994), 159.

"the Powers" provides a way to speak of the structures of human life, realities beyond the activities of individual persons or even beyond simply the sum of separate individuals. This language speaks metaphorically about the discrete "personalities" and even "wills" that these structures possess and exercise. Thus the powers include our institutions, traditions, social practices, belief systems, organizations, languages, and so on, that impact human behavior. Examples of this impacting activity might range from the spirit of a college campus that shapes informal socializing without written rules, or the atmosphere that turns a gathering of people into a hostile mob, to the feeling of citizens that if the president calls the nation to war then war is inevitable and all citizens are obligated to follow. Yoder's method is not to attempt to translate the biblical imagery of powers directly into a modern setting, but to ask what Paul and other New Testament writers mean with this vocabulary, and how that meaning might translate to the modern scene.[16] This use of the recent Powers scholarship is a further application of Yoder's methodological comments described in chapter 1 about not translating the specific language of "pre-existence" or involvement of the Son in creation into our modern language.[17]

The analysis of the six points here reflects Yoder's description of the Powers from Pauline writings.

(1) *The Powers are part of the good creation.* They were brought into being by God as a "divine gift" that makes human social life possible. When God created human beings, necessarily elements of human life such as language, traditions, and ways of ordering community life all came into existence alongside of and as a part of the normal functioning of individual human beings. And like the original human beings, the Powers were also good.[18]

This aspect of created reality is linked with Jesus Christ himself in Colossians 1: "He is the image of the invisible God, the firstborn of all creation; for in him all things in heaven and on earth were created, things visible and invisible, whether thrones or dominions or rulers or powers—all things have been created through him and for him. He himself is before all things, and in him all things hold together" (Col 1:15–17). Here the "Powers" include "thrones, dominions, rulers" and "the elemental spirits" in Galatians 4:3, 9. Today, Yoder suggests, we may want to say that

16. Yoder, *Politics of Jesus* (1994), 136, 138.
17. In chapter 1, see the text related to notes 57 and 132.
18. Yoder, *Politics of Jesus* (1994), 140–41, quote 141.

this "Powers" language metaphorically describes the necessary "regularity, system, and order" that human beings require in order to function socially. The Bible teaches that God has provided for these needs via the Powers. The provision is part of the goodness of creation.[19]

(2) *The Powers are fallen.* They are so closely linked with humanity that when human beings turned from God—spoken of traditionally as "the fall" and described in the story of Adam and Eve—so, too, did the Powers. It is as if the Powers, as part of created reality, turn against human beings when humans are alienated from God. The fallen Powers then seek to take God's place as the center of human devotion, often becoming idols. Yoder writes,

> The Powers are no longer active only as mediators of the saving creative purpose of God; now we find them seeking to separate us from the love of God (Rom 8:38); we find them ruling over the lives of those who live far from the love of God (Eph 2:2); we find them holding us in servitude to their rules (Col 2:20); we find them holding us under their tutelage (Gal 4:3). These structures which were supposed to be our servants have become our masters and our guardians.[20]

(3) *The Powers remain necessary.* In spite of their fallenness, the Powers retain their original function. Human beings still require the "regularity, system, and order" that only the Powers provide. "Even tyranny . . . is still better than chaos." Human life still requires ordering; the Powers are still used by God in the sustenance of human social life. In spite of their fallen condition, God "is still able to use them for good."[21]

Consequently, the Powers are *both* a huge part of the problem we face in living in our fallen world *and* a necessary part of whatever solutions we might find. The human dilemma in relation to the Powers is that they are simultaneously a necessary part of our God-ordered existence and an inevitable force that seeks to corrupt this existence and separate us from God. "Our lostness and our survival are inseparable, both dependent upon the Powers."[22]

---

19. Ibid., 140–41.
20. Ibid., 141.
21. Ibid., 141–42.
22. Ibid., 142–43, quote 143.

(4) *The Powers must be "put in their place."* Since the Powers are necessary for ordered existence, Yoder said, they cannot simply be abolished or ignored. With order a necessity for human existence, we must continue to understand ourselves as subject to the Powers. "Subordination to these powers is what makes us human, for if they did not exist there would be no history nor society nor humanity. If then God is going to save his creatures *in their humanity*, the Powers cannot simply be destroyed or set-aside or ignored. Their sovereignty must be broken."[23]

In other words, the Powers must be "put in their place." Ultimately, the Powers have only the power that we give them by our allegiance and acceptance of their distorted portrayal of reality. We need them but they should be our servants, on behalf of life, not our masters and idols that make us become like them. Putting the Powers in their place and revealing their true character is what Jesus has done.

(5) *Jesus conquered the Powers.* Paul asserts that Jesus in fact has done precisely what was needed. He lived, Yoder wrote, "a genuinely free and human existence. This life brought him, as any genuinely human existence will bring anyone, to the cross. In his death the Powers—in this case the most worthy, weighty representatives of Jewish religion and Roman politics—act in collusion."[24]

In responding to Jesus by killing him, however, the Powers actually facilitated their own defeat. Although as a human being he submitted to them, he rejected their authority. "Morally he broke their rules by refusing to support them in their self-glorification." Thus his death was the basis of his victory. "Therefore his cross is a victory, the confirmation that he was free from the rebellious pretensions of the creaturely condition." In his submission to death by the Powers, Jesus demonstrated that he was not a slave to any human institution, whether of "any power, of any law or custom, community or institution, value or theory." This refusal to conform to the Powers even to save his own life was Jesus' exercise of "authentic humanity." Yoder thus proclaims that Jesus' death enables his victory: "Wherefore God has exalted him highly, and given him the name which is above every name . . . That every tongue might confess that Jesus Christ is Lord" (Phil 2:9–11).[25]

---

23. Ibid., 144.
24. Ibid., 144–45.
25. Ibid., 145.

By submitting to death by the Powers, Jesus brought to light their true character. Yoder cited Colossians 2:13–15 to encapsulate the work of Christ. In Yoder's version, verse 15 contains the threefold action: "He disarmed the principalities and powers and made a public example of them, triumphing over them in him."[26]

Yoder followed this biblical citation with a long citation from Hendrik Berkhof to fill out the actions of disarming, making a public example, and triumphing. The Powers all too often are accepted as "the gods of the world." Jesus' faithfulness to the death shows that such an exaltation of the Powers is based on deception. God's presence in Jesus reveals that the Powers that kill Jesus are not God's servants but rebels against God. The religious and political leaders of Jesus time served death, not the God of life. "Obviously, 'none of the rulers of this age,' who let themselves be worshiped as divinities, understood God's wisdom, 'for had they known, they would not have crucified the Lord of glory' (1 Cor 2:8). Now they are unmasked as false gods by their very encounter with Very God; they are made a public spectacle."[27]

Christ's victory over the Powers, already present in their unmasking by the cross, becomes even more clear when God raises Jesus from the dead. In the resurrection, it becomes clear that Jesus' challenge to the Powers was endorsed and vindicated by God. In Jesus, God has ventured into the Powers' territory, remained true to God's loving character, and defeated, that is, disarmed them. They were allowed to defeat themselves by crucifying Jesus. The Powers' main weapon—deluding people into giving the Powers loyalty—was taken from them. Christ's death exposed their illusion. No Powers can separate us from God's love unless we let them. "The cross has disarmed them: wherever it is preached, the unmasking and the disarming of the Powers takes place."[28]

(6) *The Christian vocation is to live in freedom from idolatry of the Powers.* Jesus' followers are called to proclaim and embody his victory. We do so for the sake of giving a witness to the entire world of the truthfulness of God's message of mercy and wholeness. This witness is for the sake of the nations, and indeed for all of creation.

---

26. Ibid.
27. Ibid., 146.
28. Ibid., 146–47.

A crucial part of faithful witness to the Powers, the nations, and all of creation is the formation of the church, namely communities of liberated people whose life together manifests their freedom from idolatry to the powers. For Paul, the way messianic communities include reconciled Jewish and Gentile followers of Jesus stands at the heart of the gospel—reflecting his own transformation from violent zealot to nonviolent servant of Jesus. This social reconciliation, as we saw above, reflects what Paul considered justification to be about. Yoder used Berkhof's words to summarize:

> The very existence of the church in which Gentiles and Jews, who heretofore walked according to the *stoicheia* ('elemental spirits') of the world, live together in Christ's fellowship, is itself a proclamation, a sign, a token to the Powers that their unbroken dominion has come to an end.... All resistance and every attack against the gods of this age will be unfruitful, unless the church herself is resistance and attack, unless she demonstrates in her life and fellowship how men can life freed from the Powers.[29]

The church that embodies the work of Christ does not attack the Powers. Christ has already attacked and defeated them. Rather, "the church concentrates upon not being seduced by them. By existing the church demonstrates that their rebellion has been vanquished." In this demonstration the church is fully involved in the world. It is "a sample of the kind of humanity within which, for example, economic and racial differences are surmounted."[30]

The following chapter considers Yoder's use of the Powers as a function of his ecclesiology. In this present chapter, the emphasis has fallen on demonstrating that for Yoder, the Pauline concept of the Powers constitutes another instance to show that Paul extended and reinforced the social message of Jesus, and did so in language that is relevant in society today. As Yoder concluded, when the language of the Powers is made relevant for the contemporary world,

> we have found one more point at which the ethical relevance of the stance of Jesus breaks through in a segment of the apostolic literature with which for generations most Protestants did not know how to deal. The Powers have been defeated not by some kind of cosmic hocus-pocus but by the concreteness of the cross;

---

29. Ibid., 147–48.
30. Ibid., 150.

the impact of the cross upon them is not the working of magical words nor the fulfillment of a legal contract calling for the shedding of innocent blood, but the sovereign presence, within the structures of creature orderliness, of Jesus the kingly claimant and of the church who herself is a structure and a power in society. Thus the historicity of Jesus retains, in the working of the church as it encounters the other power and value structures of its history, the same kind of relevance that the man Jesus had for those whom he served until they killed him.[31]

Revolutionary Subordination: Neither Fight nor Flight

Yoder used the *Haustafeln* to demonstrate in yet another way both that Jesus had a social ethic, and that Paul and other New Testament writers continued that ethic. Frequently identified with the German term *Haustafeln*, several lists of "household rules" or expectations for interpersonal relationships are attributed to Paul and other New Testament writers. Yoder quoted the lists from Colossians 3:18—4:1, Ephesians 5:21—6:9, and 1 Peter 2:13—3:7.[32] He showed that the writers' use of the *Haustafeln* was not a borrowing of rules from Stoic or non-Christian sources that reinforced the existing social order. Rather, he argued, these lists continue Jesus' social message in a way that challenges the social order.

In his analysis of the *Haustafeln*, Yoder not only stated once again the social ethic of Jesus. He also used this argument to display in another way that no chasm existed between Jesus and Paul, and that in fact Paul was extending the social ethic of Jesus. Yoder argued that these rules, when read in the broader context of the New Testament, constitute a message of what he called "revolutionary subordination."[33] The household rules call upon Christians to walk with Jesus in their responses to social situations. Rather than merely endorsing status quo power arrangements, Yoder said, they call on all parties—both those in the "lower" or subordinate position and those in the "superior" or dominant position—to challenge the status quo.

In Yoder's interpretation, in contrast to their lack of power in the wider society, Paul addressed those of lower social standing as free "moral

31. Ibid., 158.
32. Ibid., 162–63.
33. Chapter 9 is titled "Revolutionary Subordination," in Yoder, *Politics of Jesus* (1994).

agents." The wife or other person in this lesser social status is addressed not as one who merely lives out a predefined role, but as one who is a "decision maker," a woman who has "personal moral responsibility." Yoder noted that Paul's term *hypotassesthai* does not mean "subjection" or "submission," but is better rendered as "subordination." "Sub*ord*ination means the acceptance of an *order*, as it exists, but with the new meaning given to it by the fact that one's acceptance of it is willing and meaningfully motivated."[34] Paul is thus telling the lower status persons that rather than claiming that their new freedom in Christ called for efforts to overthrow or rebel against the existing order, they are called to choose to live within it. In this subordination, their model is the person of Christ, who subordinated himself to the existing order even when unjustly accused.[35]

Yoder calls this subordination revolutionary for two reasons. In contrast to the prevailing society, it addresses the lower status person as a free moral agent, and it calls on these persons to live within rather than attempt to rebel against the social order.[36] Thus these addressees have indeed been liberated in Christ and welcomed into membership in Christ's assembly. However, quite likely they are not in positions to claim that liberation fully in the wider society while at the same time remaining (as they must) wholly committed to Jesus' path of loving their neighbors.

But revolutionary subordination applies not only to those of lower status as defined by the wider society. The "dominant partner" in a relationship is also called to a kind of subordination that actually expects more of the dominant partner than of the lower partner. In the newness of the messianic community, Paul called on husbands, masters, and parents also to practice subordination to those "below" them. This subordination is revolutionary. It is anything but an acceptance of roles defined by the wider society. This subordination "relativize[s]and undercut[s] this order." "For a first-century husband to love (*agapan*) his wife, or for a first-century father to avoid angering his child, or for a first-century master to deal with his servant in the awareness that they are both slaves to a higher master, is to make a more concrete and more sweeping difference in the way that husband or father or master behaves than the other

---

34. Ibid., 171, 172; Yoder's italics.
35. Ibid., 176.
36. Ibid., 171–73.

imperative of subordination would have made practically in the behavior of the wife or child or servant."[37]

As understood by Yoder, subordination does not connote slavish obedience or submission. Yoder defines it in relation to Jesus, and it can and even should include active resistance. In an extended note, Yoder quoted from work by Johannes Hamel, who referred to Philippians 2:5ff. Hamel concludes that when applied to Jesus, *hypotassesthai* "is in every situation a free, extremely aggressive way of acting, taking very clear account of the situation, including feeling and understanding and will, always including the possibility of a spirit-driven resistance, of an appropriate disavowal and a refusal, ready to accept suffering at this or that particular point."[38] Chapter 9 to follow develops this activist dimension of Yoder's ethic derived from Jesus' rejection of violence and subordination to Roman authorities.

With this interpretation of the *Haustafeln* in view, Yoder noted that its ethical structure occurs in other texts of the New Testament as well. He writes that with such texts, "the Christian is called to view social status from the perspective of maximizing freedom." If an opportunity occurs for more freedom, by all means take that opportunity. "But that freedom can already be realized within his present status by voluntarily accepting subordination [within the structure of the social order], in view of the relative unimportance of such social distinctions when seen in the light of the coming fulfillment of God's purposes." Without any specific linkage to the texts of the *Haustafeln*, Romans 13 expresses their call for subordination to the government, which concerns the next section of this chapter. Different from the *Haustafeln* structure, however, is that subordination to government is not reciprocal. There is no call for "the king to conceive of himself as a public servant."[39]

In his summary of the meaning of voluntary subordination, Yoder writes: "It is natural to feel Christ's liberation reaching into every kind of bondage, and to want to act in obedience with that radical shift. But precisely because of Christ we shall not impose that shift violently upon the social order beyond the confines of the church." Nonetheless, this new way of living within the church is a missionary witness to the wider world. When the believing spouse is subordinate to the unbelieving one,

37. Ibid., 177–78.
38. Ibid., 180 continuation of note 40.
39. Ibid., 182–83.

"the voluntary subjection of the church is understood as a witness to the world." Yoder calls this way of living a "creative transformation" of the social order from within. "Since in the resurrection and in Pentecost the kingdom which was imminent has now in part come into our history, the church can now live out, within the structures of society, the newness of the life of the kingdom." The voluntary subordination of believing spouse to unbelieving one, the mutual subordination of spouses, of parents and children, and of slaves and masters is a demonstration to the social order of the new way of freedom that is found in Christ. They can live with this attitude toward the world's structures because of the "radicality of the call of Jesus." "It is precisely this attitude ward the structures of this world, this freedom from needing to smash them since they are about to crumble anyway, which Jesus had been the first to teach and in his suffering to concretize."[40]

Yoder's final point concerning revolutionary subordination concerns the primary point of his chapter, which is also the theme of this chapter. Paul and other New Testament writers did not borrow the *Haustafeln* from Stoic sources and use them to conform the early church to the norms of the social order. Rather, the structure learned from the *Haustafeln* actually challenged the social order from within, and witnessed to the freedom in Christ of what Yoder called revolutionary subordination. This guidance comes, Yoder asserted, not from a betrayal of the ethic of Jesus by the apostles. On the contrary, revolutionary subordination challenged the social order with the ethic of Jesus. "Where the New Testament did offer specific guidance for its own time, that guidance confirmed and applied the messianic ethic of Jesus."[41] Thus Yoder's explanation of the *Haustafeln* and his concept of revolutionary subordination provide another example of his argument that Paul continued the ethics of Jesus.

Romans 13: Overturning the Tradition

The discussion thus far leads to Yoder's treatment of Romans 13. He notes that the majority Christian tradition has appealed to Romans 13:1–7 as

40. Ibid., 185, 187 Alongside the interpretation here of "revolutionary subordination" that includes an active challenge to the imbalances and abuses of the status quo, the suggestion of chapter 13 is also appropriate, namely, that we use less easily misunderstood terms of reciprocity and power-sharing. (See chapter 13, the context of note 51.)

41. Ibid., 187.

the "foundation of a Christian doctrine of the state." In line with this view, it is claimed that God has established civil government. The divine establishment, then, requires Christians to obey it, "not only because they fear the state's sanctions but because they conscientiously support its functions of suppressing evil and encouraging the good." The implementation of this obedience means that when the government wields the sword in war or in policing and capital punishment, these actions are "exempted from the general prohibition of killing." There is thus a "moral obligation" to support the state's legal killing, even as that is contrary to the teaching and example of Jesus.[42] It is this assumption of a disjunction between Jesus and Paul of Romans 13 that Yoder addresses.

Yoder outlined six areas of misinterpretation within the traditional view. Following Yoder's argument on these points makes clear that in Romans 13:1–7, Paul actually agrees with and extends Jesus' rejection of the sword.

(1) "The New Testament speaks in many ways about the problem of the state; Romans 13 is not the center of this teaching." In fact, a "strong strand of Gospel teaching," such as the account of Jesus and Satan in the wilderness, puts secular government in "the province of the sovereignty of Satan." Romans 13 was written about a pagan government, and it is matched by the anti-imperial outlook of Revelation 13. Further, as was sketched earlier in this chapter, the state is frequently seen as one of the powers over which Christ is victorious.[43]

(2) Romans 13:1–7 must be understood in the context of the literary unity of chapters 12 and 13.

> Chapter 12 begins with a call to nonconformity, motivated by the memory of the mercies of God, and finds the expression of this transformed life first in a new quality of relationships within the Christian community and, with regard to enemies, in suffering. The concept of love then recurs in 13:8-10. Therefore, any interpretation of 13:1–7 which is not also an expression of suffering and serving love must be a misunderstanding of the text in its context.[44]

---

42. Yoder, *Politics of Jesus* (1994), 193–94.
43. Ibid., 194–96, quote 194.
44. Ibid., 196.

(3) The subordination called for "recognizes whatever power exists," but "does not affirm, as the tradition has it, a divine act of institution or ordination of a particular government."[45] A "positivistic" view that assumes that the existing government is "of God" can result in Adolf Hitler. The more frequent "normative" view that began with Ulrich Zwingli and John Calvin and continues into the present, assumes the concept of "proper government." As long as the government is then "proper" it is to be obeyed. When it becomes improper or unjust, Christians then have a duty to "rise up against it." Yoder counters that no clear criteria exist for determining when rebellion is appropriate, and more importantly, Romans 13 says nothing about rebellion. According to Yoder's interpretation, the true meaning of Romans 13 is God's ordering of the powers, telling them "where they belong, what is their place." The calling of Christians is then subordination to government. The immediate concern for the Jewish Christians in Rome was "to call them away from any notion of revolution or insubordination. The call is to a nonresistant attitude toward a tyrannical government." In an important footnote, Yoder notes that he uses "nonresistant" not as a statement of passive "acquiescence" to evil, but in the sense of refusing "retaliation in kind." Thus being nonresistant "does not exclude other kinds of opposition to evil."[46]

(4) Christians in Rome had no voice in administration. "The text cannot mean that Christians are called to do military or police service." Rome did not ask subject peoples to perform either military or police service. These were considered either "hereditary professions or as citizens' privileges," while paying taxes and revenue and rendering honor (13:6–7) are not services. "It is therefore illegitimate to extend the meaning of the text ... to other kinds of services which other kinds of governments in other ages might ask of their citizens." It is especially illegitimate to extend it to "conscription" for military service.[47]

(5) "The function of bearing the sword to which Christians are called to be subject is the judicial and police function; it does not refer to the death penalty or to war."[48] Yoder noted that the sword as symbol of judicial authority was neither an instrument of capital punishment nor of war.

45. Ibid., 198–99.
46. Ibid., 199–202 and note 14.
47. Ibid., 203.
48. Ibid.

It could be used, of course, but "was more a symbol of authority than a weapon." This text thus has nothing to do with participation in a justifiable war. It deals with the subordination to which Christians are called.[49]

(6) "The Christian who accepts subjection to government retains moral independence and judgment.... Whatever government exists is ordered by God; but the text does not say that whatever the government does or asks of its citizens is good."[50] Since not everything that the government does is good, Christians are to exercise discrimination in what "honor" or "fear" is due. The only thing due to everyone is "love"(13:8). "Thus the claims of Caesar are to be measured by whether what he claims is due to him is part of the obligation of love." Love is defined in verse 10 as doing no harm. Thus it "becomes impossible to maintain that the subjection referred to in verses 1–7 can include a moral obligation under certain circumstances to do harm to others at the behest of government." The term Paul used in Romans 13:1 does not call for "obedience." Rather he was calling for "sub*ord*ination," which has the same root as God's "*ord*ering" of the powers. "Subordination is significantly different from obedience. The conscientious objector who refuses to do what government demands, but still remains under the sovereignty of that government and accepts the penalties which it imposes . . . is being subordinate even though not obeying."[51]

With these six points, Yoder responded to the traditional view that Romans 13 obligates Christians to obey government, including "the obligation to participate in war." This traditional view presumes that a contradiction exists between the teaching and life of Jesus as exemplified by Matthew 5 and Romans 13, with resolution of that contradiction on the side of the latter since the time of Constantine. In contrast, Yoder's analysis displays clearly that no disjunction exists between Romans 13 and the Sermon on the Mount. Both Romans 12–13 as a unit and Matthew 5–7 "instruct Christians to be nonresistant[52] in all their relationships, including the social." Both call on the disciples of Jesus to reject the

---

49. Ibid., 203–4.
50. Ibid., 205.
51. Ibid., 208–9; Yoder's italics.
52. It is important to underscore that Yoder's use of "nonresistant" means rejection of retaliation in kind but does include other kinds of resistance. See the context of notes 38 and 46 above.

pursuit of "vengeance." "*Both* call Christians to respect and be subject to the historical process in which the sword continues to be wielded and to bring about a kind of order under fire, but not to perceive in the wielding of the sword their own reconciling ministry."[53] Thus Yoder's analysis of Romans 13:1–7 constitutes yet one more instance of his assertion that Paul continued and reinforced the message of Jesus.

Thus far we have noted the linking of Jesus and Paul in Yoder's early writing, namely in *Preface to Theology* and in *The Politics of Jesus*. It is important to note that this theme is underscored strongly in the chapter "Paul the Judaizer" in Yoder's posthumously published *Jewish-Christian Schism Revisited*. For example, he writes, "To believe that the messianic age has begun, and that therefore Jews can share the glories of the Law as Grace with Gentiles, was for [Paul] 'the most authentic interpretation of classical Judaism.' Far from being the great Hellenizer of an originally Jewish message, Paul is rather the great Judaizer of Hellenistic culture."[54]

Yoder noted that the mission to Gentiles had been underway before Paul came into the picture. Thus what was unique about Paul's mission was not the mission itself but what he saw as the unfolding of divine purpose in the messianic age. "*Because* this is the messianic age, initiated by the resurrection and ascension of Jesus, *therefore* the centuries-old promises of the ingathering of the Gentiles was coming true."[55] Thus the missionary power was correlated with the many people who filled the law without knowing the law. As a result, accommodations were made for Gentiles to be recognized as "God-fearers," who could attend the synagogue without following the dietary laws or undergoing circumcision.

To this time, a part of the messianic expectation had been that in the age to come, those who wanted to know the will of God would learn it by asking Jews or coming to Jerusalem. Paul simply put this expectation together with the event of Jesus. "We recognize in Jesus the inbreaking of the messianic age. It is actually happening on a greater scale than before, that Gentiles who hear about Jesus come to the messianic synagogues. Conclusion: the will of God for our age is the active ingathering of Gentiles into a new kind of body." And thus "what Paul sees happening in

---

53. Yoder, *Politics of Jesus* (1994), 210; Yoder's italics.
54. Yoder, *Jewish-Christian Schism*, 95.
55. Ibid., 95–96; Yoder's italics.

Christ and in the Christian church . . . is the fulfillment and not the abolition of the meaning of Torah as covenant of grace."[56]

On Being Peaceable in a Violent World

This chapter has focused on Yoder's argument that contrary to traditional assumptions, no chasm exists between Jesus and Paul. In fact, Paul continues and reinforces the message of Jesus. Yoder's intent with that argument was to strengthen the case for ethics based in Jesus, namely the politics of Jesus. As this chapter has discussed the relationship of Paul to Jesus, it has put that nonviolent ethic on display. It thus prepares the way for the chapters that follow.

It is the community around Jesus, namely the church, that actualizes and exemplifies the ethic of Jesus. Chapter 7 describes further the character of the church that exemplifies the politics of Jesus and resists the allure of empire.

The politics of Jesus say "no" to the politics of empire. Yoder rejected the dynamics of "lording it over" of empire and presented the norm of servanthood and subordination based on the life of Jesus. Chapter 8 describes further the way that subordination and submission is a way to see the world.

As this chapter briefly stated, Yoder believed that the ethic of Jesus, the politics of revolutionary subordination, could involve active, nonviolent resistance. Chapter 9 describes Yoder's view of active, nonviolent resistance.

56. Ibid., 96, 97.

7

The Free Church as Body Politics

Earl Zimmerman

> God Sent me to reveal the mystery that has been hidden since the beginning of time by God, who created everything. God's purpose is now to show the rulers and powers in the heavens the many different varieties of his wisdom through the church.
>
> —The Apostle Paul (Eph 3:9–10)

> Because the risen Messiah is at once head of the church and *kyrios* of the *kosmos*, sovereign of the universe, what is given to the church through him is in substance no different from what is offered to the world. The believing community is the new world on the way.
>
> —John Howard Yoder[1]

John Howard Yoder's view of discipleship to Jesus comes to its fullest expression in his understanding of the church. Chapter 1 displayed Yoder's approach to Christology and ethics and his understanding that God is present in the story of Jesus. Living in Jesus' story, following Jesus

---

1. Yoder, *For the Nations*, 50.

produces the community that is the visible church. But discipleship concerns more than the church. The church is a model for all to see of God's purposes for the world.

Yoder espoused a paradigm of the church as a voluntary fellowship of disciples of Jesus committed to the priesthood of all believers. His congregational, free church model is biblically oriented, Spirit-led, and has a shared leadership that draws on the gifts of each member, which means that it eschews hierarchical, sacerdotal, creedalist, and sacramentalist models of the church.[2] Yoder found a historical precedent for this ecclesiology in the sixteenth-century Anabaptist or radical reformation. However, he believed that the free church paradigm applied to all communions rather than being an apology for a given denomination or family of churches.[3] Any existing church, he argued, not only fails in various ways, but is in fact sinful. That is why there is a need for continual reformation and even "radical" reformation.[4]

This chapter displays Yoder's extended argument for this radical reformation, free church paradigm and its social engagement, which he called "body politics." The chapter thus fills out the description of Anabaptist ecclesiology identified in chapter 2 and that distinguished Yoder from Goshen School Anabaptism in chapter 3.[5]

The Free Church

Given Yoder's doctoral studies in sixteenth-century Anabaptist historical theology, his free church paradigm naturally draws on those sources.[6]

2. Yoder, *Royal Priesthood*, 75–78.

3. Yoder claims that his model in not an apologetic for his own Mennonite denomination and that some Mennonite denominational characteristics are irrelevant or at worst misleading. See Yoder, *Priestly Kingdom*, 4.

4. Yoder even claims that the ecclesiological vision he is espousing is dramatically visible in some developments in Roman Catholic experience. See Yoder, *Priestly Kingdom*, 5–6.

5. In addition to Walton's apt demonstration in chapter 3 of Yoder's difference from the Bender School, I also note Yoder's intense clash with Bender over church polity in my *Practicing the Politics*, 46–50.

6. Yoder translated a Swiss-German Anabaptist document on "congregational order" that, among other things, instructs congregations to center their services on the reading and exposition of Scripture, to have a shared common meal as part of their gathering, and to establish a common fund for economic sharing so that no member will suffer need. See Yoder, *Legacy of Sattler*, 44–45. The document is also included in

The Anabaptists made a definitive break with the ruling state church as unfaithful to the biblical vision of a religious community that is sociologically differentiated from the surrounding society and its structures of power. For example, Dutch Anabaptist leader Menno Simons spoke of the true church as a suffering little flock that chose the costly path of penitence and discipleship in contrast to the state churches, each beholden to a particular competing European political power. He pointedly exclaimed, "Where the papists stick with the papists, Lutherans with the Lutherans . . . etc., now build up, and anon demolish and act the hypocrite in keeping with the magistracy's wishes, everyone who is enlightened by the truth and taught by the Spirit may judge what kind of church that is."[7]

The Anabaptist emphasis on the believing community differs from the classic Protestant position that the church is present where the Word is preached truthfully and the sacraments are rightly administered. Instead, Anabaptists spoke of the church as "a gathered congregation which is built on Christ," as "an assembly of the children of God," or as "a community of saints."[8] Yoder identified the central marks of the Anabaptist vision as (*a*) a focus on the authority of Scripture, (*b*) a Spirit empowered communal discernment process, (*c*) following Christ in life, (*d*) suffering love, (*e*) a voluntary believers church, (*f*) the discipline of communal admonition sometimes referred to as "the rule of Christ," and (*g*) community of goods or economic sharing.[9]

While the sixteenth-century Anabaptist communities were a primary source for Yoder's ecclesiology, he noted that the free church paradigm has been a recurring phenomenon in church history. Instances he lifted out include the Franciscans in the eleventh century, the Waldensians in the twelfth century, the Quakers or Society of Friends in the seventeenth century, the restorationist movement in nineteenth-century America that gave birth to the Churches of Christ and the Disciples of Christ, and base communities associated with the liberation theology movement in the

---

Klaassen, *Anabaptism in Outline*, 119–20.

7. Menno Simons, *Complete Writings*, 741.

8. Klaassen, *Anabaptism in Outline*, 102–15.

9. Yoder's summary of the things that various sixteenth-century Anabaptist groups held in common is a helpful guide, but the reader needs to be cognizant of the range of diversity within those groups spread across northern Europe. For a recent primer on the early Anabaptist movement that shows the diversity and multiple origins of Anabaptists, see Weaver, *Becoming Anabaptist*.

twentieth century.¹⁰ Yoder also engaged contemporary congregations, such as the Sojourners Community in Washington, DC, which experimented with more radical, communal, and activist forms of church life. He called such churches, modeled on the life and vision of Jesus and his first band of disciples, the "original revolution" because their gathered life made concrete a radical new way of being human.¹¹

The title "free church" has been used historically to designate churches that were not established, in contrast to the official, established or state churches in European countries or in the American colonies. That definition has become thoroughly scrambled with the advent of the modern, secular nation-state and the disestablishment in a number of countries of all religious bodies. Today numerous American churches with an historical free church background actually support the social establishment of their version of Christianity—an unofficial Christian America—through government action and have become key pillars of support for an imperialist American foreign policy. And some former state or established churches have moved over to be critical of the idea of a Christian society and seek prophetically to engage official American ideologies and policies. This distinction is captured by Yoder's belief that the free church was distinguishable from churches that assume that God's rule is exercised through national offices and policies in support of a "Christian society." Debra Dean Murphy aptly captures the essence of the free church stance as it relates to church and society:

> For Christians, what is "given" (inevitable, assumed) is *not* "the secular" or the political arrangements of modern, democratic social orders but the body politic of the church across time and space. And *as* a body politic, the church engages other orders, spheres, powers, etc. in an ad hoc way: sometimes resisting, sometimes cooperating, and, when at its best, negotiating the complexity of these challenges with generosity, not hostility, practicing the way of radical, embodied, cruciform witness.¹²

As Yoder continued to develop his free church paradigm,¹³ he identified its precedents in Jewish history long before the time of Jesus and

10. Yoder, *Priestly Kingdom*; Yoder, *Royal Priesthood*, 246–47.
11. Yoder, *Original Revolution*, 28–29.
12. Murphy, "Bearing Witness," 39. Italics Murphy's.
13. Yoder variously used the terms *free church* or *believers church* for this paradigm. Historians have used the term *free church* to designate the Anabaptist or

the early church. What Jesus did in calling his band of disciples was what God had done through Abraham, Moses, and the Hebrew prophets: "He gathered his people around his word and his will."[14] The Davidic project of establishing a kingship "like the other nations" was a deviation that needs to be understood as a rejection of God's design for authentic human community (1 Sam 8:1–18).[15] The Davidic project eventually ended in failure when the Jewish people were carried into exile in Babylon; there they developed a more faithful way of forming themselves as God's people in the midst of the society where they now lived. Speaking through the prophet Jeremiah, God instructed them to "seek the welfare of the city where I have sent you, and pray to the Lord on its behalf, for in its welfare you will find your welfare" (Jer 29:7). Yoder saw the religious community model they developed, based on God's call to live in the midst of the nations as a distinct people seeking the common good of the whole society, as prefiguring the free church. Central to this way of being in the world is the conviction that God is sovereign over history and there is no need to gain political control in order to make sure God's will is done or that history comes out right.[16]

Babylon would become the cultural center of Judaism from the time of Jeremiah until well into the middle ages—an historical reality largely unrecognized by scholars. The Jews in Babylon became a multilingual people who served as cultural brokers in the ancient world. They lived without the temple or attachment to the land, which had formerly been central to their religious identity. They became innovators that developed new forms of communal identity to sustain their religious community in this initially alien setting:

- The writing, copying, and study of Scripture became the core of their religious identity. Their Scriptures could be copied and read anywhere and were not tied to ritual forms related to temple worship.

---

non-magisterial reformation groups. It eventually became imprecise when former state-churches became formally disestablished in the modern era. The term *believers church* originated with sociologist Max Weber, who used it to describe Anabaptists and Quakers. For further discussion of history and usage of these terms, see Cartwright, "Radical Reform," 23–28.

14. Yoder, *For the Nations*, 175.

15. Ibid., 60.

16. Ibid., 66–67. See also Yoder's further discussion of the Jewishness of the free church vision in Yoder, *Jewish-Christian Schism*, 105–19.

- They developed the synagogue as a center for study, worship, and community life. A congregation could be formed wherever there were ten Jewish households. No priesthood or hierarchy was necessary. If they could afford a rabbi, his role was that of facilitator, teacher, and scribe.

- Worship was rooted in the reading and singing of Scripture. International Jewish unity was sustained through visitation and rabbinic consultation as well as commercial and inter-family relationships. There was no intra-Jewish hierarchical structure or central administration.

- Jewish intellectual life involved the creativity and freedom to develop philosophical systems but it was rooted in the community's common life, its *halakah* (walk or practice), and the shared remembering of the story that formed the identity of the community.

- Nothing in the life of these Jewish communities was dependent on or pushed toward cultural hegemony or political domination. They made their home in any society in which they were accepted and were in creative dialogue with that society.[17]

The first churches that sprang up in the Mediterranean world grew out of or were coterminous with these Jewish synagogues. They shared common patterns of structuring their religious life and of relating to the larger culture and society in which they lived. Yoder noted that scholarly debates about early Christian pacifism completely miss "any recognition that Christian moral standards may have been largely derived from, and therefore could be fruitfully illuminated by, earlier Jewish models of how to relate to this world's powers."[18] Another often-missed aspect of Jewish-Christian relations (as seen in chapter 10 below) is that a Jewish-Christian common life existed at least into the fourth century and often beyond. Teasing out these historical facts enabled Yoder to make the bold claim that "the Jewish-Christian schism did not have to be" and that "for over a millennium the Jews of the diaspora were the closest thing to the ethic of Jesus existing on any significant scale anywhere in Christendom."[19]

17. Yoder, *For the Nations*, 55–60.
18. Ibid., 66.
19. Yoder, *Jewish-Christian Schism*, 81–82. While it goes beyond the focus of this chapter, the reader may be interested in Yoder's chapter "The Jewishness of the Free Church Vision," in *Jewish-Christian Schism*, 105–19.

Reading History from the Margins

John Howard Yoder read church history from the margins, enabling him to make radical determinations about what is significant outside the standard focus on rulers, wars, and empires. It enabled him to read events differently, and to draw alternative conclusions about God's purposes and how God is active in history. He learned this way of reading history from the biblical narrative where God called Abraham and Sara to leave Mesopotamia (a powerful cultural and political center in the ancient world) and live as sojourners in a strange land; where God heard the cries of Hebrew slaves in Egypt and sent Moses to deliver them from Pharaoh; where God enabled the Jewish exiles in Babylon to survive, reform their faith tradition, and creatively engage the society where they now lived; where Jesus was born to a Jewish peasant couple, called disciples, was crucified as a subversive by the ruling elites, and whose death and resurrection became the turning point in history; where the early churches lived out the gospel of Jesus as alternative communities in the heart of the Roman Empire.[20]

Yoder also learned this way of reading history from his study of the sixteenth-century Anabaptists, who called into question the political establishment of Christianity in the fourth and fifth centuries. How was it that a movement among subject peoples of the Roman Empire, namely the Christian church, formed as an intentional alternative to imperialism, had now become the official religion of that same empire? Should we read these events as the triumph of Christianity and the beginning of the millennial reign of Christ as Eusebuis, the apologist for Emperor Constantine claimed? Instead, the Anabaptists had maintained that it was a moral failure and a wrong turn in history because it made the church captive to an imperial ethic of power and violence. The voluntary, believers church, as an alternative to empire, was replaced by a state sponsored church in which it was now a civil offense not to be a Christian; within a century Augustine was even calling it a civil offense to be the wrong kind of Christian. Emperors not only supported Christianity, they insisted on having a voice in defining orthodox belief—commonly against their political enemies.[21]

20. For an insightful study of the nature of early Christian communities as an alternative to Roman imperial society, read Horsley, *Paul and Empire*.

21. Yoder, *Royal Priesthood*, 243–48. For analysis of how the patronage of the imperial family helped shape orthodoxy, see Jenkins, *Jesus Wars*.

PART THREE—EXTENDING JOHN HOWARD YODER'S THEOLOGY

According to Yoder, supporters of Constantine conferred on him near-mythological status because of the concomitant alliance of the cross and the sword. His supporters saw this alliance as ushering in the millennial reign of Christ. Long before the radical reformers, earlier monastic critics had leveled the verdict of apostasy against this alliance of corrupt clerics and princes. Later mainline Protestant historiography also used the concept of the "fall of the church" but equivocated because "they needed to retain the *consensus quinque-secularis*, the common deposit of the first five Christian centuries, the Christian Empire and the Ecumenical Councils."[22] Yoder will have none of that equivocation. He is adamant about the debilitating consequences of this wrong turn in church history. "If, as the New Testament indicates, extending certain phases of the Old, God calls his people to a prophetically critical relationship to structures of power and oppression, then the alliance between Rome-as-Empire and Church-as-Hierarchy, which the fourth and fifth centuries gradually consolidated, is not merely a possible tactical error but a structured denial of the gospel."[23]

During that era, the ecumenical councils of Nicea and Chalcedon developed the classic creedal formulations on the nature of God and of Jesus. They focused on ontological definitions and ignored the life and message of Jesus in the gospel narratives, making it possible now to weld together church and empire—cross and sword. That is why Yoder considered it necessary to decenter the creeds in the Christian imagination.[24] The welding of cross and sword, Yoder says, calls for a stance of repentance. It is not enough to parse differences dispassionately and to seek commonalities with faith communities that Christendom formerly persecuted. Christians need to receive the grace to say,

> We were wrong. The picture you have been given of Jesus by the Empire, by the Crusades, by struggles over holy sites, and by wars in the name of the "Christian West" is not only something to forget but something to forgive. We are not merely outgrowing it, as if it had been acceptable at the time: we disavow it and

22. Yoder, *Jewish-Christian Schism*, 138.

23. Yoder, *Royal Priesthood*, 245. For challenges to Yoder's view of these developments, and for responses to these challenges, see chapter 2, note 48 above.

24. For a discussion of the ways Yoder decentered Nicea, see Sider, *To See History Doxologically*, 116–17. Although Sider fails to do so, chapter 1 of this book applies Yoder's decentering of the historical creeds to his Christology, which gives primacy to Scripture and the gospel narratives about Jesus.

repent of it. It was wrong even when it seemed to us to be going well. We want our repentance to be not mere remorse but a new mind issuing in a new way—*metanoia*.[25]

The Church and the Powers

As just noted, Yoder identified the problem of the Constantinian turn as a capitulation to the domination and violence of the Roman Empire rather than remaining in prophetic engagement with it. It is a commonly held belief that the Anabaptist position on the separation of church and state has prevailed in the modern world as secular governments have gradually ended the formal establishment of Christendom. Yoder disputed this way of framing the matter. It misunderstands the central issue, he said. The state-church tie was not a self-standing issue for the Radical Reformation. Rather, it was related to their understanding of the nature of Christian discipleship that created a distinct or visible community. Furthermore, to say that the Anabaptist position has triumphed because a given society has now legally separated church and state is actually to privilege the narrative of the nation-state. According to Yoder, "these ways of stating the 'success' or the 'progress' of the free church social critique presupposes precisely what the Anabaptists and their spiritual relatives denied, namely that the course of history and the structures of society are the most significant measure of whether people are doing the will of God."[26]

With such arguments, Yoder contested the predominant way of orienting our existence in relation to the structures and ideologies of national societies and their institutions. At first glance, establishing another way appears to be an impossible endeavor. Yet posing this visible alternative is precisely what the church is called to do as an *ecclesia* or assembly that orients its communal life as a witness to empire. In this effort, Yoder drew on Dutch theologian Hendrik Berkhof's work on the biblical language of the "Powers" (Eph 6:12; Col 2:15), which had been commonly treated as vestiges of an ancient mythological worldview that had lost its meaning in the modern era. The experience of European national rivalry that erupted into two World Wars and the rise of ideologies such as fascism caused some biblical scholars and theologians to read these texts with

25. Yoder, *Royal Priesthood*, 250–51.
26. Ibid., 67–68.

new eyes. Rather than reading them as referring to disembodied spirits in a heavenly realm, they now recognized these entities as manifestations of prevailing political and economic powers.[27]

It is not that the Powers are evil in themselves. They are actually part of God's good creation in that they serve the necessary purpose of providing order and structure in human life. Paul writes, "In [Christ] all things in heaven and on earth were created, things visible and invisible, whether thrones or dominions or rulers or powers—all things have been created through him and for him" (Col 1:16). Yoder wrote that the powers are the values and structures that are necessary for human life in society. However, they entice people to serve them as though they were absolute or an end in themselves; as such they are in rebellion against the purposes of God. Even so, they continue to serve a limited good as an ordering function in society.[28] Thus the task of the church is to call the Powers to modesty and to exercise patience toward them rather than yielding to the temptation to sanctify them, and when necessary to resist them nonviolently while avoiding the temptation to challenge them with violence.[29]

The metaphorical language of Powers indicates both concrete external structures and an inner spiritual gestalt that shapes people's lives and their social consciousness. They take many shapes and can include local structures such as a town council, the municipal police, the high school, or a church. The primary manifestation of the Powers that concerns the discussion here, however, is a privileged cluster of institutional entities that dominate the life and consciousness of an entire nation or group of nations in our global era. In contemporary American society these Powers include a military establishment with a budget nearly equal to the total military spending of all the other nations combined; powerful corporate business interests that have a pervasive global reach; two dominant rival political parties; the different branches of the federal government; elite universities; the national news media; and the entertainment industry. These entities have an inner psychological and spiritual nature

---

27. Berkhof, *Christ and the Powers*, 15. The analysis here carries forward the discussion of Yoder's use of Berkhof and the Powers that was introduced in chapter 4 and begun in chapter 6, where the argument concerned Yoder's view that the Pauline concept of the powers was an extension of the social ethic of Jesus. In the current chapter, we consider the powers in the context of Yoder's ecclesiology.

28. Yoder, *Politics of Jesus* (1994), 140–44.

29. Yoder, *Original Revolution*, 149.

which is more than the sum of their parts. The external, tangible reality of their inner spiritual nature is signified by the metaphorical language that confers names on them such as "Wall Street," "The Pentagon," or "Capitol Hill." Biblical scholar Walter Wink has identified such a cluster of Powers as a "Domination System."[30]

The Powers shape all of human life in society and, consequently, cannot be either ignored or destroyed. Rather, they need to be treated as finite, human constructions that can be challenged and reformed rather than imbued with the authority of unquestioned absolutes. In theological terms, their absolute dominance needs to be broken and they need to be redeemed. Yoder notes that this is what Jesus did by living a genuinely free human existence. Treating the powers as finite rather than absolute entities challenges their authority and can be dangerous. In response to Jesus' challenge, the Powers in first-century Palestine, represented by powerful Roman functionaries and Jewish elites, colluded against him and executed him on the cross.[31] By submitting to crucifixion, Christ triumphed over the Powers by exposing their true nature as false gods, by exposing the limitation of their ability to coerce conformity to their wishes. The resurrection established and made visible what was already accomplished on the cross. In Christ, God challenged the Powers and demonstrated that God is more powerful than they.[32] The weapon of the Powers, according to Berkhof, has been the power of illusion that they used to convince people "that they were the divine regents of the world, ultimate certainty and ultimate direction, ultimate happiness and the ultimate duty for small, dependent humanity."[33] Christ's death and resurrection exposed that fiction.

Christ has already won the victory over the Powers and the existence of the church is the beginning realization of that victory in history.

---

30. Walter Wink, expanding and developing the earlier work of Berkhof and Yoder, among others, wrote extensively on the Powers as a Domination System. Drawing on Jungian psychology, Wink has understood the biblical language of Powers as the personification of an inner spiritual reality that is inextricably linked to an outer manifestation such as a concrete political/economic entity. See Wink, *Engaging the Powers*, 5–10. For Wink's trilogy on the Powers, consult the bibliography.

31. Wink, *Engaging the Powers*, 147.

32. For an atonement theology that develops this understanding of Christ's victory over the Powers, see Weaver, *Nonviolent Atonement*. The motif is briefly summarized in chapter 11 to follow..

33. Berkhof, *Christ and the Powers*, 39. Also cited in Yoder, *Politics of Jesus* (1994), 147.

According to Yoder, "The triumph of Christ has already guaranteed that the ultimate meaning of history will not be found in the course of earthly empires or the development of proud cultures, but in the calling together of the 'chosen race, royal priesthood, holy nation,' which is the church of Christ."[34] The church engages the Powers in ways that draw on Christ's victory over them. Though restrained by God, the Powers continue to control the lives and imaginations of people. Christ's victory over them, however, enables his followers to recognize the Powers' illusions for what they are and to enter the struggle to live in the world as free and humane people. Berkhof delineates some concrete manifestations of this liberation:

> Where the Spirit of Christ rules, Mammon shrivels down to "finances," conventional morality to a set of rules of thumb, subject to criticism and limited in scope and authority. Changing customs, slogans, and isms of the moment are seen as ideas which are merely "in the air," worth no more and no less than the older slogans they replaced. Where the victorious kingship of Christ is confessed, there prevails a consistent unbelief in the utility of military power, and national or international armament is at the most grudgingly accepted as a bitter duty of responsible citizenship. Anxiety before the fearsome future gives way to a simple carefulness, since we know that the future as well is in God's hands.[35]

Since the post-World War II era during which Berkhof wrote, it is becoming increasingly evident that human life shaped by the continually increasing consumption of natural resources and the accompanying pollution of our ecosystem is not sustainable and now threatens the future of the entire planet. Accordingly, to Berkhof's list of manifestations of the Powers from which liberation is needed should be added the forces of global capitalism, militarism, and nation-state competition that drive the quest for ever increasing consumption and domination. The constellation of Powers in our twenty-first century world is increasingly identified as a global "Empire." It is understood as a system of political, economic, military, and cultural interests that benefits the powerful at the expense

---

34. Yoder, *Christian Witness* (2002), 13. *Christian Witness* was first published in 1964. The fact that Yoder titled future books *The Priestly Kingdom* and *The Royal Priesthood* is an indication of how central this understanding of the church in relation to society and history is in his theology.

35. Berkhof, *Christ and the Powers*, 49.

of the most vulnerable.³⁶ Different from past empires, it is not confined to a particular nation-state or geographic center. While its most powerful center is in the United States as the last remaining superpower, it crosses national borders and is spread all over the world as a network involving the most powerful nation states and allied business, military, and political structures.³⁷ It manifests itself as a Domination System through such things as predator drone attacks against those identified as enemies in poor countries, covert cyber warfare against nations considered to be a threat, and global economics structures that favor powerful transnational corporations at the expense of poor communities.³⁸

"Body politics" is Yoder's challenge to the Dominion System. Body politics is a heuristic depiction of the life of the congregation as a model of God's design for human relations. In other words, Yoder saw the local congregation as the first level of witness about economic issues, human relations, decision making, and the nature of community that would align human structures with the reign of God.

Body Politics

As chapter 4 displayed, John Howard Yoder's vision of the function of the church in society is dependent on Oscar Cullmann's formulation of the "reign of Christ." Drawing on New Testament sources, Cullmann claimed that the reign of Christ extends to all creation, including the state and other centers of power but remains distinct from the church and the future reign of God. The church is the heart and center of the reign of

---

36. Often cited statistics such as more than one billion people who live on less than one dollar a day cannot convey the degree of suffering in the lives of poor people in our global economy. Paul Farmer's case studies of the lives of poor Haitians can help us better understand the daily struggles of such people and the structural barriers that prevent them from escaping their situation. See Farmer, *Pathologies of Power*. Journalist Katherine Boo has written an illuminating account of the lives of poor people, based on her three years of living in a Mumbai slum, which raises disturbing questions about the underside of global capitalism. See Boo, *Behind the Beautiful Forevers*.

37. Two excellent books in this vein are Horsley, *In the Shadow of Empire*, and Míguez, Rieger, and Sung, *Beyond the Spirit*; the latter offers a more detailed description of "empire in the contemporary world," 5–9.

38. For an insightful discussion of how Yoder's non-Constantinian theology fits within an age of global capital, see Dula, "Disavowal of Constantine." For a more extensive discussion of the church, which is also constantly evolving in relation to an evolving global empire, see Zimmerman, "Church and Empire."

Christ (what happens in the church has a decisive influence on the whole creation) but it is not the extent of that reign. What distinguishes the church from other entities is that church members consciously proclaim their allegiance to the reign of Christ, while others reflect the reign of God without specific awareness of it. All governments serve as God's servants within the reign of Christ even though they may not recognize or acknowledge it.[39] Working from within this formulation, Yoder makes the claim that Christ is at once head of the church and the ruler of the whole cosmos. What the church has been given in Christ is no different in substance from what is offered to the whole world; in this respect "the believing community is the new world on the way."[40]

In his small book *Body Politics,* Yoder pulls together arguments he made in previous writings to draw a sketch of what the church as the new world on the way looks like. Congregations generously embrace and seek the welfare of the towns and cities where they live and serve.[41] What is at stake is the life and witness of the church as an alternative to the oppressive reach of the Powers as global Empire that are increasingly anything but modest in the way they affect individuals and local communities.

Body Politics sketches the shape of early churches that sprang into existence through the outpouring of the Holy Spirit on the day of Pentecost (Acts 2:1–47) and quickly spread to subaltern people in the Roman Empire in the various cities around the Mediterranean basin. Each local *ecclesia* (assembly) saw itself as an alternative to the existing social and religious status quo in its respective city, including the governing assembly of the city. In that respect, they contained a revolutionary impulse but did not seek violently to usurp power. Rather, they took their assembly's common life and the welfare of each member seriously.[42]

---

39. Cullmann, *Early Church*, 128. For a more detailed analysis of Cullmann's discussion of the reign of Christ, see chapter 4.

40. Yoder, *For the Nations*, 50.

41. Some have charged that Yoder's "body politics" as a witness to the world is a reduction of theology to ethics (e.g., Martens, *Heterodox Yoder*, 138, 142, 147). For a response to this charge, see chapter 5, note 47 and the context. The charge against Yoder does not recognize that he always worked from within the theological formulation of the "reign of Christ" that he learned from Cullmann and the framework of engaging the "Powers" that he learned from Berkhof, as well as his extension of Barth's christocentric theology.

42. For a case study of the Christian assembly in Corinth as a new society alternative to the dominant imperial society, see Horsley, "1 Corinthians," in *Paul and Empire*, 242–52.

Yoder lifts out five central practices that shaped the body life of a local assembly or church. The church is a body in the sense that it is a social organism and it is political in the sense that it distributes power, defines rules, and makes decisions. It is common to make a distinction between what a congregation does in worship and its activity in ordinary life. That distinction requires some kind of bridge to span these two worlds. Yoder seeks to break down this dichotomy by relating worship elements such as baptism and communion to social practices within the church that also have relevance for the larger society.[43] These practices can be understood as sacraments in the sense that we understand God to be acting in and through that human activity.[44] It goes beyond our purposes here to dwell on each of the practices that Yoder identified, but a brief description of each gives a sense of the paradigm he developed based on the communal life of the early church.

The first practice, using ancient rabbinical language, is called "binding and loosing" (Matt 18:15–20). It involves a proscribed process of conflict mediation when one member feels wronged or injured or when serious disagreements arise. Two central elements of the process are moral discernment and reconciliation. The practice of binding and losing poses a contrast to commonly practiced retributive justice, which focuses on punishment.[45] The second practice is the Lord's Supper or breaking bread together. Drawing on the teaching of the Apostle Paul (1 Cor 11:20–33), Yoder argues that authentic communion includes making sure that the economic needs of each member are met and includes sharing resources with the poor. This sharing stands in sharp contrast to the Dominion System, which allows money to accumulate in the hands of a few to the detriment of the many.

The third practice is baptism or the creation of a new humanity where the barriers of common social divisions such as Jew or Greek, male or female, slave or free, are broken down (Gal 3:28). Here is a clear model for transcending the racial and ethnic and class conflicts that abound in the United States and in much of the world. The fourth practice contravenes structural hierarchies. Each person and all spiritual gifts are recognized and

43. Yoder, *Body Politics*, vi–ix.
44. Ibid., 1.
45. Chapter 13 points out that Yoder's own failure and the long-drawn-out disciplinary process to which he submitted indicate the need for development of additional processes for dealing with individual failures so that they do not call into question the validity of the ecclesiological model itself. See also note 53 below.

honored (Eph 4:11–13). Even those gifts that we consider to be the least are necessary and actually the most important. Recognizing the gifts of all does not of necessity do away with various church offices such as pastor but it radically reorients their role so that they serve the entire congregation through enabling its members in their ministry. This practice challenges the common attitude that some people, particularly the economically deprived and the homeless, are expendable. The fifth practice, sometimes referred to as the "Rule of Paul," is a process of decision making that honors the voice of each person and arrives at a decision through consensus (1 Cor 14:26–33). It is different from voting in the sense that it goes beyond majority rule. It considers and values the voice and the rights of the minority in any action that is taken. This final practice challenges the democratic process. It reminds winners to respect the losing side in elections and congressional votes and to take their concerns seriously rather than following the common practice of ignoring them.

Although Yoder described body politics as the practices of a local congregation, it needs to be emphasized that he intended the implications to reach far beyond the local arena. These ideas of reconciliation, sharing, overcoming differences, respect for minority voices, and valuing the contribution of every member apply as well to national and international relations. To state only one obvious example: when the United States has about six percent of the world's population but consumes 30 to 40 percent of the worlds goods, that is an accumulation of wealth in the hands of a relative few to the detriment of much of the world.

There is nothing exclusively sacrosanct about the five practices—we might also identify others—yet Yoder surmises that they may participate in a deep structure that displays God's saving purposes for the whole world.[46] By identifying these five, Yoder sought to break down the odd selectivity that lifts up rituals of baptism and communion as sacraments to the exclusion of other practices.

In light of Yoder's robust description of these five practices, the common understanding that participation in the life of a church means showing up on Sunday for worship, listening to the sermon, affirming certain dogmas, the ritual that involves water and another that involves partaking of a thin wafer of bread and sip of wine seems incredibly thin and anemic. This observation is not an outright rejection of liturgical practices but rather a plea for their transformation through consciously

---

46. Yoder, *Body Politics*, 80.

recognizing and celebrating the bond between them and the body life of the congregation and its witness.[47]

Recognizing the body life of churches formed through the Spirit-breathed practices identified by Yoder offers a robust understanding of a church and its engagement in the world. It ought not lead to triumphalism, however, since actual congregations are far from perfect and never fully live into the kind of body life that these practices cultivate. Nonetheless, we should recognize the wonderful gift that such congregations are—a living foretaste of human social life that God desires for the whole world. According to Yoder, "Church and world are not two compartments under separate legislation or two institutions with contradictory assignments, but two levels of the pertinence of the same Lordship [of Christ]. The people of God is called to be today what the world is called to be ultimately."[48]

For the Nations

In the introduction to his *For the Nations: Essays Public and Evangelical*, John Howard Yoder wrote that his position has been defined as sectarian by both critics and friends. While he had generally not contested the label for the sake of participating in the conversation under other people's rules, in this book he did choose to defend his position. Being "sectarian" is generally understood as a posture of withdrawal or of being against the larger culture in contrast to "public" or establishment forms of Christianity that affirm culture. In this sense, he explained, the way the term is used involves an a priori judgment that the so-called sectarian stance is deficient. Yoder also notes that the designation "sect" has historically been used to define movements of prophetic dissent by reference to their minority status rather than what they believed. An added problem is that establishment does not indicate the majority, as is generally assumed, but rather a minority of people in dominant social roles who assume the right to speak for everyone.[49]

47. An inspiring example is the liturgical practice of St. Gregory of Nyssa Episcopal Church in San Francisco, which has placed its altar in the center of the sanctuary surrounded by the gathered congregation during worship. At other times the altar becomes the place for the distribution of food for the congregation's food pantry, which serves over one thousand families. See http://www.saintgregorys.org/community_service/groups/name/C148.

48. Yoder, *Body Politics*, ix.

49. Yoder, *For the Nations*, 1–5.

Returning to his archetype of the Jewish exiles in Babylon, Yoder says, "They had no choice but to work out, in response to the challenge of missionary existence, whether their acceptance of the Chaldean culture around them would be grudging and clumsy or wholehearted and creative."[50] Part of their adaptive creativity involved becoming multilingual—they maintained the Hebrew language in which their Scriptures were written, but they became so fluent in the language of their host culture that they could serve as translators, educators, and diplomats, and they developed a third language that bridged between the other two. Such fluency in various languages is indicative of the wholehearted and creative response required to seek the peace and welfare of the society in which the community of faith is placed by God—"to live *for the nations.*"[51]

This way of posing the role of the community of faith in every society in which it exists breaks down the binary distinction between "sectarian" and "public" faith stances. The experience of any living community of faith involves negotiating degrees of pluralism, hybridity, and complexity. Yoder has referred to the challenge as "not a way to keep dry above the waves of relativity, but a way to stay within our bark, barely afloat and sometimes awash amidst those waves, yet neither dissolving into them nor being carried only where they want to push it."[52] This way of living in the world reflects God's stance of vulnerable love and generosity.

Living in the world in this way necessarily involves creating a space where lives centered in the way of Jesus can be formed. The church has to be distinct to have something to say as it participates in the multiple conversations taking place. This was central to Yoder's ecclesiology and the basis of his critique of Christendom. It includes the recognition that there is brokenness and even willful sinfulness in individuals and human institutions, including the church. Using the biblical language of the Powers, this sin manifests itself as what Walter Wink called Domination Systems and more recent theologians and social philosophers call Empire.[53] The faithful church collaborates with all who seek the common good and oppose imperial forces that exploit vulnerable people, the environment, and

50. Ibid., 1.
51. Ibid., 2–3. Italics Yoder's.
52. Yoder, *Priestly Kingdom*, 58; Yoder, "But We Do," *Priestly*, 34.
53. As chapters 12 and 13 indicate, it is painful but necessary to add that Yoder's own hurtful sexual behavior toward numerous women illustrates this brokenness and sinfulness within the church and calls for renewed attention to processes for dealing with such offenses.

fragile democratic institutions. It also works together in various efforts to develop communities through things such as disaster relief, affordable housing, education, food security, conflict mediation, and health care.

The missional church avoids the fallacy of conceptualizing any society or structure as monolithic or essentially sinful. It is careful about taking a social stance that is "against the nations" or overly judgmental of contemporary culture and society.[54] While it avoids sanctifying a particular society (especially in its fight against perceived enemies), it recognizes that all societies contain much that is good and true. The art of "seeking the good of the city" includes the recognition and celebration of social goods in the language, literature, art, sports, music, architecture, religion, entertainment, design, and crafts of a given culture or social grouping. These goods reflect the soul of a culture and we can rightly feel pride in being part of this larger community. The adventure of discipleship includes finding and developing these aspects of our common humanity with our neighbors.

All of this is rooted in the faith community's transcendent hope in the God of history. The life of congregations expressed through the practices of "body politics," though often faltering, offers a foretaste of what the reign of God looks like. The same is true in our active opposition to violent and exploitative forces that are not of God. Our ability to be a multilingual people at home in a given society, though not completely identified with any society, enables us to serve as emissaries of God's new world on its way. And certainly our embrace of that which is good and true in all societies celebrates the promised arrival of the eschaton as a new heaven and a new earth (Rev 21:1). God's future does not arrive as something foreign; it is integrally related to the present working of the Spirit of Christ in the church and in the world. Yoder talked of this as "suffering love" being validated by its cosmic ground, empowering us to persevere in the face of sacrifice and to be creative in the face of dismay because we know that the grain of the universe is with us.[55]

The following two chapters developed dimensions of the witness of peace and nonviolence of the church as "body politics." Chapter 8 displays how Yoder's pacifism is a way of perceiving the world. Chapter 9 develops the lesser-known activist dimension of Yoder's peace witness in a nonviolent public theology.

54. In this sense, Yoder distinguishes himself from Stanley Hauerwas, who, according to Yoder, "maximizes the provocative edge of the dissenting posture" in his writings. See Yoder, *For the Nations*, 3 n. 6.

55. Yoder, *War of the Lamb*, 62.

8

Pacifism as a Way of Knowing

GERALD J. MAST

Among the best-known claims made by John Howard Yoder is that "people who bear crosses are working with the grain of the universe."[1] This statement is a confession that the self-giving, self-emptying love of Christ makes a witness to the true direction of history—the way things really work—and is thus the ground for any honest confrontation with the darkness of sin and violence that is surely part of the world we face each day.[2]

Put differently, following Jesus in discipleship even to the point of giving up life willingly rather than clutching at it possessively is not simply a hard teaching or rule of faith that Christians should heroically follow no matter how absurd it may appear in the context of a natural world full of rivalry, competition, violence, and the survival of the fittest. Yoder's claim that cross-bearing is cosmically sensible affirms that such self-offering discipleship springs rightly from what we can know to be true about the renewal of the creation that God is bringing about all around us, despite the blindness and disobedience that are also manifested. Yielding one's

---

1. Yoder, "Armaments and Eschatology," 58.

2. An earlier version of this chapter, here revised, appeared as the essay "Bearing the Cross as a Way of Knowing," *The Cresset* 74 (2010) 6–13. Used by permission.

life to God in such a way is an alignment with truth and thereby an act of freedom in both the practical and actual sense.

This chapter explores several ways in which such yieldedness to the cross-shaped grain of the universe opens our eyes and ears and lives to a renewed and truthful knowledge about the world around us that makes for peace. This renewed way of knowing is based on what we might call pacifist epistemology—perceiving the world around us from the standpoint of an assumption that the peaceable reign of God is in fact coming on earth as in heaven, and that it is coming peaceably. Stated another way, this chapter is a multi-faceted extension and development of the ideas of submission and subordination that were introduced in earlier chapters.

Cross and Resurrection

One of the most provocative statements concerning the epistemological status of the cross is found in a well-known passage from Yoder's *Politics of Jesus*. In the final chapter of the book, where Yoder is describing a nonviolent view of history and social change, he argues that patience trumps effectiveness as the criteria for Christian faithfulness. In extending this argument, Yoder makes the claim that "the relationship between the obedience of God's people and the triumph of God's cause is not a relationship of cause and effect but one of cross and resurrection."[3]

What does this mean? More specifically what does it mean to identify obedience with the cross and triumph with the resurrection? What is the content of the obedience that can properly be called cross-bearing and what is the sort of triumph that can properly be called resurrection? What is the relationship between the cross and the resurrection?

Yoder's perspective on the cross displays how the cross may offer a way of seeing the entire cosmos as well as the particular events taking place around us in our own time and space according to a cruciform narrative. Such a narrative refigures suffering neither as fearfully evil nor as intrinsically redemptive, but rather as a site of meaningful and potentially redemptive struggle toward the reconciliation of all things in Jesus Christ.[4]

3. Yoder, *Politics of Jesus* (1994), 232.

4. Yoder's perspective broadens significantly the meaning of the cross beyond the rituals of sacrifice and scapegoating given prominence recently by René Girard and his disciples. In his work, Girard has emphasized the extent to which the work of Jesus on

In a well-known statement from *Politics of Jesus*, Yoder argues that "only at one point, only on one subject—but then consistently, universally—is Jesus our example: in his cross."[5] But this cross, for Yoder, is "no longer any and every kind of suffering, sickness, or tension, the bearing of which is demanded," rather, "the believer's cross must be, like his Lord's, the price of his social nonconformity."[6] In this text, Yoder's intent is to distinguish between suffering in general and suffering that results from obedience. In what follows, I want to extend Yoder's argument to include obedience that may occur in the midst of any kind of suffering. Obedience would then involve the adoption of a right posture toward the suffering, a willingness to discover in that suffering that which is aligned with the direction of history and the unfolding of God's reality.[7]

One way to understand suffering, for example, is as loss: loss of stability, comfort, possession, even coherence. The story of the cross on this reading is about not needing to grasp or protect those features of our social and personal world that are generally assumed to be required for health and well-being: such as food, clothing, shelter, comfort, safety, a cell-phone with a calling plan, etc., even though these are gifts to be received with gratitude when they are available to us (except for possibly cell phones!). As Yoder puts it elsewhere quite succinctly, "if you follow the risen Jesus, *you don't have to* hate or kill. *You don't have to* defend yourself."[8] The liberation from self-possession and self-protec-

---

the cross exposes the scapegoating habits of societies that seek to save themselves from mimetic violence by forging a sacrificial solidarity against a victim. As he puts it, "The gospels only speak of sacrifices in order to reject them and to deny them any validity." Girard, *Things Hidden*, 180. In this view, the cross represents what Mark Heim has called the end of sacrifice—that is, the end of the persecution of innocent victims in order to preserve social order. Heim, "No More Scapegoats," 22–29. Bearing the cross would thus not be understood to mean making a sacrifice, but rather to live a life that exposes the futility of sacrifice. Much discussion of Girard focuses around the meaning of sacrifice and of the extent to which Christ's death can properly be called a sacrifice, or to have accomplished the end of sacrifice. Bartlett, *Cross Purposes*, 30–37.

5. Yoder, *Politics of Jesus* (1994), 95.

6. Ibid., 96.

7. Early Anabaptist leader and writer Balthasar Hubmaier seemed to recognize such a possible connection between faithful martyrdom and faithful natural death when he described three kinds of baptism: "that of the Spirit, which takes place inwardly in faith; the second, of water, which takes place outwardly by oral affirmation of faith before the church; and the third, of blood in martyrdom or on the deathbed, of which Christ also speaks." Hubmaier, *Balthasar Hubmaier*, 301.

8. Yoder, "Anabaptist Shape," 339.

tion is not, according to this view, the experience of victimhood—the forceful destruction or dispossession of human beings against their will. It is rather an experience of agency, of relinquishing willingly that which is demanded by another, of making a gift of what was demanded, thus reconstituting the object of mimetic desire as a free-will offering—an excess of resources. Thus, when on October 2, 2006, the young Amish girl Marian Fisher told the gun-wielding Charles Roberts at the Nickel Mines School to "Shoot me first," she was engaging in just such an act of impossible agency, of giving away what another sought to take, thus denying the killer ultimate control of the lives he destroyed.[9]

Furthermore, the words of Marian Fisher provide a peaceable narrative leverage not just for settings of human conflict and violence, but also for our view of the natural world. As one example, I cite my colleague Angela Montel's critique of dominant war metaphors used by cell biologists to describe the relationship between white blood cells (named natural killer cells by scientists) and the so-called invading viruses and bacteria that threaten the life of the host. Montel challenges the idea that we need to understand the struggle between white blood cells and pathogens as a war taking place within the human body.[10] She argues that such a narrative frame has motivated an approach to treatment that emphasizes ridding the body and the environment of germs that are actually helpful in strengthening the immune system. She notes, for example, the increasingly high number of cases of asthma, hay fever, and other allergies associated with germ-free environments, compared with a much lower rate in contexts such as the more polluted countries of the former Eastern Bloc, on family farms, and in child care centers. She points out how the excessive use of anti-bacterial products may be destroying a protective layer of nonpathogenic organisms on our bodies and strengthening treatment-resistant forms of harmful bacteria.[11]

Montel suggests replacing the war metaphors with images of dance and struggle in accounts of cell behavior. Emphasizing the "co-evolution of human hosts and microbial pathogens," she emphasizes the mutual dependence of hosts and pathogens and argues, following the work of Nancey Murphy, that we view the dance between microbes and their hosts as an occasion to appreciate the "sacrificial suffering through to

---

9. Kraybill, Nolt, and Weaver-Zercher, *Amish Grace*, 25–26.
10. Montel, "Violent Images," 224–25.
11. Ibid., 225.

something higher" that "binds us to all creation and to the nonviolent, suffering Redeemer himself."[12]

When we recognize that the suffering encounter with natural and social forces that seem to threaten us with death provides an opportunity to bear the cross, we are enabled to face such struggles with the knowledge that we are "threatened with resurrection," as Jim Amstutz puts it.[13] An eloquent articulation of this principle is found in the christological hymn of Philippians 2, where Christ is said to have become exalted as Lord precisely in his self-emptying obedience to death. It is to this kenotic principle that I now to turn.

Kenosis and Consumption

The christological model of submission and obedience that Yoder lifts up is the obedience of Christ even unto death in Philippians 2. The most common or traditional understanding of this text pictures Christ Jesus, who was already equal with God in the upper realm, but gave up divine attributes—that is, emptied himself—to become human, and then as a human being refused to seize what was already his, namely equality with God. Yoder suggests a different approach. As noted in chapter 1, Yoder's preferred interpretation of this text sees Jesus as a parallel to Adam. As a human being Jesus refused to seize that which was not rightfully his. In contrast to Adam, who succumbed to temptation in an effort to be like God, Yoder writes, as a human being Jesus refused any effort to seize equality with God. "Jesus did 'not consider being equal with God as a thing to be seized' (Phil 2:6). His very obedience unto death is in itself not only the sign but also the firstfruits of an authentic restored humanity." With this death, Yoder says, "we have for the first time to do with a man who is not the slave of any power, of any law or custom, community or institution, value or theory. Not even to save his own life will he let himself be made a slave of these Powers." His "authentic humanity" included accepting death from the Powers. By accepting death at their hand, and refusing to bend to their threats and coercion, Jesus exposed their weakness and defeated the Powers.[14] This obedience unto death constitutes his

---

12. Ibid., 233.
13. Amstutz, *Threatened with Resurrection*, 18.
14. Yoder, *Politics of Jesus* (1994), 145.

victory. By his obedient death, Jesus attained the role of Lord, equality with God, the attribute of deity.

In *The Priestly Kingdom*, Yoder explains that the perfection of Jesus "was not a timeless divine status but was *attained* through weakness with prayers and supplications, loud cries and tears." This statement makes it clear that kenosis or self-emptying properly understood is not a divestment of power but rather an exercise of power that defeats those dominating forces that otherwise threaten to define and undermine humanity. Moreover, Jesus' kenosis demonstrates that the powers are not defeated by the strategies of violence and abuse by which the powers maintain their grip over their subjects. Rather the powers are defeated by the refusal to grasp for control and domination, by the identification of believers with the Son who is "the image of the invisible creator, holding all things together, reconciling all things, head of the body."[15]

In her book *Powers and Submissions*, Sarah Coakley offers an extensive discussion of the possible meanings of kenosis that has parallels to Yoder's analysis. Coakley's account raises an important question about self-emptying that Yoder does not address. In a discussion that ranges from the biblical account itself through the church fathers to the present, Coakley points to the argument among feminist scholars about whether the injunction to empty oneself as Christ did is properly addressed to women—or for that matter to anyone whose full humanity has been stolen by force.[16]

This question of whether self-emptying is a practice of power or disempowerment is crucial. The way of the cross is easily misunderstood as an acceptance or enablement of violence and abuse. Coakley attributes the anxieties feminists have over kenosis to an assumption that Christ was giving up power that he had possessed as a member of the Trinity when he accepted Crucifixion. That is, Christ acted in a condescending way toward us, in a way that can best be identified with those in this world who have power and the willpower to give it up. This view assumes the traditional interpretation, or to use Yoder's language, that Christ is an "eternal being who gives up his eternal attributes in order to become a man."[17]

---

15. Yoder, *Priestly Kingdom*, 51–52.
16. Coakley, *Powers and Submissions*, 3–25.
17. Yoder, *Preface* (2002), 84.

Both Yoder and Coakley prefer the interpretation in which Jesus attains Lordship because he refused to seize the role of God, or, as Coakley argues, self-emptying is no longer understood as what Jesus does in order to become human but rather what he does as human in order to become God. In other words, self-emptying is actually a means by which Jesus achieves divinity, and therefore an attribute of divinity, rather than a compromise or giving up of divinity.

According to Coakley, if the vulnerability associated with self-emptying is in fact an attribute of divinity, a feature or sign of divine power rather than a contradiction of the divine, then the vulnerability that women often exhibit is properly seen as a practice of power rather than an experience of victimage.[18] For example, when Marian Fisher said "Shoot me first," was she exhibiting patriarchal training in oppressive self-effacement or was she in fact taking charge of the situation by asserting agency in the face of a man's attempt to destroy her?

If we accept Coakley's argument, then Fisher's speech act can be seen as a "willed effacement to a gentle omnipotence which, far from complementing masculinism, acts as its undoing."[19] In fact, according to Coakley, if such vulnerability to enemies demonstrates our true humanity, then women's tendency not to take up the privileged role of the controlling Enlightenment "man of reason" gives women a particular and privileged location for realizing the empowerment associated with vulnerability.[20] Put differently, women's capacity for agency is no longer defined according to a masculine tendency to identify power with aggression or violence (as well as to define anything short of aggression as passivity). Rather, "vulnerable, non-grasping humanity" is now acknowledged to be aligned with "authentic divine power."[21]

Furthermore, the spiritual and practical disciplines involved in refusing to grasp or demand—what traditional Anabaptist conviction has named "gelassenheit" or yielding—are then to be seen as disciplines of empowerment, of receiving as gifts what others perhaps meant as harm. The practice of contemplative prayer, for example, should no longer be seen as a practice of passive withdrawal from the struggle of everyday life but rather the discovery of a renewed space within everyday life from

---

18. Coakley, *Powers and Submissions*, 25.
19. Ibid., 37.
20. Ibid., 30.
21. Ibid., 38.

which it is possible to live in a new way amidst the ruins of the world that is passing away. Such radical contemplative prayer in the service of yielding is aligned with the practice of revolutionary subordination as described by Yoder in the ninth chapter of *The Politics of Jesus*: becoming a "free ethical agent" by voluntarily acceding to "subordination in the power of Christ instead of bowing to it either fatalistically or resentfully."[22] This is because "the new world or regime under which we live is not a simple alternative to present experience but rather a renewed way of living within the present."[23]

Because this renewed way of living is precisely not an absurd idealism amidst a tragic reality but rather a quite realistic alignment with the actual direction in which the cosmos is being renewed by God, the disciple of Jesus can yield rather than fight. Or as Yoder puts it: "it is precisely this attitude toward the structures of this world, this freedom from needing to smash them since they are about to crumble anyway, which Jesus had been the first to teach and in his suffering to concretize."[24] Radical contemplative prayer or revolutionary subordination is thus a spiritual discipline that puts the disciple into the flow of God's purposes as they are being worked out.[25]

To say this yet another way: accepting God's will means accepting the way that God works in the world—not by might or by power but by the spirit. If God does not impose God's will on God's world against the will of God's disobedient creatures, then for the disciple of Jesus to willingly accept in any given moment the painful effects of disobedient practices or structures on the disciple without trying to crush them and without accepting their ultimate sovereignty is to accept the will of God,

---

22. Yoder, *Politics of Jesus* (1994), 186. The discussion here of the admittedly controversial notion of "revolutionary subordination" supplies a somewhat different, additional nuance to the understanding of this theme, which was previously referenced in chapters 4 and 6. However, alongside these various efforts to interpret revolutionary subordination in a positive light, note the suggestion in chapter 13 to move to use "less easily misconstrued terms of reciprocity and power-sharing."

23. Yoder, *Politics of Jesus* (1994), 185.

24. Ibid., 187.

25. Or as Coakley argues, following the work of the early twentieth-century Benedictine writer John Chapman, rather than being seen as the passive or apathetic acceptance of "everything that happens to one," the contemplative stance "requires a positive and participative intention to will God's will for one at this moment, and to accept (just for this one moment) that whatever is befalling one is indeed God's will" (*Powers and Submissions*, 49).

without God's will being seen as the sovereign cause of the suffering caused by disobedience. It is only in this sense that it is right to understand Jesus' crucifixion as the will of God—as a way of responding to enemies even unto death that comports most fully with the way in which God intervenes in history, with the way God brings about God's purposes amidst disobedient creatures, and with the will of God for those of us who seek to pursue God's purposes in our daily lives.

For an additional clarification of what is being advocated here, recall Martin Luther King Jr.'s speech in Memphis the day before he was assassinated where he reflected on the famous confrontation with Birmingham police chief Bull Connor. In the speech he stresses the extent to which that confrontation witnessed to the tactical alignment of the civil rights movement with God's will and with the "physics" of the cosmos:

> We mean business now and we are determined to gain our rightful place in God's world. Bull Connor would tell them to send the dogs forth, and they did come. But we just went before the dogs, singing, "Ain't gonna let nobody turn me around." Bull Connor next would say, "Turn the fire hoses on." . . . Bull Connor didn't know history. He knew a kind of physics that somehow didn't relate to the trans-physics that we knew about. And that was the fact that there was a certain kind of fire that no water could put out. And we went before the fire hoses. . . . We knew water. That couldn't stop us.[26]

Arguably, the practices of nonviolence King advocated in the context of the civil rights movement illustrate an aggressive version of yieldedness—a public and visible and persistent witness against the disobedience of racist political and institutional life which endures the suffering involved in such a witness without retaliation or self-defense. To return to Yoder's helpful phrase, "revolutionary subordination," one can imagine a range of tactical emphases which improvise on such a complex posture. King's activist stance arguably privileged the revolutionary aspect while other stances might privilege the subordinate aspect.[27] Yet,

---

26. Quoted in Buckley, "Voice of America," 24.

27. Yoder envisioned this spectrum of responses. Recall the mentions from chapter 6 of a long citation from Johannes Hamel, which contained the comment that being subordinate could include an "extremely aggressive way of acting," and his assertion that he used "nonresistant" to mean "the suffering renunciation of retaliation in kind," but that "it does not exclude other kinds of opposition to evil." See Yoder, *Politics of Jesus* (1994), 180, the continuation of note 40, and 202 n. 14.

when some measure of each emphasis is present in Christian witness—a revolutionary refusal to be defined by the fading social order and a subordinate yielding to the damaging blowback of such a refusal—then the will of God can be understood as being fulfilled. It is this sense in which Marian Fisher can be said to have known the same thing that Martin Luther King Jr., knew: neither guns nor fire hoses are effectual against the "trans-physics" of the cross.

A "Pacifist" Hermeneutics

How does a person come to see the world in this sort of a way? What is the source of strength and wisdom for managing the life of renewal amidst the corrupting and dehumanizing structures of the fading order? What concrete knowledge can infuse contemplative prayer with improvised combinations of revolutionary challenge and nonviolent subordination which flow with God's purposes?

It is clear from Yoder's writings that he believed this concrete knowledge comes from the study and practice of the Scriptures by the living body of Christ.[28] The texts of the Bible are a marvelous instantiation of the broken and renewed world that we seek to see and address rightly. Rather than function as contemporary self-help manuals, which tell us how to adjust our lives to the functional realities of the blinded world, the Scriptures empower us to align our lives with those purposes of God which challenge the disobedience of the surrounding world. This requires us to be attentive especially to those parts of the Bible that trouble us or bother us. So Yoder was also committed to a serious effort to understand the point of view from which a given biblical text was written, especially in the case of those texts that trouble us or contradict our own assumptions.[29] In what follows, I sketch briefly an approach to biblical interpretation that is consistent with the "biblical realism" advocated by Yoder, while drawing on other contemporary biblical scholars such as Walter Brueggeman and Eugene Peterson. This approach seeks to avoid imposing our own systems and demands on the text and to rather let

---

28. "It is a basic novelty in the discussion of hermeneutics to say that a text is best understood in a congregation." Yoder, "Hermeneutics of Anabaptists," 21.

29. "Gradually I have been taught that any interpretation of an apostle is unsound unless it springs from a personal (and necessarily subjective) comprehension of the apostle's point of standing within his own history." Yoder, *To Hear the Word*, 131.

the text speak to us, a position consistent with and supportive of pacifist epistemology.

The result of this hermeneutical standpoint that is open to both the congregation and the strange perspective of the Bible is that the Scriptures make readers dysfunctional, but in a way that is humanizing, that makes us into the lovely and loving creatures God intended us to be when God created us. This humanizing dysfunctionality is precipitated in the biblical text through the discursive and performative momentum created by at least three kinds of tensions found in the Bible.

The first tension is that of generic and literary difference. Like a good library, the Bible contains texts that address a variety of different human situations and problems. As such, one finds in the Bible many contrasting methods of communication and artistic appeal. For those who want to discover who they are, the historical narratives of Israel and the church provide a background against which to live out the drama of one's own life as a member of God's people. For those who struggle with the extraordinary emotions of human experience—love, hate, delight, anger, desire, fear, and more, the Psalms provide poetry and music. For those who seek practical guidance amidst the recurring patterns of human failure, the wisdom literature of Proverbs and Ecclesiastes offers rules for living and decision-making. For those who seek empowerment to challenge the sins of self and world, the prophetic texts offer judgment and hope. For those who seek spiritual counsel and admonition there are the pastoral epistles. For those who desire a perspective on how all of this going to turn out, there is the apocalyptical literature. The changing demands of human experience are addressed in all of these genres in concrete rather than general ways.

The second tension is one of perspective and conviction. The Hebrew Bible provides what Walter Brueggemann has called disputed testimony about the nature and purposes of God.[30] We find as we read that we have the experience of being in a jury box of the biblical courtroom, listening to competing arguments and being asked to decide which one to accept. Is the God of Israel an angry God who destroys the disobedient with water and fire or is Yahweh a God of mercy and love who refuses to revoke the covenant God has made with God's people? Should the alien be removed from the community or welcomed as a friend? Are we to pursue purity or hospitality? Should we fight for God or will God fight

---

30. Brueggemann, *Theology of the OT*, 82–83.

for us? These and a vast array of other disputes about God and humanity are not finally settled in the Scriptures. As James Barr has written, "the working out of the biblical model for the understanding of God was not an intellectual process so much as a personal conflict, in which men struggled with their God, and with each other about their God."[31]

Third, we discover in the biblical story changing circumstances of godly intervention and will-manifestation. At times God shows up in the earthquake and at other times through a still, small voice. In one moment, God sends plagues and in another manna. God may harden the Pharaoh's heart or God may remove the scales from the eyes of Saul. This God, in the testimony of Moses, both kills and makes alive, both wounds and heals (Deuteronomy 32:39). Perhaps most decisively, in the Christian inflection of Scripture, this God was revealed to the ancestors through the prophets, "but in these last days by a Son whom he appointed heir of all things, through whom he also created the worlds" (Heb 1:1–2).

It is against the backdrop of such difference, debate, and development in the Scriptures that we can find ourselves with the apocalyptic seer before the mighty angel wrapped in a cloud, with a rainbow over his head, with a face like the sun, and with legs like pillars of fire—one foot planted in the sea and the other in the land—holding a scroll. We hear the voice from heaven: "Go take the scroll." We hear the angelic invitation, "Take it, and eat; it will be bitter to your stomach, but sweet as honey in your mouth" (Rev 10:1–11).

Eugene Peterson's riff on this text emphasizes how consuming the biblical text through contemplative and prayerful reading opens up the true world of God—a world that is beyond our control, without obvious relationships between causes and effects, and full of upsetting miracles. This world—the real world—disrupts the dream world of our adolescent expectations, where everything works out on our behalf. "For most of us it takes years and years and years to exchange our dream world for the real world of grace and mercy, sacrifice and love, freedom and joy."[32]

Indeed, the consumption of the scriptures can be seen as a kind of antidote to the sort of corrupting consumption that ravages our everyday lives amidst the empire of the market. The scroll appears before us as a kind of truth drug, like the red pill in *The Matrix* films. We are invited

---

31. Quoted in Peterson, *Eat This Book*, 105.
32. Ibid.

to eat it, taste its sweetness and be forewarned of the bitter feeling in our stomachs.

Such scriptural consumption is dangerous, however, and not something to try out on one's own. The proper image of scriptural consumption is not so much the private dinner but the community potluck. Swallow the text whole, but make sure you are with others who can help you out if you get too sick on your stomach. When the gathered body of Christ consumes the Word of God, taking it up in discussion and taking it in through prayer, the Word becomes enfleshed again among us. The "real world" of God becomes visible once again before the blinded world.

Eugene Peterson emphasizes how the "real world" that is available to us in the consumption of Scripture is not imposed upon us: "God's word is personal address, inviting, commanding, challenging, rebuking, judging, comforting, directing. But not forcing. Not coercing. We are given space and freedom to answer, to enter into the conversation. From beginning to end, the word of God is a dialogical word, a word that invites participation."[33] Thus, the truth we discover in the consumption of the Scriptures is a truth that can only be received rightly as a gift, as good news, and only ever offered to others in the same way.

By definition, the good news cannot be offered at the point of a sword or the barrel of a gun or the threat of a lawsuit. The good news is subject to rejection, just as we must be if we are to become its body—its agency. To become aligned with the world that God is bringing about is also to yield to both the friendly and the hostile reception of that world by the worldly audience. Or, as Yoder puts it, "readiness to bear [the audience's] hostility is part of the message."[34]

It might be objected that such an approach to scripture is inconclusive, with the potential to sideline central Christian convictions, including the teachings of Jesus himself. My assumption, an important and contestable one, is that the authority and power of the life of Jesus Christ as presented in the Scriptures does not require grounding in a unified reading of the entire Bible as a noncontradictory discourse aligned with the teachings of Jesus, although that is one conclusion that might be drawn. Certainly much of Yoder's exegetical work on the Old Testament, as it appeared in chapter 4 of *The Politics of Jesus* or *The Jewish-Christian Schism Revisited*, for example, stresses the extent to which there is more

---

33. Ibid., 109.
34. Yoder, "On Not Being Ashamed," 52.

consistency than many Christians have been tempted to see between the God of Israel and the God of Jesus Christ. At the same time, Yoder acknowledges that the Bible contains trajectories of conviction (i.e. royal ideology in parts of the Hebrew scriptures) that differ from the ultimate confirmation of the prophetic and exilic posture that is found in the life of Jesus Christ.[35] My account of diversity in the Bible here allows perhaps more of an unsettled tension or ongoing argument than Yoder did between, for example, the prophetic and priestly trajectories found in the Hebrew scriptures. It also assumes a not always resolved conversation in the church about how a commitment to the God revealed in Jesus Christ assists us in entering the ongoing argument about the meaning of God's will for God's people as it was revealed to the priests and prophets and poets of the Hebrew scriptures as well as to the gospel and epistle writers of the New Testament.

As was just noted, Yoder wrote that a text is best understood within the congregation as the living body of Christ. However, as John Nugent has argued, Yoder also believed that Jesus' teachings had the authority to relativize strands of the Old Testament that contradict the posture found in Jesus Christ.[36] In this light, I am more inclined than Yoder to allow contradictory exegesis to stand, at least in the short term, in the faith that the story of Jesus Christ will ultimately prevail.

My purpose in stressing the appearance of the story of Jesus Christ amidst an ongoing scriptural argument—perhaps to a greater extent than is apparent in Yoder's writings—is to highlight the way in which the story, teaching, and life of Jesus Christ makes a powerful witness to the peaceable reign of God precisely because it does not seek to suppress all that questions it. Just as following Jesus Christ in discipleship involves acting in faith rather than from necessity, so discovering the good news found in the Scriptures invites acceptance of the gospel without requiring the

---

35. See, for example, the chapter titled "To Serve Our God and Rule the World" in *The Royal Priesthood*, in which Yoder acknowledges that "as long as the royal house of Judah stood, the royal ideology could claim equal status in the same histories and in the psalms beside the prophetic one" (133). John Nugent has made a study of Yoder's Old Testament exegesis in which he stresses that Yoder was seeking in his interpretation to expand readers' recognition of neglected themes in the Old Testament texts that are confirmed in the life of Jesus Christ. Nugent notes that Yoder recognized rival strands within the biblical text while only granting those that are consistent with Jesus' teachings the authority to relativize those strands that contradict the posture that culminates in Jesus Christ. Nugent, *Politics of Yahweh*, 107.

36. See note 35.

overcoming of all counterarguments, even those found in the Bible. By faith, I remain confident as a Christian that the will of God as revealed in Jesus Christ is a truth that is "unkillable," even as it is revealed most fully in a context of contestation and even rejection.[37] Moreover, this "pacifist" way of knowing the truth of Jesus Christ is an expression of the peaceable way of Jesus Christ to which we are invited. And finally, even if a bit more open-ended, this "pacifist" way of knowing it is an extension of Yoder's comment quoted earlier in this volume that the truth of Jesus cannot keep dry above or overwhelm the sea of relativism/pluralism. Rather we seek "a way to stay within our bark, barely afloat and sometimes awash amidst those waves, yet neither dissolving into them nor being carried only where they want to push it."[38]

Remembrance, Forgiveness, and Obedience

The gospel epistemology that I have been describing here is a comprehensive experience of the world, even if it is as scandalously particular as a revelation of God in the life of a particular (temporarily divided) people—Israel and the church. There is a past, a future, and a present dimension of gospel consciousness, discovered first of all in the reading of the scriptures with other believers under the guidance of the Holy Spirit, but then also instantiated in the way we come to see our places in the unfolding drama of God's story in our own time and place.

The memory of the past—both that of the human societies and of our own personal histories—is for the believer embedded in the story of God's people as found in the Bible. That story is one of failure, forgiveness, and faithfulness. God's people fail God and one another while God both judges and forgives their failures. In the process of owning this story of failure and forgiveness as their own, God's people in obedience extend to one another and to their neighbors the grace and forgiveness that they have received.

In *Body Politics*, Yoder shows how the memory of God's forgiveness is represented in the practice of binding and loosing within congregational life, based on following the law of Christ. The law of Christ states

---

37. "Die Warheit ist untödlich" is an epigram that appeared in most of Balthasar Hubmaier's works, translated by Yoder as "Truth Is Unkillable." Hubmaier, *Balthasar Hubmaier*, 76–77 n. 10.

38. Yoder, "But We Do," *Priestly*, 58; Yoder, "But We Do," *Pacifist*, 34.

that we forgive others just as God forgives us, an axiom stated conditionally in the Lord's Prayer: "forgive us our sins as we forgive those who sin against us." Paul's restatement of this law emphasizes our actions in response to the forgiveness we have already received from God: "just as the Lord has forgiven you, so you must also forgive" (Col 3:13).[39]

Yoder stresses that God's forgiveness is concretely manifested through the binding and loosing process undertaken by God's people, a process whereby relationships are restored between offenders and offended through a combination of dialogue and discernment. In dialogue is established the truth of an offense; in discernment is discovered the route to restoration. Forgiveness is not simply a matter of dismissing or forgetting an offense, but rather a truth-seeking restoration of broken relationships in which a binding memory of an injury precedes the loosing forgiveness of an enemy.[40] As Yoder puts it: "there is an intimate link between forgiving and making ethical decisions."[41]

Yoder's point that binding is part of the process of loosing is helpfully illuminated by Miroslav Volf, who has argued that in order for the injuries of the past to be rightly remembered, the gospel call urges both an accurate recall of such injury and a readiness to forget it.[42] For example, the ability to forget is not unrelated to the severity of the injury. Some injuries are easier to forget than others and such distinctions regarding severity of injury must be part of any restoration process involving forgiveness. Put another way, suppressing memories of injury makes forgiveness impossible. One cannot forgive what one cannot recall.

At the same time, as Derrida has argued, forgiveness by definition is not simply a matter of justice or balancing right and wrong, but rather of giving away what cannot be restored. True forgiveness could only ever properly be offered in response to an unforgiveable offense. By contrast an action that is apparently forgiveable by definition can be compensated within an economy of exchange and justice—by reparation or restitution. Derrida thus distinguishes between pure forgiveness, which is impossible, and transactional forgiveness, which occurs in human history, but is only given meaning by reference to the horizon of the impossible form of forgiveness—forgiving the unforgiveable. He writes, "Sometimes,

---

39. Yoder, *Body Politics*, 4–5.
40. Ibid., 6–13.
41. Yoder, *He Came Preaching Peace*, 122.
42. Volf, *End of Memory*, 204–5.

forgiveness (given by God, or inspired by divine prescription) must be a gracious gift, without exchange and without condition; sometimes it requires, as its minimal condition, the repentance and transformation of the sinner." Furthermore, he argues, "It is between these two poles, *irreconcilable but indissociable*, that decisions and responsibilities are to be taken."[43]

Stated another way, the memory of God's gracious and impossible acts of forgiveness toward us provides a horizon against which it is possible to contemplate the offering of forgiveness to others—even when such forgiveness is flawed, limited, and conditional. And such a practice of both honest remembering and free forgetting is the condition of possibility for an anticipated future in which reconciled enemies make historically visible their already accomplished reconciliation in Christ. For Volf, the eucharistic body of Christ is the crucial location of such a realized future: "by remembering Christ's Passion, we remember ourselves as what we shall be—members of one communion of love, comprised of wrongdoers and the wronged."[44] Yoder frames this possibility of radical forgiveness within the context of God's excessive grace and mercy toward humanity: "We can stop loving only the lovable, lending only to the reliable, giving only to the grateful, as soon as we grasp and are grasped by the unconditionality of the benevolence of God."[45]

The astonishing presence of Amish families at the funeral of Charles Roberts is perhaps a most eucharistic instance of such practices of memory and anticipation that are energized by God's unconditional benevolence, even though communion was not served. But in more ordinary contexts, the capacity of members of Christ's broken body—alienated from one another as they might be—to gather in right relationship around the Lord's table is indeed a practice that makes visible the cross-formed grain of the universe. And any such miraculous actions that yield one's memories to God, in the hope of the world to come, whether they take place in the sanctuary or the marketplace, are evidence of the possible obedience that right remembering and hopeful anticipation make visible.

Mennonite missionary David A. Shank tells the story of attending one of Karl Barth's seminars in the early 1950s with John Howard Yoder. Barth was discussing with students the relationship between the memory

43. Derrida, *On Cosmopolitanism and Forgiveness*, 44–45.
44. Volf, *End of Memory*, 119.
45. Yoder, *Original Revolution*, 48.

of the cross and resurrection on the one hand and the anticipation of the future coming of the Lord on the other hand as the basis for Christian hope. When a student asked what the task of the Christian is during the meanwhile, between the past event of the cross and the anticipation of the second coming, Barth responded, "In-between we look back and remember, and we look forward and hope. We remember . . . and hope." David Shank recalls, "I was sitting beside John Howard, and close enough to hear him mumble under his breath, 'We obey!'"[46]

There are several ways to read Yoder's interjection during Karl Barth's lecture. Obedience can be posed as a kind of action-focused alternative to belief-centered Christianity, orthopraxy trumps orthodoxy. Obedience can also be understood as the next thing that follows once remembering and hoping have happened: Action must be rooted in correct theology, especially eschatology. But this essay has shown that instead of replacing or following faithful contemplation, the patient yet revolutionary yielding associated with practices of remembrance and hope is itself an act of obedience, whether it is an organized experience of worship, a prayerful meditation, or an act of social protest. Knowing the reconciled creation is the same thing as yielding to it, the same thing as making the peace that Jesus Christ gives.

Where earlier chapters described the patience of revolutionary subordination, this chapter has developed that patience into a pacifist epistemology derived from John Howard Yoder's way of knowing from Jesus Christ.[47] The following chapter deals with the activist and public dimensions of Yoder's pacifist way of knowing.

---

46. David A. Shank, "Another Grandpa David Story . . . We Obey!" Memo in the possession of the author.

47. Although this chapter may have presented a technically correct interpretation of Yoder's understanding of revolutionary subordination, the variations in applying this term evident between chapters 4 and 6 and here indicate that no clear consensus exists on how best to understand and apply it. These variations demonstrate that the language is easily misconstrued, and thus chapter 13 suggests using a better choice of words, particularly when addressing women who have experienced patriarchal abuse and misconduct.

9

A Nonviolent Public Ethic[1]

GLEN HAROLD STASSEN

This chapter has a twofold agenda. For one, it develops the nonviolent public ethic that emerges from Yoder's focus on a more historically grounded, more Jewish-rooted, more particular, thicker Jesus. This Christology was sketched in the Introduction and developed more fully in chapter 1. Second, in developing this public ethic, the chapter will also respond to a number of the prejudices and false assumptions that have kept people from hearing this Jesus from Yoder. Carrying out these two agenda items then speaks to the agenda of Yoder's ethics, namely to show what the "politics of Jesus" have to offer contemporary church life and the world. This description of Yoder's nonviolent, activist public ethics complements the previous chapter, which displayed Yoder's pacifism as a patient and defenseless way to view the world.

---

1. This chapter draws on "Jesus Is No Sectarian: John H. Yoder's Christological Peacemaking Ethics," which is my Introduction to Yoder, *War of the Lamb*.

Overcoming Prejudices

The Prejudice of Effectiveness

Yoder wrote that the last chapter of *Politics of Jesus*, which argued for faithfulness over effectiveness, unsettled some readers because they erroneously thought it was a call for withdrawal from social involvement. It was "offensive to contemporaries because it seemed to some to constitute an *argument* to the effect that even in other times and settings, such as our own, withdrawal from social involvement" was mandated. "It was not that, as my other writings make clear, but it is fascinating that readers thought so."[2] His other writings do make that clear.

Yoder's argument on behalf of an ethics of faithfulness rather than effectiveness is well know.[3] However, what he meant has been misconstrued. In *The War of the Lamb* he described how Tolstoy, Gandhi, and King had a "cosmological conversion," in which they each saw God as the ruler of the universe. Therefore, they believed that action faithfully in tune with God's rule is likely to be more effective. Yoder agreed. He noticed the theme of God as ruler of the universe and highlighted it in Tolstoy and King because it was a central theme in his own faith, and he saw something analogous in Gandhi. Thus Yoder wrote,

> To say "the means are the ends in process of becoming" is a cosmological or an eschatological statement. It presupposes a *cosmos*—a world with some kind of discernible moral cause-effect coherence. Unlike Kant, for whom the hereafter was needed to make the moral accounting come out even, this view claims coherence within history. But for this claim to work, one must believe that in some sense suffering is redemptive, or (as King will say it) "there is something in the universe that unfolds for justice" . . . For King it was the Black Baptist vision of another Moses leading his people from Egypt, another Joshua fighting at Jericho, a promised land we can see from the mountain top, a cross on Golgotha from which one can see the heavens opening. King also said it in terms of the American dream, the humanism of the fathers of the Republic, and even in terms of the federal politics of the Kennedy brothers.
>
> To say with King that "love is the most durable power in the world," or that "there is something in the universe that unfolds

---

2. Yoder, *War of the Lamb*, 64; Yoder's italics.
3. Yoder, *Politics of Jesus* (1994), ch. 12.

for justice," is not to claim a sure insight into the way martyrdom works as a social power, although martyrdom often does that. It is a confessional or kerygmatic statement made by those whose loyalty to Christ (or to universal love, or to *satyagraha*) they understand to be validated by its cosmic ground. Suffering love is not right because it "works" in any calculable short-run way (although it often does). It is right because it goes with the grain of the universe, and that is why *in the long run* nothing else will work....

Perseverance in the face of sacrifice and creativity in the face of dismay are heightened for those who believe that the grain of the universe is with them.[4]

In *The War of the Lamb*, Yoder made several arguments for nonviolent action as usually more effective than violent action. And he argues insightfully for accurate, balanced ways of assessing that comparative effectiveness. He was not giving up effectiveness; he was restoring it to its proper, but limited, place within sound theological and eschatological ethics.

Reinhold Niebuhr's Marginalizing of Pacifism

Reinhold Niebuhr marginalized nonviolence as an idealism without responsibility for effectiveness. He wrote of "the failure of liberal Protestantism to recognize the coercive character of political and economic life. To refuse the use of any coercive methods means that we do not recognize that everyone is using them all the time, that we all live in and benefit or suffer from a political and economic order that maintains its cohesion partially by the use of various forms of political and economic coercion."[5] Niebuhr argued from the need for coercion to the need for force, and then violence, and then war (often eliding these different categories into one).[6] He argued that "responsible" Christian ethics must

---

4. Yoder, *War of the Lamb*, 61, 62.

5. Niebuhr, "Why I Leave the F.O.R.," 254–55, first published in *Christian Century*, January 3, 1934.

6. See discussion in Stassen and Westmoreland-White, "Defining Violence." For an argument that challenges the single continuum assumption described here for Niebuhr and counters with a two-continua solution in line with the activism described for Yoder in this chapter, see Weaver, "Living in the Reign of God," 187–90. A brief discussion of one versus two continua appears in Weaver, "Response to Hans Boersma," 76–77.

recognize that national policy needs to be pragmatic, and to have a strong sense of sin, the tragic, and the ambiguous. Thus, as Yoder has pointed out, the test that Niebuhr applied to Christian ethics was its adequacy for national policy, not for Christian witness in churches. By contrast, Yoder showed ways that nonviolent witness can claim "responsible" political involvement, over against Niebuhr as well as over against a sectarian ethics of withdrawal.

Niebuhr believed that Christian pacifism was based on a legalistic absolute—love as pure unselfishness, nonresistance, or nonviolence, absolutistically understood.[7]

Religious absolutism in its pure form is either apocalyptic or ascetic. In either case, it is not compatible with political responsibility. When apocalyptic, as in the thought of Jesus, it sets the absolute principles of the coming Kingdom of God, principles of uncompromising love and nonresistance, in sharp juxtaposition to the relativities of the economic and political order and assumes no responsibilities for the latter.[8]

The effort to achieve a standard of perfect love "could only be done by disavowing the political task and by freeing the individual of all responsibility for social justice."[9] Moral absolutes have no place in the necessary pragmatism of public policy, Niebuhr said. "We can find no stable absolute in the shifting situation of the social struggle where everything must be finally decided in pragmatic terms."[10] Yoder confronted this stereotype at four key points:[11]

1) He rejected the idea that suitability for adoption as national policy was the proper test for Christian ethics. Christian ethics is for the witness made by churches, not for national political leaders. The test of its adequacy is not whether national policy will adopt it, but whether it is faithful to the gospel of Jesus Christ. We cannot make the interests of the president of the United States, or of a party in Congress, with all their mixed motives and pragmatic or nationalistic calculations, into the judge of the adequacy of Christian witness. To do so is to fall into the error of

---

7. Niebuhr, "Why the Christian Church," 8, 10.

8. Niebuhr, "Pacifism Against the Wall," 261, reprinted from *The American Scholar*, Spring 1936.

9. Niebuhr, "Why the Christian Church," 4–5.

10. Niebuhr, "Pacifism Against the Wall," 257.

11. Yoder, *Christian Attitudes*, chs. 18–20.

Constantinianism, making Christian ethics into a chaplain for Christendom. Jesus Christ is Lord, not the president or Congress.

2) Yoder had a realistic, not idealistic, view of churches as well as of national policies. He argued realistically in *The War of the Lamb* that churches and nations have usually acted neither on the basis of nonviolence nor even of just war theory, but on the basis of nationalism, right of state, or crusade.

3) Yoder rejected the idea that Christian ethics was based on an absolutist ideal. Ernst Troeltsch and most ethicists he influenced, including Niebuhr, claimed that churches of the sect type depend on norms that take the form of absolute legalism. Since the society will not accept absolute norms, the argument goes, these witness groups must either withdraw from responsible engagement in society, or try to force their norms on society by authoritarian takeover. So Niebuhr wrote of "religious absolutism as expressed in the Sermon on the Mount." This is not only an outdated, nineteenth-century idealist interpretation of the Sermon on the Mount.[12] For Yoder, the norm was not a legalistic absolute, as Niebuhr thought, but Jesus Christ as Lord.[13] With Jesus Christ as norm, a thick exegesis of the way of Jesus Christ is required, as Yoder famously had done in his *Politics of Jesus*. And it requires a hermeneutic for what witness to Jesus as Lord means in societies such as ours. The Jesus of the gospel story

> is not simply different from the Jesus of the liberal optimism that Niebuhr attacked. He is also different from Niebuhr's ethic of responsibility, by being a much more consciously political figure, in his statements, public action, and formal teaching, than Niebuhr was willing to admit. Therefore the Jesus of this story represents an option Niebuhr did not have on his scale.[14]

Jesus Christ does not proclaim or constitute an absolute rule. He is rather a proclamation of kingdom breakthroughs, hope in the Holy Spirit, a hope that churches can sometimes respond to the gospel.

---

12. Stassen, *Living the Sermon*; Stassen, "Fourteen Triads"; Stassen, "Concrete Christological Norms," 172–73.
13. Yoder, *Nevertheless*, 96–97, 133–38.
14. Yoder, *Christian Attitudes*, 317.

4) Yoder consistently called for the Christian witness to the state, as his book by that title indicates.[15] There he wrote, "Our purpose is to analyze whether it is truly the case that a Christian pacifist position rooted not in pragmatic. . . but in christological considerations is thereby irrelevant to the social order."[16] He did not expect the state to follow a legalistic or perfectionistic absolute, or to understand and submit to the gospel of Jesus Christ. Nonetheless, a witness shaped by the gospel of Jesus Christ to the state is quite possible.

Yoder names political leaders who have been faithful, including my own father—for which I am grateful.[17] He rejected the label "sectarian" for his own method,[18] and instead intentionally advocated a method in which a Christian pacifist does not seek to control history, but does advocate peacemaking practices that are effective in reducing the society's and the government's violence. Thus, in *The War of the Lamb*, he offered one section on pacifism, a second section on just war, and a final section on peacemaking practices that are proving effective. This means churches are not faced with the absolute either/or choice of asking the government to become nonviolent, or having nothing to say to them. We can develop an ethic that prods politicians to be less violent, and to engage in justice-making and peacemaking initiatives that are effective in decreasing war and violence.

These four points make clear that Yoder's ethics is not susceptible to Niebuhr's claim that pacifists are perfectionistic absolutists who have nothing to say to the "real" world. It is important to notice that Yoder's refutations of these first two misunderstandings are based on a historically contextualized understanding of Jesus as revelation of God's way and of God's kingdom breaking into our world, as described in the Introduction and chapter 1.

The Sectarian Stereotype

Numerous mainline ethicists have categorized Stanley Hauerwas as a sectarian who focuses only introspectively on the church and who then

---

15. Yoder, *Christian Witness* (2002).
16. Ibid., 7.
17. Yoder, *Priestly Kingdom*, 180–81.
18. Yoder, *For the Nations*, 3–8.

opposes the development of a public ethic for the society. These writers then stereotype Yoder as identical with Hauerwas but without evidence of having read Yoder carefully. They thus deprive themselves and their readers of learning from Yoder. Without here engaging the rightness or wrongness of their criticisms of Hauerwas, it can be said that Hauerwas himself has acknowledged that articles pointing out the contrast between Yoder and himself have become a "minor publishing industry."[19] At this writing, I have read seven such articles.

It is simply irresponsible for any scholar to stereotype Yoder as approaching the question of a public ethic in the same way as Hauerwas. In fact, this is precisely the question on which Yoder was distancing himself from Hauerwas in his last ten years. In five comments in the beginning of *For the Nations*, named to distinguish his social ethics from Hauerwas's *Against the Nations*, Yoder explicitly distanced himself from Hauerwas on precisely the point of sectarianism. Responsible scholars need to "take up and read"—for their own good and to save their students and churches from decline into thin vacuousness without a thicker Jesus. Hauerwas, deeply and sincerely loyal to much that he has learned from Yoder, would agree with this stated need for a thicker description of Jesus.

In his plans for *The War of the Lamb*, Yoder wrote that the title intentionally points to the Quaker understanding, symbolized by William Penn as Governor of Pennsylvania and Roger Williams as Governor of Rhode Island, that nonviolence does not require us to withdraw from having and carrying out an effective public ethic in pluralistic society. Nor is it based on weakness. It is based on the triumph of the crucified. This counters the dualistic view, especially articulated by Reinhold Niebuhr, that there are two kinds of ethics: effectiveness and principled purity, and that nonviolence has to belong to the second kind. Yoder referred both to Gandhi's concern for effectiveness and to Gene Sharp's massive study of the effectiveness of nonviolent action. These advocates of the effectiveness of nonviolence break apart Niebuhr's dichotomy.[20] Here Yoder's emphases on the dynamic providence of God, the resurrection triumph of the crucified Jesus, and the effectiveness of nonviolence, guide us in making a public witness.

In the chapter titled "The Science of Conflict" in *The War of the Lamb*, Yoder argues that we need to incorporate research by political

---

19. Hauerwas, *Hannah's Child*, 246.
20. Yoder, *War of the Lamb*, ch. 7, esp. 102–4, and chs. 11 and 14.

scientists like Robert Johansen on new theories in international relations and on a nonviolent world police force, and research in anthropology, sociology, and psychology on aggression and conflict resolution. Christians should not withdraw from or ignore such research, he said, but incorporate its truth into our thinking, our theories, and our theological ethics.[21]

When Yoder and I were planning our book, *Authentic Transformation: A New Vision of Christ and Culture*, I wanted to conclude the book by offering our own revised typology of relations between Christ and culture so readers could visualize how we would correct H. R. Niebuhr's typology with a better typology. But Yoder was so genuinely troubled by how Niebuhr's typology was being used to convince Mennonite students to desert their own tradition and its pacifism that he refused to include even an alternative typology.[22] I then began to urge, "Let's not cop out . . ." Yoder immediately flushed bright red. I knew what he was thinking of—the Niebuhrian stereotype of Mennonites as "copping out" from responsible engagement in the social struggle. I rushed to explain that I meant we should not cop out from at least providing a typology of ways churches *evade* the way of Jesus. Yoder immediately accepted this—and the red subsided. When the book was finished, he said to me and coauthor Dianne Yeager, "I am so glad we set Glen free to write the concluding chapter."

As this incident shows, Yoder was deeply opposed to being understood as an advocate of an ethic of withdrawal. He was deeply committed to developing an ethic loyal to the Lordship of Christ, which covered not only private life or the life of the churches, but envisioned and covered all of life. His themes of the Lordship of Christ, the normativity of the way of Jesus for all Christians, including Christians beyond the peace churches, and at least six of his books *The Christian Witness to the State*, *The Politics of Jesus*, *Priestly Kingdom*, *Body Politics*, *For the Nations*, and *The War of the Lamb*, all point to a witness in pluralistic society. This witness includes a public ethic expressed in both pluralistic language as well as in the language of Christian discipleship. Since Yoder said this in at least these six different books, it is no minor theme, despite its being

---

21. Following Yoder's lead on the intersection of theology with the social sciences, J. Denny Weaver showed the correlation between his view of atonement theology, as sketched in chapter 11 below, and recent research on forgiveness in psychology. See Weaver, "Forgiveness and (Non)Violence," and Weaver, *Nonviolent God*, ch. 8.

22. See Yoder's explanation in Stassen, Yeager, and Yoder, *Authentic Transformation*, 82.

overlooked by inattentive interpreters. In *Authentic Transformation* and in *Priestly Kingdom* he wrote that we need to be able to speak the languages of the society in order to develop articulateness about which languages in pluralistic society are useful for communicating our witness, which languages first need to be transformed, and which must be flatly rejected. In chapter 1 of this book we observed Yoder's use of multiple languages in the discussion of Christology—the several translations that went into the New Testament images and then again in Yoder's reference to the language of pluralism/relativism in our contemporary context. Yoder is quite clear about the need to understand and assess the society's languages in order to develop antibodies against being manipulated into supporting unjust ideologies of the powers and authorities.[23] He wrote about the lordship of Christ for all Christians in all of life, and for all persons and all powers and authorities in all of life. A following section explains that for Yoder, displaying the Lordship of Christ for all dimensions of life was an extension of the incarnation.

Churches can witness publicly by *modeling innovation*, by their own faithful practices inside the church communities. As chapter 7 explained in some detail on the basis of *Body Politics*, churches can advocate the societal implications of Christian normative practices for such social concerns as racial inclusion, conflict resolution, feeding the hungry, and democratic decision-making.

External actions also provide models. Churches have taken action to found orphanages, hospitals, universities, and in practicing agricultural missions, and more. Governments have noticed such works, and church practices have stimulated innovations in state policies. This is one form of public witness that Yoder advocated.

As Mark Thiessen Nation depicted Yoder's public witness,[24]

> Our life together is comprised of "a covenanting group of men and women who instruct one another, forgive one another, bear one another's burdens, and reinforce one another's witness."[25] This community provides mutual support and accountability.
>
> It is also the case that this "alternative community discharges a modeling mission. The church is called to be now

---

23. Ibid., 67–71.

24. Nation, "Politics of Yoder," 45–46. References in the quote are to Yoder's texts cited by Nation.

25. Yoder, *Nevertheless*, 135.

what the world is called to be ultimately."[26] In fact, "the existence of a human community dedicated in common to a new and publicly scandalous enemy-loving way of life is itself a new social datum."[27] And because the existence of this community is a result of "the priority of God's grace," we are emboldened to say that the practices of the church "are actions of God, in and with, through and under what men and women do."[28] Thus it is important to realize that the Christian community, empowered by the Holy Spirit, exists as a witness to the gospel of Jesus Christ. And it is precisely in giving this witness—embodying love for neighbors and even enemies—that this community gives its life for a society.[29] And this community gives its life for the world around us, we still must still nurture the identity of this community because "only a continuing community dedicated to a deviant value system can change the world."[30]

Churches also witness publicly by *translating multilingually*, making selective and tactical use of normative language in the society. "The Christian can speak to the statesman, without failing to take account of their differing presuppositions, using pagan or secular terminology to clothe social critique without ascribing to those secular concepts any metaphysical value outside of Christ."[31] We should learn to speak the language of the society where we are, adopting a multilingual method.[32] "Every secular hope is true and necessary as a criticism of ingrown and complacent 'religion.'. . . Secular hopes are necessary because secular language is the only language there is. If we do not say 'Jesus Christ is Lord' in language that men can understand, then we are not saying it at all." The problem is not translation; it is whether the translation "is big enough and true enough to say everything that the name Jesus Christ must mean."[33] We must assess translation languages by the norm of the

---

26. Yoder, *Priestly Kingdom*, 92.
27. Yoder, *Nevertheless*, 136.
28. Yoder, *Body Politics*, 72–73.
29. Yoder, *Nevertheless*, 135.
30. Ibid., 136.
31. Yoder, *Christian Witness* (2002), 73.
32. Yoder, *For the Nations*, 2–3.
33. Ibid., 121.

way of Jesus, affirming what is helpful and correcting or criticizing what is not.[34]

Speaking multiple languages enables making tactical alliances with secular assumptions such as relativism, liberation, Gandhi, or the Enlightenment.

> We may be tactical allies of the pluralist/relativist deconstruction of deceptive orthodox claims to logically coercive certainty, without making of relativism itself a new monism. We will share tactical use of liberation language to dismantle the alliance of church with privilege, without letting the promises made by some in the name of revolution become a new opiate. . . . We may then find tactical alliances with the Enlightenment, as did Quakers and Baptists in the century after their expulsion from the Puritan colonies, or with the Gandhian vision, as did Martin Luther King, Jr.[35]

In *For the Nations*, Yoder criticized "communitarians" for focusing exclusively on the strategy of modeling internally, and he criticized liberals for focusing exclusively on secular political witness. The communitarians among us

> will not risk the challenge of telling the world that servanthood, enemy love, and forgiveness would be a better way to run a university, a town, or a factory. They pull back on the grounds that only they have already experienced the power and novelty of that threefold evangelical cord in the worship and ministry of the church. They affirm integrity but at the cost of witness.

The "public Catholics" and liberals among us

> are concerned not to look foolish to their sophisticated neighbors by making any claims or promises linked to the particularity of the Jew Jesus (or of their own denominational past). By dropping the particular baggage of normative servanthood, enemy love, and forgiveness, they think they might make it easy . . . to talk their neighbors' language, but they do so at the cost of having nothing to say that the neighbors do not already know.[36]

A third way is called for. When the church that lives in Jesus Christ has learned the multiple languages of its society, this third way can be

---

34. Stassen, Yeager, and Yoder, *Authentic Transformation*, 67–71.
35. Yoder, "But We Do," *Priestly*, 61–62; Yoder, "But We Do," *Pacifist*, 38.
36. Yoder, *For the Nations*, 49.

found in a free-church community that witnesses to the Lordship of Christ over all of life—in the community and in the world. "Only a believing community with a 'thick' particular identity has something to say to whatever 'public' is 'out there' to address. And . . . only the community that welcomes the challenge of public witness can justify . . . its distinctive witness."[37]

"The entire Christian community is sent into the world to 'communicate a message and gather its hearers into communities' . . . What we do about social justice or about education should then be no less 'missionary' than what we do about crossing linguistic or political borders and communicating our convictions to unbelievers."[38]

Experiencing Overpowering Grace

In the baccalaureate sermon at Associated Mennonite Biblical Seminary, May 19, 2000, I said, "A call has come from Steven Dintaman, Ted Koontz, John Roth, Duane Shank, Duane Friesen [and now I add Paul Martens[39]] for a clearer emphasis on grace." Some of the papers from the wonderful conference at Elizabethtown College on revisioning the Anabaptist vision[40] "argued that Harold Bender and John Howard Yoder and the Concerns group have put their emphasis on deeds of discipleship and have neglected the need for grace—the need for a personal relationship with Jesus, the need for the presence of the living Christ, and the presence of the Holy in our lives."[41]

I have argued that, in fact, Yoder has written more about grace and the Holy Spirit than people realize, and I prodded Yoder himself to emphasize this yet further. I have also urged those who sense this need not simply to criticize, but to develop those themes themselves in ways faithful to Yoder's loyalty to the living Christ, and to Jesus Christ as revelation of the character of God as present in our lives and history. Now Paul Martens and Jenny Howell have published *Essential Writings*, filling in these themes from Yoder's own writings.[42]

37. Ibid., 42.
38. Ibid., 7.
39. Martens, "Discipleship."
40. Papers in *The Mennonite Quarterly Review* (July 1995).
41. Stassen, "Grace as Participation," 64.
42. Yoder, *Essential Writings*.

Part Three—Extending John Howard Yoder's Theology

Yoder displayed a major dimension of his own spirituality when he wrote:

> Hugh Barbour's exposition of the subjective religious experience of radical Puritanism in England, under the heading "The Terror and Power of the Light," interprets profoundly the rootage of the renunciation of violence in the inner experience of overpowering grace. What the Anabaptists of the sixteenth century called *Gelassenheit*, or what the early Dunkards called *perfect love*, or what frontier farmer preachers of the nineteenth century called *humility*, or what their Wesleyan contemporaries called *sanctification*, represent closely related but distinguishable labels for the view of human dignity that frees the believer from temptations to feel called to set the world right by force. Probably this commonality is more important subjectively for the peace churches' peace witness than any of the more standard ethical issues I was reviewing before.[43]

In the essay just cited, Yoder had been reviewing and analyzing the ethical argument of the U.S. Catholic bishops' *Challenge of Peace*. But he was dissatisfied with a purely ethical analysis; it overlooked a deeper faith dimension that was important for him and for the religious experience of the historic peace churches—the experience of God's grace that underlies the peace churches' peace witness. Yoder realized that the experiential dimension and spiritual commitment crucial for peace church traditions cannot be reduced to ethical argument.

In his book *Nevertheless*, and elsewhere, Yoder said that nonviolence is not adequately understood as an absolute ethical rule; it is loyalty not to a law but to Jesus. Here, in succinct form, he differentiated his own self-described position from other kinds of pacifism, and I think it important to describe it at length with multiple and extended quotes.[44]

The pacifism of the Messianic community depends "on the confession that Jesus is the Christ and Christ is Lord. . . . It is therefore in the person and work of Jesus, in His teachings and His passion, that this kind of pacifism finds its rootage, and in His resurrection that it finds its enablement. . . . It follows that the character of such a position can be known only in relation to Jesus Christ. This simple sentence is a statement first of all about the nature of revelation. Just what it means to believe in Jesus as

---

43. Yoder, *War of the Lamb*, 106.

44. The quotations in the following paragraphs are all drawn from Yoder, *Nevertheless*, 133–38.

Christ, just what it means to follow Jesus Christ as revealer of the nature and will of God, cannot possibly be figured out on our own resources." It is not based on a tablet of stone but on the full humanity of a unique and yet complete human being responding to needs and temptations of a social character. "When we confess Jesus as Messiah we find His uniqueness and His authority not alone in religious teachings or in spiritual depth but in the way He went about representing a new moral option in Palestine, at the cost of His death."

It is not moralism, the stuffy fear of ever making a mistake, nor is it reducible to living by rules; it is participation "in that human experience, that peculiar way of living for God in the world, of being used as instruments of the living of God in the world, which the Bible calls *agape* or *cross*."

> When we speak of the pacifism of the messianic *community*, we move the focus of ethical concern from the individual asking himself about right and wrong in his concern for his own integrity, to the human community experiencing in its life a foretaste of God's kingdom. The pacifistic experience is communal in that it is not a life alone for heroic personalities but for a society. It is communal in that it is lived by a [community] of men and women who instruct one another, forgive one another, bear one another's burdens, reinforce one another's witness....
>
> The existence of a human community dedicated in common to a new and publicly scandalous enemy-loving way of life is itself a new social datum. A heroic individual can crystallize a widespread awareness of need or widespread admiration: only a continuing community dedicated to a deviant value system can change the world....
>
> Those who uphold it would affirm that the discipleship of which they speak is a necessary reflection of the true meaning of Jesus and that the call to follow Jesus is a call addressed to all.... But the standards by which such a life is guided are not cut to the measure of [people] in general. They can be clearly perceived—to say nothing of being even modestly and partially lived—only through that reorientation of the personality which Jesus and His first followers called repentance. Repentance initiates that true human existence to which all are called. But as long as a given [individual] or a given society has not undergone that change of direction, it is not meaningful to describe how ... they would live as pacifists. It is thus not possible to extrapolate from this stance of faith a strategy for resolving the urban

crisis tomorrow. It is not a position which can be institutionalized to work just as well among those who do not quite understand it or are not sure how much they believe in it. . . .

Another disadvantage of this position is that it does not promise to work. The resurrection is not the end product of a mechanism which runs through its paces wherever there is a crucifixion. There is about the Christian hope in the kingdom that peculiar kind of assurance which is called faith, but not the preponderant probability of success which is called for by the just war theory or by a prudential ethic.

"*Nevertheless,*" Yoder concluded, "this position is closer than the others to the idiom of the Bible and to the core affirmations of the Christian faith." Here is his use of the word *nevertheless*, from which the book gets its title, to point to the core affirmations of Christian faith. These words constitute the core statement, in *Nevertheless*, of Yoder's own faith.

Twice in *The War of the Lamb* Yoder emphasized that the stances of Tolstoy, Gandhi, and Martin Luther King Jr. were deeply grounded in their faith in God who rules the cosmos, God who is much bigger than a particular ethical law. Yoder meant that Tolstoy, Gandhi, King, and the Puritans, Anabaptists, and Pentecostals, as well as ordinary farmers, have an experiential faith in God as Lord of the universe. For the peace churches, it is a faith in God, and in who God is, as revealed in Jesus Christ.

Chapters 4 and 5 described Yoder's learnings from Karl Barth and Oscar Cullmann. Since these two theologians emphasized the Lordship of Christ over all, Yoder's faith in the Lordship of Christ was no doubt strengthened by his engagement in PhD seminars with Karl Barth and Oscar Cullmann at the University of Basel. Barth drafted the Barmen Confession of those pastors who resisted Adolf Hitler and he resisted relegating Christ's Lordship to a private or inner-churchly realm. Along these lines, Yoder has influenced Anabaptists and many others to move from a two-kingdoms dualism in which Christ is Lord over only an inner realm to emphasizing the Lordship of Christ over all of life.

Hence, as chapter 1 demonstrated, Yoder argued in *Preface to Theology* that the main point of the doctrine of the Trinity is to make clear that the revelation in Christ is the revelation of who God really is. To claim an ethic based on God as Creator that contradicts the revelation in Christ is to deny the unity of the Trinity. Like his teacher, Karl Barth, Yoder emphasized God's unity and guarded against those interpretations of the Trinity that he saw moving toward tritheism.[45] The central point throughout *Preface to Theology* is that the God revealed in Christ, and in the Spirit, is really who God is; God is not a distant Ruler whose ethics differs from what is revealed in Jesus Christ.[46]

John Yoder himself had a deep experience of the sovereignty of God as revealed in Jesus Christ. This was why he flushed bright red when he was shocked to think I was saying pacifism "cops out" from responsible action in the public sphere. If I had meant that, it would have denied Yoder's cosmic faith in the sovereignty of God in the whole universe, grounded in God's revelation of Christ. It would have denied his commitment to serving God faithfully in all of life. It would have accepted a raft of unfriendly stereotypes of Anabaptists as "irresponsible" in a major part of life. It would have attacked their faith in God.

Many in the Anabaptist tradition are affirming a need for greater attention to the experience of the Holy Spirit in their lives.[47] Such an articulation is implied by and needed for what Yoder speaks of as the deep subjective experience of "the inner experience of overpowering grace." He identified this experience of God's presence as important for radical Puritans, Anabaptists of the sixteenth century, the early Dunkards, frontier farmer preachers, their Wesleyan contemporaries, and Pentecostals around the world whose experience of God's presence in the Holy Spirit is also an experience of Jesus Christ as Lord, powerfully present and sovereign. In chapter 10 of *For the Nations*, he concluded, "The closest the Jesus of the Gospel accounts came to projecting the shape of the church was the description in Matthew (18:15–20) and in John (14–16; 20:19–23) of the Paraclete [Holy Spirit] to empower forgiveness and discernment. That is the warrant for continuing prophetic clarity."[48] In chapter 11 of *For the Nations*, called, "The Spirit of God and the Politics of Men," Yoder referred to the work of the Holy Spirit seventeen times. He focused on the Holy Spirit's work for grace-based justice and forgiveness. "The Spirit of God on the other hand enables a justice of grace. We pray

---

45. See Stassen, Yeager, and Yoder, *Authentic Transformation*, 61–65, 84–87, 141–42.

46. Yoder, *Preface* (2002), 202. He argues similarly in Stassen, Yeager, and Yoder, *Authentic Transformation*, 61–65. See 138–42 for a qualification of how this argument applies to H. Richard Niebuhr.

47. For a recent example, see context of note 39 above.

48. Yoder, *For the Nations*, 217.

to be forgiven as we forgive others."[49] Throughout his writings, he emphasized that congregations need to be organized to practice discernment of the guiding of the Spirit, listening carefully to all members who have a word to share, and seeking clarity together. Additionally, the experience of Jesus Christ as Lord, powerfully present and sovereign, is in *The War of the Lamb*. Those of us loyal to Yoder should develop it further, with special attention to the experience of the Holy Spirit.[50]

Honoring Jesus' Roots in Judaism

Anabaptist theology has been criticized for neglecting the Old Testament and focusing on the New Testament. However, in an essay in *War of the Lamb* on the roots of nonviolence, Yoder emphasized Jesus' roots in Judaism. "Since the Middle Ages, Christians are so accustomed to considering their origins in contrast to Judaism that we often ignore the great extent to which the early Christian attitude toward the Roman Empire was simply the attitude of faithful Jews." The nonviolence of Jewry since Jeremiah "depends on a Jewish worldview uniquely tuned to befit the Jewish sociology of dispersion and the synagogue."

> The life of every human being is sacred; blood is the presence of life given by God alone and only God is entitled to take it back. Any bloodshed is sacrifice. Long before the rise of Christianity, Jewish saints and sages had mitigated judicial power through more careful rules of evidence and warnings against the dangers of bias and self-interest; by rabbinic times the actual execution of capital punishment was practically excluded by their understanding of Torah.
>
> God is sovereign over the cosmos in general, and therefore also over our oppressors as well as over us.[51]

Yoder spelled out several corollaries that follow. He based some arguments on God the Creator rather than limiting it only to God the Son. He emphasized "Jesus the risen, cosmic Lord, whose ultimate control of the world can be trusted when we cannot govern the world."[52] "The early

---

49. Ibid., 228.

50. Chapter 13 is one such development, in the context of Yoder's own coercive behavior toward a number of women.

51. Yoder, *War of the Lamb*, 46–47.

52. Ibid., 46.

Christians were Jews, and . . . Jews since Jeremiah believed that God had abandoned kingship and war as instruments of God's concern for justice within history. . . . Jesus' pacifism was not an innovation; it was an intensification of the nonviolence of Jeremiah, Ezekiel, and the singer of the Servant passages of the book of Isaiah."[53] Yoder's posthumous book, *The Jewish-Christian Schism Revisited*, argues for "Jesus the Jewish pacifist," and for continuity between the prophet Jeremiah and Jewish pacifism after the Roman destruction of the temple in 70 CE. In *For the Nations*, Yoder identified the prophet Jeremiah as one of the "two most important landmarks outside the New Testament itself for clarifying what is at stake in the Christian faith." Jeremiah is "more basic" than the Reformation and the Enlightenment.[54]

In the several dialogue lectures that Yoder and I did in various locations about 1976 and 1977, I urged him to ground his interpretation of Jesus not only in Jubilee, but more deeply in Isaiah. I argued that all of the themes he developed in *Politics of Jesus* were in Isaiah, and that he could get a significantly surer base for his argument if he would make that connection. The last four chapters of *For the Nations* are based in Isaiah. He chose two chapters written previously, in which he had made Isaiah central. After our lecture tours, he wrote chapters 10 and 11 on Isaiah.

In line with the argument in chapter 1 for the centrality of Yoder's historically contextualized interpretation of Jesus, Yoder interpreted the Old Testament from the perspective of Jesus Christ as Lord, and he enriched and thickened his interpretation of Jesus by grounding him historically in the Old Testament and especially the prophets. The implications of the Jewish roots of Jesus are further developed in chapter 10 to follow, which explores how Yoder's Christology lends itself to interfaith dialogue with Judaism, Islam, and Hinduism.

---

53. Ibid., 105. Yoder developed these themes more fully in *For the Nations* and in *Jewish-Christian Schism*.

54. Yoder, *For the Nations*, 8–9. For his extensive emphasis on Jeremiah, see pages 1, 9, 17, 33, 36 n. 44, 41, 51–55, 56 n. 9, 65–75, 76 n. 60, 77, 86, 136, 237, and page 2, where he advocates his crucial methodological emphasis on translation into languages of our pluralistic culture as exemplified by Jewish polyglossia. Also see not only the Scripture index, but also the names index under Jeremiah, Jeremiah (poem-drama), and Jeremianic model.

PART THREE—EXTENDING JOHN HOWARD YODER'S THEOLOGY

Letting Just War Theory and Pacifism Be Friends

Some who are loyal to just war theory let that loyalty close them off from Yoder. Yet Yoder probably pays more respectful yet critical attention to just war theory than any other pacifist. He argues that just war theory and pacifism should not be seen as enemies, but as complementary. When just war theory is properly understood, they both battle side by side against the usual war ethic, which is either crusade or justification of whatever wars the state has decided to wage. Yoder also performed immanent criticism of just war theory within its own terms, showing how it could be improved. Just war theorists have much to learn from Yoder.

Yoder commented, "Childress is right." That is, Yoder agreed with James Childress that just war theory, rightly understood, is based on the presumption against violence. Yoder argued this point in an essay that he labeled "A think piece on how just war thinking and pacifism coinhere."[55] And he commented: "Take note of other parallel efforts by Duane Friesen in [the] Whitmore Book and by Richard Miller in [his] book; possible paper on the theme of bridging over. Bounce it off Paul Ramsey on 'come clean.'" With these comments Yoder was referring to other writing where pacifism and a presumption against violence in just war theory would be working in the same direction.

Yoder's main point was that

> the Just War people who invest all their energy in discussing their relationship to the few pacifists on their left are in political reality tacit allies to the unjust warriors on their right. My purpose here is not to make debating points, but to clarify the substance of a perennial debate by looking at the diverse ways in which language is used to attempt to make sense of the debate but at the same time also (often unintentionally) tends to obfuscate.

In other words, Yoder was observing that just war theorists who attempted to refute pacifism actually ended up supporting those who used just war theory as the language with which to justify the state's war of the moment. Yoder's intent in this discussion was to prod just war theorists to think critically and incisively, to take their own principles seriously,

---

55. These comments are in Yoder's letter to friends asking for their suggestions about what to include in *The War of the Lamb*, and are reflected on pages 86, 98, and 115 of that book.

and to build the church practices needed actually to reject war when it is unjust. Anything less is not honest.

Two examples clearly display Yoder's intent to assist just war theorists with more honest application of the theory. One is the trips he sometimes made to talk to the cadets at Culver Military Academy in Indiana. His intent was not to convert the cadets to pacifism but to heighten the awareness of these future officers about true just war logic. If they actually applied it, the result would be less violence and fewer wars. The second example is Yoder's book *When War Is Unjust*.[56] In the book, he showed how the theory of just war has shifted from an earlier understanding that war was evil but sometimes necessary to the contemporary view in which just war language is the way that modern statesmen justify their chosen wars. The import of the description is that recovering the true meaning of just war theory would result in much less war. In the Preface to the book, a Lutheran spokesman wrote, "He [Yoder] asks us, for the sake of the world, to demonstrate the credibility of our ethic, to put it to the test, to be honest about where it leads us. . . . I am grateful to him for the gift he offers us."[57]

Entering into New Settings as Incarnational

This section reviews issues treated in another way in chapter 1. However, it is important to state again Yoder's core conviction on the Lordship of Jesus Christ since it underlies his public ethics.

Perceptive interpreters of Yoder point out that he regularly adapted to the particular cultural context and the particular set of questions that characterized the audience he was asked to address. He did not bring simply a pre-set lecture and present it regardless of the concerns of his audiences; he entered into their perspectives, and sought to speak specifically to them. He often began his lectures by discussing some dimensions of their kind of thinking and questioning, and then fashioned his lectures to answer those questions. He learned a number of languages in order to do that, including French, Spanish, German, and Dutch, and also methodological languages in ethics or philosophy or interreligious dialogue. Some have called this his "ad hoc" way of writing and speaking. However, we should interpret these wide-ranging discussions more deeply as

56. Yoder, *When War Is Unjust*.
57. Ibid., xx.

evidence of Yoder's being formed by the incarnation. His intent was to bring God's presence in Jesus the Jewish Galilean into particular human history and into particular human lives with the capacity to speak to all their concerns and needs. His willingness to use other languages and to address any issue reveals his core conviction on the Lordship of Jesus Christ and its capacity to address any setting with the gospel. Here again we see Yoder's attachment to Jesus Christ, the root of Christian faith and practice, which makes Yoder a radical theologian.

Another way of interpreting Yoder's use of other languages is to say that his whole career was a deepening entry into the meaning of the core conviction of the Lordship of Jesus Christ. His intent was to show what that Lordship meant for ever-increasing and widening areas of inquiry. Every new audience, every new subject matter, was another opportunity to show a dimension of the implications of the Lordship of Christ for all of life.

In my review of *Preface to Theology* for *Modern Theology*, I began thus: "Yoder distinguishes two teaching functions in the New Testament: catechist and coherence-tester. The catechetical function began as an effort to teach 'what is sufficient for a Christian to know in order to be baptized. . . . So the process of passing on the tradition is first. . . . The second process tests the tradition for coherence' (pp. 380–81), like the Hebraic prophet, measuring present practices for their coherence with original teachings."[58]

I also wrote,

> Contrary to some tendencies to emphasize "the 'religion *of* Jesus' reported in the Gospels [over] the religions *about* Jesus . . . in the later church," Yoder shows that "'high Christology' is present in the *oldest* documents we have" (139). It was later, in the Gospels, that the early Christian communities found it indispensable to reaffirm "the earthliness of the man Jesus, the story of his doings, and the memories of his own words" (140).[59]

Crucial is Yoder's remark on "'incarnation in its double meaning of genuine humanity and genuine divine presence' (288-9, 305-6, et passim)."[60] Yoder's historical perceptiveness and correction of Platonism is not an argument against Jesus Christ as the fully incarnational revela-

---

58. Stassen, Review of *Preface*, 519
59. Ibid., 520.
60. Ibid.

tion of God, but just the opposite. Yoder's understanding of the Lordship of Jesus Christ as the presence of God in the world is intrinsic to his advocacy of active peacemaking

Advocating Active Strategies in Peacemaking

Yoder planned the three sections of *The War of the Lamb* in memos dated "4 September 97" and "November 1997." His third section, on "Nonviolent Action and Conflict Management," developed a positive theology of peacemaking, or what we have come to call just peacemaking. It includes the just peacemaking practices of nonviolent direct action, conflict resolution, democracy and justice, support for the United Nations, international cooperation, and participation in alternative communities. Yoder's active peacemaking included four components.[61]

1. He argues that we should speak not simply of nonresistance or nonviolence, but of *nonviolent direct action*. "Nonviolence means active strategies: So what is normally meant as an alternative is specific undertakings, initiatives, strategies, procedures, nonviolent action and not simply nonviolence as a negative, abstract term. . . . Think of all the trouble we would have in developing a Christian understanding of marriage if the only word we had for it were non-adultery and we had to make our affirmations in the form of negations." Therefore, Yoder defines nonviolent action as "involvement and not withdrawal. It is a form of involvement to maintain, as all serious nonviolent activist strategies have done, a broad range of forms of pressure within the existing order, at the same time that one seeks to replace it." He defines nonviolence not simply as a deontological obligation of faithfulness, but as a teleological action designed for the purpose of allowing peacemaking initiatives to work: "I propose to use [nonviolence] here . . . [as designating] modes of activism that renounce violence, in order that other kinds of power (truth, consent, conscience) may work."[62] And as Yoder himself says,

> Nonviolent action is in any case involvement and not withdrawal. It is a form of involvement to maintain, as all serious nonviolent activist strategies have done, a broad range of forms

---

61. The four descriptions are lifted from my Introduction to Yoder, *War of the Lamb*, 23–24.
62. Ibid., 85.

of pressure within the existing order, at the same time that one seeks to replace it. The work of Martin Luther King included a very strong affirmation of the use of the American courts and appeal to the American constitution against specific injustices within the American system. Likewise, King's activity presupposed strong investment in obtaining and using the vote, and in calling the courts to implement the Constitution.

Gandhi had his reasons for trusting less to litigation than King was later to do, but he created his own political party, which ultimately became the governing party, and before that he brought into being (first of all in South Africa) the powerful educational instruments of the Ashram and popular journalism.[63]

2. Similarly, Yoder writes extensively on *conflict resolution*. Both nonviolent direct action and conflict resolution go beyond the debate between just war theory and pacifism to develop a proactive peacemaking ethic. Both are practices not only for Christians, but are normative for public ethics. Both call for peacemaking practices and initiatives by nonchristians as well as Christians in the secular world.

3. His positive peacemaking ethic also emphasizes *practices of justice*. He praises the development of religious liberty, of egalitarian democracy anti-authoritarian education, the humanizing of corrections, and raising the status of women, slaves, and original Americans. "These specimens of critical social impact may be thought of as second-order nonviolence. . . . They reflect patterns of loving community in the wider society, which are first meaningful within the faith community." They are expressions of normative New Testament practices in public ethics—as expressions of the normativeness of Jesus' lordship in society.[64]

4. Yoder advocates United Nations peace brigades, and commends Robert Johansen's work in international peacemaking.

For all these are practices of the new paradigm of just peacemaking, Yoder and I were dialoguing in my home about just peacemaking theory as it was developing. He urged that the new paradigm of just peacemaking clearly state that it does not replace the paradigms of pacifism and just war theory, but adds a crucial additional dimension, peacemaking action. I was clear on that, and John expressed his support for the project.

63. Ibid., 156–57.
64. Ibid., 50.

It enables pacifists as well as just war theorists to advocate a much-needed public ethic, with practice norms rather than legalistic absolutes, and therefore not to be marginalized as in Niebuhr's stereotype, without a relevant word to say to the state. That is what John was working to develop in his third section of *The War of the Lamb*.

This third section of *The War of the Lamb* thus shows that nonviolence is not passive but active, not withdrawn or sectarian but engaged in the world and communicating with social science studies. Indeed, the theme of the whole book as Yoder planned it is engagement, interaction, dialogue. John Howard Yoder was no monolinguist: he spoke English, French (every day with his wife, Annie), German (he wrote his first two books in German, now translated by my son), Spanish (in order to lecture in Argentina), and he learned to read Dutch in order to translate Berkhof's *Christ and the Powers*, thereby influencing us to make "the powers" a significant category in our ethics. He advocated a multilingual method in Christian ethics.[65] That included learning from and dialoguing with social science, anthropology, just war ethics, Catholics, Protestants, experts in diverse religions, and humanists. The theme of multilingual dialogue runs throughout *The War of the Lamb*—by intention.

This description of Yoder's advocacy of a public ethic should lay to rest any arguments that his commitment to the Lordship of Jesus Christ resulted in opposition to public ethics. On the contrary, his core conviction of the Lordship of Jesus Christ over all of life opposed any such two-realm dualism or sectarianism. At the end of his life, he was extending his investigations ever farther into the public ethics of just peacemaking, as displayed in this chapter and in *The War of the Lamb*, and into dialogue with Jewish thought, as displayed in *The Jewish-Christian Schism Revisited*.

Chapter 10 now makes significant and specific use of *The Jewish-Christian Schism Revisited* in exploring the implications of Yoder's Christology for interfaith dialogue.

---

65. Yoder, *For the Nations*, 2, 6, 7, et passim.

10

Interfaith Conversations
Judaism to Islam to Hinduism

J. Denny Weaver *and* Earl Zimmerman

John Howard Yoder's analysis of the Jewish-Christian schism opens doors to what promises to become an important series of conversations in North America. Most Americans in past generations had little direct contact with people of other faiths. But the era of interfaith isolation has changed dramatically as new information technologies, increased travel, trade, and immigration have made our world a smaller place. The "Pluralism Project," led by Diana Eck, has mapped the changing face of religion in America. These scholars make the surprising claim that the United States has now become the most religiously diverse nation on earth. For example, Muslims (about 6 million) now outnumber Episcopalians.[1] Christian understanding of other faiths has not kept pace with these changes. However, John Howard Yoder's theological initiative in exploring the schism between Christians and Jews opens up a space for a new and more fruitful conversation between groups whose boundaries have long been considered mutually exclusive, even as Yoder respected the differences of each group. Some comments on Yoder's website extend

---

1. Eck, *New Religious America*, 2–4.

the implications even farther. This chapter explores the link between Yoder's analysis of Christology in chapter 1 and the doors he opened to interfaith dialogue.

In his seminal book, *The Politics of Jesus*, John Howard Yoder located the rejection of violence in the narrative of Jesus of Nazareth and pictured what Christian ethics would look like if the earthly Jesus were accepted as ethical norm. Chapter 1 of the book in hand showed how the story of the earthly Jesus emerges from the New Testament as the basis of Yoder's theology. With this focus on the significance of Jesus as ethical and theological norm, it might come as a surprise that in his assessment of the Jewish-Christian schism, Yoder wrote, "It did not have to be."[2] The current chapter shows how Yoder's contextualizing or relativizing approach to classic Christology allowed him to say that it did not have to be, and then extends the analysis to dialogue with Islam and Hinduism.

The argument has several parts. The first puts Yoder's analysis in *The Jewish-Christian Schism Revisited* alongside that of orthodox Jewish scholar Daniel Boyarin's analysis of the schism in his book *Border Lines*.[3] Their remarkable agreement, written without either having knowledge of the other's work, underscores Yoder's discussion.[4] The second section recalls elements from chapter 1 that contribute to Yoder's approach to the Jewish-Christian schism. This discussion reviews Yoder's relativizing of the classic christological statements from the fourth and fifth centuries, along with a brief discussion of Trinitarian terminology. The next section presents Yoder's critique of historical determinism. These sections focus two dimensions of the theologizing that enabled Yoder to say that the schism "did not have to be." Following this discussion of Yoder's theology, the chapter introduces a further argument from Yoder concerning approaches to ecumenical conversation and applies it to the Christian conversation with Judaism, and then to Islam and Hinduism.

---

2. Quote from the title of the first chapter of Yoder, *Jewish-Christian Schism*.

3. Boyarin, *Border Lines*

4. Boyarin's agreement with Yoder's analysis is described in Boyarin, "Judaism as a Free Church," published in *CrossCurrents*. The essay was reprinted as Boyarin, "Judaism as a Free Church," in Dula and Huebner, *The New Yoder*. Quotes in what follows are from *The New Yoder*. Some parts of the material on Yoder and Boyarin in this chapter are expansions of material from Weaver, "A Footnote on Jesus," *CrossCurrents* 56 (2007) 22–35. This essay was a comment on Boyarin's essay in *CrossCurrents*.

PART THREE—EXTENDING JOHN HOWARD YODER'S THEOLOGY

"It Did Not Have to Be"

A striking confluence of historical argument appears in the independent but parallel accounts of the parting of the ways of Judaism and Christianity in Daniel Boyarin's *Border Lines* and John Howard Yoder's *Jewish Christian Schism Revisited*. Both Yoder and Boyarin agreed that the beginning of the parting involved Justin's effort to drive a wedge between Christians and Jews.

Boyarin described the driving of that wedge in exquisite detail. He noted a centuries-long status of disagreement and multiple views within the early Jewish-Christian community that did not result in mutual rejection or excommunication. Boyarin located the beginning of the schism with Justin's effort to define the Logos as an exclusively Christian possession, even though many or most Jews did believe in the Logos. A long process followed, in which each side came eventually to mutual exclusion sometime after the fifth century. As one piece of evidence that Jews believed in the Logos, Boyarin noted the Jewish philosopher Philo, whose view of the Logos "is surely on a way that leads to Nicaea and the controversies over the second person of the Trinity."[5] From their side, the rabbis reciprocated the Christian claim to exclusive possession of the Logos by abandoning the Logos to the Christians.

Boyarin depicts a part of that process of abandonment as the work of fifth and sixth century rabbis who projected their view back to the first century and created the myth of Yavneh as a first century synod that enshrined truth in the perpetual debate of the rabbis about the meaning of Torah, which exists on earth. Thus truth could not be lodged in a heavenly Word, outside of Torah. "The Talmud raises [an] ever-unresolved dialectic to the level of a divine principle."[6] The idea of perpetual dialogue was intended as a contrast to the Christian's establishment of a claimed uniform orthodoxy.

The Christian side, Boyarin argued, created its own myth. A close reading of the writings of Athanasius by Virginia Burrus shows that the idea of the council of Nicea as a unified rejection of the Arians was a literary creation of Athanasius some twenty-five years after the council, and was motivated in part by his desire to support his claim to be the

---

5. Boyarin, *Border Lines*, 114.

6. Ibid., 193. Boyarin's description of this myth is in chapter 7, "The Yavneh Legend of the Stammaim: On the Invention of the Rabbis in the Sixth Century."

legitimate successor to his bishop Alexander.[7] Boyarin used this argument from Burrus and other scholars to depict the emergence in Nicene Christianity of the idea of a "traditionalist, and miraculously authorized monovocal truth." It is the opposite of the rabbi's assertion of "ever-unresolved dialectic." Boyarin adds, somewhat ruefully, that debate did not cease with this assertion of Nicea's authority, but rather "on the ideological level, debate was no longer considered appropriate for the determination of Christian truth."[8]

In depicting the emergence of two mutually exclusive attitudes toward the Logos, with both views claiming divine authority and the weight of tradition,[9] Boyarin noted that each side rejected what he called the "hybrids," those positions that in some way belonged simultaneously to each side. Rejection of the "hybrids" had two results—the positions that had concerned a disagreement within the community were now pushed outside the community into the territory of heresy, and without the hybrids what remained were two pure, mutually exclusive traditions. The existence of these two pure religions, with Judaism designated by Christians as the false one, was given the status of imperial law in the Code of Theodosius of 438.[10] Even as the conclusion gave him pause, Boyarin acknowledged that his historical analysis raised the possibility posed by Yoder, namely, to contemplate the prospect that it was not inevitable that this story end with a mutually exclusive parting of the ways. Nevertheless, as is explained further below, Boyarin believes it important to maintain his identity separate from Christians.[11]

Yoder of course knew nothing of Boyarin's analysis. Nonetheless, Yoder's discussion parallels Boyarin's. One piece of Yoder's belief that the schism "did not have to be" came from a historical observation. He states that incompatibility of Christian faith with Jewish identity is not the beginning of the schism. For at least a century, he said, Jews who confessed Jesus as Messiah and those who did not could attend synagogue together without that disagreement resulting in one or the other being expelled from the community. Living with this disagreement was a fact

7. Burrus, *"Begotten, Not Made"*, ch. 1.

8. Boyarin, *Border Lines*, 192–96, quotes 193.

9. Ibid. See also Boyarin, "Tale of Two Synods." In addition to Burrus' analysis, for the political machinations from which a uniform orthodoxy emerged, see Jenkins, *Jesus Wars*.

10. Boyarin, *Border Lines*, ch. 8.

11. Boyarin, "Judaism as a Free Church," *CrossCurrents*, 11–12.

of Jewish-Christian common life. Since this co-existence was historically possible, Yoder argued, it "cannot be excluded theologically. If it cannot on historical grounds by excluded for then, it cannot on theological grounds be forbidden tomorrow."[12]

Although Yoder named Justin as the one who began to drive the wedge between Jews and Christians, he also claimed Justin in support of his thesis. Since Justin mentioned "Jewish Christian believers" who were not rejected by their synagogues, that is evidence for the thesis that there was a Jewish-Christian common life. Thus, a century after Pentecost, Justin is driving a wedge between two kinds of Christians: those who follow Paul in keeping the border "between them and Jewry open," and those "like himself . . . who turn their back on the Jews in the interest of making more sense to the Gentiles."[13]

Yoder noted and rejected other arguments that supposedly make Jews and Christians mutually exclusive groups. One concerned the claim that Jesus was the Anointed One, the Messiah, which Christians have claimed was a rejection of Judaism. Yoder points out, however, that other individuals had claimed to be Messiah or were acknowledged as potential Messiah by others, and such claims did not result in expulsion from or denial of Jewishness. "Thus it is not true either in theory or in actual experience that to affirm the messianity of a man made anyone less Jewish, in the first or second centuries."[14]

Another argument for the inevitability of separation into mutually exclusive groups is that Christians called Jesus "Son of God." Yoder writes that this argument would be true if "son" had the meaning attributed to it in the christological controversies of the fourth century. However, in the first century the term did not have that meaning. In Psalm 2, the king is designated "Son of God," and in the narrative of the temptation of Jesus, Satan's use of the title would make Jesus a Zealot king.[15]

To this discussion of the development of the term "Son of God," Yoder adds an additional question, whether the "'high trinitarian' language of the post-Constantinian creeds should in principle be regarded as counter to monotheism and as offensive to Jews, if properly understood." While these formulas have been offensive to Jews and later to Muslims,

12. Yoder, *Jewish-Christian Schism*, 53.
13. Ibid., 54.
14. Ibid., 54–55, quote 55.
15. Ibid., 55.

who consider them a threat to monotheism, Yoder implies that more careful understanding of these formulas would certainly render them less offensive.[16]

Yoder rejected two other arguments for the inevitability of schism. One such argument was that the existence of disagreement within a group leads inevitability to schism. In response, Yoder suggests that argument does not always prove that people are in incompatible movements; in fact, "it may prove just the opposite." The rabbis were particularly adept, Yoder said, "at managing contradictory views within the one social process." Further, Yoder called for a need to distinguish kinds of conflicts within Jewish identity in the first century. For example, the fact that the prophets scolded their own people harshly does not place them in different, mutually exclusive groups. Christians also experienced conflicts, but were still recognized as Christians. Yoder thus concludes that schism into mutually exclusive groups between Jews and Christians was not inevitable. Supporting that conclusion from the Jewish side is that there has been no consensus on when the break became irrevocable.

Yoder located the culmination of the schism earlier than did Boyarin (although Yoder also acknowledged that at least some elements did not separate until much later), but even that disagreement contributes to one of Yoder's points, namely that the absence of a consensus among historians on when it occurred points to the fact that it did not have to be. Where Boyarin considered the schism final with the promulgation of the code of Theodosius in 438, Yoder could "suspect" that the division became final when Christians gained political power in the fourth century and thus could change the social meaning of their own group. "Jewish Christian" groups such as "Ebionites" still existed, Yoder noted. However, the "Hellenizing apologetes" produced more literature. When they came to define orthodoxy, Jewish Christians disappeared from view. Yoder wrote that the stories of the "'middle party' experience" can be "salutary," if it brings us to realize that the "'main-line' perspective," which is best known because it is our dominant story, was not dominant at the time. Thus when Hellenized Christians were beginning to deny any place to Judaism in the purposes of God, and when the most radical rabbis were reciprocating by building in a corresponding rejection, each side still had members that accommodated the other side, namely as messianic Jews

---

16. Ibid., 56.

and as Gentiles who attended the synagogue with its restraints. It was these "middle party" people who were rejected by both sides.[17]

Boyarin and Yoder agree on the beginning of the schism, that it involved elimination of the "hybrids" or "middle parties," and they agree that there is no consensus on the point at which the schism became final, which supports Yoder's thesis. It is a unique confluence of historical observations. In describing Yoder's approach that has so much in common with his own, Boyarin writes that Yoder had "an entirely different account of the relationship of Judaism to Christianity than I have seen anywhere else."[18]

Meanwhile, according to the standard account, which both Yoder and Boyarin dispute, Jesus and Christology are presumed to be the decisive dividing point between Christians and Jews. Yet Yoder and Boyarin, without surrendering their particular identities, can each say (or at least imply) that Jesus per se need not be the agent that puts Judaism and Christianity in mutually exclusive camps, and they arrive at that realization without stooping to a fuzzy ecumenism of mutual tolerance that either ignores differences or declares them unimportant. That Jesus and/or Christology need not be the agents of mutual exclusion may surprise those new to this conversation. The focus of the chapter now shifts specifically to the theology of John Howard Yoder. The following section elucidates further how John Howard Yoder can both profess belief in Jesus as Christian norm and say, "It did not have to be."

The Theology of "It did not have to be"

Christology

As just noted, in *Jewish-Christian Schism Revisited*, Yoder acknowledged that the "high trinitarian" language of the post-Constantinian creeds has been offensive to both Jewish and Muslim commitments to monotheism, but raised the possibility that there would be less offensive ways for Christians to talk about Jesus and Jesus' relationship to the God of Abraham. A brief survey of Yoder's approach described in chapter 1 indicates what he had in mind.

---

17. Ibid., 57–58.
18. Boyarin, "Judaism as a Free Church," *New Yoder*, 9.

Yoder certainly believed that one line of development from the New Testament did pass through the Nicene formula. However, the more important point for present purposes is that without rejecting Nicea and the other classic formulas, his relativizing of those formulas kept the door open for other lines of development.

In a class discussion of Christology in the course that produced *Preface to Theology*, which Weaver took with John Howard Yoder nearly forty years ago, Yoder said that a crucial issue concerned the category that we should use to talk about continuity between God and Jesus. The classic statements from the fourth and fifth centuries (Nicea, the Cappadocian's terminology for Trinity, Chalcedon) used ontological categories. Yoder suggested that we did not need to be bound to those categories. "For us," he said, "perhaps the category of continuity is 'ethics' or 'history.'" That long-remembered class comment has a parallel in a published comment from the same epoch and quoted in chapter 1. In *The Original Revolution*, Yoder wrote, "The concept of Incarnation, God's assuming manhood, has often made us direct our thought to metaphysics. . . . But when, in the New Testament, we find the affirmation of the unity of Jesus with the Father, this is not discussed in terms of substance, but of will and deed. It is visible in Jesus' perfect *obedience* to the *will* of the Father."[19]

Concerning the Trinity, whose codification as "official doctrine" emerged from the discussion of Nicea, Yoder called it a "deformation" to think that "threeness-in-oneness is itself something that saves us," as though "the truth that God is three persons is one that can only be known by revelation." He wrote: "As a matter of fact, it [doctrine of the Trinity] was not given to us by revelation. . . . It is something the Cappadocians figured out in the fourth century. . . . The doctrine of the Trinity is the solution to an intellectual difficulty that arises if we accept the statements of the Bible. It is not *itself* a revealed truth, but the solution[20] to the word problem we get into when we accept revelation in Jesus, the continuance of that revelation in the Holy Spirit, and hold to monotheism at the same time."[21]

In discussing the authority of the Nicene Creed, Yoder gently chided those "many Christian groups and thinkers," who reject in principle the

---

19. Yoder, *Original Revolution*, 136; Yoder, *Royal Priesthood*, 185; Yoder's italics.

20. At this second occurrence of the phrase "the solution," the original, unedited version reads "a solution." Yoder, *Preface* (1981), 140.

21. Yoder, *Preface* (2002), 204; Yoder's italics.

claim of Roman Catholicism to establish normative biblical interpretation, yet "still give the Nicene creed and its trinitarian statements equal authority with the Bible. If we look back at the politics between 325 and 431, at some of the theologians' methods and motives, at the personal quality of Constantine, . . . then we have to be dubious about giving this movement any authority."[22] A bit later Yoder noted that the development of views is more clearly understood when each view is seen as a response to a preceding one. Then in a statement that foreshadows Daniel Boyarin's observation about the multiplicity of views on both sides in the centuries before the parting of the ways, and the comments of Virginia Burrus and Boyarin about the development of the myth of Nicea as a unifying statement of what was always believed, Yoder wrote,

> It should, however, not be thought that just one line of development existed in which one view succeeded another. Neither should it be thought that there was just one population in which such a conversation went on. The total Christian community in the early centuries was enormously varied and enormously scattered. . . . Thus the clarity of types in logical sequence which is useful for our purposes should not be misunderstood as an actual description of what went on.[23]

Yoder returned again to the question of the authority of the classic creeds at the conclusion of his *Preface* lectures on Chalcedon. He noted that for the Catholic tradition, "the creeds *are* the history of the church" [Yoder's italics]. Then speaking for Anabaptists he said,

> Probably, if we were to be fully honest, we would need to challenge more clearly the Catholic axiom that assumed the authority of the councils and therefore of the creeds. We would need to challenge it more clearly at the point of automatic authority, while being still quite interested in listening to that history, learning from it, and sympathizing deeply with what it tried to say. But it must mean something to us that the Arians and the Nestorians—each in their own age[24]—were less nationalistic,

22. Yoder, *Preface* (2002), 204.

23. Ibid., 205

24. It is important here to note that Yoder refers to "in their own age" and is not making a blanket statement that would cover all appearances of these rejected positions, particularly in light of the fact that the Nestorian position condemned was not the view of Nestorius. Also relevant is Hanson's statement on the relationship of ecclesial authorities and the emperor: "Neither East nor West formulated any coherent

less politically bound to the Roman Empire, more capable of criticizing the emperor, more vital in missionary growth, more ethical, and more biblicist than the so-called orthodox churches of the Empire. At the most, these creeds fruitfully define the nature of the problem with which we are struggling. They are helpful as a fence, but not as a faith.

Readers of Yoder who want to retain the creeds as a foundation can take consolation in his concluding statement:

> The creeds are helpful as fences, but affirming, believing, debating for, and fighting for the creeds are probably things on which a radical Anabaptist faith would not concentrate. . . . A lot of dirty politics were involved in defining the creeds, in explaining their meaning, and still more in applying their authority, but this is the history with which God has chosen to lead a confused people toward at least a degree of understanding of certain dangers and things not to say if we are to remain faithful.[25]

That final caveat notwithstanding, it seems unmistakably clear that Yoder relativized the standard formulas of Nicea and Chalcedon, as well as for the Trinity. That is, he saw these formulas as true answers in the language of the time to particular questions that emerged from a particular historical context, but without transforming those answers into the only possible answers. That relativizing of these formulas is one factor in enabling Yoder to say of the Jewish-Christian schism, "It did not have to be."

Another indication that Yoder could contemplate other theological expressions alongside classic Nicene-Chalcedonian Christology was his purpose for studying Anabaptist history, as explained in detail in chapter 2 of this volume. Making use of Yoder's newly available correspondence, Earl Zimmerman makes clear that Yoder's dissertation in Swiss Anabaptism was an effort to produce Anabaptist theology as the beginning of an alternative to the standard theology of Christendom. When Yoder discovered that his European professors did not consider Anabaptist theology a

---

theory during the period under review of the relation of church and state. When the state brought pressure to bear on them bishops of every theological hue complained. When it used its power to coerce their opponents, they approved." Hanson, *Search for the Christian Doctrine*, 854.

25. Yoder, *Preface* (2002), 222–23. On the "dirty politics," see Jenkins, *Jesus Wars*.

valid topic in systematic theology, he did an end run around that obstacle by entering Anabaptist theology through Anabaptist history.[26]

The *Preface* lectures follow up that use of Anabaptism. In a comment on the authority of the classic creeds, Yoder wrote, the Anabaptists

> assumed the Apostolic Creed. . . . But they did not give it any final authority. . . . So although most of the Anabaptists would have accepted this as part of the tradition and not debated it much, they gave the creed no dogmatic quality. They gave no special importance to the fact that the church had made decisions about phrasing in the fourth or fifth century. . . . In what sense are we bound to doctrinal definitions of the fourth century, or the fifth, or the sixteenth? Is it only in the sense that they are useful documents of how the church struggled to keep the centrality of Jesus straight in the language of their time? Or do we, without thinking, take over from fundamentalism, which took it over without thinking from Calvinist Orthodoxy, which took it over without thinking from the Middle Ages, the idea that there is a certain amount of post-biblical dogmatic substance that all true Christians have to believe?[27]

Already in a 1967 article, Yoder implied the relativity of doctrine. He questioned the adequacy of any denomination's theology to present the fullness of the meaning of scripture. "Is the inherited doctrinal system of a given denomination, which claims to be identical with the total teaching of Scripture, really that accurate as a portrayal of what the Bible says? Does this not need to be tested again in every generation?"[28] Rather than seeing the development of doctrine like the ongoing growth of a tree, Yoder used the image of a vine that requires continual "pruning and a new chance for the roots" to push out new growth. He called this appeal to origins "a 'looping back,' a glance over the shoulder to enable a midcourse correction, a rediscovery of something from the past whose pertinence was not seen before, because only a new question or challenge enables us to see it speaking to us."[29] The final norm for this looping back is the scripture. With such statements, Yoder was not providing a "how to" statement of biblical authority. However, these statements do illustrate his presumption of the relativity of doctrine and assume the prerogative

26. See ch. 2 above, and Zimmerman, *Practicing the Politics*, ch. 5.
27. Yoder, *Preface* (2002), 222–23.
28. Yoder, "Hermeneutics of Anabaptists," 293.
29. Yoder, "Authority of Tradition," 69.

of using new language to enable the biblical message to address new challenges, which was demonstrated in chapter 1.[30]

John Howard Yoder's relativizing of the standard Nicene Christology in no way results in a so-called low Christology. In *Jewish-Christian Schism Revisited*, he wrote, "All of the 'high' statements about Jesus as the Anointed which we find in the New Testament were made by radically monotheistic Jews and were not, when made, seen by those who said those things to be in any sense polytheistic or idolatrous."[31] He provided an exposition of five such texts with a high Christology in the essay, "'But We do See Jesus': The Particularity of Incarnation and Universality of Truth."[32] The "high Christology" of these texts, written centuries before Nicea, Yoder called the "natural cultural ricochet" of taking the ecclesiology built on Jesus into other cosmologies.[33]

Another comment that belongs to the discussion of Yoder's high Christology and relativizing of Nicea and other classic formulas appears in *Politics of Jesus*. He wrote that the view he presents in *Politics of Jesus* "is more radically Nicene and Chalcedonian than other views. I do not here advocate an unheard-of modern understanding of Jesus. I ask rather that the implications of what the church has always said about Jesus as Word of the Father, as true God and true Human, be taken more seriously as relevant to our social problems, than ever before."[34] Those sentences have been cited supposedly to show Yoder's adherence to the classic formulas. In fact, however, they are a corrective of the classic tradition. Rather than affirming the classic language, the comment displays an adherence to ideas behind these formulas. Thus, such statements leave the door wide open, in words just cited, to "other solutions, words, phrasings or ways" to express the ideas behind these formulas.[35]

Yes, John Howard Yoder had a high Christology. But the point to underscore is that his high Christology did not depend on the classic formulas that Yoder in one way and Boyarin in another identified as the culmination of the wedge between Christians and Jews. Yoders's relativizing of the classic formulas that belonged to the wedge constitutes one

30. For Yoder's own description of having taken a "relativizing" approach to the history of doctrine, see notes 7 and 8 and the accompanying text in the Introduction.

31. Yoder, *Jewish-Christian Schism*, 106.

32. Yoder, "But We Do," *Priestly*; Yoder, "But We Do," *Pacifist*.

33. Yoder, *Priestly Kingdom*, 54; Yoder, *Pacifist Way of Knowing*, 31.

34. Yoder, *Politics of Jesus* (1994), 102.

35. Yoder, *Preface* (2002), 204.

dimension of Yoder's argument that the Jewish-Christian schism "did not have to be."

On Historical Determinism

This discussion of the relativizing of classic christological vocabulary complements, or is complemented by, Yoder's challenge to historical determinism. In *Jewish-Christian Schism Revisited*, Yoder raised the possibility that "it did not have to be." One principal aspect of that argument came from his challenge to the common approach to historical writing that identifies a contemporary situation, and then searches for the cause of that situation. The common assumption, Yoder said, is that "events had to go the way they did." The historian then seeks to explain the factors that led to that causation. Yoder's argument is that the personalities involved in the events did not think that they were involved in a scenario with an inevitable outcome, that they did not know how things would come out, and that they in fact faced real choices and could have made other decisions, and events could have come out differently.[36] Thus the historian is most true to the events when he or she acknowledges those choices and the possibility of other outcomes. This is the historical perspective from which Yoder said of the Jewish-Christian schism, "it did not have to be."

In a 1992 conference presentation, Yoder expanded on the discussion of reading history from the viewpoint of the protagonists and their genuine choices rather than from the perspective of a presumed inevitable outcome.[37] For that setting, Yoder used two primary historical examples. One involved the radicals' break with Ulrich Zwingli and Michael Sattler's parting from the reformers in Strasbourg in the emergence of Swiss Anabaptism in the sixteenth-century. The other example Yoder cited was the Jewish-Christian schism. A third set of examples come from the 1992 conference agenda. The conference was called to explore the possibility of writing American history from a nonviolent perspective. One of the questions for the conference was to show that, contrary to the common assumption, United States wars were not inevitable. Conference organizer James Juhnke wrote, "In the new history we are envisioning, American wars will be exposed as the human failures they were rather than

---

36. Yoder, *Jewish-Christian Schism*, 43–44.
37. Yoder, "Burden and Discipline."

acclaimed as triumphs for human freedoms otherwise unattainable."[38] In *Jewish-Christian Schism Revisited*, Yoder echoed Juhnke's challenge to inevitability. As examples of cases where other outcomes were possible, Yoder noted the American Revolution, the American Civil War, and the First World War, and said that "at least some Christians in Germany were ready to say that there did not have to be an Auschwitz."[39]

Yoder did challenge historical determinism, and he envisioned and participated in discussions that revealed choices rather than inevitable outcomes. From this challenge to historical inevitability and the examples provided, it is only a short step sideways to reach a challenge to the inevitability of the development of the standard doctrine represented by Nicea and Chalcedon. In the previous section, it was said that he relativized these supposed foundational statements. It is a parallel argument to say that Yoder's rejection of the idea of historical inevitability leaves wide open the possibility of other theological formations alongside those from the fourth and fifth century that from the Christian side became the wedge that made the parting from Judaism appear inevitable. This challenge to the inevitability of these formulas is even more relevant in light of arguments that appeared after Yoder's death, namely the discussion from Virginia Burrus and Daniel Boyarin, which indicate that the existence of Nicea as the unifying document of a unified tradition was in large part a myth created by Athanasius.

Implications for Christians and Interfaith Dialogue

Christians and Jews

Yoder's theology is rooted in the claim that the life and teaching of Jesus of Nazareth demonstrate that he is Messiah and, in that sense, God with us. This claim about Jesus was initially made by Jews within a monotheistic Jewish world and was not based on the ontological suppositions of later creedal formulations that developed in the fourth and fifth centuries. Consequently, in spite of his high claims about Jesus, claims not shared by Daniel Boyarin, Yoder can proclaim that faith in the Jewish pacifist Jesus is not something that puts him outside the people of Israel. Likewise, neither does Boyarin's rejection of these high claims about

38. Juhnke, "Manifesto," 8.
39. Yoder, *Jewish-Christian Schism*, 44.

Jesus place him outside of the people of Israel. The point of the historical analysis by both Boyarin and Yoder was that the conversation between Jews and Christians could and would change if the focus shifted away from the wedge that both Yoder and Boyarin identified and that Theodosius pounded in, and toward the question of whether Jesus was Messiah, whether or not the messianic age had begun in Jesus. As both Yoder and Boyarin are teaching us, this conversation should happen without the mutual exclusion of Christians and Jews.

Both Boyarin and Yoder point to belief in the Logos among both Jews and Christians in the first three centuries. In fact, according to Boyarin, given the multiple views on both sides of the line between Jews and Christians, including for some Jews worship of an entity distinct from God, a "second person," the vital difference between Christians and Jews concerned details of the incarnation. Thus Boyarin says, "This leads me to infer that Christianity and Judaism distinguished themselves in antiquity not via the doctrine of God, and not even via the question of worshipping a second God . . . but only in the specifics of the doctrine of this incarnation. Not even the appearance of the Logos as human, I would suggest, but rather the ascription of actual physical death and resurrection to the Logos was the point at which non-Christian Jews would have begun to part company theologically with those Christians—not all, of course—who held such doctrines."[40] In his specific response to Yoder, Boyarin stated it thus: "Indeed, I would assert that there is no particular theological claim or expectation that marks Christianity as 'other' to the Judaism of its time, excepting, of course, the claim that Jesus of Nazareth is the one."[41]

Discovering that this disagreement need not mean mutual exclusion in no way indicates that the disagreement lacks ultimate meaning. On the contrary. In fact, discovering this disagreement to be a "family argument" that can proceed without the ominous ending of mutual excommunication from the family may allow genuine conversation between Christians and Jews about this highly significant difference for the first time in fifteen to eighteen centuries.

Yoder raised the option that "it did not have to be." Boyarin recognizes the logic and the attractiveness of that position, but resists it because it would mean at least a partial surrender of his own distinct tradition. Is

---

40. Boyarin, *Border Lines*, 124–25.
41. Boyarin, "Judaism as a Free Church," *New Yoder*, 5.

there not value in diversity in and of itself and the maintaining of diverse traditions, Boyarin asks. Rather than seeking to undo the schism, which implies that his Jewish tradition is unnecessary, Boyarin suggests that we "live it differently."[42] Stated more sharply than Boyarin does, Christians must be very careful that Yoder's "it did not have to be" not become what people in the minority Jewish tradition may hear as one more effort of the majority Christian tradition to tell Jews who they are. Stated another way from the Christian side, how can Christians continue to be other without implying that Jews have abandoned God or that the promises to Abraham have been superseded for Jews?

Yoder is not here to respond for himself. In his place, we suggest a partial answer. Yoder's relativizing of the classic language of the ultimate wedge and his subsequent shifting of the discussion to whether Jesus the Jewish pacifist is the Messiah clearly locates Christians in the tradition of Israel. Yoder has brought the Hebrew Scripture along in his treatment of Jesus, and he intends to see Jesus as a continuation of the story of the people of God whose father is Abraham. Therefore, there can be absolutely no question of supersessionism, no question whether God has abandoned the Jews or whether the promises to Abraham have been shifted uniquely to Christians. The belief that the age of the Messiah had begun with Jesus was a new stream within Judaism. Some Christians might thus imply that a certain sense of going beyond the stream in which Daniel Boyarin stands seems inevitable. But whatever language we might ultimately use for it, this "going beyond" may not be one of replacement nor a declaration that denies God's promise in the other stream. It is a going forward that calls forth continuing conversation and cooperation. It is a going forward that respects differences without a perceived need to convert the other side. In Yoder's sense, it is an undoing of the schism that did not have to be. For Boyarin it is preserving traditions. And it may well be that the most fruitful conversation can occur when identities are respectfully maintained. And the fruitful and freeing dimension of the conversation is that disagreement and maintaining of identity can proceed without mutual exclusion from the people of God as we discuss together what it means to live as the people of one God.

---

42. Boyarin, "Judaism as a Free Church," *CrossCurrents*, 11–12, quote 12.

PART THREE—EXTENDING JOHN HOWARD YODER'S THEOLOGY

Christians and Muslims

Yoder's (and Boyarin's) analysis of the Jewish-Christian schism suggests a model for use with other religions as well. It displays a capacity to pass over into the religious world of the other and then return to one's religious homeland with new insight and self-knowledge. Theologian John Dunne describes this interfaith journey from a Christian perspective. "One has to pass over, to shift standpoints, in order to enter into the life of Jesus, even if one is a Christian, and then one has to come back, to shift standpoints again, to return to one's own life. From this point of view all the religions, even one's own, become part of the wonderland in this odyssey. One's own life is finally the homeland."[43]

A particular aspect of this passing over is to recognize the element in one's own religion that constitutes offense to the other. In Christian perspective, as both Yoder and Boyarin indicated, it means recognizing the extent to which the classic formulas of Christology and Trinity have posed a particular problem for Jews. But the implications of this insight for interfaith dialogue do not stop with Judaism. As both recognized, there are also implications for conversations with Islam, and Yoder extends it to Hinduism.

One of Islam's standard accusations against Christians is the charge of tritheism. This concern is visible in the dialogue between Badru Kateregga, a Muslim scholar in Islamic studies and comparative religions, and David W. Shenk, a former Christian mission administrator involved in interfaith conversations. Shenk carefully seeks to explain the New Testament claim that Jesus was the Son of God through his intimate relationship with God and being the perfect image of God.[44] Kateregga, attuned to the issue of tritheism, responds. "This is the point where Muslims and Christians painfully part company. The issue is deeply theological and anthropological. The Christian view of incarnation seems to compromise God's transcendence and sovereignty while at the same time exalting a mere man to God-like status."[45] Shenk agrees that to think of Jesus' sonship as "God begetting a son" would be heretical. He makes the claim, "Jesus the Messiah, as Son of God, reveals something completely different. He reveals a perfect relationship between God and the Messiah. The

43. Dunne, *Way of All the Earth*, ix–x. For a further discussion of "passing over" and "coming back" in interfaith conversations, see Clasper, *Eastern Paths*, 122–36.
44. Kateregga and Shenk, *Muslim and a Christian in Dialogue*, 163.
45. Ibid., 166.

sonship of Christ is a description of perfect love and relationship between God and the Messiah."[46]

In a personal conversation with Weaver, Shenk explained the importance of using this kind of understanding of Son of God.[47] To paraphrase the conversation, Shenk explained that for Islam, the Word is the guarded book in heaven. Mohammed was commissioned to be the channel through whom the final portion of the eternal Word was sent down; that final Word is the Qur'an, an exact copy of the heavenly original. The Qur'an says that the Word created Jesus, which means that Jesus was created by the Word in Mary's womb, parallel to the Word creating heavens and earth. For Islam, God cares enough for the world to send the Word in the form of the Qur'an. In contrast, for Christians God cared enough to come in person in Jesus and to share the human condition, which included suffering and death. Resurrection is then the victory over weakness, an overcoming of the evil that oppresses humanity. The cross shows the love of God for humanity, being willing to share the human condition. In a conversation with Shi'a Muslims, Shenk explained this contrast and shared the Christian message about God coming and sharing the human condition. In response, one Muslim listener said that he could now see how God was related to Jesus, that God and Jesus were one, and that this view of the relationship of God to Jesus was not tritheistic.[48] This story illustrates the wisdom of speaking of the relationship of God and Jesus in terms of a relationship rather than in terms of the classic terminology of being and person. This conversation by no means represents an agreement between Islam and Christianity. However, understanding "Son of God" as a New-Testament term expressing a relationship rather than in the later usage of "offspring" lessens the offense to Islam and is in line with Yoder's treatment of Nicene and trinitarian language. Recall, for example, Yoder's comment that rather than using the language of "substance" to affirm the unity of God and Jesus, the New Testament describes that unity in terms of "will and deed," which is "visible in Jesus' perfect *obedience* to the *will* of the Father."[49]

46. Ibid., 167. For an extended, parallel discussion of the significance of interpreting "son of God" in terms of relationship and obedience, see Cragg, *Jesus and the Muslim*, 189–209, and esp. 285–94.

47. Conversation on July 7, 2011.

48. Parallel comments in Shenk, *Journeys of the Muslim Nation*, 163, 166–67.

49. Yoder, *Original Revolution*, 136. Reprinted in Yoder, *Royal Priesthood*, 185; Yoder's italics.

In his *Preface* lectures, after describing the shift in form from narrative to ontological categories with the language of Nicea and Trinity, Yoder notes that a second "moving away from the biblical center" occurs with the term "person" as used for trinitarian doctrine. In its original sense, person meant something on the order of ways of being. Yoder calls it a "deformation" when it takes on the modern meaning of person as "a center of consciousness, a will distinct form other wills." In some versions of Trinity, then, it is said to refer to three "personalities," and some icons have depicted the Trinity as three identical human figures. Yoder notes that this usage, which has modern manifestations, was present already for Islam. As a result, Yoder says, it may well be the source of the "tritheism Mohammed thought he perceived," which has produced a "strong anti-Christian, pro-monotheist Muslim movement." And in the case of Mohammed, Yoder says, "He may have been right."[50]

The most common response of Christians to Islam is to attempt to explain that "Trinity" or "three in one" does not mean three Gods.[51] This approach, while well intentioned, still claims the right of Christians to define the terms of the discussion. Yoder's relativizing of the classic language, that is, displaying it as a correct answer within its context but as not the only possible answer, opens the door to a different, less defensive approach. By not making a given (an "absolute") out of the traditional language, Yoder suggests finding an earlier place to begin the conversation. Similar to the way he could say that the schism between Jews and Christians did not have to be, it is possible to envision a conversation between Muslims and Christians in which there was still disagreement within a "family" context about the nature of God and of the rule of Jesus but without the terminology which virtually requires the two sides to be mutually exclusive.

In fact, Yoder envisioned the possibility of such a conversation. In an item on his website, he discussed issues in missions. Even as he stated in a note that he considered Nicea and Chalcedon to be "valid enculturation" in their own world, he wrote that "subservience to hellenistic thought

---

50. Yoder, *Preface* (2002), 203.

51. As one such example, see Hoover, "Islamic Monotheism," in which the author, a participant in a Mennonite-Shi'a dialogue, attempts to make Athanasian, Nicene, and trinitarian language palatable to Muslims. Another example comes from Miroslav Volf, who attempts to define the term *Person* as well as the threeness of God and the language of the Athanasian Creed in ways palatable to Islam. See the chapter titled "The One God and the Holy Trinity" in Volf, *Allah*, 127–48.

forms" had been a "hindrance" in Christian mission. "Would Islam have taken on the belligerent shape it did, if it had not been for the ease with which trinitarian language could be interpreted as forsaking monotheism?" The anecdote just cited from David W. Shenk demonstrates the wisdom of Yoder's suggestion. And in a similar question that leads to the next section of this chapter, Yoder wondered, "Might the missionary encounters with the Hindu world, or with traditional religious cultures, have taken a different shape if the Gospel texts had been the springboard, if the ontological definities [sic] of *physei* and *ousiae* and *hypostaseis* had not had to be part of the message?"[52]

Historical determinism also powerfully shapes Muslim-Christian relationships, which is often depicted as a clash of civilizations. It is common to assume that the long history of warfare between Islam and Christian Europe was an inevitable outcome of two clashing civilizations. Muslim scholar and activist Rabia Terri Harris challenges such assumptions. She reminds us that the historical spread of Islam has mostly been peaceful through the travel and work of merchants and teachers. People came into Islam by choice and not by force. Harris also interprets the life of the prophet Muhammad and the early Islamic community as a noncoercive struggle to form a community that submits to Allah (God).[53] The kind of historical imagination and reconstruction that Boyarin and

---

52. Yoder, "Confessing Jesus." A statement of Christology by Monika Hellwig has many parallels to that of Yoder. As Yoder did, Hellwig relativizes the language of Nicea and Chalcedon, but searches for new language to proclaim in our world Chalcedon's concern for the humanity and the deity of Jesus. Her answer is to call Jesus "the compassion of God." Hellwig has an application to dialogue with Jews and Muslims that is a parallel to Yoder's. Like Yoder, she recognized that "son of God" in the New Testament has a different meaning than the divinity claim it has for Nicea-Chalcedon, which is the offensive point for both Jews and Muslims, particularly when attached to the term *person*. Parallel to Yoder's suggestion to shift categories from metaphysics and substance to will and deed, Hellwig suggests that we recall that "son of God" has a metaphorical meaning, and should not be interpreted as implying a preexistent continuity of consciousness in Jesus from eternity. Hellwig also recognizes that Christianity, Judaism, and Islam all claim ultimacy for their view of revelation. There is thus no higher authority that can adjudicate these claims. Her answer is also like Yoder's—convictions of truth comes from reflection on the practice of the tradition, and one testifies to that tradition by continuing to live in it. See Hellwig, *Jesus*, esp. 109–23, 138–45.

The parallels between Hellwig and Yoder are not merely a product of academic comparisons made by Weaver and Zimmerman. Many years ago, Yoder recommended Hellwig's book to Weaver as an example of how to do Christology in our modern context.

53. Harris, "Nonviolence in Islam."

Yoder brought to the Jewish-Christian schism is also needed to move beyond such common impasses with Muslims.

Christians and Hindus

Yoder's relativizing of the classic categories opens new opportunities for conversations between Christians and Hinduism. A brief historical sketch provides the background to that assertion.

Zimmerman has repeatedly heard from Hindus in India the criticism that both Christianity and Islam are exclusivist and imperialist. Such charges certainly have some basis in fact. They reflect the Indian's historical struggle against the Muslim Mughal Empire that began in the sixteenth century, and then struggles with the British East India Company that gained a foothold in the seventeenth century, eventually to be replaced by the British Empire which gradually gained control of most of South Asia by the nineteenth century.[54] The close historical relationship between Christianity and empire is clearly on display in Kolkata (formerly Calcutta) India. The massive Victoria Memorial was built in the nineteenth century to honor Queen Victoria and the success of the British colonial regime in India. The impressive edifice dominates the large open park in the city known as the Maidan. Nearby is St. Paul's Cathedral, an Anglican Cathedral of the Church of North India. The entry to the cathedral is filled with plaques and statues honoring various important British church leaders, governors, and soldiers who served during the colonial era. It lucidly illustrates the strong link between empire and a Christian mission that has a culturally triumphant, exclusivist theology.[55]

But a different story of the spread of Islam and Christianity in India does not display this relationship to empire. Muslim merchants and Sufi mystics arrived on the Malabar Coast of India as early as the seventh century, spreading their faith throughout India long before the arrival of the Mughals in the sixteenth century. Followers of Jesus arrived even earlier. The Mar Thoma Church in South India traces its founding to the arrival of Jesus' disciple Thomas in Kerala, India in 52 CE. Though it is

---

54. For a good one-volume history of India, read Wolpert, *A New History*.

55. For insightful case studies of nineteenth-century Christian mission in India, see Copley, *Religions in Conflict*. For an excellent study of late nineteenth- and early twentieth-century Baptist and Mennonite mission efforts in the present state of Chhattisgarh, see Dube, "Issues in Christianity."

impossible to verify this account, it is within the realm of historical possibility. It is known that there were Jewish communities in India before the birth of Jesus and it appears that the first followers of Jesus (later known as Christians) emerged from these communities. It is also known that by the fourth century the Mar Thoma churches in India were connected to the Syrian Church.[56]

This history, situated within the distinct religious and social context of South Asia, complicates Hindu-Christian relationships. As seen in the above brief historical overview of Islam and Christianity in India, the Hindu conversation with both religions can benefit from Boyarin's and Yoder's ability to look at history in a way that rejects historical determinism or the notion that things had to turn out as they did. Just as the Jewish-Christian schism did not have to be, the sad history of Muslim and Christian exclusivism and religiously supported imperialism in South Asia did not have to be.[57] Some strong historical precedents indicate what an alternative history might have looked like had religious communities been more faithful to their foundational religious convictions. Hindus easily identify with the person who told the missionary E. Stanley Jones, "Jesus is ideal and wonderful, but you Christians—you are not like him."[58]

It is widely recognized that Mahatma Gandhi, the father of Indian independence remained a devout Hindu but drew inspiration and the methods for his nonviolent struggle from various religious and secular sources. He had an extraordinary ability to pass over to another religion through sympathetic understanding and come back to his own with new insight. This indicates that Yoder's focus in his conversation with Judaism on the narrative of Jesus the Jewish pacifist is also a fruitful avenue for conversation with Hindus. Yoder drew on the interrelated examples of

---

56. See Griffiths, *Christ in India*, 49–50.

57. An excellent source on the religious sensibilities of India is Dalrymple, *Nine Lives*. There is a long history of popular combined Hindu-Muslim devotion in India. One of Dalrymple's stories concerns a Sufi shrine frequented by both Muslim and Hindu religious seekers. Dalrymple writes, "The Sufis believed that [the] search for God within and the quest for *fana*—total immersion in the absolute—liberated the seeker from the restrictions of narrow orthodoxy, allowing the devotee to look beyond the letter of the law to its mystical essence. This allowed the Sufis for the first time to bring together Hindu and Muslim in an accessible and popular movement which spanned the apparently unbridgeable gulf separating the two religions" (113).

58. Jones, *Christ of the Indian Road*, 114.

Leo Tolstoy, Mahatma Gandhi, and Martin Luther King Jr. who represent the kind of religiously motivated social activism he commends.[59]

Yoder recognized that Gandhi lived at the intersection of two pluralistic worlds or cultures. One was Gandhi's native Hindu society and the other was the occupying world of British colonialism. According to Yoder, "Hindu society seemed stagnant, defeatist, and stratified; yet its fundamental religious vision, far less debilitated by the acids of modernity than religion in the West, bore the seed of its own renewal." British colonialism was infused with a similar imperial orthodox vision of Christendom that Tolstoy had struggled against in Russia. It was necessary to cut through that to the gospel narrative of the life and teaching of Jesus. Britain also had a system of legal institutions that could be used to struggle against the injustices of the oppressive colonial structures. Gandhi learned from both worlds and used each as "the fulcrum against which to move the other."[60]

Gandhi's life was a series of repeated conversions or, as he said in his autobiography, "experiments with truth." According to Yoder, "Gandhi sees the cosmos as a unity of spiritual powers, interwoven in an unbroken nexus of causation, making sense of the notion that fasting, prayer, or sexual continence, and above all the active renunciation of violence, can exert spiritual power—'soul force'—upon the adversary one desires not to destroy but to restore to his or her right place in a fuller human community."[61] Gandhi's active program involved the development of a set of social strategies that fit his cosmology. Yoder writes:

> Out of the religious holiday of *hartal* there springs the strategic work stoppage. Out of purity rituals there springs the boycott. Going to jail for refusal to obey an unjust law applies moral pressure to the judge and thereby to the legislator (especially in a democratic society). The illegitimate assembly or procession provokes the oppressor to unveil his illegitimacy by lashing out. It also seizes the attention of the public, including the newspaper readers of London.[62]

The gospel narrative of Jesus who lived and taught the reign of God was the core of what Gandhi took from Tolstoy. It resonates with a

---

59. Yoder, *War of the Lamb*, 52–65.
60. Ibid., 57.
61. Ibid.
62. Ibid., 57–58.

Hindu cosmology and social program in which *ahimsa* (nonviolence) is the active negation of *himsa* (violence) that fails to recognize the unity of all beings and acts in ways that do harm.[63] Hindu conceptions of the divine are of "the one and the many"—as the ultimate reality beyond any names and yet recognized in many forms. The *Trimurti* or three forms of God—creator, sustainer, and destroyer—help us conceptualize the Hindu understanding of God's manyness.[64] Within this Hindu cosmology, a Christian triune conception of God does not create the problems that it does within the strictly monotheistic cosmologies of Islam and Judaism. What is offensive and hardly comprehensible is religious exclusivism. For example, Zimmerman met a young Hindu woman in the Himalayan foothills who professed a deep devotion to Jesus but was distressed when Christian acquaintances told her she needed to renounce Hinduism and became a Christian. She said she was being asked to give up her very identity, which she could not do.

Yoder's ability to engage Judaism in a way that respectfully maintained both Jewish and Christian identities also suggests an approach to a fruitful and freeing conversation with Hindus. What needs to be overcome is the proclivity to exclude the other from the people of God. Parallel to his remarks concerning dialogue with Judaism and Islam, Yoder's recognition of the contextual or relativized character of the classic language of Christology and Trinity enabled him to suggest that conversation with Hinduism would have proceeded better "if the Gospel texts had been the springboard" rather than requiring the ontological definitions of "*physei* and *ousiae* and *hypostasis*" to be a required part of the message. We see the beginning of such a conversation in Yoder's discussion of Gandhi's Hindu faith and its positive contributions to nonviolent social action designed to create a more just and peaceful world.

Conclusion

John Howard Yoder's analysis of the Jewish-Christian schism, along with that of Daniel Boyarin, initiates a new epoch in conversations between Christians and Jews. Further, comments by Yoder extend the possibility of new stages of dialogue to Islam and Hinduism. Yoder opens the doors to such conversations without surrendering the claims of Christians

---

63. Shastri and Shastri, "Ahimsa and the Unity of All Things."
64. Eck, *Encountering God*, 63–73.

about the uniqueness of Jesus. These conversations reflect the approach to Christian witness in the context of the modern context of pluralism/relativity sketched in chapter 1.

Christianity, Judaism, Islam and Hinduism each make claims of ultimacy. Although the claims differ, each religion has a sense of being the source of the one, ultimate, supreme truth. The modern context of pluralism/relativism means the recognition that there is no universally recognized and universally accessible higher source of appeal to justify or validate such claims of ultimacy, either for themselves or against each other.

Competing claims seem intractable. In different ways, Judaism, Islam and Hinduism all object to what they understand as the ultimate claims of the classic terminology of Nicea and the Cappadocians's Trinity formulation. In Boyarin's and Yoder's analysis, the final wedge between Christians and Jews was Theodosius' declaration that the formula from the Council of Constantinople was imperial policy. For Islam, the Cappadocian's language of "three Persons" was a statement of three gods. Hindus are offended by Christian claims of religious exclusivism, which Yoder tied to requiring the Nicene and Cappadocian (trinitarian) terminology.

We point to two ways that Yoder's theologizing has addressed these offenses, the competing ultimate claims, and the seemingly inevitable conflicts, and has made new conversations thinkable. Although in different ways and at different points, the classic categories of Christology and Trinity have been problematic for Judaism, Islam, and Hinduism. One way that Yoder has opened the doors to new kinds of conversations was his recognition of the contextual character of the classic formulas of Christology and Trinity. This analysis was the focus of chapter 1 and was summarized in the current chapter. This recognition means that interfaith conversations need not start by imposing the offensive categories and calling on the dialogue partner to accept them. Conversations would be different, Yoder suggested, if Christians began instead with the story of Jesus. And that beginning point in the story of Jesus—the root of Christian belief—is what makes Yoder a "radical theologian."

Yoder's second suggestion that enables new forms of dialogue concerns the way one testifies to the truth of one's beliefs. In light of awareness that no universally recognized and accessible norm exists by which to adjudicate ultimate claims, Yoder abandons the search for such a norm and abandons the idea of finding a way to win the argument by coercive discussion. Chapter 1 explained this move as well. Rather, he said, we witness to the truth of our convictions about Jesus by being willing to live in his story when it is not required and even when it is costly or dangerous. This is a lived witness to truth rather than an effort to coerce the other into belief. The import of this stance is that it does not deny the ultimate claims of the other faiths. When properly understod, this stance cannot be one of imperial power. Rather it accepts the other as an equal seeker in a shared search for truth. Further, since Yoder's stance has acknowledged the impossibility of "winning" by force or by a coerced argument, it is by definition a nonviolent stance. For those who live in Jesus' story, it is a extension of the nonviolence of Jesus. For Christians in the line of John Howard Yoder, it is a testimony to the uniqueness of Jesus as the presence of God on earth. And at this juncture, those who live in the story of Jesus display a different version of Christianity than that encountered by those who claim that Jesus is "wonderful" but Christians "are not like him."

11

A Model in Conversation with Black and Evangelical Theology[1]

J. Denny Weaver *and* Gerald J. Mast

Chapter 1 established the theological foundation of John Howard Yoder's approach to theology and ethics in the narrative of Jesus. The discussion showed his use of New Testament writers to illustrate how theology developed as additional meaning was derived from that narrative, and then his extension of that demonstration to the development of the classic statements of Christology and Trinity that emerged in the fourth and fifth Christian centuries. This analysis displayed Yoder's twofold stance toward the classic formulas. On the one hand, he exhibited obvious respect for the classic formulas. He clearly recognized that they dealt with important issues raised by the New Testament text, and that they were true answers within their context and frame of reference. But on the other hand, Yoder also relativized the classic formulas (as well as all theology) and thus kept open the possibility of using new terminology and images to express the New Testament issues in other, different contexts. As he said in the memo quoted at the end of the first chapter, he could "recount supportively the development of early Christian dogma

1. Original condensed version of this article appeared in *Direction: A Mennonite Brethren Forum* 41.1. © 2012 *Direction* (Winnipeg, MB). Used by permission.

without being tied to the adequacy of those formulations in all other times and places." With this chapter we demonstrate and push farther these elements of Yoder's approach.

In his memo on methodology, Yoder also wrote that he could "affirm the priority of the gospel" in a way that intersects and transforms culture. Here gospel refers to the good news about Jesus, which is contained in the narrative that identifies him, and which is the root of Christian faith. The aim of intersecting and transforming culture would be the driving force behind his seminal book, *The Politics of Jesus*, and is reflected in *Preface to Theology*, in which he began his christological analysis with the narrative outline of the sermons in Acts. This current chapter begins with a theological sketch that follows Yoder's example, namely developing theology from the narrative of Jesus.[2] It presents a summary of the gospel narrative, which then becomes the basis for statements of atonement and Christology that are not beholden to the classic categories or language. The application of these statements to the issue of racism illustrates their capacity to engage issues in the modern world. Different from the first ten chapters, the current chapter is not an analysis of Yoder's theology. It is rather an attempt to illustrate or model the several dimensions of his theological methodology. The first section of the chapter models a theology that has gone through the door opened by his relativizing of theology, including that of the classic formulas, but a theology that nonetheless clearly reflects Yoder's comment that our theology should be "specific to Jesus."

However, this theological model can also be adapted to fit other agendas as well. In the memo on methodology just cited, Yoder also wrote that rather than seeking to establish a foundational beginning point, his style was to take on issues "in the categories of others" or in "the other guy's terms." Following sections of this chapter provide two examples of the possibility of joining a conversation in the categories of others. One opportunity is with the writers of what one reviewer called "the new black theology."[3] The other conversation is with the position that Roger Olson

---

2. This sketch uses a summary of Yoder-shaped and -influenced statements of atonement and Christology based on earlier discussions in Weaver, *Nonviolent Atonement*. We believe that this work can serve to illustrate both dimensions of Yoder's methodology. For the earlier, condensed version of the article that discussed one of the applications presented here, see Weaver and Mast, "Anabaptist Christology."

3. Tran, "New Black Theology."

called "postconservative evangelical theology."[4] Fitting the theological proposal of this chapter into these conversations illustrates what Yoder said about taking on issues "in the categories of others."

This chapter now moves to the model and then its several possibilities for appropriation.

The Narrative

The Gospel writers identify Jesus with a narrative of his birth, life, death, and resurrection. Since the story is well known, for purposes here we offer only a brief thematic sketch of that narrative, in line with the outline of the Synoptic Gospels. Following the birth narratives, on which the Gospels differ markedly, and the testimony of John the Baptist, and the temptation in the wilderness, Jesus inaugurated his mission in the synagogue in Nazareth. He read from Isaiah 61:1–2, which promises good news for the poor, release of captives, recovery of sight for the blind, and freedom for the oppressed. Then Jesus proclaimed, "Today this scripture has been fulfilled in your hearing" (Luke 4:18–19, 21). In other words, in his person and in his activity Jesus' mission was an enactment of these ancient prophetic concerns. He is identifying with and extending the story of Israel.

These words cited from Isaiah put on display that Jesus' mission had obvious social connotations. His mission would touch the daily walk of people. Reading through the Gospel then brings out aspects of this social mission. Jesus developed a community by calling followers. He healed people. He cast out demons. He continued preaching and teaching. He confronted oppressive tax structures, as demonstrated by the repentance of Zacchaeus. He forgave sins. He sent out followers, the twelve and then seventy, to proclaim that the kingdom of God has come near. In his dealings with women and Samaritans, he lived out ethnic reconciliation by crossing gender and ethnic boundaries.

Although it is the resurrection that ultimately validates the claim, we can say at this juncture that the God of Israel was present in this story. And since God is present in Jesus, the person, teaching and activities of Jesus show the character of the reign of God on earth. Thus as the disciples and crowds follow Jesus, they are being introduced into and begin to participate in the presence of the reign of God on earth.

4. Olson, *Reformed and Always Reforming*.

Jesus' activities had confrontational elements. They challenged the religious establishment. One clear example of this confrontation comes from the story in Luke 6:6–11 of healing the withered hand. The scribes and Pharisees were waiting to catch him in a Sabbath violation, and Jesus knew he was being watched. But he had the man come stand with him where all could see, and asked the congregation if it was lawful to do good or harm on the Sabbath. Only then, with all eyes on him, did he heal the hand. Since Jesus is chastised by the synagogue leader in another account of Sabbath healing, in Luke 13:10–17, it is clear that Jesus rejected advice to wait until the following day, and that he specifically chose to confront and challenge the religious leadership.

The culminating act of confrontation is the event called "cleansing of the temple." Saying that the money changers and merchants had turned the house of prayer into a den of robbers, he overturned their tables covered with money and used a whip to chase animals out of the area. The high priest was appointed by the Roman rulers. The temple rulers taught that access to God was through the sacrificial system administered by temple authorities. Thus Jesus' ministry of challenge to Sabbath laws, of forgiving of sins and displaying direct access to God, and culminating with the disruption of the functioning of the temple, had both religious and political implications. As such it was a direct threat to the temple authorities.[5] This culminating act in the temple precipitated the plot to have Jesus' arrested, tried and killed.

Jesus was arrested and passed from the Jerusalem religious authorities to the Romans for condemnation in their court. The religious leadership wanted Jesus convicted and executed but Pilate declared him innocent of the charges. Nonetheless, at the insistence of the leadership and a mob, Pilate did condemn him to death. Roman soldiers carried out the execution, the cruel death by crucifixion. For the soldiers it was a routine assignment, one carried out hundreds of times by the Romans as a tactic for terrorizing an occupied population into submission. For the Romans and for those who wanted to dispose of Jesus, this crucifixion was an end of the story, a seeming victory.

But for those that today are called Christians, the story was far from finished. The true culmination came three days later when Jesus was raised from the dead and left an empty tomb, an apparent victory for the reign of God. Over the next forty days or so, he appeared to a number

---

5. Horsley, *Jesus and Empire*.

of women, to his disciples, and to other followers. This part of the story of Jesus concludes with his ascension to heaven, as recounted in Acts 2.

The Beginning of Theologizing

Our theologizing—thinking theologically about the meaning of this story—begins with the resurrection. God's resurrection of Jesus from the dead is what puts God's blessing and validation on Jesus as the presence of God in the world. In other words, resurrection certifies that God was present in the life of Jesus, and that Jesus' life and teachings make present the reign of God on earth. The resurrection is the ultimate validation of Jesus as God's anointed one, Israel's Messiah, the Christ. In traditional language, resurrection testifies to the deity of Jesus.

Resurrection means that this narrative of Jesus is a story of the victory of the reign of God over the powers of evil. It is a victory over the worst that evil can do, namely to take life and thus to deprive someone of existence. As a consequence of carrying out his mission to witness to the reign of God, Jesus lost his life. Perhaps better stated, Jesus' life was taken from him. Jesus' confrontation of the powers of evil resulted in his death. His life was annihilated. And the response of God was to restore Jesus' life. Death was not the final word. The final word was God's restoration of life. Visible here is the omnipotence of God—the capacity of God to respond to human resistance to the reign of God and to the annihilation of existence by restoring life in the face of that resistance. Those who live in Jesus today then participate in and experience this victory as well.

Resurrection is thus an invitation to us to experience the reign of God by identifying with the life and witness of Jesus. Jesus called followers and taught them how to live in the reign of God. Those who would be Jesus' followers today are similarly called to live in the life and the teaching of Jesus. Resurrection is the invitation and the guarantee that those who live in the life of Jesus will experience resurrection with Jesus. At least that is what Paul argues in 1 Corinthians 15:1–19, where he says that to deny a general resurrection is to deny the resurrection of Jesus, and to believe in the resurrection of Jesus is to affirm belief in a general resurrection.

Since the resurrection poses an invitation to live in the story of Jesus, this narrative has an intrinsically practical dimension, and theology derived from the narrative then has an intrinsically moral dimension.

One relates to Jesus and to the God revealed in Jesus by accepting the invitation to live in the story of Jesus. To tell the story is to describe how one defined by Jesus Christ—a Christian—should live. And the answer to the question, "How should we live as Christians?" comes from recounting the narrative of Jesus.

The resurrection thus makes the story of Jesus a story of salvation. A sinner leaves the sinful life and experiences salvation in the reign of God by accepting the Jesus of this story as the presence of the reign of God, by accepting Jesus as God's anointed one—the Savior of the world. And that acceptance means believing strongly enough in resurrection's testimony that Jesus is God's anointed one to live in Jesus' story, when it is not required and even when it means hardship.

This leaving of a sinful life and beginning a new life engages the personal responsibility of the individual. That free engagement of the will appears in the call to "Follow me," which Jesus addressed to those who became his disciples. Would-be followers of Jesus today must also engage their personal responsibility—their free will—by making a decision to accept that invitation.

On the other hand, the pervasive reality of sin means that an individual alone, on his or her own initiative, is helpless to overcome the reality of sin. Only the active presence of God in the world—the Spirit of God—can enable a sinner to resist the power of sin and to begin to live in the reign of God. As is implied in writings of John Calvin, since we cannot save ourselves but we discover that we believe, it must be that God has elected and saved us.[6] These two impulses—human responsibility and God's electing grace—together constitute the paradox of grace. Paul situated himself in this paradox when he wrote: "But by the grace of God I am what I am, and his grace toward me has not been in vain. On the contrary, I worked harder than any of them—though it was not I, but the grace of God that is with me" (1 Cor 15:10).

Atonement Imagery

The narrative and its theological implications sketched here can be read as an atonement image. In making that suggestion, we see this chapter as an example of continuing an exploration or going through a door opened by John Howard Yoder.

---

6. See Calvin, *Institutes*, 964–72.

The Introduction to this book mentioned the 1980 believers church conference at Bluffton College (now Bluffton University). This conference posed the question, "Is there a believers church Christology?" Yoder gave the keynote address. The long opening sentence of the address applauded the innovation of the conference question.

> We should commend the planners of this conference for daring to go at the notion that there might be such a thing as an identifiable "concept of the believers' church" not from the narrative historical roots of specific Christian communities, nor from the obvious formal differentiae of adult membership and separation from the state, but from the middle of ordinary dogmatic debate, where the debaters are hardly aware of any direct correlation of their differences with ecclesiology.[7]

It is appropriate to ask, he continued, whether there are "points ... within the bread and butter basics of ordinary belief where the church's freedom, her voluntariness, and her not being established, would correlate logically with some trends and tenets more than others." In other words, it is appropriate to ask whether the ecclesiology that Yoder found in Anabaptism and that is expounded as "body politics" in chapter 7 of this volume might produce theological formulations different from those of standard orthodoxy.[8] In a postscript added after the conference to the text of the address on his website, Yoder wrote that previous Believers Church conferences had focused on clarifying this ecclesiastical concept and their "witness to Christians of other traditions." But the Bluffton conference reversed the direction of the question, asking "whether churches of this kind would properly have distinguishing orientation within the realm of confession and dogma."[9] Yoder's ecclesiology of "body politics" that is a consequence of living out of the story of Jesus (as developed in chapter 7) is a believers church ecclesiology. In suggesting formulations of atonement and Christology derived from the narrative of Jesus and focusing on living in that narrative, the chapter in hand is thus a continuation of the exploration that Yoder commended in his 1980 address.

As an atonement image, the narrative version recited in the previous section belongs to the category of "Christus Victor." The name comes from the idea that the resurrection of Jesus was a victory over the powers

---

7. Yoder, "'That Household We Are,'" 1.
8. Ibid.
9. Ibid., 9.

of evil and the devil who killed Jesus. This motif had a number of historical formulations—Jesus handed over to Satan as a ransom payment to the devil in exchange for the release of the souls of humankind held captive; or Jesus was killed by Satan in a cosmic battle between the forces of God and the forces of evil. Versions of the motif appeared in the writings of early church fathers, such as Irenaeus, Gregory of Nyssa, Augustine, and others.

An important characteristic of the narrative-focused version of Christus Victor sketched here is that it begins not with a restatement of one of the church fathers, but with the narrative of Jesus itself. It is a motif derived from the gospel narrative. Apart from using a historically meaningful name, "Christus Victor," if there is a relationship between narrative Christus Victor and the later images, it is that the later motifs have departed from the narrative foundation described here. In other words, the later motifs are derived from or are perhaps a stripped down version of this interpretation of the narrative of Jesus.

A second important characteristic of narrative Christus Victor is that it understands the presence of evil, not first of all as a personified and cosmic devil, but rather in terms of the actions of people who opposed the reign of God. These actions combine to form the spirit of any institution or structure—business, athletic team, city, nation, church—which has a material impact on the lives of people.[10] Of course one can then extend the understanding of evil to include a cosmic level, but it is important to locate evil in the world in a way that is seen to ensnare the lives of all human beings. Ultimately, given the universality of sin, all people are captive to the powers of evil that bound the people who killed Jesus. With the resurrection, the reign of God is victorious over the powers of evil, however one might want to understand evil. Accepting the invitation of the resurrection then enables followers of Jesus to begin to experience and participate in a partial way in the victory over evil as well. The important point is that although sin is universal, locating it first of all in the world where people live means that with the power of God evil can also be overcome in the world to the extent that people live into the loving and evil-confronting life of Jesus.[11]

10. This is a brief description of the idea of the Powers, a concept that Yoder learned from Berkhof, *Christ and the Powers*, as discussed in chapters 6 and 7 above. For the extensive discussion of the Powers as a "Domination System," see the three-volume series by Walter Wink: *Naming the Powers*; *Unmasking the Powers*: *Engaging the Powers*.

11. In addition to the full treatment of "narrative Christus Victor" in Weaver,

PART THREE—EXTENDING JOHN HOWARD YODER'S THEOLOGY

Atonement, Race, and Ethnicity

We use the issue of racial and ethnic reconciliation to illustrate the relevance of narrative Christus Victor as a theology for living. Since it is derived from the narrative of Jesus, which includes his crossing of racial and ethnic boundaries, racial and ethnic reconciliation are intrinsic to this narrative atonement image. Jesus' parables and his acts display challenges to racial and ethnic stereotypes and discrimination of his day. There is the well-known parable of the Good Samaritan, the account of the Samaritan who helped an injured man found lying in the road when leaders of the religious establishment passed by on the other side. From this parable, the term "good Samaritan" has passed into the English language as an expression for a helpful person.

Less often recognized, however, are the anti-racism implications of this parable. The Samaritans of Jesus' day were thought to be of mixed ethnic origin rather than truly Israelite. As a result, Samaritans were despised and experienced discrimination. According to the strict purity code, they were considered unclean. It is a challenge to this discrimination and these attitudes when Jesus' story makes the Samaritan out to be the good person in contrast to the failures of the perceived religious leaders of society. The good neighbor, the despised Samaritan, has now become the object of love, the one whom the lawyer has just been told to love as himself (Luke 10:27). If the parable were told today, it might feature a so-called illegal alien in the role of the Samaritan, with the priest and Levite played by members of congress in coat and tie who are known to demand loudly that measures be instituted against undocumented people. Or perhaps the role of the Samaritan is taken by a person from a country accused of terrorism with the other roles played by the political leaders who call for ever tougher sanctions and military measures against that country. Or perhaps the Samaritan is played by an African American woman, invisible to a white mayor and city council president, visiting in town to recruit a new industry but concerned about how to ensure that the new business will hire employees of the "the right kind"—that is, white ones.

The story in John 4 of Jesus' encounter with the Samaritan woman at the well at Sychar adds an additional dimension to his challenge of discrimination based on race or ethnicity. As depicted in this narrative,

---

Nonviolent Atonement, a short summary is available in Weaver, "Atonement and (Non) Violence" and Weaver, "Violence in Christian Theology."

Jesus not only used a Samaritan as a good example and as the enemy to be loved. He actually traveled in Samaria and interacted with a Samaritan woman. In other words, he crossed real boundaries of geography, ethnicity (and gender). In contrast, those who wished to avoid ritual contamination from the supposedly unclean Samaritans avoided traveling through Samaria. They walked out of their way to the east side of the Jordan river and made their way on that side of the Jordan when traveling from Judea in the south of Palestine to Galilee in the north. In making this journey Jesus crossed a geographic boundary that was also an ethnic boundary, and his interaction with the Samaritan woman put this crossing of racial or ethic boundaries on display.

As the one who makes the reign of God visible in his person and his acts, Jesus' parable and travel put the reign of God on the side of confronting racial and ethnic discrimination. The parable and the journey through Samaria exemplify that confronting this evil requires a change in attitudes and practices. His example in the parable challenged prevailing attitudes and his trip through Samaria illustrated the need for prevailing practices to change.

These boundary crossings are an example for Christians in the twenty-first century. But crossing of boundaries and racial or ethnic reconciliation are also visible in the theological formulation of a narrative atonement image. Racism belongs to the powers that killed Jesus. The resurrection's victory over the powers of evil is thus a victory over racism. The resurrection shows that Jesus' making present of the reign of God includes overcoming racism. Our participation in the reign of God requires us to "change sides," to switch loyalties from whatever is opposed to God to the side of the reign of God. This participation thus calls for racial and ethnic reconciliation, and to deny or to ignore this reconciliation is to place ourselves outside of the reign of God. Racial reconciliation is an ineradicable dimension of God's reign. Resurrection is then the invitation to identify with Jesus and to participate in the ethnic and racial reconciliation that is present in Jesus and that God is now already accomplishing in the world.

Paul expressed this ethnic and racial reconciliation. As John Howard Yoder reminds us, the rite of baptism introduces the believer into "a new world" (2 Cor 5:17 NEB) that God is creating through the work of Jesus Christ. Whereas previously they were separate, Paul writes that Jews and Gentiles now pray and eat together. They are reconciled. They now constitute a "new humanity" (Eph 2:15), or in Yoder's translation of Galatians 3:27–28, "Baptized in Christ, you are clothed in Christ, and there is neither slave nor free, neither male nor female, you are all one in Christ Jesus."[12] These individuals retain their particularity, but they have been joined by God into a new community of interethnic inclusivity.

It is important to state specifically that confronting and overcoming racism are explicit dimensions of the reign of God. Drawing on elements of Jesus' story concerning his teaching and interaction with Samaritans and then Paul's appropriation of the work of Christ locates a challenge to racism and ethnic discrimination as an inseparable and intrinsic element of theology derived from the narrative of Jesus. James Cone has lamented the absence of such challenges and the invisibility of racism as an ethical issue in most traditional theology.[13] Our intent with a lived theology derived from the narrative of Jesus is to put on display what Cone's black theology makes visible, namely that confronting and overcoming racism belongs to salvation in the reign of God that is made visible in the person of Jesus.

Since living in the story of Jesus requires a change in loyalty to the reign of God, it is clear that racial and ethic reconciliation is no easy declaration of tolerance or merely claiming to like everyone or pretending that color does not matter. It is necessary to become anti-racist. True reconciliation requires recognition of the existence of racism, and the way that it has been accommodated and supported or ignored in traditional theology. Reconciliation thus requires a change in the status quo of both theology and practice. Not to challenge the systemic injustice of racism is to condone it. In North America, racial and ethnic reconciliation requires those who belong to the dominant, white culture to take specific steps to challenge the attitudes and practices that surround us—our own attitudes as well as the structures and philosophies of the institutions in which we participate. This specific action to counter racism and to enact race reconciliation makes this a lived theology. If this dimension of the story of Jesus is not lived, then the telling of the story of Jesus is not fully Gospel.

---

12. Yoder, *Body Politics*, 28–40, quotes 28–29.
13. Cone, *God of the Oppressed*, 106–7, 180–87.

Parallels in Black Theology

This sketch of a theological model derived from the narrative of Jesus has significant parallels to points emphasized by James H. Cone, who is often recognized as the founder of the black theology movement. He sought to construct a black theology over against traditional theology that was white theology without the label. Cone identified this European tradition as white in one way, and J. Kameron Carter and Willie James Jennings, whose writings are summarized in a following section, identify its whiteness in a more profound and theoretical way. Our religious identity gives us a certain empathy for these projects.

We locate our religious identity in historic Anabaptism, a religious tradition often perceived as marginal to the supposed normative, European theological tradition. Earlier chapters of this book noted that sixteenth-century Anabaptists rejected the established church and were thus perceived as a threat to the social order. As a result, several thousand were executed at the hands of political authorities, usually with cruel torture. *The Martyrs Mirror* preserves stories of these martyrs.[14] Martyrdom is no longer a reality for the heirs of Anabaptism in modern North America. However, hearing martyr stories and belonging to a tradition whose origins placed it outside of or on the underside of mainstream theology have fostered our capacity to raise questions concerning mainstream or standard theology. In chapters 2 and 4, it will be recalled, John Howard Yoder's Anabaptist roots propelled him to pursue an Anabaptist theological construction that would bypass the inherited theology of Christendom. That same impulse energizes the theological model posed in this chapter. And this identity with a perceived marginal tradition gives us empathy for the efforts of Cone, Carter, and Jennings to construct alternatives to white theology from which they are excluded.[15]

As is the case for our model, for Cone Christian theology also begins with the Jesus of history. It is in the story of Jesus in history that one sees liberation from oppression taking place. And the God that Cone sees present in Jesus is the liberating God who saved Israel in the exodus. For

---

14. van Braght, *Martyrs' Mirror*.

15. Along with this statement of empathy, it is important to emphasize that the stance of Anabaptists on the margin was different from that of African Americans. Anabaptists chose to place themselves on the ecclesiological margin, and since they knew that stance was risky, in one sense their suffering was voluntary. Enslaved Africans were forced to the margin violently and their suffering was always involuntary.

Cone, as for our lived theology, theology that does not deal with the reality of liberation—salvation—in history is not true theology.

> Fellowship with God is made possible through God's activity in history, setting people free from economic, social, and political bondage. God's act of reconciliation is not mystical communion with the divine; nor is it a pietistic state of inwardness bestowed upon the believer. God's reconciliation is a new relationship with *people* created by God's concrete involvement in the political affairs of the world, taking sides with the weak and the helpless."[16]

In the language of black theology, Cone expresses what we called the need for white people to challenge the racism of the status quo.

> When whites undergo the true experience of conversion wherein they die to whiteness and are reborn anew in order to struggle against white oppression and *for* the liberation of the oppressed, there is a place for them in the black struggle of freedom. Here reconciliation becomes God's gift of blackness through the oppressed of the land.[17]

The evil of racism still colors American society. It is present in the fact that for the vast majority of people, whether Caucasian or African American, unconsciously the first characteristic accounted for when meeting a person for the first time is skin color. Racism is present in the reality of "white privilege," the assumption of many people that the United States is a "white" society and that wherever one goes, one should be able to carry on all daily affairs with white people, accompanied by the assumption that one need make no effort to understand or know about cultures that differ from white culture. Racism is present in the common perception that since the disappearance of legal segregation and discrimination, the problem of racism has been solved and thus racism now involves only the commission of specific acts judged to have a racial bias. This perception is reinforced repeatedly by the way the news media report incidents, as though a perpetrator acts individually with no reflection of or reinforcement from the social ethos. The assumption that racism applies only to individual incidents renders invisible, for example, the prejudice behind the assumption of white privilege, as well as the mostly unacknowledged but real systemic racism that produces higher unemployment among African Americans, defacto segregation

16. Cone, *God of the Oppressed*, 209.
17. Ibid., 222.

in housing, an achievement gap in schools, lower average wages for African American workers, and such things as the claim that speculation about Barack Obama's supposed foreign birth was not fueled by racism. Recently Michelle Alexander has described the racial bias in the pursuit of "the war on drugs."[18] True reconciliation requires confession of past injustice, whether by individuals or the church or the national culture. And it means acknowledgment of current injustice, which is the heir to past discrimination. The beginning of reconciliation means recognizing the injustice that exists and making changes to achieve reconciliation.

It is not as though only those who belong to the dominant culture are guilty of participation in the evil of racism. James Cone writes that God is on the side of the oppressed who struggle for justice, which means that God enters history to break down the hostility and racism of white people. From their side, the oppressed people must accept this new existence wrought by God "by struggling against all who try to make us slaves."[19] The implication of Cone's position is that not engaging in the struggle for liberation is to accept the oppression practiced by the dominant society, which is to participate in the evil—the sin—of oppression. In other words, a claimed reconciliation that does not challenge an unjust status quo is not true reconciliation.

Comments from Garth Kasimu Baker-Fletcher, a second-generation black theologian, make explicit the implication that the oppressed can participate in their own oppression. He writes of the need to be delivered from the desire to conform to white societal expectations and values. Through hearing the word of Jesus Christ there is a deliverance that results in one becoming a Christian. And there is a second deliverance that is an extension of the first. It is "hearing the word of Blackness, which is a cry to leave Euro-dominated Space and return to God's affirmation of your Afrikan self.... It is a deliverance because after it occurs, one is no longer bound by the mental, cultural, and spiritual shackles of Euro-dominators."[20] Baker-Fletcher also writes that it is easy for African Americans to use this domination to claim the status of victims, but he emphasizes the problem of "self-imprisonment." "We are not wholly innocent." he writes. Self-imprisonment comes from accepting the views that white society has placed on black women's bodies and the abusive

18. Alexander, *New Jim Crow*.
19. Cone, *God of the Oppressed*, 215–18.
20. Baker-Fletcher, *Xodus*, 86.

system of patriarchy as well as the inheritance of "generations-long intertribal hatred" from Africa. Self-imprisonment also involves an inherited subordination of women, and the "sin of irresponsibility, abusiveness, and sexist behavior" by African American men, including the black on black violence of gang warfare.[21]

Although in different ways, racism is a sin that touches all people. True reconciliation occurs when people recognize their kinds of accommodation and participation in it, and then consciously chart a new direction of confronting racism. Their individual acts will not immediately change the systemic racism of the society that surrounds us, but with this change their participation becomes involuntary. And true reconciliation is achieved, not when racism is fully overcome—that goal is far from achieved—but when from their several sides, all these participants in racism are now joined together in a common bond to confront it. This is the racial and ethnic reconciliation to which the resurrection of Jesus Christ calls every Christian.

Resurrection is the invitation to participate in this reconciliation, and the church consists of these reconciled people. Their mission is to live in such a way—to put on display—the nature of reconciliation in the reign of God, and to provide a view of the future reign of God.[22] Racial and ethnic reconciliation is a part of what the church is about. If the church does not put this racial and ethnic reconciliation on display it is not living in nor making a living witness to what Jesus was about. Or in the words of John Howard Yoder, "If reconciliation between peoples and cultures is not happening, the Gospel's truth is not being confirmed in that place."[23]

A second way in which this narrative atonement image responds to racism and includes racial reconciliation appears in conversation with Delores Williams' womanist challenge to traditional substitutionary and satisfaction atonement imagery. We engage that discussion after a brief display of the contrast between the narrative Christus Victor motif and traditional satisfaction atonement.

---

21. Baker-Fletcher and Baker-Fletcher, *My Sister, My Brother*, 124–26.

22. Chapter 7 above on "body politics" described additional ways in which the church makes visible and testifies to the future of the reign of God in the present.

23. Yoder, *Body Politics*, 38.

Narrative versus Satisfaction Atonement

The ransom version of Christus Victor was rejected by Anselm (ca. 1033–1109) and replaced by the idea that Jesus' death satisfied the offended honor of God, which restored the order of creation. Stated rather crassly, in the ransom version of Christus Victor, God handed over Jesus to the devil as a payment to ransom the souls of humankind held captive by Satan. However, when God raised Jesus, Satan was defeated and souls were rescued from the clutches of Satan. In rejecting the ransom version of Christus Victor, Anselm argued that Satan had no rights that God was bound to honor. Thus Anselm removed the devil from the equation and argued that the sin of humankind had offended the honor of God. Thus humankind owed a debt to God that they were unable to pay. God then sent Jesus as a human being to supply the human death that would satisfy God's honor and restore the distorted order of creation.

Putting the narrative version of Christus Victor side-by-side with Anselm's satisfaction theory reveals an important difference. In Anselm's understanding, sinful humans owe God but cannot pay that debt. Therefore Jesus the Son is sent in order to die to supply the debt that God needs. The internal logic of this scenario makes God the one who is ultimately responsible for the death of Jesus—God needed a death to satisfy God's offended honor and God sent Jesus to provide the death that sinful humans could not supply. Thus the salvific component of Jesus' work is his death. In contrast, for narrative Christus Victor, human sin is responsible for the death of Jesus, and the action of God is to restore the life of Jesus in the face of that sin and to invite sinners to participate in the life of God as it is visible in the life of Jesus. The saving act in this scenario is God's resurrection of Jesus. People are saved when they accept God's invitation of the resurrection to live in the reign of God made visible in the life of Jesus.

The import of this comparison is to see that narrative Christus Victor has the image of a God who saves without sanctioning violence in contrast to the God of satisfaction atonement who sanctions violence and uses it to satisfy the divine need. Thus narrative Christus Victor projects an image of God that is consistent with Jesus' rejection of violence. This nonviolent image of God is what must be the case if God is indeed truly revealed in Jesus. Space forbids an in-depth discussion in this essay of the idea of the nonviolence of God.[24]

Another problematic dimension of satisfaction atonement in any of its forms is the image of Jesus that it presents. Along with the violent image of God in the satisfaction atonement images, this motif pictures Jesus as a model of voluntary submission to innocent suffering. The Father needs the death of Jesus to satisfy divine honor in order to restore the order of creation; as innocent victim Jesus voluntarily agrees to submit to this death needed by the honor of God. Or as innocent victim Jesus voluntarily agrees to undergo the punishment deserved by sinful humankind in order to meet the demand of divine justice. Because Jesus' death is needed, Jesus models being a voluntary, passive and innocent victim, who suffers because a higher authority—the Father—needs it.

This passive suffering differs significantly from the suffering that one chooses to accept as the consequence of living as a witness to the visible reign of God. It can be properly said that God suffers with us in this choice to suffer, even as God suffered with Jesus in his mission to make visible the reign of God in human history. This suffering is not the purpose of living in the will of God but is rather the consequence of being identified with God's reign. It is not God's will that anyone should suffer, but God redeems the suffering of those who experience it as a consequence of working for the reign of God.[25]

Feminist and Womanist Responses

It is important to underscore those for whom the images of a God who needs death and of a Jesus as innocent, passive sufferer pose a particular concern. Applying these images can foster injustice. Living in the model of Jesus in satisfaction atonement means to submit passively and

---

24. For longer discussion of the implications of atonement images for the violence-oriented images of God, see comments throughout Weaver, *Nonviolent Atonement*, as well as Weaver, *Nonviolent God*. The latter features a conversation about God and violence in the Old Testament, with nonviolent images of various kinds pictured alongside the well-known view of violence in the Old Testament. It is the life of Jesus that makes clear that it is the nonviolent side of this conversation that most truly pictures the image of God. For nonviolent versus violent images of God in forgiveness, see Weaver, "Forgiveness and (Non)Violence." An argument for the nonviolence of God is a departure from the perspective of John Howard Yoder on this point. See Gingerich, "Theological Foundations."

25. On witness to the reign of God in the midst of suffering, see chapter 8 above.

to endure injustice. There are many examples. Feminists and womanists have said that God the Father in atonement theology projects an image of divine child abuse. This image, along with the image of Jesus as innocent and passive victim, are unhealthy models for a woman abused by a man or a child violated by her father. They constitute double jeopardy when attached to hierarchical theology that asserts male headship over women.[26] A model of passive, innocent suffering poses an obstacle for people who encounter conditions of systemic injustice, or an unjust status quo produced by the power structure. Examples might be the legally segregated, American south prior to the civil rights movement; the silent but real oppression of "white privilege"; global marketization that favors big business and disadvantages peasant farmers;[27] military-backed occupation, under which land is confiscated and indigenous residents crowded into enclosed territories, called "reservations" in North America and "autonomous areas" in Palestine. James Cone linked substitutionary atonement specifically to defenses of slavery and colonial oppression. He called Anselm's atonement image "A neat rational theory but useless as a leverage against political oppression. It dehistoricizes the work of Christ, separating it from God's liberating act in history."[28]

Womanist writers have stressed a threefold agenda of opposition to racism, sexism, and poverty. They have protested the male dominance of some elements of the black church, and have protested claims of feminists to speak for all women. The poorer economic status of black women has meant that they have long worked outside the home, womanists said, often as domestics and serving people in white homes and establishments. Prominent womanist Delores Williams includes these forms of oppression and more in her description of "surrogacy," the numerous ways in which black women have been forced to fill roles properly belonging to white men and women and black men.[29] Williams says that to accept satisfaction or substitutionary atonement and its image of Jesus—the

---

26. Brown and Parker, "For God"; Hopkins, *Towards a Feminist Christology*, 50–52; Brock, *Journeys by Heart*, 55–57; Heyward, *Saving Jesus*, 151; Williams, *Sisters in the Wilderness*, 161–67.

27. Harder, "Violence of Global Marketization."

28. Cone, *God of the Oppressed*, 211–12.

29. See comments throughout as well as indicated pages in Williams, *Sisters in the Wilderness*, 22–29, 62–74, 178–203.

"ultimate surrogate figure"—is to validate all the unjust surrogacy to which black women have been and still are subjected.[30]

Mennonite womanist Nekeisha Alexis-Baker suggests that Yoder's treatment of the cross supports the womanist critique of the passive suffering modeled by satisfaction atonement imagery. Yoder emphasized, Alexis-Baker writes, that not all suffering is parallel to Jesus' cross. Rather the cross was "the result of Jesus' voluntary decision to reject violence, hate, hostility, and non-involvement in confronting the powers." Likewise, "when one takes up the cross and follows Christ, one makes a conscious choice to vulnerably resist injustice and renounces the paths of premature peace and violent insurrection." Thus only the suffering that results from this kind of resistance to injustice is the cross that Christians bear in imitation of Christ. And very importantly, by naming what the cross is not, namely all suffering, "Yoder subverts the hermeneutics of sacrifice that sanctifies Black women's pain and encourages resistance to oppression as a way to follow Jesus." In this way, Yoder's understanding of the cross "undercuts religious rationales for Black people's subjugation precisely because the suffering they experience is not a valid 'way of the cross.'" And when Yoder identified the kind of suffering

> manifest in Jesus' cross, his theology supports womanist work to liberate Black women from viewing our violated bodies, surrogacy, and oppression as our cross to bear. Furtheremore, Yoder's emphasis on the voluntary nature of the cross enables Christians to thoroughly denounce any and all abuses that are imposed upon Black women and other underprivileged groups.[31]

The womanist concerns about modeling passive submission to unjust suffering and surrogacy are addressed by the image of Jesus in narrative Christus Victor. In this narrative version, Jesus is not passive, supplying the death that the Father needs. Rather in making the reign of God visible, Jesus confronts oppressive structures and codes, and crosses unjust racial boundaries. His life thus displays the reconciled way of living in the reign of God.

This discussion of atonement leads into a discussion of Christology. Our proposal began with a sketch of the New Testament's narrative of Jesus, and then showed how that story could be read as an atonement

---

30. Ibid., 60–83, 161–67, 178–99.
31. Alexis-Baker, "Freedom of the Cross," 87–88.

image. These same items—the narrative and the atonement motif—can also be identified as the basis of a narrative-oriented Christology.

Christology and Trinity

In the standard approach, classic theology appeals to several early christological formulas as norms or as minimal statements to affirm about Jesus. These formulas include the language from the council of Nicea (325 CE) and repeated at Constantinople (381 CE) and the language of the council of Chalcedon (451 CE). These councils used the category of ontology to declare Jesus to be *homoousios* or "one in being" or "of the same substance" or "same essence" as God and as humankind. These are commonly referred to as affirmations of the deity and the humanity of Jesus. The Cappadocian Fathers' language of "one God in three Persons"—one essence and three *hypostases* or persons—is used to extend the same deity to the Holy Spirit. The Athanasian Creed (fifth or sixth century CE) asserts the equality of the three Persons and asserts that nothing can be in one that is not in the others.

Our proposal for a narrative-based theology is distinguishable from the classic formulations at several junctures. These differences all reflect or extend farther the influence of Yoder's contextualizing methodology described in chapter 1 and applied to interfaith conversations in chapter 10.

One such juncture concerns the approach to the threeness of God, commonly referred to as the Trinity. It is the God of Israel who is also present in and raised Jesus and who is still immediately present today as God's Spirit in calling disciples. This depiction of a threefold presence of God in time reflects the previously quoted comment by Yoder that Weaver recalls from the class lectures that were eventually published as *Preface to Theology*. In class, Yoder said that the early fathers used the category of ontology to depict the continuity of Jesus with God the Father. But since that philosophical system and its cosmological context were not ours, other categories might be appropriate to affirm the continuity of Jesus with God. For us, he suggested, Trinity was a "time problem"—understanding that the God of Israel was the God of Jesus and accessible to us today—and the category of continuity might be "ethics or history." That remark corresponds to his published comment that while the early fathers turned to "metaphysics" to discuss Jesus' humanity, deity, and relation to God, that was not the category used in the New Testament. There we find "the affirmation of the unity of Jesus and the Father" in terms of "will and deed" and "in Jesus' perfect *obedience* to the *will* of the Father."[32] Our proposal constitutes a narrative approach to Trinity in time, and is done with Yoder's caution in mind from chapter 1. There it is stated that "threeness-in-oneness" in itself does not save, and that the idea that "God is three persons" was "not given us by revelation."[33]

A second distinction concerns the visibility of ethics in our theological proposal. Our proposal uses the narrative of Jesus as its beginning point, which gives our proposed theology an intrinsically practical or moral dimension. The primary ethical dimension presented in this essay has concerned racism and racial reconciliation.[34] These explicit ethical dimensions are lacking from the abstract categories of being that define Jesus in the classic creedal statements of both Christology and Trinity. When these formulas are considered the sufficient norm of truth concerning Jesus, then ethical implications are not intrinsic to theology governed by these supposed, universally accepted classic formulas.

John Howard Yoder noted the absence of the narrative in the Nicene formulation when he wrote, as quoted in chapter 1, that "*in form* we are moving farther and farther away from the Gospel story. The form of the confession is still used, but it has been so padded out with statements about the essence of Christ that one recognizes no narrative to it any more."[35] That is a significant observation in light of our intent to produce a lived theology.

Other writers have also observed the absence of an explicit ethical dimension in the classic formulas. We note two. James Cone remarked that lack of attention to the particular history of Jesus in Palestine and the focus on the abstract issue of Jesus' deity has produced a mainstream or standard theology in which the sin of racism and the issue of poverty were invisible or ignored. He writes that although Athanasius stressed the humanity of Jesus as the basis of salvation,

---

32. Yoder, *Royal Priesthood*, 185; Yoder, *Original Revolution*, 136; Yoder's italics.

33. Yoder, *Preface* (2002), 203, 204.

34. Additional important dimension of this ethical orientation would include (but not be limited to) gender issues, economic exploitation and inequality, poverty, and the rejection of violence (discussed in chapters 8 and 9 of this volume), and the challenge to usurpation of religious authority by political powers, which has been visible but not emphasized in this chapter.

35. Yoder, *Preface* (2002), 202.

few, if any, of the early Church Fathers grounded their christological arguments in the concrete history of Jesus of Nazareth. Consequently, little is said about the significance of his ministry to the poor as a definition of his person. The Nicene Fathers showed little interest in the christological significance of Jesus' deeds for the humiliated, because most of the discussion took place in the social context of the Church's position as the favored religion of the Roman State.

With Jesus defined as "the divinizer" of humanity, "Christology is removed from history, and salvation becomes only peripherally related to this world."[36] In a later chapter, Cone writes that Constantine's participation in the Arian controversy influenced "the ethical import" of the church's theology.

> That was why the early Church Fathers could ask about the Son's relation to the Father and later the Holy Spirit's relation to both without connecting the question to the historical freedom of the oppressed. Since the Church and its bishops . . . were not slaves, it did not occur to them that God's revelation in Jesus Christ is identical with the presence of his Spirit in the slave community in struggle for the liberation of humanity."[37]

Joerg Rieger offered similar comments in the context of an effort to find resources within the classic formulations that would challenge empire. He finds one possibility in Nicea's *homoousios*, since it has the potential to introduce Jesus into the Godhead, with "Christ's life in all its complexity, divine and human, including his resistance to the powers that be." However, that potential was not pursued at that time, Rieger said. "It is hardly an accident that the life of Christ is not mentioned in the creeds. . . . The challenge to empire posed by the life of Christ would have just been too great." That potential challenge to the religious and political establishment depends on a link to the "deeper realities of Christ's particular life (in solidarity with the outcasts of his time)." But "where the creeds without particular attention to the life of Christ are considered sufficient, . . . this challenge is lost, which makes the 'orthodox' position so convenient for empire."[38]

---

36. Cone, *God of the Oppressed*, 106–7.
37. Ibid., 107, 181.
38. Rieger, *Christ and Empire*, 96–97.

Our proposal that begins with the narrative of Jesus makes visible the element that Yoder and both Cone and Rieger noted was missing from the classic formulations. The contrast between our beginning theological formulation and the classic statements indicates what has changed (and perhaps even gotten lost) between the New Testament and the fourth- and fifth-century acceptance of the conciliar statements as authoritative.

The comment on the difference between the New Testament theological formulations and the classic creedal statements reveals another characteristic with at least as much significance. It reveals that the creedal statements have a context. As Cone and Rieger noted, they reflect a particular social milieu, and served the interests of some elements of the church—such as powerful rulers—more than others, namely the poor and those without political power. Yoder's analysis pointed to another aspect of their context. These statements use the philosophical category of "ontology" or *ousios*, meaning "essence" or "being" as the category with which to define Jesus' relationship to God the Father and to humanity, and presume a three-decker hierarchical universe in which the being or essence of God above is the same being or essence of Jesus in our world below. Yoder's analysis made clear that these are not universal, transcendent categories, but rather reflect a particular time and place. As he was quoted in text and a note in chapter 1, all participants to the conversation in the first centuries lived in cosmologies "with the top open for transcendent validation." And as just noted, the New Testament affirmed the unity of Jesus with the Father in terms of "will and deed" and "obedience" rather than "substance."

However, Yoder also took pains to make clear that awareness of the social milieu of these categories and their worldview in no way render these statements false. On the contrary, if one wants the answer about Jesus' relationship to God in terms of ontological categories and presuming a tiered universe, then these are the correct answers. However, recognizing the particularity or the context of the creedal statements opens the door to the possibility of other ways of responding to the same questions in other contexts. Our approach sketched above illustrates such an alternative. It indicates two ways to affirm that the God of Israel is fully present in the story of Jesus, one theological and one practical. For one, the resurrection validates the life of Jesus as the life and the presence of God and the reign of God on earth. There is also a lived, practical version of this confession that Jesus is God's anointed one. One professes and confesses belief that Jesus is the Christ by committing oneself to live in the story of Jesus when it is not required and even when it is costly. This is a lived version of the truth of Jesus.

This proposal for theologizing—for writing theology—is distinct, if not quite unique. It is not a restatement of classic theology based on the classic formulas for Christology, Trinity, or atonement; neither is it an attempt to explain differently or to broaden these classic formulas. In fact it does not begin with these formulas or with classic theology, and it does not link salvation to right doctrine.

This proposal for theologizing is distinct because of its claimed beginning point. With Yoder, we purport to begin theologizing with the life and story of Jesus. The result is an intrinsically practical theology, a lived theology or a theology for living. It has extracted an atonement image from the New Testament that bypasses the traditional images. This image is compatible with Jesus' rejection of violence. Going through a door opened by Yoder, this proposal poses a narrative-based approach to both Christology and Trinity that reflects the life of Jesus, and thus has an intrinsically practical approach. It has the potential to address any ethical issue. In this chapter we have chosen to illustrate the practical dimension with a discussion of racism. This is indeed the proposal of a theology for living. In line with John Howard Yoder, because it theologizes on the basis of the narrative of Jesus, our proposal could be called a radical theology.

Again with Yoder, this approach addresses the same issues as the classic formulas—identifying Jesus as human and as identified with God, while preserving monotheism—but is not specifically beholden to the classic language. This is an indication of a distinct theological direction, with racial reconciliation and rejection of violence as intrinsic or ineradicable elements. Although not entirely new, it is certainly distinguishable from the received tradition of what Yoder could identify as standard theology. And although we have not made a point of it, it is an Anabaptist theology in the sense that that sixteenth-century movement is one historical precedent that points to Jesus as the norm of theology and ethics.[39] Sixteenth-century Anabaptism was one of the sources of Yoder's theology, and as chapter 2 recounted, Yoder pursued its history to get access to a theological perspective different from mainstream theology. In these ways, this proposed theology represents an effort to extend one di-

39. For our statement of sixteenth-century Anabaptism as a movement that points toward the narrative of Jesus as the norm for theology and ethics, see Mast and Weaver, *Defenseless Christianity*.

mension of Yoder's methodology that was depicted in chapter 1, namely to pose a theology that establishes a distinct theological archetype, one in conversation with but not beholden to the classical approach to theology.

The "New Black Theology"[40]

Thus far, the theological proposal of this chapter has pursued the inquiry commended by Yoder in 1980 to explore the extent to which a believers church or voluntary ecclesiology can or does produce dogmatic images that are distinguishable from the classical images of Christendom. However, Yoder also wrote of entering a conversation in the categories of others. As was made clear in chapter 1, Yoder also demonstrated how to reform the classical images from within. For example, the often-quoted statement by Yoder that his view was "more Nicene and Chalcedonian than others"[41] was an encouragement to take seriously the human narrative of Jesus, and in particular his rejection of the sword, in expounding the meaning of the humanity and deity of Jesus. This would be entering a conversation in the categories of the standard or traditional Christology.

Writers of the "new black theology" exhibit both dimensions of Yoder's methodology, restoring or reforming the standard expressions as well as calling for new formulations. Yoder and the model just sketched can enter these discussions in their categories. J. Kameron Carter and Willie James Jennings both describe the development of the standard theological tradition to show that its separation of the work of Jesus from his Jewishness privileged whiteness and supported racism.[42] The result of this separation was a supposed universal Jesus, in which the various European national entities could define the mission of Jesus in a way that supported the colonial organization and domination of native peoples in South America and Africa and supported the slave trade and the enslavement of Africans in the Americas. Both writers share with Yoder the idea that theology should derive from Jesus, with Carter more on the side of reforming the standard formulations from within while Jennings is

---

40. The descriptor "new black theology" comes from Jonathan Tran's review of J. Kameron Carter and Willie James Jennings rather than the two authors themselves. See Tran, "New Black Theology." When the label is used occasionally for easy reference in this chapter, we put it in quotation marks to indicate that it is not Carter and Jennings' own description of their work.

41. Yoder, *Politics of Jesus* (1994), 102.

42. Carter, *Race*; Jennings, *Christian Imagination*.

closer to the side of advocating a new theological project. As with Yoder, for Carter and Jennings understanding their methodology is at least as important as content.

The thesis of J. Kameron Carter is that "modernity's racial imagination has its genesis in the theological problem of Christianity's quest to sever itself from its Jewish roots." This happened in two conceptual but related stages. First, Jews were cast as a "race group," in contrast to the Western Christians, who with the assistance of discourses in theology and philosophy, were also subtly "cast as a race group." Thus the European and eventually Euro-American Occident could conceive itself racially and religiously different from Jews, who were oriental. And then second, as a religion of the east, "Jews were then deemed inferior to Christians of the Occident or West." Thus was forged the racist imagination that led eventually to the racist imagination of white supremacy.[43]

Carter provides a devastating critique of Immanuel Kant's Enlightenment philosophy. With Jesus separated from his Jewishness, Kant developed a view that led to Christianity as the religion of whiteness, with whiteness as the norm of racial perfection but also existing above racial identity itself. This stance supported the colonial enterprise of European dominance. At three separate locations in the book, Carter does readings of Irenaeus, whose response to Gnosticism depended on the Jewishness of Jesus; Gregory of Nyssa, the Cappadocian father whose understanding of Jesus in the Trinity included the Jewishness of Jesus, and whose view of Jesus led him to oppose all slavery; and Maximus the Confessor, a seventh-century monk in the Eastern Church, whose inclusion of the covenant with Israel in his understanding of Jesus displays Maximus as a prototype of the kind of theology based on the Jewish flesh of Jesus that Carter is proposing. The analysis of these three demonstrates that the separation of Christianity from its Jewish roots and the descent into a generic Jesus that sponsored white supremacy was not inevitable, and also points the way to a theology that overcomes the whiteness of traditional theology.

Part Two of Carter's book deals with contemporary black theology, including a chapter on James Cone. Carter affirms the intent of Cone to counter white theology, and affirmed Cone's early intent to base the incarnation of God in Jesus of Nazareth as a Jew. Cone comes under critique, however, for switching from the Jewishness of Jesus to the abstract

---

43. Carter, *Race*, 4.

category of "black" in making Jesus relevant for the contemporary struggle of liberation. Thus "although there is much to celebrate in black theology," it "is not radical enough" because "it ironically leaves whiteness in place."[44] In Carter's analysis, Cone's black theology is still within the orbit of white theology or defined in relation to standard white theology that denies its whiteness.

Carter uses Part Three of his book to do a theological reading of three antebellum, "Afro-Christian" writers, namely Britton Hammon, Frederick Douglass, and Jarena Lee. In these writings, Carter sees efforts "to understand themselves as theological subjects, the meaning of whose bodies could only be understood in relationship to the economy of Jesus' Jewish body." Their endeavor to reshape theology on the basis of the Jewish flesh of Jesus, Carter believes, align them with the earlier efforts of Irenaeus, Gregory of Nyssa and Maximus the Confessor.[45]

The readings of the three early writers, the three antebellum Afro-Christians, and contemporary black theologians all contribute to Carter's solution to the problem of whiteness in standard theology. His proposal is to do Christology that takes seriously the Jewish flesh of Jesus. To counter whiteness requires "an understanding of Christian existence as ever-grounded in the Jewish, nonracial flesh of Jesus and thus as an articulation of the covenantal life of Israel."[46] By "nonracial flesh of Jesus," Carter means Jesus understood not as a member of an ethnic group, but as the bearer of the covenant between God and Israel. It is this Jewish Jesus that is, as Carter says in relation to the Christology of Irenaeus, "the locus from which to understand all created reality in relationship to YHWH, its Triune Creator."[47] Paul's mission to the gentiles was to invite them into this covenant. Since Gentiles are incorporated into this covenant, this Jewish flesh of Jesus has universal implications. Holding the Jewish flesh of Jesus in view means that Jesus is a continuation of the covenant with Abraham. Identifying Jesus as Jewish and as the bearer of the Abrahamic covenant locates Jesus in history. The standard theology has thus gone wrong in reducing this theological Jewishness to an ethnic identity, which could be abandoned along with the "dark people"

44. Ibid., 192.
45. Ibid., 344.
46. Ibid., 192.
47. Ibid., 14.

as "aliens" to the western theological imagination.⁴⁸ It was replaced by a supposed universal Jesus redefined in a way that privileged whiteness. It is recovery of the Jewishness of Jesus in history, of Jesus as the bearer of the covenant with Israel, that Carter sees as the basis for reconstructing Christian theology beyond white privilege.

The reconstruction of theology envisioned by Carter on the basis of the Jewishness of Jesus is theology done from the perspective of identification with the poor, theology that arises from "the everyday practices of the very people" forgotten by elitist theology of whiteness. It is theology done with the theological imagination shaped "*from within* the crises of life and death" rather than theology done by a scholastic elite. This theology will be tied not simply to the resurrected Jesus, "but to the Christ who was resurrected *from the dead* and in whose Jewish (nonracial) flesh, Christian thought claims, all of creation lives and moves and has being." The theology of whiteness forecloses such a theology. This reconstituted theology will "take its bearings from the Christian theological languages and practices that arise from the lived Christian worlds of dark peoples in modernity and how such peoples reclaimed . . . Christian theology from being a discourse of death—their death." The language of dark people, of whom Carter claimed Hammon, Douglass and Lee as examples, is the beginning of theology beyond race, "beyond the theological problem of whiteness."⁴⁹

In his book, Willie James Jennings exposes the problem "in which the Christian theological imagination was woven into processes of colonial dominance." As European colonialists carried Christianity to the rest of the world, "it claimed to be the host, the owner of the spaces it entered, and demanded native peoples enter its cultural logics, its way of being in the world, and its conceptualities." This colonial Christianity was one that assumed white superiority. Jennings goal is "to paint a portrait of a theological problem in order to suggest a way forward."⁵⁰

Like Carter, Jennings recognizes the formative contribution of Enlightenment philosophy to a theology of whiteness. His main thrust, however, is to demonstrate that this theology, which supported the several colonial enterprises propelled by a belief in white superiority, existed much earlier. For that demonstration, Jennings analyzes the theology

---

48. Ibid., 373.
49. Ibid., 374, 377, 378, 379. Carter's italics.
50. Jennings, *Christian Imagination*, 8, 9.

that supported Henry the Navigator's launching of the Portuguese slave trade as depicted by his chronicler, Gomes Eanes de Zurara; the devastating impact on the native peoples of Peru by the educational endeavors of Jesuit José de Acosta; and the program of Anglican bishop John William Colenso in South Africa. Even when Colenso finally saw the great harm done to native peoples by the colonial enterprise, his inherited theology provided no resources for his change of mind or efforts to assist the native peoples. Finally Jennings assesses the writing of Olaudah Equiano, who was captured by slavers as a small boy in Nigeria, who experienced purchase by four different masters and eventually purchased his own freedom. His narrative depicts the disjuncture, which Equiano never fully surmounted, between his profession of Christianity and coming to that profession through the tutelage of his masters/owners and under a theology that defended his enslavement.

Like Carter, Jennings also locates the development of a theology that privileges whiteness in the separation of Jesus and his work from his Jewishness. Israel was God's elect. Citing another author, Jennings states, "Israel exists only because of God's choice, and apart from God, it has no existence at all." However, this election was separated from Israel and from Jesus, and attached to other peoples. Divine election through the church was then claimed by the various nation-state subjects, which fueled the colonial enterprise that claimed European, white superiority.[51]

To counter this theology of dominance and white superiority, Jennings argues, Christian theology needs to recover the Jewishness of Jesus. With Jesus, the election of Israel was extended or opened to all peoples, and thus specifically to gentiles. Jesus' election was "in the heart of Israel's space," and created a new identity within Israel. With Jesus it becomes clear that the God of Israel is the God of all peoples who are reconstituted within Israel. With Jesus, there is a new way of being within Israel. A "new family" is formed around Jesus. This is not a destruction of Israel, but a "rebirth" of Israel in Jesus. It is now the case that around Jesus, within the continuation of Israel, many languages join together in worshiping the God who was witnessed to in Jesus. "This is the coming of the one new reality of kinship." The old cultural identities do not disappear in the new identity. Rather they are born anew in a community that honors and respects them. People defined by their cultural differences "enfold the old cultural logics and practices inside the new ones of others, and

---

51. Ibid., 254.

they enfold the cultural logics and practices of others inside their own." The result is a "community seeking to love and honor those in its midst." None is superior, all are equal and exist within the new Israel as a gift of God's election, with "the possibility of love and kinship."[52]

Recognition of the theology of whiteness and the colonial movement, Jennings believes, requires a reconstruction of Christianity and of theology "within the Gentile-Jewish relational matrix." The theology of presumed white superiority that governed the colonial enterprise separated Jesus from his Jewishness. Jennings calls for recognition of "the grotesque nature of a social performance of Christianity that imagines Christian identity floating above, land, landscape, animals, place, and space, leaving such realities to the machinations of capitalistic calculations and the commodity claims of private property."[53] The antidote is to do theology that locates Jesus in history, in his Jewishness as the bearer of God's covenant with Israel.

Conversation with the "New Black Theology"

The theological sketch of this chapter, as well as the theology of John Howard Yoder that stands behind it, can join a conversation with Carter and Jennings. Albeit with significant differences, these all advocate that the beginning point for Christian theology is the Jesus of history rather than now classic formulas that emerged some centuries later. Carter and Jennings appeal to the Jewishness of Jesus to begin to develop a theology beyond whiteness. Our sketch, along with Yoder, appeals to the particularity of the life of the human Jesus to show that rejection of the sword is intrinsic to Jesus' mission. Our sketch also displayed that efforts to confront racism are intrinsic to our understanding of Jesus' mission.[54]

52. Ibid., 259, 263, 266, 273, 274.
53. Ibid., 291, 293.
54. Jonathan Tran writes that the arguments of Carter and Jennings make clear that the label of "black" theology, while giving African Americans a voice, enables white theologians to marginalize it, while denying the whiteness of their own theology. He thus suggests that "the new black theology is best described as the new theology, no (dis)qualifying adjective necessary." In other words, when it is done properly there is only "Christian theology." As a minimum, Tran suggested, European theology should have acknowledged its own label as "colonizing theology." Tran, "New Black Theology," 27. Such labels do appear in Weaver, *Nonviolent Atonement*, 126–27, 150, 151. However, while Tran's point is well taken, rejecting the idea of labels and calling for theology to be "theology" or "Christian theology" does not quite solve the problem.

These parallel appeals to different aspects of the particular narrative of Jesus hold the potential for a mutually enriching conversation. Making the narrative of Jesus the initial base from which Christian theology develops gives our sketch an intrinsically ethical element. To ask how Christians should live requires telling the story of Jesus. And reciting that narrative holds up the model that Christians live by. Although Carter and Jennings rightfully stress the particularity of Jesus in his Jewishness, they deal little with the narrative of Jesus itself. Attention to the ethical dimensions of that narrative beyond racism would add additional elements to their arguments.

On the other hand, while we affirm the emphasis on the Jewishness of Jesus, that element was implied but not developed in our theological sketch. That dimension could be expanded considerably. Yoder's work certainly assumed the Jewishness of Jesus. Recall the material quoted above in chapter 6 from Yoder's essay, "Paul the Judaizer." Since the messianic age had begun, it was natural for Paul to believe that "Jews can share the glories of the Law as Grace with Gentiles." Therefore, "Far from being the great Hellenizer of an originally Jewish message, Paul is rather the great Judaizer of Hellenistic culture." Because this is the messianic age, "the centuries-old promises of the ingathering of the Gentiles was coming true." And since Gentiles are coming to the messianic synagogues in greater numbers than before, "what Paul sees happening in Christ and in the Christian church . . . is the fulfillment and not the abolition of the meaning of Torah as covenant of grace."[55] That Jesus was a continuation and not a break from Israel is clear in Yoder's assertion that Christian nonviolence did not begin with Jesus. Rather Jesus was extending a stance located at least as early as Jeremiah. He counselled the exiles in Babylon that although they did not control the reins of power they should "seek the welfare of the city" (Jer 29:7), which entailed the stance of nonviolent cultural resistance exhibited in the stories of the Hebrew captives in the

---

One has only to recall the conservative, quasi- or neo-fundamentalist meanings attached to the label "Christian" in the popular media to realize that something more is needed. All theology represents and reflects and comes out of a context. Inevitably there will be an assertion of criteria that reflect a context and which will be called into service to identify and validate that particular "theology." Recall, for example, Carter's argument that theology beyond whiteness must be done "from within the crises of life and death." Thus at some remove, even if we do not lead with them, labels do serve a purpose.

55. Yoder, *Jewish-Christian Schism*, 95–97.

books of Daniel and Esther.[56] The analysis of Yoder's treatment of the Jewish-Christian schism in chapter 10 makes clear his belief that Jesus was a continuation of the covenant with Israel. However, we need to add that Carter and Jennings theorize the problem of race in theology far beyond anything in Yoder or our sketch, which indicates to us an avenue for future development.

Carter and Jennings share another parallel with Yoder, which is also visible in our sketch. As demonstrated in chapter 1, Yoder's theologizing emphasizes methodology—deriving theology from the narrative of Jesus—as much as content. The books by Carter and Jennings project methodology more than content. Both point the way to produce a theology beyond whiteness, but neither actually develops that theology. Carter goes the farthest by providing examples of three pre-Enlightenment theologians who appeal to the Jewishness of Jesus and show the way to avoiding a theology of white superiority. Carter also asserts that Chalcedon's language of "fully human and fully divine" and trinitarian language can be reformulated to include the Jewishness of Jesus. For example, "Understood in the light of YHWH's covenant with YHWH's partner Israel and thereby with the world, Chalcedon is to be conceived of as witnessing to a theology of covenantal participation in which the life of YHWH is thoroughly implicated in and suffuses the life of Israel."[57] Thus while Carter does not develop a systematic theology beyond the theology of whiteness, his analysis and methodology show the way to a renewal or reforming of orthodoxy from within. His "reconceived practice of theology" is certainly "not opposed to classically articulated theology," as the engagements throughout his book indicated. On the other hand, it does not do to "simply repeat them [writers of classic orthodoxy] in fidelity to a 'language game.'" What matters," Carter says, "is the disposition out of which they are read."[58] This stance is in line with Yoder's comment about giving a sympathetic treatment to the development of the classic tradition, and being "more Nicene and Chalcedonian than others."

On the other hand, Carter's work aligns with Yoder's critique of classic orthodoxy as well. Carter's need to mention that which was not included in traditional interpretations of Chalcedon, namely the Jewishness

---

56. "Jesus the Jewish Pacifist," in Yoder, *Jewish-Christian Schism*, 69–89; also "See How They Go with Their Face to the Sun," in ibid., 183–202.

57. Carter, *Race*, 191.

58. Ibid., 378.

of Jesus, and his statements of reformulation display a relativizing of the classic formulas in line with Yoder. Further, in line with the argument of our sketch above, Carter's frank admission that although Gregory of Nyssa opposed slavery, the two remaining Cappadocians (Basil and Gregory of Nazianzus) both accepted slavery as a given,[59] displays pointedly that the classic language itself lacks an explicit ethical dimension. Meanwhile, Jennings's final chapter offers no specific models for reformulation but extensive discussion of what transformed theology will look like. His projections are thus in line with the contention of our sketch that in light of new understandings and developments, as Yoder indicated, it is quite appropriate to develop new formulations that expressed elements of the narrative of Jesus missing from the standard formulations.

Postconservative Evangelical Theologizing

The theological proposal sketched in this chapter can enter another conversation, in a quite different way than that proposed for Carter and Jennings. This second conversation is with Roger Olson and the segment of the evangelical tradition that he identified as "postconservative evangelicals."[60] The entry to this conversation is not at the level of appropriation of the particularity of Jesus as with Carter and Jennings but at the level of affirmation of classic theological professions.

Olson accepts a description of evangelical Christianity from David Bebbington, who listed "four hallmarks or 'core convictions'" that identify it. These four are: "biblicism, conversionism, crucicentrism (cross-centered piety), and activism in evangelism and social transformation." These four can cover a wide range of evangelicals. Olson uses a quote from Mark Noll to say that in and of themselves these four characteristics cannot sustain evangelical structures, but they do serve to identify evangelicals working within a variety of structures.[61]

Under the umbrella of these four core convictions, Olson positions what he calls "postconservative evangelicals." Over against conservative evangelicals, who would understand the four in terms of "correct doctrine," postconservative evangelicals "tend to regard the essence of

---

59. Ibid., 232.
60. Olson, *Reformed and Always Reforming*. For definition of postconservative evangelicalism, see 26–27, 43.
61. Ibid., 26–27.

authentic Christianity and evangelical faith as transforming experience and a distinctive spirituality (e.g., a personal relationship with Jesus Christ that results in amendment of life toward holiness)." Thus "orthopathy (right experience) is prior to orthodoxy in defining true Christianity. The influence of pietism is evident in postconservative evangelicalism." And this orientation then also means that for postconservatives "the main purpose of revelation is transformation rather than information." Postconservatives do not deny a propositional element to revelation, "but many are uncomfortable with the conservative emphasis on propositions as the most important feature of revelation."[62]

From here Olson describes the postconservative approach to theology as one that recognizes the possibility of change in theology within the limits set by scripture. Postconservatives want "to make the Word of God fresh in a new and constructive encounter with culture. They tend to think the constructive task of theology is always unfinished and that the call of the theologian is to rethink traditional concepts and categories in every generation and culture. They are not relativists, but they eschew an absolutism that enshrines human formulations of belief in incorrigible terms as if theology were a museum."[63] Although postconservatives comprise a diverse group,

> All are committed to the Bible as theology's primary and controlling source and norm. All work within a supernatural life- and worldview centered on God's revelation of himself in Jesus Christ "in [whom] all things hold together" (Col 1:17 NRSV). All proclaim salvation through Christ and conversion as a supernatural work of the Holy Spirit by grace through faith alone. . . . All feel perfectly free and even compelled to move beyond traditional boundaries when the Spirit calls through Scripture, for all of them believe there is a difference between every human interpretation of Scripture and revelation itself. No doctrine is in itself sacrosanct; all doctrines are open to reexamination, and the constructive task of theology is never finished because God always has new light to break forth from his Word.[64]

On the basis of this characterization of postconservative theologizing, Olson added an additional, fifth characteristic. He recognizes that revelation is "not a closed book" nor "a set of commandments written

62. Ibid., 28.
63. Ibid.
64. Ibid., 29.

in stone." Rather, "orthodox doctrine is the product of human reflection on God's revelation and therefore is open to reconsideration in light of faithful and fresh readings of God's Word." Thus to the four characteristics just mentioned, Olson adds a fifth, namely "deference to traditional, basic Christian orthodoxy within a higher commitment to the authority of God's Word in Scripture as the norming norm of all Christian faith and practice."[65] This characterization of four plus one constitutes Olson's description of postconservative evangelical theology within the broad family of evangelicalism.

Conversation with Postconservative Evangelical Theology

Our proposal is not linked to correct doctrine as occurs in some versions of the evangelical tradition. Neither is it based on a distinct conversion experience, as is specified in some versions of evangelicalism; nor is it defined by a broader and more inclusive kind of inner and transformative religious experience of Jesus Christ, which is a primary characteristic of what Roger Olson called postconservative evangelicalism, and which he poses as the alternative to evangelicalism identified by correct doctrine.[66] On the other hand, the theology of our proposal meets the five criteria of evangelical theology suggested by Olson, and our experiences in church with what some would call evangelical piety, our involvement in the evangelical network, and our institutional location with Bluffton University, an institution of the Council of Christian Colleges and Universities, identifies us as evangelicals with the sort of credentials called for by Olson. Thus our proposal engages a conversation both within and against evangelical theology.

The theology of our project can be said to fit within Olson's four plus one characterization. The sketch of the life of Jesus and the theologizing derived from it are clearly biblical. We assume that being identified with Jesus produces a changed life or conversion. Since a willingness to die as a consequence of witnessing to the reign of God is intrinsic to living in the story of Jesus, our sketch is crucicentric, although the theological focus falls on resurrection rather than on the cross. And our vision of an

---

65. Ibid., 43.
66. Olson, *Reformed and Always Reforming*, e.g., 51–52.

activist Jesus that is a model for Christian activism fits within the fourth core conviction of activism and social transformation.

The theology of our sketch aligns with both parts of Olson's fifth characteristic of postconservative evangelical theology. The confession that God and the reign of God are present in the life of Jesus and certified by the resurrection are equivalent to the creedal assertions of the deity of Jesus. The threefold view of God in time then aligns with the three traditional Persons of God as Father, Son and Spirit, and is fully compatible with the equality of presence and activity among the three Persons. These observations demonstrate that our proposal is compatible with, as Olson was just quoted, "basic Christian orthodoxy within a higher commitment to the authority of God's Word in Scripture." And with postconservative evangelicalism we also believe that "theology is always unfinished and that the call of the theologian is to rethink traditional concepts and categories in every generation and culture." Thus under the guidance of the Bible, we have offered some new formulations that subject some orthodox assumptions to biblical authority but which can nonetheless be incorporated by proponents of postconservative evangelicalism.

At the same time, the theology of our proposal is not fully defined by or contained within Olson's description of postconservative evangelical theology. Rather than being based on a pietist-oriented transformative experience, our theology is expressed via a life lived in the narrative of Jesus. To develop theology based on the New Testament's narrative of Jesus is to sketch the way that a person identified by Jesus Christ should live. It is to sketch a life of discipleship to Jesus. And to ask how a Christian should live returns us to telling the story of Jesus. The examples in this particular chapter focused on racism and racial reconciliation. It pictures the narrative of Jesus as a norm for the Christian life into which God's Spirit transforms the believer. This is what we have called a lived theology or a theology for living. Theology and ethics are inseparable, they are two sides of the same proverbial coin, a lived and a written expression of the commitment to Jesus Christ as Lord. Lived theology, theology that takes the narrative of Jesus as its point of departure, is of a different genre from theology based on the options Olson described of either personal experience or doctrinal propositions.

Although the power of the gospel transforms individuals, which is an evangelical point, it is important to state that in our formulation, the proper subject of theological instruction is the church more than the individual. God's agent in the world today is Christ's body and God's people who have joined to that body. Their action is primarily collective and even when we act as individuals we are representing that body and our actions are empowered by the spirit of God that flows in that body as the presence of God today.

We can identify with the evangelical emphasis on salvation as a gift from a gracious God and on our reception of this gift as an experience of conversion. However, somewhat different from evangelicalism, we believe that this conversion is a social and practical event that involves our joining a new primary community whose existence arises from the birth, life, teachings, actions, death and resurrection of Jesus Christ. This social understanding of conversion gives our theology a different orientation from much of evangelical and orthodox theology, even if it does not necessarily contradict it.

The emphases on living out of the story of Jesus Christ and on the church as the proper subject of theological instruction are where our Anabaptist identity appears. Both authors have done extensive research and writing in Anabaptist theology. Like John Howard Yoder, the subject of this book who has been classed with evangelicals but also retained an Anabaptist identity, the authors can fit with evangelicals but have a clear Anabaptist identity. Our view on the nature of Anabaptism is that it is the sixteenth-century Reformation movement whose focus was on a return to the Jesus of the New Testament, and that this Jesus was the norm for Christian faith and practice. The result of Anabaptists' attempts to live out the New Testament story of Jesus was the emergence of a church that separated from the established church and that lived as a witness to the social order.[67] Thus the proposal for a lived theology sketched in this chapter can be properly characterized as an "Anabaptist theology." At the same time, since this chapter has not quoted sixteenth-century Anabaptist sources, it has demonstrated that one does not need first to be a student of Anabaptist history and theology in order to understand or, it is suggested, adopt our theological proposal. However, if a reader wants a historical precedent, one is found in sixteenth-century Anabaptism. Many of John Howard Yoder's writings model this approach.

An article current as this chapter is edited into its final formulation illustrates well what we believe is our Anabaptist contribution to this

---

67. For our extended statement of sixteenth-century Anabaptism from this perspective, see the title in note 39.

conversation with postconservative evangelicalism. Mark Galli, editor of *Christianity Today*, both supports and challenges a recent book by evangelical writer Rob Bell.[68] Bell has an experiential approach to knowledge of God that in Galli's words, is based in "our experiences and our intuitions." This experiential approach to knowledge of God and his willingness to offer fresh interpretations of orthodox doctrines clearly locate Bell in Olson's category of postconservative evangelicalism.

Galli's comments in critique of Bell exhibit problems addressed by elements of our proposal. Galli provides a brief history of "a religion of felling . . . shared by American evangelicals." It began with the "bornagain experience" of the Great Awakening of the 1740s, which was then reduced to the product of a "mere technique" by Charles Finney. It has been used by revival preachers ever since. The revivals of Billy Graham were noted by "his refusal to manipulate emotions" in favor of a rational "decision" for Christ. However, as typified by the Second Great Awakening it has been common to produce conversions based on emotional despair. In some circles, the authenticity and depth of one's conversation was defined by the felt experience of remorse. More recently, Galli said, the experiential element has shifted from the supposed one-time experience of a graphic conversion to a search to "experience God 24/7/365." In other words, there is now a search for daily experiences of God as the basis of assurance of one's relationship to God. Galli's point with this history is to demonstrate that experience is quite varied as well as to acknowledge that it is impossible truly to have a profound experience repeatedly on a daily basis.[69]

Although not discounting some vivid experiences, Galli notes that the experience of God "will be fully realized only when sin and death have been defeated and love and peace reign in the coming kingdom." He cites Paul's characterization of the current age as "groaning," and suggests that rather attempting to live each day in a present experience of *redemption*," on the basis of Christ's death and resurrection made known by the Holy Spirit, we live in "*hope* that redemption is coming." Instead of striving with our wills to experience God or experience redemption, we should "wait in patience" for future redemption. Citing Paul, Galli asserts that the admonition to wait in patience "suggests that it's normal

---

68. Galli, "What We Talk About." Galli's article responds to Bell, *What We Talk About*.

69. Galli, "What We Talk About," 36–37.

not to have such experiences." Our calling as Christians is to "love" the needy, dying to self as Jesus did. We carry out this loving life, Galli suggests, without a continuing emotional experience of God to validate it but confident in the hope of future redemption.[70]

The problem described by Galli is addressed by two, closely related elements from our proposal for an Anabaptist theology. In response to the vagaries of experience as a source of validation, the narrative of Jesus in our proposal can serve as a norm or reference point for experience. All Christian experience is measured by or takes its meaning from that story, and separated from that story it can take on the exaggerations Galli cautions against. This observation leads to the second point. The measuring of the experience of Jesus Christ occurs within the community created by living in his story. As noted a few paragraphs above, the experience of Jesus Christ is a social and practical event that involves joining a new primary community whose existence arises from the birth, life, teachings, actions, death and resurrection of Jesus Christ. Stated differently, the experience of Jesus Christ in our Anabaptist understanding is not an individual experience but a communal one. It thus provides a vivid and visible alternative to Galli's sense that "the road of experience leads nowhere except to the barren desert of the self." (39) We suggest, therefore, that attention to an Anabaptist component would strengthen the post-conservative evangelical movement, which Roger Olson characterized by "transforming experience and a distinct spirituality" over against evangelicalism defined in terms of assent to correct doctrine. An Anabaptism understood in terms of living within the narrative of Jesus shows the way beyond the Scylla and Charybdis of defining a relationship to Jesus Christ as either assent to correct doctrine or a proscribed experience.

Conclusion

The fact that the model proposed in this chapter is an "Anabaptist" approach but that one need not come to it through historic Anabaptism leads to our final point, namely that our theological proposal offers itself as an ecumenical beginning point that can bring together the different trajectories of this chapter. Every person who claims the name "Christian" has an interest in Jesus. Thus to propose that *Christ*ian theology begins with the story of Jesus *Christ*, which John Howard Yoder demonstrated

---

70. Ibid., 38–39. Galli's italics.

in *Preface to Theology*, is to propose a theological beginning point open and accessible to every Christian. The fact that Christians disagree on the meaning of Jesus does not alter their common foundation in the story of Jesus. Rather, it poses the story of Jesus as the beginning of a conversation about the meaning of Jesus.

This chapter has demonstrated three such conversations. The model with which the chapter begins concerns an effort to construct a distinct theology from the New Testament narrative in conversation with but not beholden to the classic formulas, in response to a modern context that differs significantly from the context that produced the classic formulas of Christology and Trinity and atonement. The second section entered a conversation with proposals for theology beyond the whiteness that characterizes the classic or standard theology of the Christian West. The third part of this chapter presented a proposal to enter, and even be incorporated into, a conversation with postconservative evangelicalism. All three conversation trajectories take the Bible seriously. Although with different emphases and approaches, all conversations find a common point in Jesus the Jewish messiah. All conversation trajectories reflect aspects of the theology and methodology of John Howard Yoder. Seeing that all trajectories radiate from John Howard Yoder points again to the difficulties scholars have had in trying to produce a coherent synthesis of Yoder's theological perspective. Since the developing vectors of these trajectories point in different directions, it is not possible to synthesize Yoder's theology into one coherent system that incorporates all possible projections. One can however identity what is common to all the trajectories, namely Yoder's roots in the story of Jesus the Jewish Messiah, which is what makes Yoder a radical theologian.

Chapters 12 and 13 now turn to developing Yoder's theology in a different way.

12

Reflections from a Chagrined "Yoderian" in Face of His Sexual Violence

TED GRIMSRUD

The Yoder Dilemma

In June 1992, in a series of investigative articles by reporter Tom Price, *The Elkhart Truth*, John Howard Yoder's hometown newspaper, reported on widespread allegations of coercive sexual activities by Yoder. These allegations led to a disciplinary process from the Indiana-Michigan Mennonite Conference in relation to Yoder's ministerial credentials.[1] In the years since, debate has continued concerning the nature of Yoder's offenses and their implications for the use of his theology.

In a helpful discussion Glen Stassen and Michael Westmoreland-White define violence as "destruction to a victim by means that overpower the victim's consent." This definition is meant to include domination and

---

1. These articles may be accessed online: peacetheology.net/john-h-yhoder/sexual-misconduct/.

psychic damage as well as bodily harm.[2] What is known of the specifics of Yoder's actions is discussed in a following section. It suffices here to say that by this definition, these actions were most certainly psychologically, if not physically, violent.

I was a student of Yoder's at Anabaptist Mennonite Biblical Seminary in the early 1980s and have long been deeply influenced by his peace theology. And, as a consequence, I have been troubled by what I have learned of the sexual misconduct of my peace teacher.

For all of my adult life, ever since I was nearly drafted into the Vietnam War in the early 1970s, I have thought constantly about issues of violence, its effects and how to overcome the problems it causes. Most of my focus has been on violence in relation to war, but I have thought about violence more generally as well. John Howard Yoder's theology has been influential for me, but others have perhaps influenced me even more in thinking about violence's origins and impact on our world.

This conversation about John Howard Yoder as doer of violence links in with my interests on several levels. One is certainly on the level of how to make sense of the actions of my teacher who helped me learn so much about peace theology. This problem calls attention to the fact that theology—at least our Anabaptist theology—is not merely abstract theory, but is also about our life and actions as Christians. Another interest is the broader level of thinking about a terrible and oh so personal aspect of the phenomenon of violence—men acting violently toward women, especially in Christian communities. And finally, there is the discussion of how to apply things I have learned about violence from many sources over the years.

Important Sources for Understanding and Responding to Violence

I have found four writers to be especially helpful for my thinking about understanding and responding to violence and seeking peace: Walter Wink, Alice Miller, James Gilligan, and Howard Zehr. They complement many of Yoder's *ideas*, but they also help us to think about Yoder's *actions*—and about our responses to Yoder's actions. How do we hold *together*, if we can, our hatred of violent acts, our commitment to the

---

2. Stassen and Westmoreland-White, "Defining Violence," 18.

healing of those hurt by such acts, our on-going respect for the humanity of the violator, and our hope for creating whole communities?

(1) Walter Wink's *Engaging the Powers* has long been an inspiration and guide for me. Its beginning sets the tone for much of my work: "One of the most pressing questions facing the world today is, How can we oppose evil without creating more evils and being made evil ourselves?"[3] Wink provides a profound and practical effort to answer this question, still enormously useful now over twenty years after publication of the book.

Wink himself, and I strongly agree, starts with the assumption that as human beings, we all have a basic responsibility to do what we can to "oppose evil." Passivity and resignation are not acceptable options, nor—of course—is complicity with evil. However, Wink insists, we must oppose evil in ways that actually do diminish (if not fully overcome) the evils we oppose. All too often, we oppose evil in ways that actually heighten the evil—as when our nation goes to war to defeat Nazi and Imperial Japanese oppression and ends up unleashing new and still spiraling oppressions and violence.[4]

Wink's book focuses more on macro-level issues. However, the problem of how to oppose evil in genuinely healing ways applies to all of life. I believe it surely must apply to how we approach sexual violence. Wink's first point (or at least my first point drawing on Wink) is that we must oppose the evil of sexual violence. We should seek a world (and certainly seek churches) with zero tolerance for sexual violence, where all vulnerable people are safe, where perpetrators of sexual violence are held accountable and prevented from repeating the harm they have done. However, I think we should honestly recognize that here too we likely will find it challenging and difficult to do this work in ways that truly are healing—that actually are effective and that do not set off another spiral of violence toward violence-doers and turn those who do the necessary work of resisting evil into evil-doers themselves.

(2) Alice Miller has also long been an inspiration and guide. The Swiss psychotherapist, who died in 2010, wrote and spoke on behalf of the most vulnerable of the vulnerable, children. Her book that speaks most

---

3. Wink, *Engaging the Powers*, 3.
4. Grimsrud, *Good War That Wasn't*.

directly about the origins of violence is called *For Your Own Good*.⁵ For my purposes here, one of Miller's key insights was that even the most violent of people were not born violent but were made violent. She argues that our tendency simply to condemn violators as "bad apples" keeps us from learning much from their actions and, more importantly, makes it much more difficult to understand how to break the cycle of violence.

Miller sees the roots of violence in violent treatment of young children. In *For Your Own Good*, she even examines the early life of Adolf Hitler. She, of course, does not excuse Hitler (in fact, Miller herself grew up Jewish in Poland and lost her entire family in the Holocaust). But she insists we must bracket our understandable revulsion at Hitler's deeds and try to understand. If we do so, we discover (she argues, controversially) that the roots to the sociopath that Hitler became lay in the violence he experienced as a child. So, for Miller, one of the key steps we must take to prevent new Hitlers from arising is to end violence against children.

The point I am particularly interested in here is Miller's insistence in seeking to understand, to go beyond condemnation and stereotyping and learn about each person and the dynamics that shaped their lives. While often focusing on extreme cases to make her points, Miller suggests that most other less extreme cases of violent patterns in life also stem from early childhood—a major dynamic in violent behavior being a lack of empathy for the recipient of the violence. She resists retributive thinking toward offenders, seeking to create a sense of empathy toward even the cowering little boy that had been Adolf Hitler. In this way, she hopes, the spiral of violence might be broken. That said, Miller's main concern is with protecting children from violence. She believes that this will best happen by breaking free from any kind of violence, even violence against violent offenders.

(3) After Alice Miller, I read James Gilligan's important book, *Violence*,⁶ and found Gilligan (himself a psychiatrist as well, who worked in the Massachusetts state prison system for many years) to offer a parallel analysis. Like Miller, Gilligan focuses significant attention on the worst of the violent offenders. And like Miller, Gilligan argues for seeking to understand, empathize with, and not simply stereotype and punish these offenders. And like Miller, Gilligan's agenda is seeking to find the most effective and transformative way to overcome the problem of violence.

---

5. Miller, *For Your Own Good*.
6. Gilligan, *Violence*.

Gilligan advocates taking what he calls a "public health" approach to what he sees to be the "disease" of violence—in contrast to what he calls a "moral" approach (I would prefer the term "moralistic") that focuses on assessing and punishing guilt. His book is challenging in how he, like Miller, empathetically deals with people who have committed horrendous acts of violence. He also suggests that the worst way to deal with violence is by adding to the cycle of violence by punishing wrongdoers.[7]

The most powerful pathogen in creating the disease of violence, Gilligan suggests, is shame. This is why ostracism, punishment, and hostility toward wrongdoers tend to be counterproductive. Punitive approaches often exacerbate the shame and actually intensify the impulse to act violently—rather than effectively serving as deterrents to more violence.

(4) Howard Zehr's pioneering work on restorative justice is the final source of insight I will mention. Zehr's central book is *Changing Lenses*,[8] in which he outlines the philosophy of restorative justice and its theological grounding in Christian sources—though he certainly does not believe that only Christians may practice restorative justice. A later book, *Transcending*,[9] adds important first-person accounts from those who have been hurt by violent crime and a perceptive essay by Zehr that reflects on the needs of those hurt by violent crime. Restorative justice, as presented by Zehr, has at its heart the concern for the healing of communities that have been disrupted by hurtful wrongdoing.

One of the key points I have gained from Zehr's work is that, contrary to many misrepresentations of the approach, the people who matter the most in restorative justice are those who have been hurt by the wrongdoing. There is an underlying assumption that true healing of the brokenness ultimately requires the healing of all parties involved in the problem, but the healing of wrongdoers is, in a sense, secondary to the healing of those who were wronged. One of the main reasons punitive, retributive approaches to wrongdoing are challenged by restorative justice is that causing pain to wrongdoers generally does not in itself bring healing to the wronged. It often may even add more pain to the already

---

7. My recent book, *Instead of Atonement*, draws on Gilligan and others in challenging traditional Christian atonement theology and presenting a different reading of the biblical story that supports a non-punitive approach to wrongdoing as grounded in the Bible's portrayal of God.

8. Zehr, *Changing Lenses*.

9. Zehr, *Transcending*.

harmed—not to mention the way the prison-industrial complex in the U.S. that feeds on the drive toward punitive responses to crime has damaged our broader society.

At times, restorative processes are short-circuited by hasty efforts to bring "closure," to pressure the wronged to "forgive," and to "restore" wrongdoers to the community prematurely. Such short-circuiting should not be seen as a reason to abandon restorative justice approaches but rather as a challenge to learn evermore about processes that foster genuine healing.

As I think about Yoder's actions in light of these four writers, I conclude that still all these years later much may be done to help bring more healing for those Yoder hurt. And, certainly, we must learn from these events how better *now* to overcome sexual violence. However, we should also work hard to understand as best as we can Yoder's actions in ways that respect his own humanity and that resist adding to the spiral of violence with our own reactions to his wrongdoing.

Thinking about Sexual Violence

I believe these ideas that in my work I have applied mostly to war and the death penalty and criminal justice must also be applicable to sexual violence—though I do not pretend to speak as a particularly knowledgeable person about sexual violence. My desire to make as much sense as I can of Yoder's theology in relation to Yoder's behavior, though, challenges me to think about sexual violence.

It seems like one key theme that arises in just about all accounts of violence is a dynamic (not necessarily obvious) of beginning with lack of empathy and moving on to stereotyping and "othering" and dehumanizing and violence. Certainly this dynamic happens in warfare and it seems to be a central factor in many cases of sexual violence. In general, violence usually requires some kind of diminishing of the humanity of the other.

We live amidst many currents in church and society that push us to label and stereotype, to objectify and impersonalize. Empathy for others, especially others who are different in significant ways, seems fairly rare in our broader society (and all too rare in Christian communities). So a major challenge that fits directly within Walter Wink's insistence that morally responsible human beings must commit ourselves to opposing evil to find ways to resist "othering" dynamics and to encourage empathy.

Most centrally, this task should focus on resistance to othering dynamics that lead to harm to vulnerable people—specifically, in the context of the current discussion, the dynamics that lead some men to violate some women.

At the same time, the on-going presence of vulnerable people in our communities means we cannot simply wait for growth in empathy and resistance to othering and dehumanizing to make our communities safer. We continue to work to create safe environments and to empower people who have been hurt to speak out, to tell their stories, to be respected and listened to. It is a kind of dialectic, where our communities need to evolve to be more empathetic toward all people and at the same time more explicitly and practically opposed to actions that harm.

One important aspect of opposing evil without adding to it is to seek to cultivate empathy and resist "othering" and dehumanizing even those who themselves "other" and dehumanize vulnerable people, and who with their own lack of empathy hurt others by transgressing boundaries they are oblivious to or disdainful of. Alice Miller and James Gilligan, for example, offer us models of writers who are strong in their opposition to violent behavior yet understand that the cycle of dehumanization itself should be resisted through treating offenders as human beings—responsible for their acts and needing to be stopped in their hurtful acts but still individual human beings who should be understood and helped to heal, not simply condemned.

I think Wink's challenge to oppose evil without adding to it is a call to find ways to resist violence and people who act violently while at the same time becoming ever more compassionate and creative in breaking all cycles of violence.

The Allegations about Yoder

I remember back in the mid-1980s when I learned that John Howard Yoder would no longer be teaching at Associated Mennonite Biblical Seminary in Elkhart, Indiana. My wife, Kathleen, and I had attended AMBS in the 1980–81 school year because Yoder was teaching there. Right after our time at AMBS we decided we wanted to become Mennonites.

Once he started teaching at Notre Dame in nearby South Bend in the 1970s, for a number of years Yoder had taught only one class a semester at AMBS. I first assumed when he left AMBS that he had decided himself to focus only on his Notre Dame responsibilities. However, I began to hear from friends at AMBS that this move was not Yoder's decision, but that AMBS had decided to end the relationship. However, the reasons for this termination were top secret. No one I talked with had any sense of what the problem had been, only that AMBS administrators were indicating that there had to be no information given due to legal confidentiality purposes.

I was troubled, but for many years I had no idea what the problem might have been. Then, Kathleen and I returned to AMBS for a semester in the spring of 1992. And the other shoe dropped. Yoder had been invited to speak at Bethel College in Kansas, and due to voices of protest raised by women whom Yoder had hurt and their allies, Yoder's invitation was rescinded. We had a forum at AMBS shortly afterwards that was the first time I heard a more detailed explanation (though still pretty cryptic) that the reason that Yoder was no longer teaching at AMBS was sexual misconduct.

Then, in June 1992, Tom Price wrote his series of articles based on interviews with three of those directly hurt by Yoder as well as numerous church leaders. One article included a summary of one of Yoder's unpublished essays that seemed to give an indirect rationale for Yoder's actions. Price's articles have remained the main source that I am aware of with specific information on Yoder's actions. A few years ago, a friend of Yoder, the prominent theologian Stanley Hauerwas, included a short but informative discussion of Yoder's situation in his memoir *Hannah's Child*.[10]

Price and Hauerwas give us our main public knowledge. I have learned a few other things from reliable sources and, of course, heard many rumors and much hearsay. I have become convinced that Yoder did engage in coercive and sexually inappropriate behavior that caused serious emotional harm for several women.

The extent of this behavior remains a matter of speculation. Hauerwas states that Yoder "began his seductions of 'weighty' Mennonite women—women of intellectual and spiritual stature" in the 1960s.[11] As far as I know, it has not been established when he stopped, but there is reason to believe that he continued at least well into the 1980s. Price reports that eight women together brought charges of sexual harassment against

---

10. Hauerwas, *Hannah's Child*, 242–47.
11. Ibid., 244.

Yoder that resulted in a disciplinary process undertaken by a committee from the Indiana-Michigan Mennonite Conference. We may safely assume that the number of women whose boundaries Yoder transgressed was much greater than the eight who brought formal complaints.

Price's articles detail strange and clumsy attempts at physical intimacy along with unwelcome and invasive conversations, letters, and phone calls. Part of what made these advances traumatic for their recipients was the respect many of these women had for Yoder as a teacher and scholar. They saw him as an advocate for peace—advocacy they affirmed. So they felt a strong sense of trust that was then violated in hurtful ways.

In the years since 1992, I have been part of many discussions regarding the level of harm caused by Yoder's actions. Price's articles do not suggest that there was profound physical harm. In the end, though, we simply have to accept that Yoder's actions were significant violations—he did cause harm, and we should not try to minimize the seriousness of his violations.

My own understanding of the hurt that Yoder caused was deepened by one conversation I had with a woman who, as a young seminary student, had been accosted by Yoder and seriously traumatized. Our conversation happened decades after the event and many years after Yoder's death. But the pain was still present in obvious ways. There is no way to explain away this transgression, and it seems clear that we could multiply the trauma my friend had experienced perhaps numerous times with other women Yoder treated similarly.

Why Did It Happen?

From what I understand, Yoder's explanation for his behavior (which he seems not to have seen as the violation that it was) was that he was testing his theory that Christians of the opposite sex could have intimate physical relationships that did not involve overt sexual intercourse. Hauerwas refers to this, as does Price in his summary of Yoder's ideas.

Yoder's "theory" is interesting and does not seem on the surface to be utterly outlandish (though it is not a theory I am personally attracted to). I know from my own experience in intentional Christian communities in the 1970s that the issue of close friendships between non-married people was a theme for long conversations.

What made Yoder's theory so problematic, I sense, is that when he tried to implement it he tended to be oblivious to the lack of interest and even active resistance from his would-be partners. This is when he became especially coercive—according to Price, physically forcing himself on at least one of the women Price interviewed and violating emotional boundaries with numerous others.

Chillingly, even when resisted and challenged, Yoder did not seem to express regret or an awareness of the pain he had caused. On Hauerwas's account (confirmed by a few other sources), Yoder continually defended his actions in terms of experimenting with his theory of intimacy. He does not seem to have sought to understand the feelings of trauma and betrayal he left in his wake.

One aspect of the story I know next to nothing about is whether there were women who did not resist Yoder's advances. I have heard one reliable account of a woman who did have a relationship with Yoder that she welcomed. There may have been others over the decades during which Yoder sought such partners.

As I reflect on my struggle with Yoder's behavior in relation to Yoder's theology, I have concluded that it is best to accept that he was indeed psychologically violent, over and over. Regardless of whatever fine line we might want to make concerning degrees of transgression, he was way over the line between innocent, if clumsy, attempts at friendship and hurtful, coercive acts of sexual violation. I would identify three different areas of concern in relation to what Yoder's sexual harm-doing means for us today.

(1) The first is the general issue of sexual violence in our churches and church-related settings. I hope that the ferment around Yoder's acts can serve as a fruitful catalyst to stimulate more conversation, reflection, and action in addressing the on-going problems of sexual violence. Maybe we can be energized to devote more of our best energies to what obviously continues to be a living issue.

Yet, I do worry a bit that all the focus on Yoder and events from the now fairly distant past might divert some of that energy. I am not sure that there are a lot of specific lessons to be learned from Yoder's story that apply directly to our needs today beyond the general lesson that sexual violence must be confronted quickly and decisively. It seems unthinkable that a parallel situation could arise at the Mennonite school where I teach given the decisive action that has been taken time after time since the mid-1990s in cases of sexual misconduct. I hope talking about Yoder can trigger a move to then go on to talk about our present—a conversation that would eventually have little to do with Yoder.

(2) The second is the issue of telling and learning from the story of the past. Yoder remains an extremely important figure in Mennonite history of the second half of the twentieth century. He also remains an important figure in the world of Christian theology and peacemaking. So his story is of intrinsic interest—like the stories of all influential people. And, certainly this issue of his sexual violations is part of the story of his life. But it is only part of that bigger story.

Yoder's life story, I think, is not important because of his sexual violence. It is important most of all because of his intellectual endeavors and his influence on Christian theology and ethics. We should not, however, try to tell the story without this problematic part. So it is worthy of attention to fill out our account of this challenging person.

The story of Yoder's sexual misconduct is also of historical interest in the context of tracing the general story of North American Mennonites in the second half of the twentieth century. We learn from this story about how Mennonites and their institutions have (and have not) responded to sexual violence. I hope for perceptive, careful, well-researched historical writing on the Mennonite story in relation to John Howard Yoder's life and thought.

(3) Third, the issue that has motivated my own reflections more than any other, is the question of what our knowledge of Yoder's actions means for how we approach his theology. I struggle to make sense of the paradox of how the theology I love coexists with the behavior I hate. I am moving more toward being content that I have to accept the paradox, recognize the difficulty of resolving that struggle, and thus focus mainly on Yoder's ideas. Others may respond differently. The following chapter, for example, suggests possible avenues of research into connections between Yoder's failures and both limits and possibilities of radical Anabaptist theology in the vein of Yoder.

The purpose of focusing on his ideas, though, is not to construct a Yoderian theology. Rather, it is to move beyond Yoder. He gave us his legacy of theological writing (which is, I believe, profound indeed) for the purpose of our learning and then moving on to do our own work. Yoder's ideas help us do that. But there is a sense that as time passes it becomes less and less important where the ideas came from (and what kinds of terrible things the originator of the ideas might have done) and more and more important how the ideas stimulate further ideas and—more importantly—peaceable living.

What about Yoder's Theology?

Yoder's theology has been quite important for my life and work. So, how do I reconcile this influence with such deeply problematic behavior? I have been reflecting on the behavior, and now I want to take some time to reflect on the theology—to sketch why I have found it so valuable. It's not just that Yoder is famous and important and widely read and cited. It is that his work has had a profound effect on my own life and thought in many, many ways.

I began to read Yoder in the fall of 1976. A few years later, I moved to Indiana to study with Yoder at AMBS. I have continued to read Yoder and absorb his theological insights. I would like to believe, though, that I have followed a path he would have approved of, which is using his ideas as stimulants to develop my own. Yoder himself did very little writing where he focused in detail on other people's theology. He mostly referred to the Bible, history, and to the practical outworking of the ideas. It was not theology about theology but theology about life.

As Earl Zimmerman presents it in his fine book on Yoder's intellectual development, *Practicing the Politics of Jesus*,[12] Yoder's decision to become a theologian came as a young adult working in post-World War II western Europe. He became convinced that the epic disaster of that war was an indictment on Western Christianity. What the world needed was a different way to think about faith and social life. Yoder believed that the sixteenth-century Anabaptists provided a good model, but that what was needed was something more universal that he found in the life and teaching of Jesus. This root in the life and teaching of Jesus is what characterizes the radical theology of the book in hand.

So, Yoder modeled an approach to theology that cares deeply about contributing to peaceable social life in the world for the sake of the world and draws deeply on the Bible and the Anabaptists. Yoder's theology was anything but "sectarian." The on-going power and influence of his work

12. Zimmerman, *Practicing the Politics*.

witnesses to his perceptive his insights. I have been influenced by his method to construct theology that is socially engaged, based especially on the Bible, and inspired by the Anabaptists. Yoder's ideas are catalytic for my own constructive work—which I would call "peace theology," not "Yoderian theology."

What I Have Learned from Yoder's Theology

To make this specific, I will briefly mention ten of Yoder's key contributions to my theology. This present list is drawn quickly, and I could mention many more contributions.

(1) Surely the most important for me is Yoder's presentation of the case that Jesus was indeed "political"—and political in a specific way. Yoder took the imagery of God's "kingdom/empire," "messiah/king," "savior/ liberator," "gospel," and "congregation/ekklesia," in the political sense they had in the first century. Jesus—and the rest of the Bible—are political through and through. Political, that is, in the sense of "politics" referring to how people operate socially. The politics of Jesus is indeed about how people relate—with its main emphasis on compassion and caring for others. So it is a "kingdom" and Jesus is a "king," but in ways that overturn the ways of power politics.

(2) Yoder has helped me to view everything through the lenses of my pacifist commitment—what I now call a pacifist way of knowing.[13] We may understand pacifism as an orientation toward the world wherein we see that nothing takes precedence over the call to love the neighbor. This should effect everything—including how we read the Bible and how we construct our theology, not to mention, of course, every aspect of our social lives. Chapter 8 touches on aspects of this knowing.

(3) The book of Yoder's I read first was *The Original Revolution*.[14] The chapter that had the most impact initially for me was the discussion of violence in the Old Testament. I have developed my thinking beyond Yoder's ideas in that chapter, but his emphasis (leaning heavily on the work of his colleague Millard Lind[15]) on how the Old Testament presents

---

13. See Grimsrud, "Pacifism and Knowing," and Yoder, *Pacifist Way*.
14. Yoder, *Original Revolution*.
15. See Lind, *Monotheism, Power, Justice*.

an alternative sense of political power to the ways of the nations, and puts God and Torah at the center instead of king and state, remains central to my own thinking about how to navigate the Old Testament-as-violent conundrum. Yoder and Lind helped me to see that the Old Testament should be approached as a positive asset for peace theology, not a problem to overcome.

(4) Toward the end of his life, in essays published posthumously in the book *The Jewish-Christian Schism Revisited*,[16] Yoder developed further his way of reading the Old Testament as being in continuity with the politics of Jesus. He points to the words of Jeremiah during Israel's time of exile: "seek the peace of the city where you find yourselves." These words offered a programmatic call for God's people to give up on channeling the Promise through a traditional kind of kingdom. Instead they were to embrace the calling to be prophetic minorities in various settings that they do not try to rule.

(5) Yoder introduced me to the exceedingly fruitful way of analyzing power through use of the language from the Pauline letters of "principalities and powers." Walter Wink's later work,[17] in part inspired by Yoder, fleshes out the ideas much more. And both Yoder and Wink are indebted to the earlier pioneering work of Hendrik Berkhof.[18] Use of the "powers" motif helps us understand the institutional and cultural dimensions of life, especially of the dynamics where the "fallenness" of the powers shapes us in profound ways (for example, the dynamics of racism, militarism, sexism, et al, that in a genuine sense transcend individual choice and action). Several chapters above reference Yoder's use of the powers.

(6) Yoder's writings address the challenge people who have a vision for biblical shalom face in trying to embody that vision in a broken world. One motif he addressed often is the notion of "patience," where we cultivate a sense of trust in that the "grain of the universe" runs toward wholeness (I am more comfortable using this more imprecise language; Yoder would often talk more directly about trusting in the sovereignty of God). Such trust helps guard against the constant tendency to try to take things into our own hands, to seek to "be in charge," a tendency

---

16. Yoder, *Jewish-Christian Schism*.
17. See especially Wink, *Engaging the Powers*.
18. Berkhof, *Christ and the Powers*.

that often leads to violence and ultimately self-defeating compromise and exaggerated senses of self-importance. He refused to accept an absolute dichotomy between faithfulness and effectiveness, insisting that in the long run faithfulness is our most effective approach.

(7) Yoder helped me understand that the vision for salvation in the writings of Paul stands in harmony with Jesus' vision and, overall, with the Old Testament vision. Paul's sense of "justification" was not strictly about an individual getting right with God, but as with the rest of the Bible Paul believed salvation is a social event. For Paul, the key effect of Jesus' ministry was to empower enemies to be reconciled, Jew and Greek to become part of one community, even ultimately blessing all the families of the earth. Chapter 6 explores Paul's continuation of Jesus' vision.

(8) Yoder also helped me understand that the biblical themes of eschatology and apocalyptic have a lot to do with how to understand God's work in the present and not only in the future. He stated that these themes in the Bible, especially in the teaching of Jesus, are not focused on the idea that history is ending but rather they are emphasizing why history continues—that people of faith might embody biblical shalom in history.

(9) Yoder helped me understand that Judaism and Christianity should be seen as more complementary than has traditionally been the case. His discussion of what he calls the "Jewish-Christian schism" concludes that "it didn't need to happen." This view challenges many received ideas about Christian origins and the disastrous idea that Christianity "replaced" Judaism. These issues are discussed at some depth in chapter 10 and the insight extended to Islam and Hinduism. This motif is not only interesting for historical purposes but it actually provides a challenging angle for better understanding how the Old Testament can work as a Christian book and for enhancing the unity of beliefs with practices in Christian understandings.

(10) Finally, as is detailed in chapter 2 above, Yoder is an important resource for sustaining a continuing affirmation of the present relevance of the sixteenth-century Anabaptists. His dissertation, written in German and only recently published in English, provides an important study of how the Anabaptists remained committed to continue talking with mainstream reformers in pacifist ways.[19] Among other things, Yoder ar-

19. Yoder, *Anabaptism and Reformation*.

gues that it is a mistake to see in the Radical Reformation an inevitable separatism and inclination toward withdrawal. He suggests that in the early years at least, Anabaptists actually modeled ecumenical initiative and a vision for social transformation.

As I reflect on Yoder's theology and its impact on my work, summarized in these ten points, I conclude that his theology (as with all other good theology) is best approached as a catalyst for on-going constructive work that builds on earlier theology but does not keep its focus on that earlier theology. That catalytic quality is underscored by the way other chapters of this book also reflect aspects of these learnings. Yoder's ideas, I believe, are best appropriated in ways that move theology beyond Yoder. Chapter 11 illustrates one such example of "going beyond." Yoder's method was to draw especially on the biblical story, informed by later theological work, and apply theology to fruitful living. When our theology imitates this method we will not be writing a lot about Yoder but using Yoder's insights along with other sources to create new theology, radical theology that depends on the root, Jesus Christ.

Theology and Practice

So, we continue to struggle with the issue of what we do with Yoder's theology in light of his hurtful sexual behavior. These are my tentative conclusions:

(1) The reality of Yoder's sexual violence is, of course, very relevant for accounts of Yoder's life story. I welcome careful biographical studies of that story because of Yoder's importance for the Mennonite world and beyond. And such studies will be useful for any theological reflection that draws on Yoder's writings.

(2) The relevance of Yoder's hurtful sexual behavior seems more complicated when we focus specifically on approaching Yoder's theology itself as the object of study. If Yoder's theology becomes the object of our study, then we surely do need to consider the possible implications of his problematic behavior for how he construed theology. My sense of the discussion so far, though, is that people tend to pick up on themes in Yoder's theology that they already have questions about and suggest that that is where the link with his hurtful behavior might be found. I am not sure

how fruitful that approach will be. I still tend to suspect that the roots of Yoder's actions lie elsewhere than his theology and are not likely to be visible in the theology. But it is totally appropriate to scrutinize the theology with this problem in mind. For those interested in such a project, the following chapter suggests questions to explore that are raised by the problem of sin and failure in Anabaptist theology.

(3) How I want to approach Yoder's theology in my own work is to draw on his ideas more in ways that emphasize the insights and apply the helpful aspects than thorough analysis of Yoder's thought for its own sake. For this kind of work, his sexual violence is less relevant. The ideas, such as those listed above, remain perceptive and helpful regardless of what I learn about his life. This makes the details of his life of less interest to me theologically. Those details are interesting, of course, but the interest runs the risk of being prurient and to that extent should probably not be cultivated.

13

Sin and Failure in Anabaptist Theology

GERALD J. MAST

Sin and Grace-Empowered Discipleship

Anabaptists from the sixteenth to twentieth centuries have sometimes encountered charges of perfectionism or Pelagianism. Such charges arise because they have emphasized the ontological transformation made possible in human beings by the work of Jesus Christ. Although Anabaptist reformers and Anabaptist theologies did insist that God's grace as manifested in the life, death, and resurrection of Jesus Christ makes it possible for disciples to change sinful behaviors and to live a victorious Christian life, the charges of perfectionism or professed sinlessness are generally not true.[1] Rather, Anabaptist theologies usually acknowledge

---

1. For a discussion of charges that Anabaptists are Pelagians and a careful accounting of what sixteenth-century Anabaptists actually believed about freedom from sin, see Beachy, *Concept of Grace*. For a rich contemporary discussion of the assumption that Anabaptism is perfectionist, see J. Lawrence Burkholder's autobiographical reflections and a number of responses collected together in Sawatsky and Holland, *Limits of Perfection*.

that believers continue to struggle against sin, needing God's grace both as leverage for the will's triumph over sin and also as forgiveness for repeated failures to win the battle against sin.[2]

The first section of the chapter will display the discussions of grace, free will, and efforts to overcome sin in Anabaptist theology, which have opened the door to the charges of perfectionism or Pelagianism. That description then constitutes the wider context in which to consider John Howard Yoder's failure to live up to his own theology. From this discussion there then emerge four questions that indicate avenues for further research in development of Anabaptist ecclesiology and efforts to live as disciples of Jesus Christ.

Menno Simons asserts that the "sinful nature" is not entirely destroyed in baptized believers, who are often "overcome by sin," even though they profess a desire to master it.[3] Menno distinguishes between "lapses" that are due to a "defective and weak nature" and intentional or purposeful sin, undertaken against better judgment.[4] The former are the focus of daily struggle and penitence; the latter risk God's judgment. Following Menno and most early Anabaptist writers, John Howard Yoder acknowledges that "there is pride and selfishness in every action" and that there are therefore "no perfectly loving agents," even if this does not prove that "there cannot be a loving act" nor constrain what is possible "in Christ."[5]

Because it has been guided by the life and love of Jesus Christ as a positive example of God's will being done on earth, Anabaptist theology has tended to stress the extent to which sin is a failure to love rather than a mere transgression of rules. J. C. Wenger, for example, claims that "sin is any failure to love God and man with a perfect heart, which lack of love leads to attitudes and deeds which are displeasing to God."[6] John Howard Yoder expands and simplifies this statement as follows: "We can never remind ourselves often enough that sin for the Christian disciple is not a matter of doing what is forbidden. Sin is doing anything less than

---

2. For a more thorough exploration of early Anabaptist understandings of sin and evil, see my chapter on the topic in a multivolume work on evil in the West: Mast, "Anabaptism."

3. Menno Simons, *Complete Writings*, 245.

4. Ibid., 564.

5. Yoder, *Reinhold Niebuhr*, 17–18.

6. Wenger, *Introduction to Theology* (1966), 93.

the very best one knows."[7] Such statements illustrate how Anabaptist theology tends to ascribe sin to a much broader range of actual human actions even while it rejects sweeping doctrinal claims about the total depravity of humans.

Anabaptist thinking and writing has been deeply shaped by its ongoing argument against Protestant capitulation to the necessary evils of a fallen world. Rather than focus on the ongoing failure of even profoundly gospel-centered church communities to follow Christ consistently, the stress in Anabaptist theology has typically been on the capacity of grace-enabled human beings to live according to the good news of the gospel. In fact, this emphasis in Anabaptism on God's empowering grace and on following in the footsteps of Jesus Christ is one of the attractive features of the Anabaptist vision for those who are weary of Christendom's compromises with the empires of this world.[8]

Yoder's writing certainly features this emphasis on grace-empowered discipleship.[9] A powerful rhetorical theological gesture that is repeated again and again in Yoder's writing is the systematic demolishing of every structured excuse provided by Christians over the centuries for disregarding various teachings of Jesus Christ as unrealistic or unattainable in this world.[10] In the theological project of Yoder, the gospel is good news precisely because of the new world that it announces, which is already dawning in actual human history and in real human communities.

Although Yoder focuses his proposals for grace-empowered discipleship on the life of the church and its witness to political authorities and institutions, other writers and practitioners have advanced these ideas into emerging frameworks of active peacemaking, conflict transformation, and restorative justice, as described in chapter 9. More recently, Cynthia Hess pushes beyond Yoder's focus on actions that challenge external violence and restore relationships broken by such violence, to an account of communal practices that contribute to the healing of internalized violence and trauma.[11]

---

7. Yoder, *Radical Christian Discipleship*, 64.

8. Murray, *Naked Anabaptist*, 28–31.

9. For me, "grace-empowered discipleship" is an effort to distill into a phrase the posture announced in *The Politics of Jesus*: following the service-offering and enemy-loving way of Jesus Christ in the context of a community that announces in its words and deeds the already accomplished work of Jesus Christ in reconciling sinners to God and to one another, making God's grace and reign visible to a watching world.

10. Yoder, *Politics of Jesus* (1994), 1–20.

11. Hess, *Sites of Violence*, 11–32.

Yoder and those who follow his theological direction tend to understand sin in terms of social processes and systems that have become corrupted by violence, power, and injustice. The redemption of these systems involves the appearance on the horizon of human history of a new social reality whose appeal and truthfulness counteracts the force of overextended and dehumanizing power that characterizes the systems of the world.[12] Thus, the church's response to the imperial and dominating forces of this world is to make visible in its own life the new humanity to which the whole world is called.[13] This public example includes such practices as breaking bread together as an act of economic sharing and actions of binding and loosing whereby offenses are named, forgiveness is offered, and reconciliation is achieved—thus modeling restorative justice for the watching world.[14] Yoder's argument seems to be confirmed by numerous actual examples of churchly witness influencing worldly political systems for the better, including the adoption of some restorative justice models in the criminal justice system and the application of peace-building models in the context of military policies.[15]

However, when we look honestly at the actual life of real church communities and church members, we are able to see that much of the time the church manifests many of the same symptoms of corrupted social processes, division and violence that so tarnish the more general human experience in communities and societies. Ephraim Radner, for example, has called attention to such failures of the church in the context of some of the most notable instances of massive violence in the modern world—including the American Civil War, the German Holocaust, and the Rwandan Genocide. In each of these cases, the church is not only complicit with the violence of state authorities, but is actually a significant contributor to mass violence through impoverished communal and biblical discernment.[16]

---

12. As noted in chapters 4, 6, and 7, Yoder's view of the Powers as overextended concentrations of legitimate authority is derived from Hendrik Berkhof, whose work on the Powers Yoder translated. See Berkhof, *Christ and the Powers*.

13. Yoder, *For the Nations*, 46. Chapter 7 deals extensively with this new ecclesiology.

14. Yoder, *Body Politics*, 1–27.

15. For restorative models of criminal justice, see Zehr, *Changing Lenses*. For the influence of Mennonite church practices of peacemaking on international peacebuilding, see Lederach and Sampson, *From the Ground Up*.

16. For a discouraging but important account of how the German Mennonite church capitulated to the Nazi regime, see Lichti, *Houses on the Sand?*.

A traditional Anabaptist response to such obvious corruptions of the church is to distinguish between a faithful, Jesus-following, cross-bearing New Testament church and "nominal" Christianity compromised by Constantinian capitulation to the war and violence of worldly political authorities.[17] While this approach does have some merit and has certainly empowered conventicles of radicalized Christians through the ages to recover lost elements of the apostolic vision, it does not adequately address the ways in which even peace churches who have successfully refused to participate in the violence of the state nevertheless display the iniquities of power and violence within their own body politics. In the Anabaptist stream of church and congregational history, one could cite many examples of overextended and hurtful practices of church discipline that exhibit the arbitrary power of stubborn and ungraceful church authority, or conflicts between church members that divide congregations and devastate families, or the covering up of abuse and violence by influential leaders of the church's institutions and networks.[18]

Yoder's Failures in Theological Context

The expectations for changed behavior that characterize Anabaptist theology in general and the radical Christian theology of John Howard Yoder in particular constitute the context in which to consider the sexual misconduct of Yoder toward numerous women, along with the Mennonite Church's flawed response. Details of Yoder's appalling behavior appear in the previous chapter. For current purposes it is sufficient to say that the abusive behavior of which Yoder was accused and to which he admitted in a church discipline process appears to have been addressed by the church only after a great deal of harm was done that might have been prevented had Yoder been held accountable in a more urgent fashion.[19]

17. Marpeck, "Exposé," 38–39.

18. For a sociological account of conflict in Mennonite church communities, see Kniss, *Disquiet in the Land*. Also, see a special issue of *Mennonite Quarterly Review* devoted to multidisciplinary evaluations of a variety of Mennonite conflicts (April 1998). Most of these cases turn out not to be inspiring Anabaptist models of conflict transformation for a watching world. For a documented historical account of incest by a Mennonite college president, the ensuing cover-up by denominational leaders, and the resulting long-term devastation and trauma, see Sharp, *School on the Prairie*, 189–93.

19. Tom Price wrote a series of investigative articles for *The Elkhart Truth* in June and July 1992 that document the accusations against Yoder and the church

Moreover, the disciplinary process, once it was initiated, unfolded in ways that sometimes extended rather than curtailed the hurt and sorrow that resulted from Yoder's behavior. For some who were impacted by Yoder's behavior, the four-year disciplinary process was agonizingly long; for others, it was inadequately conclusive. Yoder's actual misconduct appears to include both consensual extramarital intimacy and unwelcome sexual advances that were hurtful and abusive. In any event, it seems evident that neither Yoder's acknowledged hurtful behaviors, nor the initial responses of his institutional employers, nor the timetable for the disciplinary process to which Yoder submitted conform very well with the politics of Jesus or the body politics of the church that Yoder's theology advocates. Moreover, even if Yoder's original motivations for some of his behaviors appear to have been theologically driven, this hardly excuses his refusal to accept for many years the counsel of colleagues and church authorities that his actions were doing great harm.[20] Arguably

discipline process that resulted. These articles appear to me to be the most reliable source of public knowledge about Yoder's misconduct. The information provided in these articles is the primary, although not the only, basis for my characterization of what happened. The articles are available online and indexed on Ted Grimsrud's *Peace Theology* blog: http://peacetheology.net/john-h-yoder/john-howard-yoder's-sexual-misconduct—part-five-2/.

20. At least some of the time, Yoder appears to have been seeking new approaches to the need for intimacy among single people, especially women, in the church. However, his experimentation appears not to have accounted meaningfully for his own marriage vows, family responsibilities, or the power associated with his stature as a church leader and renowned theologian. The details are documented in part two of Tom Price's articles printed in *The Elkhart Truth*, accessible on Ted Grimsrud's *Peace Theology* blog: http://peacetheology.net/john-h-yoder/john-howard-yoder's-sexual-misconduct—part-two/. A line of inquiry not yet pursued in any venue of which I'm aware is the possible influence on Yoder of early Anabaptist practices of sexual utopianism, such as the Davidites (followers of David Joris) who apparently engaged in communal nudity without arousal in order to prove their triumph over lust, and the Dreamers who by contrast sought to redeem sexual intercourse in the context of spiritual marriages that were regarded as trumping their official, worldly marriages. For discussion of Davidite communal nudity, including Joris's teaching (according to Nicolaas Blesdijk) that the proof of a believer's rebirth was his ability to "stand in front of or sleep with naked women without becoming sexually aroused," see Waite, *David Joris*, 122. For a discussion of the Dreamers and of Anabaptist sexual utopianism more broadly, see Roper, *Oedipus and the Devil*, 79–103. According to Roper, a theme in Anabaptist sexual utopianism is the interest by male leaders in managing or redeeming female sexuality—a theme that bears an uncanny resemblance to Yoder's interest in the intimacy needs of unmarried women. Also, in the case of Joris, he apparently only taught communal nudity without arousal to a select inner circle of his followers, a practice that is comparable to Yoder's reservation of his unorthodox sexual teachings

the outrage, hurt, and betrayal felt by the victims of Yoder's misconduct, by their allies, and by scholars and students who encounter information about these events reflect the contradiction between Yoder's actions and the expectations for grace-empowered discipleship that Yoder himself helped to strengthen among several generations of students, pastors, and church leaders.

For Anabaptist theology as interpreted by John Howard Yoder, the good news of the gospel includes liberation from such offenses as sexual predation, the honest confrontation and persistent reformation of networks of power that enable and sustain such behaviors, and the truthful restoration of offenders and victims who are ensnared by this sin.[21] When disciples or their church communities fail to act according to this liberating and reconciling gospel, the gospel has been contradicted, and this requires a response that addresses the contradiction, a response that involves repentance and "amendment of life."[22] From what I can tell, this

---

and practices for a select circle. According to one of Yoder's former students, Yoder shared with Donald Durnbaugh, Church of the Brethren historian, an interest in the sexual irregularities of the radical streams in Pietism and Anabaptism; this interest remained merely historical for Durnbaugh but for Yoder became part of his own pursuit of what he called "Friendly Relations" with "Sisters" who shared his radical vision. I make these observations not to justify Yoder's behavior but rather to suggest a line of inquiry into the way that sin may be expressed in Anabaptist communities and cultures—not merely as a failure to live up to certain rules of conduct, but also as the harm associated with excessive zeal or with the determination to resist conformity. Was Yoder's unwillingness to listen to the counsel of colleagues and leaders regarding his sexual conduct related to his conviction that he was simply acting as a radical Christian nonconformist who was certain to encounter resistance and misunderstanding concerning his actions? For those of us who identify with the drama of Anabaptist nonconformity and martyrdom, and with the victims of magisterial power, might it be difficult to acknowledge the ways in which we might harm others by our stubborn refusals to conform to social norms that we deem "worldly" or conventional? In some cases, might such harms be as egregious as the harms perpetrated by the systems of social and political power that we want to reject? Is it therefore possible that we may as easily sin in our nonconformity as we sin in our conformity to popular or conventional morality?

21. While Yoder did not directly address the offense of sexual misconduct in his published discussions of church discipline, he does make it clear that the process of binding and loosing must be directed in a singular way at the goals of reconciliation and restoration. Among the concerns that often get dragged into disciplinary processes but that are not valid from a New Testament perspective, Yoder lists "the purity of the church as a valuable goal in its own right" and "protecting the reputation of the church before the outside world." See Yoder, *Royal Priesthood*, 335–36.

22. The phrase "amendment of life" is taken from article six of the Dordrecht

commitment to actual changes in practice and to true reconciliation appears to drive ongoing calls to complete unfinished work in the church's process of addressing the hurtful misdeeds of one of its leaders—even though that leader is now deceased. In her extensive examination of the possible therapeutic explanations for Yoder's abusive behavior, for example, Ruth Krall poses the following question as one of the motivating concerns for her study: "What can we learn from his life that will help the church to prevent future instances of abuse that resemble his?"[23] This all seems consistent with Anabaptist convictions that redeemed people are empowered to challenge sin and failure, to expect accountability, and to continue the process of reforming the church to more fully reflect God's will for human wholeness and well-being.

At the same time, we might ask why processes of this nature have been such a challenge for the church. Perhaps one reason for the difficulty is the shame associated with sin in a community where sin is seen as conquered or seldom discussed any longer. We might ask whether Anabaptist theologians and church leaders shaped by Yoder's legacy have adequately acknowledged the persistence of sin and failure in the life of the church and its members. Have we oversimplified the Christian struggle against sin and implied that well-intentioned people can simply decide to be disciples of Jesus Christ by exercising our redeemed wills? If so, it would not be surprising to discover that when the reality of sin and failure is unacknowledged, we might be tempted to disproportionately amplify the significance of any particular sin—such as sexual misconduct—in ways that overstate the power that such behaviors should be permitted to exert over the spiritual imagination of church members or the tactical decisions of its leaders. We might be tempted, for example, to ignore evidence that church members or leaders are doing harm because such evidence may contradict our naïve expectation that sin is rare in the church. We might be tempted to avoid confessing our own sin in the context of a community of such naïve expectations, because such a confession may make us seem like unusual failures in comparison to the routine ethical rigor of those around us. And if we are church leaders, we might be tempted to suppress knowledge of sin and failure because we fear for the reputation of the church and of the sin-conquering gospel the church proclaims. To sum up, when the particular realities or experiences of sin's

---

Confession of Faith. Horst, *Mennonite Confession*, 28.

23. Krall, *Elephants in God's Living Room*, 12.

persistence are silenced then victims of sin are discouraged from telling their stories, perpetrators of sin are ashamed to confess, and sin's power in the life of the church grows in direct proportion to the church's success at covering it up.

Sin persists in the life of the church and we should be neither scandalized nor paralyzed by its routine appearance, even when to our chagrin sin overtakes those leaders and mentors who have contributed greatly to our discovery and understanding of the way of Jesus Christ. We should be clear that, as the gospel writer John confirms, "everyone who commits sin is a slave to sin," but the truth makes us free. The truth here is identified with Jesus Christ, but this is because Jesus is a discloser of truth while the devil is the "father of lies." Hiding sin makes us its slave; acknowledging sin and Jesus' triumph over it, makes us "free indeed" (John 8:31–47).

Some scholars have argued that failures in the church of the kind exhibited in the Yoder misconduct case raise serious questions about the validity of Yoder's theology, or even of Anabaptist theology more generally.[24] While such a line of inquiry should certainly be considered seriously by Anabaptist scholars and theologians, it is also possible and valuable to examine how cases like that of Yoder's misconduct provide an opportunity to correct and qualify and strengthen Anabaptist theology and practice, along the lines already opened up by Yoder's writings and in the deeper Anabaptist theological heritage.

I choose this line of inquiry because I am convinced that the church and its leaders and members can do better in the grace-empowered struggle against sin—a conviction I continue to embrace partly because of the influence of Yoder's theological legacy. This approach seeks to be clear that failing to achieve perfection or even to go very far down the road toward it should not be an excuse for neglecting the ways in which partial righteousness has been achieved, and therefore can also be extended and deepened. For example, it appears to me that while the church and its members failed in some significant respects when responding to Yoder's misconduct and to the accusations brought against him, the church also acted rightly, in some respects. While it acted too late and perhaps with

---

24. For a rant about how Anabaptist communities are compromised by power, even though they claim to be free from such power, and therefore have little credibility in their political critiques, see Hunter, *To Change the World*, 150–66. Hunter also repeats the perfectionist charge against neo-Anabaptist communities and theologians, including Yoder.

less urgency and thoroughness than might have achieved a fuller reconciliation and a greater healing, the church and its members did in fact initiate a process of accountability to which Yoder was urged to submit, and to which he did finally submit, although perhaps too reluctantly and without adequate vulnerability. This process clearly did not achieve resolution or reconciliation for everyone who was impacted by Yoder's offenses, yet it did begin to establish some truthful acknowledgement of what in fact took place: for example, characterizations of actions to which Yoder admitted or which he did not dispute. Surely such truth telling and discovery is important ground for future work in discerning the church's institutional and collective responsibility for the failures that are associated with the church's response. In other words, perhaps we should not draw the conclusion that because the church only partially succeeded in holding Yoder accountable for his actions, such processes of accountability are simply signs of hypocrisy or Anabaptist over-optimism about the struggle against sin. To use Yoder's words, "that (the) triumph over sin is incomplete changes in no way the fact that it is possible."[25]

In this spirit, the remainder of this chapter proceeds along the lines of the assumption that in the power of God and through the life of discipleship, it is possible to do better, even though this doing better may involve more than simply trying harder or making greater demands. In what follows, I explore four questions about the ways in which sin and failure are experienced in actual human life that suggest emerging theological tasks for radical Christian theologians shaped by the grace-empowered discipleship focus in Anabaptist theology and in particular by Yoder's writings. These questions arise to a significant extent in response to the failures of the church—especially Anabaptist-minded churches—to act according to the proclamation of the church that Jesus Christ is Lord and that he is our peace. These questions do not assume that because the church fails repeatedly it must adopt an ethics of compromise or realism. Rather, these questions assume that God has more light yet to break forth from God's Holy Word and that all baptized believers are still called to follow after Jesus Christ in life, even when it is costly or risky or frustrating to do so.

---

25. Yoder, *Reinhold Niebuhr*, 22.

Does Anabaptism Display an Overly Muscular Communal Will?

Brethren pastor and theologian Scott Holland has repeatedly raised the question of whether the framing of the Anabaptist Vision in the twentieth century along the lines established at Goshen by Harold Bender and Robert Friedmann asserts an overly confident picture of the authority of the church community over individual actions as a basis for authentic discipleship. In Holland's account, the reception of Anabaptism through the "Goshen school" tradition risks becoming "a religion of the superego wherein all individuals must find their plot and place in the story of the communal soul."[26] From this perspective, Anabaptist communities easily become artless communities committed to The Way We Must Follow, as my colleague Jeff Gundy states it with affectionate sarcasm.[27] Such communities can become unhealthy when they neglect the beauty and delight of human and earthly realities expressed in such crafts as poetry and creative writing, not to mention the awareness of the failures and problems of language that are never far from the consciousness of skilled poets.

According to this view, the voices of poets and artists attend more readily to the ambiguities of actual human existence and real experiences of faithful action than do the writings of many theologians, especially those who seek to provide normative visions against which church communities can judge their successes and failures. Advocates of theopoetics like Holland and Gundy suggest that a strong community that demands accountability may not be a sufficient or even the most helpful leverage against the power of sin and corruption, especially when there is no attention to the romance and delight of faithfulness, to the inner experience of spiritual attachment, or to what Holland calls "the epistemology of the heart."[28] Moreover, Holland raises the question of whether this version of Anabaptism is simply wrong to assert, as Yoder did, that "the church precedes the world epistemologically . . . and axiologically."[29] For Holland, the human body, not just the churchly body, is also a site of divine

---

26. Holland, "Pietist as Strong Poet," 169.
27. Gundy, *Songs from an Empty Cage*, 184.
28. Holland, "Pietist as Strong Poet," 172–76.
29. Holland, "Communal Hermeneutics," 101–2. For Yoder's claim about the church preceding the world, see Yoder, *Priestly Kingdom*, 11.

revelation and truthful knowledge, which is confirmed by the fact that in the Bible "the grand story of creation precedes the story of the church."[30]

Might those who advocate theopoetic Anabaptism be right that discipleship is often more a matter of art than of will, of desire than of submission? If so, Holland might then also be correct that the resources of Pietism should be seen not as an enemy but an ally of Anabaptist conviction. This is a possibility that I am willing to entertain, so long as the strong poet of Pietism does not simply replace the muscular community with the muscular individual.

In historic Anabaptism, there is no premium on correct theology; rather there is the marshaling of any text or vision or practice that can enable discipleship. A poem or a story will do as well as a theological treatise, and sometimes better, in the struggle for reconciliation. Inner resources of emotional motivation are as important as outer resources of communal accountability, and perhaps more so, at least for some people.

The case for a theopoetic course correction in Anabaptist Vision practice is strengthened by the recent work of Lisa Schirch, a peacebuilding practitioner who advocates for the importance of symbolic and ritual activities in bringing together parties to a conflict. Schirch writes that "our bodies may, in some cases, learn more quickly than our brains," and that "humans are by nature both sensual and emotional"; therefore "peacebuilders should engage people in conflict with processes that address the full range of ways that humans know and make sense of their world, through traditional lectures and writing activities, as well as activities such as drama or theater, sports, eating, dancing, and walking outside together."[31] For the church more fully to address the deep and complex human realities of sin and brokenness, it will no doubt need to offer a more eloquent and artful witness, one that draws on the resources of artists, poets, storytellers, coaches, and performance artists, not just theologians and theorists.

Is Sin More than Corrupted Practice?

Another critique that has sometimes been leveled at the kind of Anabaptist theology advocated by Yoder is that it incorrectly assumes a strong personal will with sufficient agency to reform or exceed corrupted social

30. Holland, "Communal Hermeneutics," 102–3.
31. Schirch, *Ritual and Symbol*, 43–44.

processes. By emphasizing the external and visible manifestations of sin in documented social practices and relations, it is argued, contemporary Anabaptist theology describes a triumph over sin that can be cast primarily as a matter of changed behavior, rather than of changed inner motivations.

Stephen Dintaman takes up this position in a well-known essay titled "The Spiritual Poverty of the Anabaptist Vision." In this essay, Dintaman claims that the generation of Anabaptist scholars and theologians who followed Bender and his Anabaptist Vision neglected to give adequate attention to the work of the Holy Spirit in transforming people, a spiritual work that Dintaman claims was vital in Bender's theological vision. As a result, those schooled in more recent versions of the Anabaptist Vision learned little about "sin and the dynamics of inner bondage to death and violence" and instead saw behavioral change as "simply a matter of seeing a better way and deciding to do it."[32] This "just do it" approach exhibits little patience for people who are "deeply wounded" or who are struggling with enslaving habits and addictions. Although Dintaman criticizes contemporary Anabaptism's overemphasis on the individual will rather than the dependence on the communal will highlighted by writers like Gundy and Holland, he arrives at Pietist conclusions similar to that of Holland: "Until we can think and talk as passionately about receiving and being as we do about strategizing and doing, until we get as passionate about praise and prayer as we do about socio-political analysis, we will remain spiritually impoverished."[33]

In my own writing on this topic, I have been hesitant to grant that the experience of "spiritual poverty" is necessarily a problem for Anabaptist theology, but I have seen it instead as an opportunity for humble acknowledgement of our own limits and a motivation for extending ourselves toward others in love.[34] As the renowned social theorist Slavoj Žižek has stated, "Only a lacking, vulnerable being is capable of love: the ultimate mystery of love is that incompleteness is in a way higher than completion."[35] Žižek's work is shaped by a Lacanian psychosocial evaluation of selfhood that stresses the abyss or event dividing social identity

---

32. Dintaman, "Spiritual Poverty," 2. For the original Anabaptist Vision text, see Bender, *Anabaptist Vision*.
33. Dintaman, "Spiritual Poverty," 3.
34. Biesecker-Mast, "Slavoj Žižek," 188.
35. Žižek, *Fragile Absolute*, 147.

between an articulated self and a disavowed Real, a traumatic abyss that both founds and threatens the structured self.[36] Put more simply, selfhood is a fragile and unfinished project whose claim to sovereignty and agency is mythic or rhetorical, not actual. We are not in control of our lives, even though we are compulsive about finding ways to maintain such control, including the construction of immortality projects that are in denial about the reality of death.[37] In other words, sin is surely not reducible to corrupted social processes, but is also a reality that characterizes the inner experience and motivations of individuals, who are divided against themselves, doing what they do not want to do, and not doing what they want, to paraphrase Paul the apostle (Romans 7:19).

However, any recovery of theological language that seeks to heal the diseases and quench the thirsts of a sin-corrupted inner life must be attentive to the ways in which such language can also obscure the limits and harms of human agency and willpower, even when rooted in the work of Jesus Christ and the power of the Holy Spirit. In other words, these spiritual resources alone are not the answer to a sin-corrupted life. Hence, I am reluctant to name such resources as "spiritual capital" that needs to be recovered; instead I would rather consider such resources as practices that cultivate patience and humility.[38]

Alex Sider gets it right when he argues that in Yoder's theology of fallibility, he describes human brokenness "as *both* painful *and* potential for newness of life" and therefore church communities are actually dependent on "continuing to encounter new brokenness," as they proclaim a gospel that is offered without control or condition, and therefore open to rejection and susceptible to abuse. This is why I am hesitant to recover too quickly any triumphalist sense that the work of Jesus Christ and the power of the Holy Spirit fixes me or fixes my community; many times this christological work and pneumatological power appears in human history amidst scandalously frustrating and spiritually impoverished conditions—the gospel, we must remember, proclaims the vindication

---

36. Ibid.

37. For a discussion of Ernest Becker's concept of immortality symbols and the denial of death in an Anabaptist perspective, see Liechty, *Theology in Postliberal Perspective*, 1–12.

38. Dintaman uses the phrase "spiritual capital" to refer to doctrines of the Holy Spirit and the work of Jesus Christ. Dintaman, "Spiritual Poverty," 3.

of weakness, and therefore only when received in weakness can its appearance in time and space be a truthful occasion for prayer and praise.[39]

If sin is more than corrupted social processes, and is a condition that clings to selfhood, then we should expect that our struggles to "fix" either worldly or churchly structures and systems will have no more closure than our efforts to establish coherent selves. Thus, we should not be surprised when a church disciplinary process that had been declared closed is discovered not to be. Nor should we be surprised to know that the process both succeeded in some respects and failed in others. Rather, the discovery of ongoing brokenness offers new opportunities for the church to make visible God's reconciling work, a work that is most authentically proclaimed when undertaken in weakness and lament, with an honest recognition of our own complicated and not fully redeemed motivations.

Does Anabaptism Serve an Angry Father?

In the conclusion to his book on Yoder's ecclesiology, Sider repeats a statement made by Rowan Williams that "the substance of the gospel has to do with God's giving up possession or control, the Father giving up or giving over the Son to the cross, or Christ giving up his 'wealth,' security, life for the sake of human beings."[40] This statement makes clear an implicit concern that emerges from explorations of the previous two questions. A significant sin problem is the human compulsion to control outcomes, to save the self, to manage others, and to rule the surrounding world. According to Yoder's account of the politics of Jesus, God's way of intervening in human history is to give up control and to serve humanity and the cosmos, even unto death.[41]

However, as Jeff Gundy has noticed, some of Yoder's metaphors for the Rule of God seem to contradict this vision of humble and nonresistant service. For example, in his essay "But We Do See Jesus" Yoder describes the project of the early church in terms of having "seized" the categories of the world and "hammered them into other shapes," thereby witnessing to the ways in which the Rule of God has "defeated" the "rebellious" cosmos.[42]

39. Sider, *To See History Doxologically*, 206–97.
40. Ibid., 207.
41. Yoder, *Politics of Jesus* (1994), 233–40.
42. Gundy, *Songs from an Empty Cage*, 189–90. For the passage from Yoder

This raises the question of whether Yoder contradicted in his rhetorical and literary style the theological commitments to nonviolence and weakness to which his theological project appears committed. This is a difficult and challenging question that requires attention to Yoder's method of reading the Bible, in particular the Old Testament accounts of God's violent actions on behalf of Israel's liberation or humanity's punishment. John Nugent has offered a cogent account of Yoder's reading strategy, highlighting his focus on the trajectory in Old Testament narratives that featured trust in a saving God rather than in human violence and power and culminating in Jesus' rejection of violence altogether.[43]

At the same time, Yoder's unwillingness to confront directly the violence of Old Testament stories that contradict the loving God revealed in Jesus Christ, as Brethren in Christ scholar Eric Seibert has had the courage to do, might offer an explanation of why military metaphors and images of control creep back into Yoder's account of God's peaceable reign.[44] In fact, as I reread my summary of Anabaptist understandings of sin in the first paragraph of this chapter, I wonder how much the broader Anabaptist tradition, as well as my own account of it, remains trapped in a metaphorical family system governed by a controlling Father.

A more decisive theological rejection of the image of an angry, controlling and violent God, following in Yoder's footsteps but taking his critique much farther, is found in the groundbreaking work of J. Denny Weaver, both in his evaluation of standard Christian atonement motifs and more recently in his biblical reconstruction of a peaceable God who comprehensively reflects the nonviolent image of Jesus Christ displayed in the gospel stories. Weaver makes no effort to rehabilitate any of the violence found in the Old Testament, even as lessons in trusting a sovereign God, opting instead to acknowledge that to live in the story of Jesus is to accept his validation of that stream of scriptural witness that unambiguously displays God's peaceable and everlasting love for the whole cosmos, both in terms of God's peaceable purpose and in terms of God's nonviolent strategies for achieving that purpose.[45]

Weaver's work can be seen as one correction of a latent tendency in Yoder's theologizing to exhibit habits of speech that reflect divine images

---

containing military metaphors, see *Priestly Kingdom*, 54.

43. Nugent, *Politics of Yahweh*, 86–87.
44. Seibert, *Violence of Scripture*.
45. Weaver, *Nonviolent God*, 13–28.

of the violent and controlling Father rather than of the defenseless and peaceable Lamb. If a feature of the church's failure to address the sin that its members exhibit is the desire of its leaders and members to manage outcomes, to engage in damage control, and to stay in charge, Weaver's account of a nonviolent God who truly reflects the serving life offered by Jesus Christ may assist the church in its struggle to speak the truth in love.

How Do We Confront the Powers in the Church?

While Yoder never claims that the church is free from the failures of the surrounding world, the drama that typically unfolds on his theological stage features the church as a righteous and faithful protagonist, encountering and witnessing to an unrighteous and disobedient world. In Yoder's theological imagination, the concentration of corrupting power that leads to the dehumanizing empire of the Powers is typically found out there in the state or in the judicial system or in large economic structures.[46]

Yet, as feminist scholars are often more likely to point out, the Powers out there are already inside the church, fostering exclusion, enabling unaccountable and arbitrary processes, and reproducing unwarranted and unjust privilege. Dorothy Yoder Nyce and Lynda Nyce name this reality with convincing clarity: "Power, which is inherent in all social relationships, actively shapes church life, whether church members and leaders own, confront, deny, or ignore the extent of its influence within ecclesial settings."[47] Nyce and Nyce go on to describe how unacknowledged power in Anabaptist churches, including patriarchal power that maintains inequitable relations between men and women, becomes perverse and destructive precisely because church leaders and members are reluctant to recognize it or speak about it. These scholars provide a particularly prescient example of how calls for servant leadership often provide a rhetorical disguise for stubborn patterns of dysfunctional domination by leaders "who depend on others to be dependent upon them."[48] And they suggest more radically egalitarian models of decision-making

---

46. According to Yoder, the Powers out there have been defeated by the presence of Jesus and the church, "which is itself a structure and a power in society." Yoder, *Politics of Jesus* (1994), 158.

47. Nyce and Nyce, "Power and Authority," 155.

48. Ibid., 160–61.

and authority distribution that would "help to counter the sin of violence and abuse that has thrived within structures that discriminate."[49]

This move to acknowledge the Powers within the church may be the most urgent course correction required of the radical theological vision associated with Yoder and with the Anabaptist Vision. As I write this, the failure of the broader historic Anabaptist movement to confront the sin of corrupted power within the church is increasingly visible, perhaps most strikingly among some traditional Mennonite communities where the virtues of humility and service have been so thoroughly cultivated.

In a recent letter to the *Canadian Mennonite*, Canadian Mennonite poet Di Brandt calls attention to a description by reporter Jean Friedman-Rudovsky of the ongoing traumas associated with the "ghost rapes" of scores of Mennonite women by Mennonite men in a traditional Mennonite colony in Bolivia.[50] This horror went unchallenged for far too long, Brandt writes, in part because of such systemic factors as a "lack of checks and balances," a "warped use of forgiveness," the normalization of suffering, and a group identity that "sees itself as outside the limits of the rest of society and that values the reputation or integrity of the group over the safety and protection of the individual." Brandt concludes, "I hope the Mennonite church-based communities of North America take this story and insightful analysis as a challenge and opportunity to embark on a serious process of self-reflection and wide scale internal revisioning—since these 'systemic factors' and attitudes (and harmful effects on the intimate and social lives of women and men, even if not as dramatically expressed as in Bolivia) are widely prevalent throughout the Mennonite world."[51]

Confronting the Powers within the church is every bit as urgent as confronting the Powers concentrated in the State and in the Empire. And these grace-empowered actions must now take account of revisions to Anabaptist theologies of reconciliation that feature, as does Cynthia Hess's work, the "reconstitution of shattered agency" that is often an outcome of trauma in the experience of victims.[52] Binding and loosing will now involve particular attention to the lives of those traumatized by violence, offering respect and affirmation, and inviting the work of the Spirit into the community's processes and decisions. Even though lan-

49. Ibid., 170.
50. Friedman-Rudovsky, "Ghost Rapes."
51. Brandt, "On Line Article," 13.
52. Hess, *Sites of Violence*, 96.

guage of "revolutionary subordination" may be a technically correct way to speak of a yielding that empowers (see chapters 4 and 6 as well as 8 for nuanced discussions), new, less easily misconstrued terms of reciprocity and power-sharing will be used to describe the church's response to the abuses of Power.[53] The church's public witness will now not only include a prophetic critique of overextended Powers out there in the world, but will also lift up the stories of suffering experienced by its own traumatized members—including those traumatized by the abuses and violence of the church itself—thus showing how the truth indeed does make free.[54]

Considering the question of power in the church opens the door to a discussion of power in church-related institutions, such a colleges and universities, where much of the twentieth century recovery of the Anabaptist Vision, including the Yoder theological legacy, took place. To what extent is contemporary Anabaptist theology overly dependent on the flawed resources of an academic culture steeped in powerful Enlightenment assumptions about the divisions between mind and body, reason and emotion, spirit and flesh, an academic culture that historic Anabaptism largely rejected and that remains hostile in many ways to women?[55] Does contemporary Anabaptist theologizing accept too readily a regime of truth that privileges abstraction and theory over lived experience? Does the success of Anabaptism in the academic guilds of theology and ethics obscure the everyday reality of ordinary life in which early Anabaptist conviction thrived? Is the lived reality of academic culture—its status obsessions, its intensely erotic dimensions, its obscure conflicts—inadequately acknowledged in the evaluation of theologies and theoretical frameworks that were birthed amidst the twentieth-century Mennonite embrace of higher education as a mission of the church?

On the one hand, the development of Mennonite colleges and seminaries provided an opportunity for the more systematic and organized exhibition of Anabaptist convictions whose deeper consideration was truncated by the sixteenth- and seventeenth-century persecutions and the

---

53. Ibid., 100. Nekeisha Alexis-Baker argues that Yoder's understanding of "revolutionary subordination" can further a womanist agenda, but also points to the easy misunderstanding of the term and suggests a more positive expression such as "creative transformation." Alexis-Baker, "Freedom of the Cross," 89–94, quote 93.

54. Hess, *Sites of Violence*, 103.

55. For a recent case study of the ongoing struggle to achieve gender equity in one challenging context of higher education, the Harvard Business School, see Kantor, "Harvard Case Study."

departure of Anabaptism from European cities and universities.[56] On the other hand, no doubt many sixteenth-century Anabaptists would be appalled by the embrace of abstract theological and intellectual projects that are often relatively inaccessible to those who are not educated in specific disciplinary vocabularies, a concern that could be applied to the volume in hand.[57] Certainly much of Yoder's work seeks to exceed such abstraction; nevertheless, Anabaptist theology shaped by Yoder continues to be primarily read and studied by seminarians, graduate students, and other academicians. There is no doubt that such academic and intellectual witness is an important ministry of the church; at the same time, a tradition that has always been suspicious of the *schriftgelehrten*—the privileged scribes— should be vigilant about the blind sides of academic culture: its hierarchies of power and privilege, its disciplinary arrogance and petty conflicts, and, perhaps especially, its unhealthy suppression of the deeply emotional and sensual dimensions of the drive for truth and knowledge.

Conclusion

This chapter has been, for me, a display of my own deep formation in the fallible theological vision of John Howard Yoder and the Anabaptist Vision that it extends and clarifies. I hope to have displayed something of the prayerful humility that I believe is called for when exploring the problems and possibilities of any inspiring yet limited human vision. Sin clings to Yoder's radical Anabaptist theology, as it does to every human vision and practice of the good, including grace-empowered discipleship; moreover, sin clings in particular historical and concrete ways, including in the appalling and hurtful actions of this radical vision's sinful human vessel. Those of us who continue to think and act within the light cast by Yoder's profound legacy must also, with prayers and tears, attend to the legacy's shadows, as well as to our own sins and failures, in the hope of salvation.

---

56. J. E. Hartzler, writing in 1925, stated the hopes associated with Mennonite higher education succinctly: "To study in an atmosphere in which the ideals, doctrines and history of Mennonitism are constantly emphasized is a most worthwhile opportunity for any person preparing for service within the denomination." Hartzler, *Education among the Mennonites*, 179.

57. For an example of the skewering of the *schriftgelehrten* in an early Anabaptist collection of writings, see Valentin Ickelshamer's poem on "The Learned Ones, the Wrongheaded Ones," in Rempel, *Jorg Maler's Kunstbuch*, 37–60.

Conclusion

J. Denny Weaver

This book began with an analysis of both content and methodology in Yoder's class lectures published as *Preface to Theology*, and in the article "But We Do See Jesus," which displays Yoder's application of the methodology of *Preface*. Use of the much-neglected *Preface* and tying it to the essay reveals a different picture of Yoder's theology than that contained in any other publication.

Earlier scholarship dealt with Yoder primarily as a major proponent of peace theology. That characterization is true, of course, but is not the complete picture. More recent writing has identified a number of other "Yoders." He has been depicted as both a proponent of standard Nicene orthodoxy and judged somewhat deviant or heterodox because he did not stand on standard Nicene orthodoxy. As has been demonstrated in several locations in this book, each of these characterizations contains a modicum of truth. Those who claim Yoder's orthodoxy are correct that he did not reject Nicene Christology outright. Those who proclaim Yoder's deviation from orthodoxy are correct that he did not build his thought on Nicene Christology. At the same time, neither is an accurate picture of Yoder's theology and methodology. Because of the wide range of issues Yoder addressed, his ethics has been labeled "ad hoc." Others have claimed Yoder as a postmodern thinker who can be brought into conversation with other postmoderns. These characterizations all contain a grain of truth, but likewise all fail properly to identify Yoder's methodology and theology, at least as he is discovered in this book.

Chapter 1 presented an extensive examination of Yoder's theology and methodology visible in *Preface* and the essay 'But We Do See Jesus." It is important to underscore the term "methodology" in the last sentence. Both these writings reveal and illustrate his theological methodology as well as his theological views.

What has been missed, and what these two writings reveal, is that virtually the only fixed point in Yoder's theology and ethics is his understanding of the significance of the narrative of Jesus. A tour of Yoder's writing is, at least in part, a tour of the many ways that he discussed and applied the meaning of that narrative. In the part of *Preface* that deals with the Bible, he began by constructing the outline of what the early church said about Jesus in the weeks and months after his death and resurrection. The rest of Yoder's discussion of New Testament material was a display of the way the New Testament writers dealt with that story. The Gospel writers expanded the outline visible in Acts. The writers of the Epistles drew meaning from that story, for example, as Paul did in his defense of a general resurrection.

Yoder's exposition of how the New Testament writers drew meaning from the story of Jesus reached a climax of sorts in the essay, "But We Do See Jesus." He pointed to five different New Testament christological images that emerged when the writer took the narrative into a different cosmology. This methodology then models the way that we should do Christology today. One important point of that essay with real contemporary impact is the injunction not to copy either their language or their imagery, exemplified by the notions of "preexistence" or "participation of the Son in creation," language which reflect a cosmology and context different from our own. Rather we should recognize the worldview in which we live today, which Yoder called pluralism/relativism, and then figure out how to express the meaning of Jesus in that context. In a worldview characterized by pluralism/relativism, there is no universally recognized and universally accessible norm of appeal by which to coerce skeptics into accepting our version of truth. Thus in this relativist/pluralist milieu, the way to testify to the truth of Jesus, Yoder indicated, is to live by his story when it is not required and may even be dangerous.

Yoder's description of drawing out the meaning and of changing the means of expressing the story of Jesus appeared in the discussion of the formulas of Nicea, Trinity, and Chalcedon in *Preface*. On the one hand, he recognized that these were valid efforts to state and preserve

New Testament understandings of Jesus. But on the other hand, he also pointed to the way that they reflected a particular context. Thus they were the best answer in that context, but in other contexts other expressions were clearly thinkable. And at that level, 'But We Do See Jesus" was an example. In it Yoder wrote of "high Christology," meaning Christology that linked Jesus to God, which was visible in the New Testament, but there was no mention of Nicea as the required means to validate that high Christology.

The chapters of Part Two discussed four important sources for Yoder's theology and ethics, namely, sixteenth-century Anabaptism, the Goshen School of Anabaptism, the biblical scholarship of Oscar Cullmann, and the theology of Karl Barth. In each case, the analysis showed, Yoder drew on and learned from these sources, but was not simply adopting or using them as a foundation. Rather, he used learnings from these sources to craft his own expression of the meaning and application of the narrative of Jesus.

The discussions of Part Three extended Yoder's work in two ways. Chapters 6 through 11 dealt with his interventions into theology, and provided further demonstrations of the way that he drew meaning from the story of Jesus. Chapter 6 pointed to Yoder's understanding that Paul was not the beginning of separating Christianity from Judaism, but rather Paul was extending and expounding the narrative of Jesus as a continuation of the story of Israel. Discipleship to Jesus produced the visible church, which was described in chapter 7. Chapters 8 and 9 developed two dimensions of Yoder's understanding of pacifism, peace and nonviolence that were derived from his Christology. Chapter 8 displayed the yieldedness of a life lived within the nonviolent narrative of Jesus, while chapter 9 displayed the activist dimension of the commitment to live within the narrative of Jesus. Chapter 10 drew out the implications of Yoder's understanding of the narrative of Jesus and his relativizing of classic Christology for interfaith conversations with Judaism, Islam and Hinduism. Finally, chapter 11 identified three different ways to extend or appropriate Yoder's theology and methodology. It suggested a model for a distinct theology on the other side of the door opened by Yoder's relativizing of the classic formulas of Christology and Trinity. But it also discussed two different conversations that could be joined by a contemporary, Yoder-stimulated, theological application of the narrative of Jesus. Chapters 12 and 13 extended the discussion of Yoder's theology into a previously unexplored area. In light of the high expectations for a nonviolent life raised by Yoder's theology, chapter 12 dealt with the profound disappointment caused by Yoder's failure to live up to his own theological insight. In the final chapter, it was suggested that the outrage in response to Yoder's failure actually reflected the wide-ranging influence of the high expectations raised by his theology. The chapter concluded with suggestions for developing additional resources to deal with such failures.

The one constant throughout these chapters, whether dealing with his intervention in theology or his failures, which may also be linked to his methodology that included some unusual theological defense of sexual experimentation, is Yoder's view that theology and ethics express and draw meaning from or are reflections on the narrative of Jesus. With that priority or "root" beginning point in view, theology generally and Christology in particular come to be seen as the language that draws out and expresses the meaning of Jesus. The classic language for Christology, Trinity, and Chalcedon then appear as valid and true efforts to explain the meaning of Jesus and his relationship to God within the context and world view of the early Christian centuries. But seeing the contextual nature of these statements also opens the door to developing other language in a different or modern context for answering the questions left open by the New Testament.

Identifying the "root" of Yoder's theology and ethics also brings his methodology into focus. This "root" enabled Yoder to face in multiple directions and to enter a wide variety of conversations in the already existing terms of that conversation, using that terminology to move the conversation in the direction indicated by the gospel. In characterizing Yoder as ethicist or theologian, it is thus as important to recognize Yoder's methodology as it is to find the fixed point in his theology and ethics. He faced multiple ways and entered multiple conversations. Mistaking one of these ways or directions for *the* Yoder stance has enabled writers erroneously to label him in diverse but incomplete and sometimes contradictory ways as peace theologian, as orthodox, as heterodox, as "ad hoc" thinker, or as postmodern theologian.

What the volume in hand has made clear is that methodology is as important as content in understanding Yoder's theology and ethics. When his methodology comes into full view, it also becomes visible that it is impossible to synthesize Yoder's theological writings into one coherent system. The fact that he entered multiple conversations on the terms of the conversation and opened multiple doors makes quite plain the impossibility of synthesizing all his statements into the one, comprehensive statement of his theology. Rather, what is visible throughout is his location in or position of "standing on" the narrative of Jesus, and his willingness to take that narrative anywhere and express its meaning in any context or use it to address any question asked.

Here I state only the obvious example of pointing in different directions most often referenced in this book. For those so inclined, on the basis of the narrative of Jesus Yoder demonstrated how to reform the standard or "orthodox" christological formulations from within. When he wrote that his view was "more radically Nicene and Chalcedonian than other views," he was offering a corrective and a way to reform the standard or classic Christology. As he said, "I do not here advocate an unheard-of modern understanding of Jesus. I ask rather that the implications of what the church has always said about Jesus as the Word of the Father, as true God and true Human, be taken more seriously as relevant to our social problems, than ever before."[58] At the same time, Yoder also opened the door to a christological expression that was, as he put it, "not beholden" to the standard formulas. That approach was on ample display in his essay, "But We Do See Jesus." With these two approaches in view—reforming Nicea and Chalcedon from within, and Christology not beholden to Nicea and Chalcedon—it becomes obvious that one cannot then systematize all Yoder's answers or statements into one coherent theological whole as *the* theology of John Howard Yoder. There is however a consistent methodology, that of taking the narrative of Jesus into any milieu and using it to address any question. And posthumously it also challenges his own conduct, which fell well short of expectations.

This book was originally constituted as a conversation of one school of Yoder interpreters, namely those who saw Yoder the radical theologian, with another school of Yoder interpreters, those who believe that Yoder based his theology on Nicene orthodoxy. The book has fulfilled that agenda, as well as addressing some additional interpretations.

---

58. Yoder, *Politics of Jesus* (1994), 102 This comment was quoted in chapter 1, note 107, and discussed there in the context of *Preface*. For those who appropriate this statement in defense of standard or orthodox Christology, it also needs to be underscored that it is not a declaration to use to affirm Yoder's agreement with the creedal traditions. To follow Yoder at this point actually calls one to challenge the way the creedal traditions have removed the narrative from the standard formulation.

It is important to be clear about the theologizing of Yoder the radical theologian.

However, as the Afterword shows, there is much more to parsing Yoder's theology than this particular discussion. As the exclusively male list of chapter authors in this book plainly exhibits, the school of thought reflected in portraying Yoder the radical theologian has not included women as prominent or persistent participants. This absence of women's voices and perspectives has undoubtedly impoverished the discussion of Yoder's theology more broadly, as well as the discussion represented in this particular book. Moreover, texts are not read in isolation, and Yoder's writings are now being read in light of his abuse of many women. Thus the Afterword by Lisa Schirch is a fitting and important final word. Even as she recognizes the value of the scholarship presented in this book, Schirch points out the unfinished agenda of the book and the important conversations yet to come.

John Howard Yoder was a Christian who sought to express the meaning of Jesus in any and all contexts. In that way, if a label besides "Christian" applies to Yoder's theologizing, it is the term "radical." Following the meaning of radical as coming from the root, Yoder's theology was radical, radically Christian. It went to the root of the Christian tradition, namely the story of Jesus. If he were with us today, John Howard Yoder would tell us not to copy his views and certainly not his actions. Rather he would want us to follow his way of being radical, that is, to begin our theologizing with the root of the Christian tradition, namely the story of Jesus told in the New Testament.

Let it be so.

Afterword

To the Next Generation of Pacifist Theologians

Lisa Schirch

Yoder, the radical follower of Jesus—the Jewish pacifist. Yoder, the brilliant and prolific theologian. Yoder, the awkward and sexually abusive man. Yoder, the man whom the church protected. This book paints a portrait of an exceptionally complicated, gifted, and troublesome man.

The talented male authors of the book are long on their contribution to the study of Yoder and his many contributions. Their careful scholarship brings out an important analysis of key themes in Yoder's many publications, particularly the fact that Yoder draws attention to Jesus as the primary source for Christian theologians as opposed to those who simply build on Nicene orthodoxy. It is a positive step forward that these male authors condemn Yoder's abuse in these chapters. The stated agenda of the book was to describe Yoder's methodology. But by virtue of their identities, the authors in this book cannot speak from the perspectives of women, a problem addressed in this Afterword. A book in 2014 on any topic, but particularly a book on John Howard Yoder, requires an analysis from women scholars, including victims of Yoder's assaults, as well as from Latino, African, Asian, and Pacific theologians, from people of diverse sexual orientations, and from peacebuilding practitioners who draw inspiration from Yoder to translate pacifist theology into pragmatic, real-world strategies.

I write this Afterword as a woman born and raised in the Mennonite Church. I have seen the negative effects of Yoder's assaults and the church's delayed response impact three generations of Mennonite women over the last thirty years in over a dozen Mennonite institutions. Some of Yoder's victims were his peers in his own generation. Some were his students, in the next generation. Women in both of these generations who spoke about the assaults experienced significant backlash. In today's world, a third generation of women theologians continues to be marginalized for their critique of Yoder and the church. I am not aware of any female Yoderian scholars, an important point that Weaver notes in the beginning of this book. Today's Bible and theology departments at Mennonite institutions are predominantly male. In my opinion, Yoder's assaults on women and the broader church's protection of Yoder at the expense of women's safety are important reasons why many talented Mennonite women pacifist theologians have left the Mennonite Church and have moved on to other denominations.

Women's voices and analysis are essential to the conversation on Yoder's role in Christian theology. Future generations of theologians reading Yoder need to hear their voices. Mennonite women such as Ruth Krall and Carolyn Holderread Heggen, Barbra Graber, Sara Wenger Shenk, Linda Gehman Peachey, Hannah Heinzekehr, Stephanie Krehbiel, Charletta Erb, and others write on sexual abuse and have made recommendations to the church on how to address Yoder's abuse. These women offer a fair acknowledgment of Yoder's contributions and his humanity. This Afterword summarizes some of the contributions of these women and includes information directly sourced from one of Yoder's victims.

I write this Afterword from the perspective of a peacebuilding practitioner. John Howard Yoder's theology positively impacted the field of peacebuilding. Peacebuilding requires a set of ethics and processes. As a pacifist, I concur with Yoder himself on the need to speak out against injustice and affirm the humanity of all people, even perpetrators. Yoder's abusive actions are a tragedy for the women victims, a tragedy for Yoder's family, and a tragedy for Yoder's legacy and those who devoted their lives to being "Yoderian" scholars. There is still important peacebuilding work for the church to do in order to address the wounds from the past and recover the integrity of peace theology. This Afterword identifies a peacebuilding agenda for the church in doing justice, loving mercy, and walking humbly.

In 2014, the Mennonite Church is undergoing a "John Howard Yoder Discernment Group." In his message to Mennonite Church USA, conference moderator Ervin Stutzman listed the shared assumptions about Yoder's behavior.[1] These include the following:

- We know abuse happened.
- We know there are victims—some known, some not known.
- We know wounds remain unhealed.
- We know that despite previous efforts by church leaders to stop the abuse and to enable healing, further work on the part of the church is being called for and is indeed needed.
- We know the truth will set us free.

The goals of the group are to listen to and contribute to the healing of all those impacted by Yoder's abusive actions and the church's response; to thank those women who have tenaciously worked to have the abuse addressed; and to prepare a churchwide process for lament, prevention of abuse, and healing for victims and offenders.

No one stands to gain from ignoring or covering up what happened. We all need healing. The victims are not responsible for hurting Yoder's reputation by reporting on his assaults. And Mennonite women writers urging the church to address victim's wounds are not guilty of defaming Yoder's name. Yoder alone is responsible for the damage to his credibility. No one stands to gain financially or politically from knowing the truth. In contrast, everyone stands to heal and recover integrity from acknowledging what happened, lamenting the harm it caused to so many, and deciding, as men and women in the church, to move the pacifist agenda forward by ensuring that sexual abuse ends.

The goal of this Afterword is not to *de-Yoderize* peace theology by taking Yoder's contributions away. The goal is to *deodorize* peace theology—healing the sickening wounds of silence requires the light and oxygen of public acknowledgment and lament. Even Yoder's most ardent male supporters seem to agree that the soul of Yoder's pacifist, radical Christian theology depends on a critical analysis of Yoder's actions toward women and the church's equally appalling actions in protecting

1. See Stutzman, "John Howard Yoder Discernment Group."

Yoder at the expense of the safety of his women students and women in the church. If theologians fail to understand fully the causes and consequences of Yoder's abuse and the church's long delays in justice, what hope is there for the future of pacifist theology? For the next generation of theologians reading this book, here are six ideas to consider if the church wants to recover the integrity of pacifist theology from this tragedy.

(1) *Yoder committed both sins of sexual immorality and acts of domination in sexual assaults.*

Sexual immorality and sexual assaults are two different types of behavior and imply different types of harm. Evidence seems to suggest that Yoder had extramarital relationships with women who desired a relationship with Yoder and pursued his attention. At the very least, this was immoral sexual behavior. But at least some of these women were admiring students who came to Yoder to be mentored. Excerpts of their adoring letters can be found online. Scholarly research on sexual abuse details that people in positions of power may use that power to attract sexual attention. No relationship involving a differential of power (such as a professor and an admiring student) can be truly consensual.[2] But between fifty and a hundred other women theologians indicated to Mennonite leaders that they did not invite sexual advances from Yoder, yet he forcibly kissed them, groped their private parts, wrote them sexually explicit letters, seemed to stalk them on their way to their homes late at night, and even physically jumped on them.[3] These are acts of domination that tore at the dignity of the brilliant and potentially powerful women Yoder deliberately chose to violate. Yoder's violence changed the lives of these women.

New York Times writer Mark Oppenheimer's 2013 article on Yoder's sexual assaults asks the remaining critical question about Yoder's scholarship: "Can a bad person be a good theologian?"[4] At what point does our bad behavior overwhelm or negate our writings about doing good? In today's world, Yoder's actions would be legally identified as sexual harassment and sexual assault. It is appropriate then to speak of Yoder's crimes against women. In today's world, institutions are legally responsible for addressing sexual harassment and sexual assault. Thus church leaders who knew of Yoder's actions but did not take aggressive action would

2. See for example Heggen, *Sexual Abuse in Christian Homes*.
3. Krall, *Elephants in God's Living Room*, 370.
4. Oppenheimer, "Theologian's Influence," A13.

also be criminally liable in today's world. Having new language and laws to identify Yoder and the church's actions offers us more insight on the seriousness of their actions. It is not anachronistic to name behavior as criminal just because the laws on sexual harassment have evolved. Slavery was always criminal even though slavery was technically legal for centuries. Naming an action as criminal helps the church recognize the seriousness of the situation and the need to take preemptive action to ensure the safety of women in the church. Despite the seriousness of Yoder's actions, I am not aware of anyone asserting the need for any type of formal criminal justice process against Yoder or the church. No one suggests that Yoder's theology should be thrown out because of the abuse or that he did not make other positive contributions in his personal life.

Excuses for Yoder abound. Some blame the victims, suggesting they all wanted Yoder's sexual attention. Some downplay the harm from his "sexual experiments." Some blame his Asperger-like symptoms of social awkwardness. Yoder's followers are eager to move back to their main pursuit of discussing Yoder's pacifist theology. But to name Yoder's behavior as "abuse" is more honest. Yoder was self-aware about what he was doing to women, as he offered elaborate justifications for it in his final posthumous writings on punishment.[5]

In her book on Yoder's abuse titled *The Elephant in God's Living Room: The Mennonite Church and John Howard Yoder—Collected Essays*, Ruth Krall asks critical questions about what shaped Yoder's view of women and what went wrong in his life that led to his sexual assaults on women. Krall's book is by far the most helpful clinical and psychological analysis of what Yoder himself may have suffered or experienced that influenced his abusive actions. Krall and others note that Yoder had many normal, healthy, and even pastoral social interactions and was not abusive in all aspects of his life. Krall writes, "While occasionally his harassing actions may have been opportunistic ones, in most reported situations they appeared to be pre-planned and methodically carried out. Potential victims were identified and they were groomed for acts of victimization."[6]

In the tradition of great pacifists who reach out to those causing harm, women writers like Ruth Krall have gone out of their way to affirm Yoder's humanity and to lament that the church failed not only the victims but also Yoder and his family by not stopping his abuse sooner.

5. Yoder, "Chapter 5: With and Beyond Girard."
6. Krall, *Elephants in God's Living Room*, 14.

Future generations of pacifist theologians should not diminish or excuse the harms Yoder caused but should acknowledge and lament the tragic consequences of Yoder's immoral and sexually violent actions and the effect they have had on women, his family, and the pacifist tradition.

(2) *The church itself needs to take responsibility for the institutionalized patriarchal setting that contributed to Yoder's abuse. Yoder grew out of a patriarchal church, and his writings as a white man reflect this privileged status.*

A toxic cocktail of patriarchy, sexual repression, and entitled leadership beyond reproach contributes to religious leaders around the world committing a high rate of sexual abuse. In a *Christian Century* article titled "Evangelicals 'Worse' than Catholics on Sexual Abuse," which quotes leading Christian voices working to stop such abuse, it is stated that "too many Protestant institutions have sacrificed souls in order to protect their institutions."[7] In this context, Yoder's abuse of his power as a professor was a symptom of a much wider problem.

Peacebuilding requires looking at root causes, not just symptoms of violence. Rather than blaming or diagnosing Yoder alone, a peacebuilding response to Yoder's abuse requires the church at large to examine the sickness of patriarchy. Yoder's abuse needs to be viewed in the context of the church's affirmation of patriarchy, where men are granted systematic entitlement to positions of power. Patriarchal systems limit women's access to education and positions of power and view women as second-class citizens.

Given the pervasiveness of institutionalized patriarchy, it would be surprising if Yoder's writing did not reflect patriarchal beliefs. As indicative of his patriarchal beliefs, Stephanie Krehbiel cites Yoder's description of women in his most recent, posthumous book, *The End of Sacrifice*, which seems to have been written in response to women's call for accountability for his assaults: "More recently men as a class have come to be vulnerable in a new way, as compensation for pain suffered by women, when that pain can be blamed upon the prior patriarchal tilt of our society." In the footnote to this sentence, Yoder added,

> There should be room, logically, for the objection that beneficent patriarchal care, properly understood and benevolently exercised, would not be harmful; that what has hurt women has been the violation, not the implementation, of proper fatherly

---

7. Allen, "Evangelicals 'Worse' than Catholics on Sexual Abuse," 16.

caring. This excuse would however not change the retaliatory dynamics, since the root of the power of the punitive drive is located not merely in a mistake the stronger party made but in the weaker party's anger *at being weaker*.[8]

Yoder suggests that women's anger at men is not necessarily due to men (such as he) having victimized women, but rather that women are angry because they are "weaker" than men. Yoder seems to see himself as an innocent symbol or scapegoat for women's anger at patriarchy.

Further, Yoder's earlier writing on the idea of "revolutionary subordination" did not resonate with many women, as discussed by Gerald Mast in chapter 8 of this volume ("Pacifism as a Way of Knowing"). Yoder identified patriarchy as a problem. But Yoder's writing is cryptic and a little too eager to emphasize women's subordination in biblical cultural context without providing a vision for equal relations between men and women in today's church. Hannah Heinzekehr argues, "[Yoder's] theology seemed to veer dangerously close to setting up frameworks that would not just allow . . . abuse to happen, but made it seem somehow honorable or noble."[9] Women should not suffer domestic violence or sexual assaults or view subordination of their identity as having redemptive power. In order to willfully subordinate, one must have a sense of agency and empowerment. One must feel entitled to respect in order to submit to disrespect. In this book, Weaver and Mast's chapter "Extending John Howard Yoder's Theology" makes these points in its discussion of atonement theology.

South Africans only chose nonviolent resistance after a concerted movement of Black consciousness to unlearn the oppressive practice of teaching black South African children that they were less human than white South African children. In Latin America, Paulo Freire described the process of "conscientization" as a necessary first step before impoverished Brazilians could start the revolutionary process of nonviolently questioning their oppressive government. In the women's liberation movement, developing a feminist consciousness of "women's power" is also a primary step.

---

8. Yoder, "Chapter 5: With and Beyond Girard," italics added. An adaptation of this quote can also be found in Yoder, "You Have It Coming," 183. However, in the published version, the editor, John C. Nugent, removed the three italicized words from Yoder's original text.

9. Heinzekehr, "Can Subordination Ever Be Revolutionary?"

As a woman and a peacebuilding practitioner who advocates nonviolent resistance, I believe revolutionary subordination requires two conditions.

a) Suffering requires empowerment. Empowerment comes from self-awareness and a lucid power analysis to identify that oppression is unjust and unnatural. Every human being deserves dignity. But not every person recognizes this human right in a world of social hierarchy and humiliation. Jesus critiqued the oppressive religious, social, and political powers of his day. He told downtrodden people like the Samaritan woman at the well that she was worthy of his respect and that she was a child of God. Only empowered people conscious of their right to dignity can make subordination revolutionary. Without empowerment, subordination may become internalized oppression where victims choose subordination because they cannot imagine that they deserve dignity.

b) Suffering must be a voluntary choice. In most cases, suffering is revolutionary only if there are other choices that do not require suffering. Jesus had a choice other than the cross. His choice to suffer made the subordination revolutionary. But many people do not have other choices.

As a woman peacebuilding practitioner, there are times in my life when I willfully choose powerlessness and to believe in the strategy of revolutionary subordination. When I was living in Kabul, Afghanistan, to conduct research on Afghan perspectives on peacebuilding during the years 2009–2011, I chose to live in an unarmed guesthouse, knowing full well that most foreigners had armed guards and stayed in gated hotels. Choosing subordination and vulnerability made sense—not having armed guards sent an important message to both my Afghan colleagues and to any Taliban or insurgents watching my movements that I was not part of the foreign occupation. I also choose revolutionary subordination when I provide training on peacebuilding at U.S. military bases. I am often the only woman and the only civilian in a room full of military leaders in uniforms. I make a choice to enter a space where my audience often opposes and belittles my experience. I speak diplomatically but forcefully on the rights of civilians and the alternatives to war even as I feel the silent and invisible poison darts coming at me as I speak.

In other contexts, I deliberately avoid subordination. While attending graduate school in Washington DC, there were times when I would have to walk late at night, and I chose to carry hot pepper spray so that I would be able to defend myself by nonlethal means, if necessary. When men in my church belittle my contributions, I confront the substance of their critique. While I may be willing to choose to die or suffer for my beliefs in some situations, I will not willfully submit to humiliation and violence in a context where those in my own community deny my personal agency. Most girls around the world are taught to be submissive. Their subordination is not revolutionary, as it is not chosen. When women's subordination is forced, it is violent.

People who have a critical mass of supporters in their homes and communities may develop an internal strength so that they can engage in this "revolutionary subordination" from a place of power and choice. Women tend to share their stories of sexual abuse and discrimination with each other, in order to become conscious of the systematic, impersonal denigration of our individual and collective voices. A feminist conscience and a community of other women who share a gender analysis of the church enable me to engage critically but respectfully on issues of sexual abuse. Women in the church who lack such feminist support either stay quiet and subordinate, or they walk away from an oppressive church whose "body politic" excludes and dismisses their voices.

Yoder, of course, was a white male, as are most of his followers. They operate in a patriarchal church that only recently has made important strides to include women. These patriarchal structures did not protect women in the church. Since Yoder assaulted many of his female students and rising female church leaders, his actions directly impacted a generation of women's leadership. The continuing absence of women in so many centers of pacifist theology at Mennonite institutions today means that new generations of pacifist theologians may also not be informed by a gender or power analysis or take into consideration the privilege and entitlements that males enjoy. Even putting Yoder's behavior with women aside, new generations of pacifist theologians need to bring other lenses and voices to engage with Yoder's theological concepts, including "revolutionary subordination." The church at large, and pacifist theologians in particular, need to critique patriarchy and embrace a wider set of ideas about pacifism and how it relates to people in different social positions.

(3) *Christian pacifism is not dependent on the credibility or idolatry of Yoder.*

The outline of this Afterword came together as I was explaining to my fourteen-year-old daughter the three ways Yoder's life and works impacted my life. First, I told her that Yoder's theology influenced a generation of my mentors and colleagues at the Center for Justice and Peacebuilding at Eastern Mennonite University. Mennonites worked for peace before Yoder. But without Yoder, it might have taken much longer for the Mennonite Church to translate pacifist theology into institutionalized efforts in restorative justice and peacebuilding. I have spent most of my life attending or working for Mennonite institutions. I grew up in a church that often seemed to be as Yoder-centric as it was Jesus-centric. Countless people have come to see Jesus as a "Jewish pacifist" and have understood the political message in the Bible because of Yoder. I might not be working in the field of peacebuilding had it not been for Yoder's contributions to those who mentored me. But I came to devote my life to peacebuilding and pacifism without ever having read Yoder. Other mentors and authors in the church—not Yoder—taught me to support peace and justice.

The two Mennonite professors who had the most impact on my understanding of pacifist theology were mental health clinician-theologian Ruth Krall[10] and musician Carol Ann Weaver, whose own academic training prepared them to bring a wider set of questions to teaching theology. These women steered me toward a reading list on feminist theology, liberation theology, and black theology. I read Mary Daly and Starhawk alongside Martin Luther King and Gandhi, two other powerful pacifist men from patriarchal contexts who faced allegations of sexual impropriety. From this broader theological perspective, Yoder's theses in *The Politics of Jesus* did not seem radical when I read them later in my life. The final chapter in this volume, Gerald Mast's "Sin and Failure in Anabaptist Theology," is an important effort to begin to have a dialogue between Yoder and theologians who self-identify as feminist, womanist, black or liberation theologians.

Second, I draw on Yoder's work to explain why it makes sense for me, a Mennonite, to be married to a Jew. My daughter identifies herself as both Jewish and Mennonite. Yoder's writing on Jesus as Jewish pacifist and on the Jewish-Christian schism, discussed in Weaver and Mast's and Weaver and Zimmerman's chapters, will make important contributions

---

10. Dr. Krall holds an MS in psychiatric-community mental health nursing and a doctorate in theology and personality. In addition, she taught peace studies at Goshen College for eighteen years.

to my children's ability to theologically justify their identity to the wider Christian church (if they ever care to do so!).

Third, when other Mennonites denounced my work to educate the United States government and military about peacebuilding, Yoder's theology as well as his own work with the ROTC program at the University of Notre Dame helped me articulate a theological justification to the church for this practical engagement of the U.S. military. Yoder's concept of speaking about religious ethics through secular terms or "middle axioms" gave me theological justification for talking to governments and military forces about human rights, violence against women, the structural causes of violence, and how to build peace. I did not start to work with the military because of Yoder. Rather, Yoder's writings helped me articulate the theological basis for my work to a conservative Christian audience who questioned reaching out to "the enemy."

As a peacebuilding practitioner, I recognize that all of us who work for peace are less than perfect. If we were to wait for a perfect messenger to speak on peace and justice, we would greatly hinder any progress toward improving the human condition. Yet the true measure of the quality of witnessing for peace is not what you say, but what you do. The inconsistencies in the lives of most peace and justice practitioners are far less dramatic than Yoder's.

The real-world applications of pacifist theology in the fields of restorative justice and peacebuilding provide the next generation of theologians with a much more compelling vision of pacifism. It is much easier to "see" a pacifist Jesus in the men and women who are running victim-offender reconciliation programs, facilitating dialogue between Muslims and Christians, advocating for social justice, or training the Congolese military in how to respect women's rights. I would choose to admire the silent, humble generosity of a quiet peacebuilder long before I would applaud an articulate theologian who pushed women down and jumped on them.

Yoder has a place on our bookshelves, but not on a pedestal. The integrity of pacifist theology does not depend on Yoder. Idolatry of Yoder is wrong. First, it diminishes the voices of the victims he hurt. Second, it stumbles and contorts itself to align a theology of peace with the actions of an abusive man. Third, it pulls attention away from the many other pacifist voices whose lives and writings better illuminate the pacifist path. The authors of this book deserve to be read in their own right. They make important contributions to Christian pacifism. A new generation of Christian pacifists should be read not for their insights on Yoder, but for their own unique contributions.

(4) *Pacifism and feminism require the same ethical commitments.*

"This world is crazy." My daughter shook her head as I told her of Yoder's assaults. Like most women around the world, I have a duty as a mother to prepare my daughter to live in a world where some people will devalue her humanity and underestimate her intellect. She needs to learn how to respond to the epidemic of men who assault women (approximately one in three women will be assaulted in their lifetime).

There is no gap between pacifism and feminism. Ruth Krall taught me to ask this question: "Why is sexual violence and domestic violence tolerated by Mennonites when military violence is not tolerated? Both forms of violence shared in the sinfulness of the human community. Both destroyed human life and well-being. Neither represented a divine will for the human community."[11] So I explained to my daughter that as a Mennonite pacifist, feminist, peacebuilding practitioner, I care just as much about ending war in Afghanistan and Syria as I do about the safety of girls and women who suffer a shocking level of attack on their humanity. The link between public violence and private violence is evidenced in the rape of women in the midst of war, in the alarming rates of domestic abuse on military training bases, and in the level of sexual violence in the patriarchal church.

Unlike Yoder and many other Mennonite pacifist theologians, my life's work has been about connecting the public violence of war with the private violence of domestic violence and violence against women. Pacifism and feminism both recognize the dignity and humanity of all people while seeking to end the harm that comes in any act of violence, domination, or subordination. Weaver's book *The Nonviolent Atonement* is an example of a male pacifist who embraces feminism. Mast also cites feminist and womanist writers in this book. But all too often, women alone are left to speak out on sexual violence or devote their careers to the difficult work of raising issues of sexual violence in the church.

Feminism is a call to a new relationship between men and women based on mutual respect. Feminism fosters opportunities for women's leadership and appreciation of women's contributions to society. Feminism is the radical notion that women are human beings. Feminism

---

11. Krall, *Elephants in God's Living Room*, 20.

is not about hating men. Most feminists are married to men. Men can be feminists too. Feminism is inherently pacifist. There are no calls for women to take up arms against men or to punish men.

Feminism requires a commitment to stop sexual violence against women and men. Because there is so much violence in the world against women, many feminists are indeed angry and want to stop this selective violence. Feminism requires listening to women's unique perspectives, acknowledging the differences in men's experiences and women's experiences without deeming one more valuable than the other.

Peacebuilding is a process of putting hands and feet on pacifism and feminism. Peacebuilding requires practical strategies of empowerment, building relationships that illustrate the dignity of every human being, and advocating for just social relations. Peacebuilding requires that we view as equally damaging any harm done to children, women and men, to workers, to the environment, and to countries gripped by war.

When a country invades another country to secure its oil interests, that is violence. When a corporation exploits workers and destroys the environment, that is violence. When a man pushes a woman down and gropes her in his office, that is violence too. When the church criticizes women for naming abuse committed by a powerful church leader, and when it demands harmony, silences women's voices, and protects a perpetrator, that too is violence. An engaged pacifist theology needs to be concerned about all these forms of violence.

Yet to this day, there are two places where I am usually the only woman in the room: when I am training the military in peacebuilding and when I am discussing pacifist theology. When it comes to security and theology, the men who hold powerful positions in the U.S. military and in the church's theological institutions often actively exclude women's voices and approaches. What is the explanation for this? Are women less intelligent? Less ambitious? Do we have fewer opportunities for higher education? Are many women just not interested in security and theology? Or do men actively exclude, overlook, or even denigrate women because it is easier to work with "their own kind" and it can be difficult to "fit in" a woman's perspective?

In my opinion, women are left out of discussions on security and theology because we have a different set of experiences that lead us to hold different opinions. In both settings, we define violence differently. Some men are uncomfortable with our anger and our perspectives. So we are left out of conferences, books, and collegial circles between our academic peers. Because women's understandings of security and theology are so different, women also self-select not to put themselves in situations where they will be a minority voice. Women seek safer pastures in which to tend their intellectual sheep.

Future generations of pacifist theologians need to interrogate this pattern. Pacifist theologians need to engage directly with feminist writers. Pacifist theologians need to read and engage the community addressing sexual violence with the same intensity with which they address violence by the state. They need to study women's writings, advocate among men to stop violence against women, and illustrate with their lives their desire to empower women's leadership and to make space for women's voices.

(5) *Yoder and the Church that loved him damaged a radical pacifist agenda and undermined the politics of Jesus.*

Jesus questioned the authority and self-interest of Jewish leaders in his day. Early Anabaptists shared this skepticism of church and state authorities. Like Jesus, they seemed to have no interest in creating or maintaining institutions. As part of the Anabaptist tradition, Yoder questions church and state authority with a pacifist ethic. Unlike other theologians who seem to have more interest in consolidating the power and control of the church over its followers than in following Jesus, Yoder asks Christians to question authority.

In the authority-questioning tradition of Jesus and the Anabaptists, pacifist theologians should question the self-interest of the church in addressing sexual violence. Ruth Krall documents the Mennonite Church's delays in responding to Yoder's violence:

> For more than twenty years denominational administrative personnel officers and chief executives managed allegations, rumors, and gossip about Yoder's behavior by secrecy and by facilitating geographical and professional work relocations. They chose, therefore, a preferential option to maintain Yoder's theological career as a spokesperson for a Mennonite theology of non-violence and cultural identity rather than a preferential option to provide safety to vulnerable women potentially in Yoder's grasp. Thus, denominational leaders, knowingly or unwittingly, created a hostile religious climate in which Yoder's behavior could continue and proliferate. Victims and potential victims were left to fend for themselves. Ideology, institutional authority and denominational leader power, therefore, trumped

a viable living communal praxis of justice, accountability, individual healing and collective reconciliation.[12]

Women who did try to warn other women of Yoder's potential assaults were chastised for "gossiping" and disrupting the harmony of the church. When women later brought their stories—first privately and then publicly—to the attention of Mennonite leaders in the hope that they would stop Yoder's behavior, Yoder threatened a lawsuit against them and accused some of them of not being "sophisticated." Some people in the church accused them of making up the stories or of seducing Yoder themselves, asking, "Why didn't they just say no?" (Reports suggest that Yoder accepted "no" from some women, but harassed others for many months after they said no.) Some in the church accused the women of hurting Yoder's family and spreading false rumors. In other words, Yoder and the church punished the victims and the victims' supporters for speaking the truth.[13]

Yoder is responsible for hurting his victims. Yoder, not his victims, is responsible for hurting his family. And Yoder, not his victims or their supporters, are responsible for hurting the pacifist agenda.

Krehbiel argues the church's response was "too little, too late, and more about institutional damage control than about justice or healing for Yoder's victims."[14] While the field of restorative justice drew theological inspiration from Yoder's writings,[15] there was nothing restorative about the church's process of addressing Yoder's abuse. Restorative justice is victim-centered. Church institutions offered forgiveness to Yoder, not the victims. Restorative justice does not seek to punish. Rather, in restorative justice offenders acknowledge and take responsibility for the harms they have done to others. The church "punished" Yoder in a variety of ways, including banning him from attending church. But the victims were not in the center of the church's first attempts at addressing the abuse.

Some of the women who experienced Yoder's assaults wrote letters to him, first asking him to stop writing them inappropriate letters. Yoder did not stop. Some women also assert that they themselves wrote Yoder long letters detailing the pain and harm his assaults caused in their lives.

---

12. Ibid., 10–11.
13. This information comes from an e-mail exchange with one of the women who experienced aggressive sexual behavior from Yoder.
14. Krehbiel, "The Woody Allen Problem."
15. See Zehr, *Changing Lenses*.

Reportedly, Yoder never felt remorse for his actions that caused this pain, nor did he apologize directly to these women.[16] As noted earlier, his professional writing after the church process laid out a complex justification for his behavior and seemed to blame women themselves for the pain they suffered.

The church's efforts to protect Yoder's family also seem inept at best, if not a double victimization of their own suffering related to Yoder's actions. Yoder reportedly cooperated with church leaders in what may have been numerous painful meetings at the kitchen table, most likely led by well-meaning church leaders with little experience or knowledge of sexual abuse. Krall notes, "By not recognizing Yoder's suffering and by not recognizing the women's suffering their shared faith community failed in its collective spiritual task of bringing healing to them."[17]

The church has evolved in the last twenty years. There are new safeguards in place for women in the church. The Mennonite Church's process of discernment is a positive sign that the church is taking responsibility for addressing the harms that Yoder and the church itself did to Yoder's victims. Future generations of pacifist theologians will need to continue to challenge institutions to use a moral compass and not their status, power, or financial interests to guide them through the thicket of sexual violence in the church.

It is ironic that Yoder, the radical theologian, advocated biblical teachings on justice and peace with his words but led the church away from Jesus' radical teachings with his actions. In this book, Zimmerman quotes Yoder regarding the split between Swiss Reformer Zwingli and the Anabaptists: "To place the unity of Zürich above the faithfulness of the church is not only to abandon the church; it is also the demonization of the state, for persecution becomes a theological necessity."[18] In the same way, to place the unity of the Mennonite Church above the faithfulness of the church is not only to abandon the church; it was the demonization of the church, since the required silencing of women's voices—a form of persecution—became a theological necessity.

Naming wrongdoing by Yoder and the institutional church is not out of lack of care for Yoder's legacy or the church. Rather, it illustrates that we do care about the pacifist agenda and the integrity of the church.

16. Krall, *Elephants in God's Living Room*, 109.
17. Ibid., 150.
18. See chapter 2, "Sixteenth-Century Anabaptist Roots."

Future generations of pacifist theologians can restore credibility to pacifism not by downplaying Yoder's actions but by naming the abuses, lamenting the harm done to the victims and to Yoder's family, and working to end sexual abuse in the church.

(6) *Moving forward requires all of us to do things differently.*

The magnitude of the impact of Yoder's abuse and the church's long delays in addressing it require action to make things right. Peacebuilding requires truth-telling, victim-centered restorative justice, new initiatives to prevent future sexual violence, and both lament and trauma healing for Yoder's victims, family, and the church as a whole. Krall argues that in order to move forward, we need first to collectively reflect.

> [It is in] acknowledgement of the factual truth of an abuser's fully embodied life that we and future generations begin to free ourselves and our communities to make different behavioral choices than he chose to make during his lifetime. Acknowledging the legacy of good he did in his lifetime frees us from the need to demonize him. Recognizing the legacy of harm he did to us and to others frees us from idolatry. Once free, we can view his life as a precautionary tale that teaches us, and future generations, what not to do. In recognizing and speaking the factual truth of our lives, we individually and collectively free ourselves and future generations from the tyranny of his legacy of abuse. If we allow it to do so, a perpetrator's abusive life and the harm he did to others can serve as a searchlight that reveals the fault lines in the communal realities we once shared with him. If we allow his life, in all of its complexities, to teach us, we can examine the painful realities and fault lines of our own lives.[19]

Perhaps this book is a start on that journey. I laud the authors of this book for naming Yoder's actions as abusive and beginning to question the church that protected him. But there is more work to do.

Barbra Graber lays out specific strategies for moving forward. These include the following:[20]

1. Anyone writing or speaking about Yoder should directly name Yoder's actions as "sexual assaults and abuse" rather than call it

---

19. Krall, *Elephants in God's Living Room*, 61.

20. Graber, "What's to Be Done?" Barbra Graber is a retired professor of theater at Eastern Mennonite University and Associate Editor of *Our Stories Untold* (www.ourstoriesuntold.com).

"inappropriate behavior" or other ambiguous terms relating to his social skills.
2. Journalists should acknowledge the harm Yoder did along with his accomplishments.
3. Church leaders should commit to doing justice for Yoder's victims and in every sexual abuse case.
4. Men should learn more about sexual violence against women and take steps to address it in their own communities.
5. Peace and justice educators should make clear that sexual violence is an issue of equal concern as war and public violence.
6. Church leaders should speak out on sexual violence in sermons and in their congregational life, to enable public conversation to address private violence.
7. Victims should find ways to get support and voice their experiences, so as to prevent violence against others in the future.

I would add one more to Graber's list. The widespread impact of Yoder's theology on global scholars and practitioners requires a broader set of voices from authors of diverse identities. My colleague Howard Zehr has made a commitment to question any invitation to speak on a panel that is made up entirely of white men. White men concerned about peace and justice should make a commitment to advocate for the inclusion of women's voices and men of other ethnic and racial backgrounds in their professional speaking and writing careers. Like all people, white men are not objective or neutral. We are all subjective. White men's perspectives are valid and real. But because of society's structures, white men's experiences are different from others. Some of us have institutional power and others do not. So a further strategy for addressing Yoder's impact is to make a commitment that any edited book, conference, or panel about Yoder will include the voices of women, including those named at the beginning of this chapter, who write critically on Yoder's negative impact on pacifist women in the church.

This Afterword is just the beginnings of a map for future generations of pacifist theologians to bring together orthodoxy (right belief) with orthopraxy (right action). Addressing Yoder's violence is only a part of this peacebuilding process. Our larger task is to ensure that the radical message in some of Yoder's writings gets translated into radical acts of inclusion of other voices on pacifist theology so eloquently articulated in this book. Passing the pacifist torch requires that the church itself, and those leading pacifist theology, listen to the voices of those not in power.

Bibliography

Alexander, Michelle. *The New Jim Crow: Mass Incarceration in the Age of Colorblindness.* Rev. ed. New York: New Press, 2012.
Alexis-Baker, Nekeisha. "Freedom of the Cross: John Howard Yoder and Womanist Theologies in Conversation." In *Power and Practices: Engaging the Work of John Howard Yoder,* edited by Jeremy M. Bergen and Anthony G. Siegrist, 83–97. Scottdale, PA: Herald, 2009.
Allen, Bob. "Evangelicals 'Worse' than Catholics on Sexual Abuse." *Christian Century,* October 20, 2013, 16.
Amstutz, Jim S. *Threatened with Resurrection: Self-Preservation and Christ's Way of Peace.* Scottdale, PA: Herald, 2001.
Bainton, Roland H. *Christian Attitudes toward War and Peace: A Historical Survey and Critical Re-Evaluation.* Nashville: Abingdon, 1960.
Baker, Sharon L., and Michael Hardin, eds. *Peace Be with You: Christ's Benediction Amid Violent Empires.* Scottdale, PA: Cascadia, 2010.
Baker-Fletcher, Garth Kasimu. *Xodus: An African American Male Journey.* Minneapolis: Fortress, 1996.
Baker-Fletcher, Karen, and Garth KASIMU Baker-Fletcher. *My Sister, My Brother: Womanist and Xodus God-Talk.* Bishop Henry McNeal Turner/Sojourner Truth Series in Black Religion 12. Maryknoll, NY: Orbis, 1997.
Barnes, Michel René. "The Fourth Century as Trinitarian Canon." In *Christian Origins: Theology, Rhetoric and Community,* edited by Lewis Ayres and Gareth Jones, 47–67. London and New York: Routledge, 1998.
Barrett, Greg. *The Gospel of Rutba.* Maryknoll, NY: Orbis, 2012.
Barth, Karl. "The Church between East and West." In *Against the Stream: Shorter Post-War Writings 1946–52,* 127–31. New York: Philosophical Library, 1954.
———. *Church Dogmatics.* Edinburgh: T. & T. Clark, 1956–69.
———. *Community, State, and Church.* Gloucester, MA: Peter Smith, 1960.
Bartlett, Anthony W. *Cross Purposes: The Violent Grammar of Christian Atonement.* Harrisburg, PA: Trinity, 2001.
Beachy, Alvin J. *The Concept of Grace in the Radical Reformation.* Nieuwkoop: B. de Graaf, 1977.
Bell, Rob. *What We Talk about When We Talk about God.* New York: HarperOne, 2013.
Bender, Harold S. "The Anabaptist Vision." *Church History* 13 (1944) 3–24.
———. *The Anabaptist Vision.* Scottdale, PA: Herald, 1944.
———. "The Anabaptist Vision." *Mennonite Quarterly Review* 18 (1944) 67–88.
———. "The Mennonites of the United States." *Mennonite Quarterly Review* 11 (1937) 68–82.

Bibliography

———. "'Walking in the Resurrection': The Anabaptist Doctrine of Regeneration and Discipleship." *Mennonite Quarterly Review* 35 (1961) 96–110.
Bergen, Jeremy M. and Anthony G. Siegrist, Anthony G., eds. *Power and Practices: Engaging the Work of John Howard Yoder*. Scottdale, PA: Herald, 2009
Berkhof, Hendrik. *Christ and the Powers*. Translated by John H. Yoder. Scottdale, PA: Herald, 1977.
Biesecker-Mast, Gerald J. *Separation and the Sword in Anabaptist Persuasion: Radical Confessional Rhetoric from Schleitheim to Dordrecht*. The C. Henry Smith Series 6. Telford, PA: Cascadia, 2006.
———. "Slavoj Žižek, the Fragile Absolute, and the Anabaptist Subject." *Brethren Life and Thought* 48:3–4 (2003) 176–91.
———. "Towards a Radical Postmodern Anabaptist Vision." *Conrad Grebel Review* 13 (1995) 55–68.
Black, Edwin. "The Second Persona." *Quarterly Journal of Speech* 56 (1970) 109–19.
Blough, Neal. "Introduction: The Historical Roots of John Howard Yoder's Theology." In John Howard Yoder, *Anabaptism and Reformation in Switzerland: An Historical and Theological Analysis of the Dialogues between Anabaptists and Reformers*, edited by C. Arnold Snyder, translated by David Carl Stassen and C. Arnold Snyder, xl–lx. Kitchener, ON: Pandora, 2004.
Blum, Peter C. "Yoder's Patience and/with Derrida's *Différance*." In *The New Yoder*, edited by Peter Dula and Chris K. Huebner, 106–20. Eugene, OR: Cascade, 2010.
Boo, Katherine. *Behind the Beautiful Forevers*. New York: Random House, 2012.
"Books of the Century." *Christianity Today* 44 (2000) 92–93.
Boyarin, Daniel. *Border Lines: The Partition of Judaeo-Christianity*. Philadelphia: University of Pennsylvania Press, 2004.
———. "Judaism as a Free Church: Footnotes to John Howard Yoder's *The Jewish-Christian Schism Revisited*." *CrossCurrents* 56 (2007) 6–21.
———. "Judaism as a Free Church: Footnotes to John Howard Yoder's *The Jewish-Christian Schism Revisited*." In *The New Yoder*, edited by Peter Dula and Chris K. Huebner, 1–17. Eugene, OR: Cascade, 2010.
———. "A Tale of Two Synods: Nicaea, Yavneh, and Rabbinic Ecclesiology." *Exemplaria* 12 (2000) 21–62.
Brandon, S. G. F. *Jesus and the Zealots: A Study of the Political Factor in Primitive Christianity*. New York: Scribner, 1967.
Brandt, Di. "On line article." *Canadian Mennonite*, August 2, 2013, 13.
Brock, Rita Nakashima. *Journeys by Heart: A Christology of Erotic Power*. New York: Crossroad, 1988.
Brown, Joanne Carlson, and Rebecca Parker. "For God So Loved the World?" In *Christianity, Patriarchy and Abuse: A Feminist Critique*, edited by Joanne Carlson Brown and Carole R. Bohn, 1–30. New York: Pilgrim, 1989.
Brown, Raymond E. *The Death of the Messiah: From Gethsemane to the Grave: A Commentary on the Passion Narratives in the Four Gospels*. Anchor Bible Reference Library. New York: Doubleday, 1994.
Brueggemann, Walter. *The Theology of the Old Testament: Testimony, Dispute, Advocacy*. Minneapolis: Fortress, 1997.
Buckley, William F. "The Voice of America: Two Volumes of Political Oratory, from James Otis to Bill Clinton." Review of *American Speeches*, edited by Ted Widmer. *The New York Times Book Review*, January 7, 2007, 24.

Bibliography

Burke, Kenneth. *Language as Symbolic Action: Essays on Life, Literature, and Method.* Berkeley: University of California Press, 1966.

———. *A Rhetoric of Motives.* Berkeley: University of California Press, 1984.

Burrus, Virginia. *"Begotten, Not Made": Conceiving Manhood in Late Antiquity.* Stanford: Stanford University Press, 2000.

Calvin, John. *Institutes of the Christian Religion.* Edited by John T. McNeill. Translated by Ford Lewis Battles. Library of Christian Classics. Philadelphia: Westminster, 1960.

Caputo, John, ed. *Deconstruction in a Nutshell: A Conversation with Jacques Derrida.* New York: Fordham University Press, 1997.

Carter, Craig A. "The Liberal Reading of Yoder: The Problem of Yoder Reception and the Need for a Comprehensive Christian Witness." In *Radical Ecumenicity: Pursuing Unity and Continuity After John Howard Yoder*, edited by John C. Nugent, 85–105. Abilene, TX: Abilene Christian University Press, 2010.

———. *The Politics of the Cross: The Theology and Social Ethics of John Howard Yoder.* Grand Rapids: Brazos, 2001.

Carter, J. Kameron. *Race: A Theological Account.* New York: Oxford University Press, 2008.

Cartwright, Michael. "Radical Reform, Radical Catholicity: John Howard Yoder's Vision of the Faithful Church." In John Howard Yoder, *Royal Priesthood: Essays Ecclesiological and Ecumenical*, edited by Michael G. Cartwright, 1–49. Grand Rapids: Eerdmans, 1994.

Clasper, Paul. *Eastern Paths and the Christian Way.* Maryknoll, NY: Orbis, 1980.

Coakley, Sarah. *Powers and Submissions: Spirituality, Philosophy and Gender.* Oxford: Blackwell, 2002.

Cone, James H. *God of the Oppressed.* Rev. ed. Maryknoll, NY: Orbis, 1997.

Copley, A. R. H *Religions in Conflict: Ideology, Cultural Contact and Conversion in Late Colonial India.* Oxford: Oxford University Press, 1997.

Cragg, Kenneth. *Jesus and the Muslim: An Exploration.* London: George Allen & Unwin, 1985.

Cramer, David C. "Inheriting Yoder Faithfully: A Review of New Yoder Scholarship." *The Mennonite Quarterly Review* 85 (2011) 133–46.

Cullmann, Oscar. *The Early Church: Studies in Early Christian History and Theology.* Edited by A. J. B. Higgins. Philadelphia: Westminster, 1956.

———. *Jesus and the Revolutionaries.* New York: Harper & Row, 1970.

———. "The Kingship of Christ and the Church in the New Testament." Albert J. Meyer papers, box 1/40. Archives of the Mennonite Church, Goshen, Indiana.

———. "The State in the New Testament." Albert J. Meyer papers, box 1/40. Archives of the Mennonite Church, Goshen, Indiana.

———. *The State in the New Testament.* New York: Scribner, 1956.

Dalrymple, William. *Nine Lives: In Search of the Sacred in Modern India.* London: Bloomsbury, 2009.

Dante Alighieri. *The Divine Comedy.* Translated by Allen Mandelbaum. New York: Knopf, 1995.

Derksen, Kevin. "Milbank and Nonviolence: Against a Derridean Pacifism." In *The Gift of Difference: Radical Orthodoxy, Radical Reformation*, edited by Christ K. Huebner and Tripp York, 27–49. Winnipeg: Canadian Mennonite University Press, 2010.

Derrida, Jacques. *On Cosmopolitanism and Forgiveness.* New York: Routledge, 2001.

Bibliography

Dintaman, Stephen F. "The Spiritual Poverty of the Anabaptist Vision." *Gospel Herald* 23 (1993) 1–3.

Doerksen, Paul. Review of *Anabaptism and Reformation: An Historical and Theological Analysis of the Dialogues Between Anabaptists and Reformers*, by John Howard Yoder. *The Conrad Grebel Review* 24 (2006) 81–83.

Drake, H. A. *Constantine and the Bishops: The Politics of Intolerance*. Baltimore: Johns Hopkins University Press, 2000.

Dube, Saurabh. "Issues in Christianity in Colonial Chhattisgarh." In *Sociology of Religion in India*, edited by Rowena Robinson, 231–55. Themes in Indian Sociology 3. New Delhi: Sage, 2004.

Dula, Peter. "The 'Disavowal of Constantine' in the Age of Global Capital." In *Seeking Cultures of Peace: A Peace Church Conversation*, edited by Fernando Enns, Scott Holland, and Ann K. Riggs, 62–77. Telford, PA: Cascadia, 2004.

———. "For and Against Hauerwas Against Mennonites." *The Mennonite Quarterly Review* 84 (2010) 375–96.

Dula, Peter, and Chris K. Huebner, eds. *The New Yoder*. Eugene, OR: Cascade, 2010.

Dunne, John S. *The Way of All the Earth: Experiments in Truth and Religion*. New York: Macmillan, 1972.

Durnbaugh, Donald F. *The Believers' Church: The History and Character of Radical Protestantism*. New York: Macmillan, 1968.

———, ed. *On Earth Peace: Discussions on War/Peace Issues Between Friends, Mennonites, Brethren and European Churches, 1935–1975*. Elgin, IL: Brethren Press, 1978.

Dyck, Cornelius J., ed. *An Introduction to Mennonite History: A Popular History of the Anabaptists and Mennonites*. Scottdale, PA: Herald, 1967.

Eck, Diana L. *Encountering God: A Spiritual Journey from Bozeman to Banaras*. Boston: Beacon, 1993.

———. *A New Religious America: How a "Christian Country" Has Now Become the World's Most Religiously Diverse Nation*. New York: HarperCollins, 2001.

Elliott, Neil. "Romans 13:1–7 in the Context of Imperial Propaganda." In *Paul and Empire: Religion and Power in Roman Imperial Society*, edited by Richard A. Horsley, 184–204. Harrisburg, PA: Trinity, 1997.

Farmer, Paul. *Pathologies of Power: Health, Human Rights, and the New War on the Poor*. Berkeley: University of California Press, 2005.

Friedman-Rudovsky, Jean. "The Ghost Rapes of Bolivia: The Perpetrators Were Caught, but the Crimes Continue." *Vice.com*, August 5, 2013. http://www.vice.com/read/the-ghost-rapes-of-bolivia-000300-v20n8?Contentpage=-1.

Friesen, Abraham. *Erasmus, the Anabaptists, and the Great Commission*. Grand Rapids: Eerdmans, 1998.

Galli, Mark. "What We Talk about When We Talk about Rob Bell." *Christianity Today* 57 (2013) 34–39.

Garrett, James Leo, Jr., ed. *The Concept of the Believers' Church: Addresses from the 1968 Louisville Conference*. Scottdale, PA: Herald, 1960.

Gilligan, James. *Violence: Reflections on a National Epidemic*. New York: Vintage, 1997.

Gingerich, Ray C. "Theological Foundations for an Ethics of Nonviolence: Was Yoder's God a Warrior?" *The Mennonite Quarterly Review* 77 (2003) 417–35.

Girard, René. *Things Hidden Since the Foundation of the World*. Translated by Stephen Bann and Michael Metter. Stanford: Stanford University Press, 1987.

Graber, Barbra. "What's to Be Done about John Howard Yoder?" *Our Stories Untold*, July 17, 2013, .

Griffiths, Bede. *Christ in India: Essays Toward a Hindu-Christian Dialogue*. Springfield, IL: Templegate, 1984.

Grimsrud, Ted. "Against Empire: A Yoderian Reading of Romans." In *Peace Be With You: Christ's Benediction amid Violent Empires*, edited by Sharon L. Baker and Michael Hardin, 120–37. Scottdale, PA: Cascadia, 2010.

———. *The Good War that Wasn't—and Why It Matters: The Moral Legacy of World War II*. Eugene, OR: Cascade, 2014.

———. *Instead of Atonement: The Bible's Salvation Story and Our Hope for Salvation*. Eugene, OR: Cascade, 2013.

———. "Pacifism and Knowing: 'Truth' in the Theological Ethics of John Howard Yoder." *The Mennonite Quarterly Review* 77 (2003) 403–15.

Gundy, Jeff. *Songs from an Empty Cage: Poetry, Mystery, Anabaptism, and Peace*. Telford, PA: Cascadia, 2013.

Hallie, Philip. *Lest Innocent Blood Be Shed: The Story of the Village of Le Chambon and How Goodness Happened There*. New York: Harper Perennial, 1994.

Hanson, R. P. C. *The Search for the Christian Doctrine of God: The Arian Controversy, 318–381*. Edinburgh: T. & T. Clark, 1988.

Harder, James M. "The Violence of Global Marketization." In *Teaching Peace: Nonviolence and the Liberal Arts*, edited by J. Denny Weaver and Gerald Biesecker-Mast, 179–93. Lanham, MD: Rowman & Littlefield, 2003.

Harink, Douglas. *Paul among the Postliberals: Pauline Theology Beyond Christendom and Modernity*. Grand Rapids: Brazos, 2003.

Harris, Rabia Terri. "Nonviolence in Islam: The Alternative Community Tradition." In *Subverting Hatred: The Challenge of Nonviolence in Religious Traditions*, edited by Daniel L. Smith-Christopher, 107–27. 10th anniv. ed. Maryknoll, NY: Orbis, 2007.

Hartzler, John Ellsworth. *Education among the Mennonites of America*. Danvers, IL: Central Mennonite Publishing Board, 1925.

Hauerwas, Stanley. "The Christian Difference: Or Surviving Postmodernism." In *Anabaptists and Postmodernity*, edited by Susan Biesecker-Mast and Gerald Biesecker-Mast, 41–59. C. Henry Smith Series 1. Telford, PA: Pandora, 2000.

———. *A Community of Character: Toward a Constructive Christian Ethic*. Notre Dame: University of Notre Dame Press, 1981.

———. *Hannah's Child: A Theologian's Memoir*. Grand Rapids: Eerdmans, 2010.

———. *Sanctify Them in the Truth: Holiness Exemplified*. Nashville: Abingdon, 1998.

———. *With the Grain of the Universe: The Church's Witness and Natural Theology*. Grand Rapids: Brazos, 2001.

Heggen, Carolyn Holderread. *Sexual Abuse in Christian Homes and Churches*. 1993. Reprint, Eugene, OR: Wipf and Stock, 2006.

Heim, S. Mark. "No More Scapegoats: How Jesus Put an End to Sacrifice." *Christian Century* 123 (September 5, 2006) 22–29.

Heinzekehr, Hannah. "Can Subordination Ever Be Revolutionary? Reflections on John Howard Yoder." *The Femonite*, August 9, 2013. http://www.femonite.com/2013/08/09/can-subordination-ever-be-revolutionary-reflections-on-john-howard-yoder/.

Hellwig, Monika K. *Jesus: The Compassion of God*. Wilmington, DE: Michael Glazier, 1983.

Bibliography

Hengel, Martin. *Die Zealoten*. Leiden: Brill, 1961.
Hershberger, Guy F., ed. *The Recovery of the Anabaptist Vision: A Sixtieth Anniversary Tribute to Harold S. Bender*. 1957. Reprint, Scottdale, PA: Herald, 1970.
———. *War, Peace and Nonresistance*. Scottdale, PA: Herald, 1944.
———. *War, Peace, and Nonresistance*. Rev. ed. Scottdale, PA: Herald, 1953.
Hess, Cynthia. *Sites of Violence, Sites of Grace: Christian Nonviolence and the Traumatized Self*. Lanham, MD: Lexington, 2009.
Heyward, Carter. *Saving Jesus from Those Who Are Right: Rethinking What It Means to Be Christian*. Minneapolis: Fortress, 1999.
Holland, Scott. "Communal Hermeneutics as Body Politics or Disembodied Theology?" *Brethren Life and Thought* 40 (1995) 94–110.
———. "The Pietist as Strong Poet: A Brethren Corrective to the Anabaptist Communal Soul." In *New Perspectives in Believers Church Ecclesiology*, edited by Abe Dueck, Helmut Harder, and Karl Koop. Winnipeg: Canadian Mennonite University Press, 2010.
Hoover, Jon. "Islamic Monotheism and the Trinity." *The Conrad Grebel Review* 27 (2009) 57–82.
Hopkins, Julie M. *Towards a Feminist Christology: Jesus of Nazareth, European Women, and the Christological Crisis*. Grand Rapids: Eerdmans, 1995.
Horsley, Richard A. "The Death of Jesus." In *Studying the Historical Jesus*, edited by Craig Evans and Bruce Chilton, 395–422. Leiden: Brill, 1994.
———. *Jesus and Empire: The Kingdom of God and the New World Disorder*. Minneapolis: Fortress, 2003.
———, ed. *In the Shadow of Empire: Reclaiming the Bible as a History of Faithful Resistance*. Louisville: Westminster John Knox, 2008.
———, ed. *Paul and Empire: Religion and Power in Roman Imperial Society*. Harrisburg, Pa.: Trinity Press International, 1997.
Horst, Irwin B. *Mennonite Confession of Faith*. Lancaster, PA: Lancaster Mennonite Historical Society, 1988.
Hubmaier, Balthasar. *Balthasar Hubmaier: Theologian of Anabaptism*. Translated and edited by H. Wayne Pipkin and John Howard Yoder. Classics of the Reformation 5. Scottdale, PA: Herald, 1989.
Huebner, Chris K. *A Precarious Peace: Yoderian Explorations on Theology, Knowledge, and Identity*. Scottdale, PA: Herald, 2006.
———. "The Work of Inheritance: Reflections on Receiving John Howard Yoder." In *Power and Practices: Engaging the Work of John Howard Yoder*, edited by Jeremy M. Bergen and Anthony G. Siegrist, 19–27. Scottdale, PA: Herald, 2009.
Hunter, James Davison. *To Change the World*. New York: Oxford University Press, 2010.
Jasinski, James. "A Constitutive Framework for Rhetorical Historiography: Toward an Understanding of the Discursive (Re)Constitution of 'Constitution' in the *Federalist Papers*." In *Doing Rhetorical History: Concepts and Cases*, edited by Kathleen J. Turner, 72–92. Tuscaloosa: University of Alabama Press, 1998.
———. *Sourcebook on Rhetoric: Key Concepts in Contemporary Rhetorical Theory*. Thousand Oaks, CA: Sage, 2001.
Jenkins, Philip. *Jesus Wars: How Four Patriarchs, Three Queens, and Two Emperors Decided What Christians Would Believe for the Next 1,500 Years*. New York: HarperOne, 2010.

Jennings, Willie James. *The Christian Imagination: Theology and the Origins of Race.* New Haven: Yale University Press, 2010.
Jones, E. Stanley. *The Christ of the Indian Road.* New York: Abingdon, 1925.
Juhnke, James C. "Manifesto for a Pacifist Interpretation of American History." In *Nonviolent America: History Through the Eyes of Peace,* edited by Louise Hawkley and James C. Juhnke. Cornelius H. Wedel Historical Series 5. North Newton, KS: Bethel College, 1993.
———. *Vision, Doctrine, War: Mennonite Identity and Organization in America, 1890–1930.* Mennonite Experience in America 3. Scottdale, PA: Herald, 1989.
Kantor, Jodi. "Harvard Case Study: Gender Equity." *New York Times,* September 8, 2013, 1, 18–19.
Kateregga, Badru D., and David W. Shenk. *A Muslim and a Christian in Dialogue.* Scottdale, PA: Herald, 1997.
Kauffman, Daniel. *Doctrines of the Bible: A Brief Discussion of the Teachings of God's Word.* Scottdale, PA: Mennonite Publishing House, 1929.
Klaassen, Walter, ed. *Anabaptism in Outline: Selected Primary Sources.* Classics of the Radical Reformation 3. Scottdale, PA: Herald, 1981.
Kniss, Fred. *Disquiet in the Land: Cultural Conflict in American Mennonite Communities.* New Brunswick: Rutgers University Press, 1997.
Koop, Karl. Review of *Anabaptism and Reformation: An Historical and Theological Analysis of the Dialogues Between Anabaptists and Reformers,* by John Howard Yoder. *Journal of Mennonite Studies* 23 (2005) 277–79.
Krall, Ruth Elizabeth. *The Elephants in God's Living Room.* Vol. 3, *The Mennonite Church and John Howard Yoder: Collected Essays.* N.p.: Enduring Space, 2013. http://ruthkrall.com/downloadable-books/volume-three-the-mennonite-church-and-john-howard-yoder-collected-essays/.
Kraybill, Donald B., Steven M. Nolt, and David L. Weaver-Zercher. *Amish Grace: How Forgiveness Transcended Tragedy.* San Francisco: Jossey-Bass, 2007.
Krehbiel, Stephanie. "The Woody Allen Problem: How Do We Read Pacifist Theologian (and Sexual Abuser) John Howard Yoder?" *Religion Dispatches,* February 11, 2014. http://www.religiondispatches.org/archive/culture/7544/the_woody_allen_problem__how_do_we_read_pacifist_theologian__and_sexual_abuser__john_howard_yoder/.
Lasserre, Jean. "The 'Good' of Romans 13:4." In *On Earth Peace: Discussions on War/Peace Issues between Friends, Mennonites, Brethren and European Churches, 1935–1975,* edited by Donald F. Durnbaugh, 130–35. Elgin, IL: Brethren Press, 1978.
———. *War and the Gospel.* Translated by Oliver Coburn. Scottdale, PA: Herald, 1962.
Lederach, John Paul, and Cynthia Sampson, eds. *From the Ground Up: Mennonite Contributions to Internatonal Peacebuilding.* New York: Oxford University Press, 2000.
Leithart, Peter J. *Defending Constantine: The Twilight of an Empire and the Dawn of Christendom.* Downers Grove, IL: InterVarsity, 2010.
Lesher, Emerson L. *The Muppie Manual: The Mennonite Urban Professional's Handbook for Humility and Success, or, How to Be the Gentle in the City.* Intercourse, PA: Good Books, 1985.
Lichti, James Irvin. *Houses on the Sand? Pacifist Denominations in Nazi Germany.* New York: Peter Lang, 2008.
Liechty, Daniel. *Theology in Postliberal Perspective.* Philadelphia: Trinity, 1990.

Bibliography

Lind, Millard C. *Monotheism, Power, Justice: Collected Old Testament Essays.* Text-Reader Series. Elkhart, IN: Institute of Mennonite Studies, 1990.

Marpeck, Pilgram. "Exposé of the Babylonian Whore." Translated by Walter Klaassen. In *Later Writings by Pilgram Marpeck and His Circle*, vol. 1, *The Exposé, A Dialogue, and Marpeck's Response to Caspar Schwenckfeld*, translated by Walter Klaassen, Werner Packull, and John Rempel, 19–48. Kitchener, ON: Pandora, 1999.

Martens, Paul. "Discipleship Ain't Just about Jesus: Or on the Importance of the Holy Spirit for Pacifists." *The Conrad Grebel Review* 21 (2003) 32–40.

———. *The Heterodox Yoder.* Eugene, OR: Cascade, 2012.

Mast, Gerald J. "Anabaptism." In vol. 3 of *The History of Evil*, edited by Chad Meister, Charles Taliaferro, and Daniel Robinson. Durham, UK: Acumen, forthcoming.

———. "Bearing the Cross as a Way of Knowing." *The Cresset* 74 (2010) 6–13.

———. "Jesus' Flesh and the Faithful Church in the Theological Rhetoric of Menno Simons." In *The Work of Jesus Christ in Anabaptist Perspective: Essays in Honor of J. Denny Weaver*, edited by Alain Epp Weaver and Gerald J. Mast, 173–90. Telford, PA: Cascadia, 2008.

Mast, Gerald J., and J. Denny Weaver. *Defenseless Christianity: Anabaptism for a Nonviolent Church.* Telford, PA: Cascadia, 2009.

MCC Peace Section—Conferences. Puidoux I—Reports 1955, box 1/38. Archives of the Mennonite Church, Goshen, Indiana.

McKenny, Gerald. *The Analogy of Grace: Karl Barth's Moral Theology.* Oxford: Oxford University Press, 2010.

Meier, John P. *A Marginal Jew: Rethinking the Historical Jesus.* Vol. 2, *Mentor, Message and Miracles.* New York: Doubleday, 1991.

Menno Simons. *The Complete Writings of Menno Simons, c. 1496–1561.* Edited by John Christian Wenger. Translated by Leonard Verduin. Scottdale, PA: Herald, 1956.

Meyer, Ben F. "Jesus Christ." In *The Anchor Bible Dictionary*, edited by David Noel Freedman, 3:773–96. New York: Doubleday, 1992.

Míguez, Néstor Oscar, Joerg Rieger, and Jung Mo Sung. *Beyond the Spirit of Empire.* London: SCM, 2009.

Miller, Alice. *For Your Own Good: Hidden Cruelty in Chid-Rearing and the Roots of Violence.* New York: Farrar, Straus and Giroux, 1990.

Montel, Angela Horn. "Violent Images in Cell Biology." In *Teaching Peace: Nonviolence and the Liberal Arts*, edited by J. Denny Weaver and Gerald Biesecker-Mast, 223–34. Lanham, MD: Rowman & Littlefield, 2003.

Mouw, Richard J. *He Shines in All That's Fair: Culture and Common Grace.* Grand Rapids: Eerdmans, 2001.

Murphy, Debra Dean. "Bearing Witness in Contentious Times." *Sojourners*, May 2012, 38–39.

Murray, Stuart. *The Naked Anabaptist: The Bare Essentials of a Radical Faith.* Scottdale, PA: Herald, 2010.

Nation, Mark Thiessen. *John Howard Yoder: Mennonite Patience, Evangelical Witness, Catholic Convictions.* Grand Rapids: Eerdmans, 2006.

———. "The Politics of Yoder Regarding *The Politics of Jesus*: Recovering the Implicit in Yoder's Holistic Theology of Pacifism." In *Radical Ecumenicity: Pursuing Unity and Continuity after John Howard Yoder*, edited by John C. Nugent, 37–56. Abilene, TX: Abilene Christian University Press, 2010.

Niebuhr, Reinhold. *Moral Man and Immoral Society: A Study in Ethics and Politics*. 1932. Reprint, New York: Scribner's, 1960.

———. "Pacifism Against the Wall." In *Love and Justice: Selections from the Shorter Writings of Reinhold Niebuhr*, edited by D. B. Robertson, 260–67. Philadelphia: Westminster, 1957.

———. "Why I Leave the F.O.R." In *Love and Justice: Selections from the Shorter Writings of Reinhold Niebuhr*, edited by D. B. Robertson, 254–59. Philadelphia: Westminster, 1957.

———. "Why the Christian Church Is Not Pacifist." In *Christianity and Power Politics*, 1–32. New York: Scribner's, 1952.

Nugent, John C. *The Politics of Yahweh: John Howard Yoder, the Old Testament and the People of God*. Eugene, OR: Cascade, 2011.

Nyce, Dorothy Yoder, and Lynda Nyce. "Power and Authority in Mennonite Ecclesiology: A Feminist Perspective." In *Power, Authority, and the Anabaptist Tradition*, edited by Benjamin W. Redekop and Calvin W. Redekop, 155–73. Baltimore: Johns Hopkins University Press, 2001.

Olson, Roger E. *Reformed and Always Reforming: The Postconservative Approach to Evangelical Theology*. Grand Rapids: Baker Academic, 2007.

Oppenheimer, Mark. "A Theologian's Influence, and Stained Past, Live On." *New York Times*, October 11, 2013, A13.

Parler, Branson L. *Things Hold Together: John Howard Yoder's Trinitarian Theology of Culture*. Harrisonburg, VA: Herald, 2012.

Peachey, Paul. Letter to John Howard Yoder, April 4, 1954, John Howard Yoder Papers, Archives of the Mennonite Church.

Peterson, Eugene. *Eat This Book: A Conversation in the Art of Spiritual Reading*. Grand Rapids: Eerdmans, 2006.

Reimer, A. James. "The Nature and Possibility of a Mennonite Theology." *Conrad Grebel Review* 1 (1983) 33–55.

———. "Theological Orthodoxy and Jewish Christianity: A Personal Tribute to John Howard Yoder." In *The Wisdom of the Cross: Essays in Honor of John Howard Yoder*, edited by Stanley Hauerwas et al., 430–48. Grand Rapids: Eerdmans, 1999.

Rempel, John, ed. *Jorg Maler's Kunstbuch*. Kitchener, ON: Pandora, 2010.

Rieger, Joerg. *Christ and Empire: From Paul to Postcolonial Times*. Minneapolis: Fortress, 2007.

Roper, Lyndal. *Oedipus and the Devil: Witchcraft, Sexuality, and Religion in Early Modern Europe*. London: Routledge, 1994.

Roth, John D., ed. *Constantine Revisited: Leithart, Yoder, and the Constantinian Debate*. Eugene, OR: Wipf & Stock, 2013.

———, ed. *Refocusing a Vision: Shaping Anabaptist Character in the 21st Century*. Goshen, IN: Mennonite Historical Society, 1995.

Sawatsky, Rodney J. *History and Ideology: American Mennonite Identity Definition through History*. Kitchener, ON: Pandora, 2005.

Sawatsky, Rodney J., and Scott Holland, eds. *The Limits of Perfection: A Conversation with J. Lawrence Burkholder*. 2nd ed. Waterloo, ON: Institute of Anabaptist and Mennonite Studies, Conrad Grebel College, 1996.

Schirch, Lisa. *Ritual and Symbol in Peacebuilding*. Bloomfield, CT: Kumarian, 2005.

Scott, Joan W. "The Evidence of Experience." *Critical Inquiry* 17 (1991) 773–97.

Bibliography

Seibert, Eric A. *The Violence of Scripture: Overcoming the Old Testament's Troubling Legacy*. Minneapolis: Fortress, 2012.

Sharp, John. *A School on the Prairie: A Centennial History of Hesston College, 1909–2009*. Telford, PA: Cascadia, 2009.

Shastri, Sunanda Y., and Yajneshwar S. Shastri. "Ahimsa and the Unity of All Things: A Hindu View of Nonviolence." In *Subverting Hatred: The Challenge of Nonviolence in Religious Traditions*, edited by Daniel L. Smith-Christopher, 57–75. 10th anniv. ed. Maryknoll, NY: Orbis, 2007.

Shenk, David W. *Journeys of the Muslim Nation and the Christian Church: Exploring the Mission of Two Communities*. Scottdale, PA: Herald, 2003.

Sider, J. Alexander. "Constantinianism Before and After Nicea: Issues in Restitutionist Historiography." In *A Mind Patient and Untamed: Assessing John Howard Yoder's Contributions to Theology, Ethics, and Peacemaking*, edited by Ben C. Ollenburger and Gayle Gerber Koontz, 126–44. Telford, PA: Cascadia, 2004.

———. *To See History Doxologically: History and Holiness in John Howard Yoder's Ecclesiology*. Grand Rapids: Eerdmans, 2011.

Snyder, C. Arnold. "Doing History with Theological Ethics in Mind: John Howard Yoder as Historian of Anabaptism." *The Conrad Grebel Review* 24 (2006) 3–32.

Stassen, Glen H. "Concrete Christological Norms for Transformation." In Glen H. Stassen, D. M. Yeager, and John Howard Yoder, *Authentic Transformation: A New Vision of Christ and Culture*, 127–89. Nashville: Abingdon, 1996.

———. "The Fourteen Triads of the Sermon on the Mount: Matthew 5.21—7.12." *Journal of Biblical Literature* 122 (2003) 267–308.

———. "Grace as Participation in the Inbreaking of the Kingdom: Mountains of Grace Back Home." In *Engaging Anabaptism: Conversations with a Radical Tradition*, edited by John D. Roth, 61–74. Scottdale, PA: Herald, 2001.

———. *Living the Sermon on the Mount: Practical Hope for Grace and Deliverance*. San Francisco: Jossey-Bass, 2006.

———. Review of *Preface to Theology: Christology and Theological Method*, by John Howard Yoder. *Modern Theology* 21 (2005) 519–21.

———. *A Thicker Jesus: Incarnational Discipleship in a Secular Age*. Louisville: Westminster John Knox, 2012.

Stassen, Glen H., and Michael L. Westmoreland-White. "Defining Violence and Nonviolence." In *Teaching Peace: Nonviolence and the Liberal Arts*, edited by J. Denny Weaver and Gerald Biesecker-Mast, 17–36. Lanham, MD: Rowman & Littlefield, 2003.

Stassen, Glen H., D. M. Yeager, and John Howard Yoder. *Authentic Transformation: A New Vision of Christ and Culture*. Nashville: Abingdon, 1996.

Stayer, James M., Werner O. Packull, and Klaus Deppermann. "From Monogenesis to Polygenesis: The Historical Discussion of Anabaptist Origins." *Mennonite Quarterly Review* 49 (1975) 83–122.

Stendahl, Krister. "The Apostle Paul and the Introspective Conscience of the West." *Harvard Theological Review* 56 (1963) 199–215.

Stoltzfus, Philip E. "Nonviolent Jesus, Violent God? A Critique of John Howard Yoder's Approach to Theological Construction." In *Power and Practices: Engaging the Work of John Howard Yoder*, edited by Jeremy M. Bergen and Anthony G. Siegrist, 29–46. Scottdale, PA: Herald, 2009.

Sturzo, Luigi. *Church and State*. Notre Dame: University of Notre Dame Press, 1962.

Stutzman, Ervin. "John Howard Yoder Discernment Group." *Menno Snapshots*, September 23, 2013. http://www.mennoniteusa.org/2013/09/23/11987/.

Toews, Paul. *Mennonites in American Society, 1930–1970: Modernity and the Persistence of Religious Community*. Mennonite Experience in America 4. Scottdale, PA: Herald, 1996.

Tran, Jonathan. "The New Black Theology." *Christian Century*, February 8, 2012, 24–27.

Trocmé, André. *Jesus and the Nonviolent Revolution*. Edited by Charles E. Moore. Maryknoll, NY: Orbis, 2003.

Turner, Kathleen J. "Introduction: Rhetorical History as Social Construction: The Challenge and the Promise." In *Doing Rhetorical History: Concepts and Cases*, edited by Kathleen J. Turner, 1–15. Tuscaloosa: University of Alabama Press, 1998.

van Braght, Thieleman J. *The Bloody Theater: or, Martyrs' Mirror of the Defenceless Christians: Who Baptized Only Upon Confession of Faith, and Who Suffered and Died for the Testimony of Jesus, Their Saviour, from the Time of Christ to the Year A.D. 1660*. Translated by Joseph F. Sohm. Scottdale, PA: Mennonite Publishing House, 1950.

Volf, Miroslav. *Allah: A Christian Response*. New York: HarperOne, 2011.

———. *The End of Memory: Remembering Rightly in a Violent World*. Grand Rapids: Eerdmans, 2006.

Von Muralt, Leonhard, and Walter Schmid, eds. *Zürich*. Quellen Zur Geschichte der Täufer in der Schweiz 1. Zurich: S. Hirzel, 1952.

Waite, Gary K. *David Joris and Dutch Anabaptism, 1524–1543*. Waterloo, ON: Wilfrid Laurier University Press, 1990.

Walton, Robert C. "Was There a Turning Point of the Zwinglian Reformation?" *Mennonite Quarterly Review* 42 (1968) 45–56.

Walton, Zachary J. "Achieving an Anabaptist Vision: The Constitutive Rhetoric of Goshen Circle Mennonite Leaders." PhD diss., Southern Illinois University, 2011.

Ward, Graham. *Barth, Derrida, and the Language of Theology*. New York: Cambridge University Press, 1998.

Weaver, Alain Epp. "Missionary Christology: John Howard Yoder and the Creeds." *Mennonite Quarterly Review* 74 (2000) 423–39.

Weaver, J. Denny. *Anabaptist Theology in Face of Postmodernity: A Proposal for the Third Millennium*. C. Henry Smith Series 2. Telford, PA: Pandora, 2000.

———. "The Anabaptist Vision: A Historical or a Theological Future?" *Conrad Grebel Review* 13 (1995) 69–86.

———. "Atonement and (Non)Violence." *Epworth Review* 36 (2009) 29–46.

———. *Becoming Anabaptist: The Origin and Significance of Sixteenth-Century Anabaptism*. 2nd ed. Scottdale, PA: Herald, 2005.

———. "A Footnote on Jesus." *CrossCurrents* 56 (2007) 22–35.

———. "Forgiveness and (Non)Violence: The Atonement Connection." *The Mennonite Quarterly Review* 83 (2009) 319–47.

———. *Keeping Salvation Ethical: Mennonite and Amish Atonement Theology in the Late Nineteenth Century*. Studies in Anabaptist and Mennonite History. Scottdale, PA: Herald, 1997.

———. "Living in the Reign of God in the 'Real World': Getting Beyond Two-Kingdom Theology." In *Exiles in the Empire: Believers Church Perspectives on Politics*, edited by Nathan E. Yoder and Carol A. Scheppard, 173–93. Studies in the Believers Church Tradition 5. Kitchener, ON: Pandora, 2006.

Bibliography

———. *The Nonviolent Atonement*. 2nd ed. Grand Rapids: Eerdmans, 2011.
———. *The Nonviolent God*. Grand Rapids: Eerdmans, 2013.
———. "Response to Hans Boersma." In *Atonement and Violence: A Theological Conversation*, edited by John Sanders, 73–79. Nashville: Abingdon, 2006.
———. "Violence in Christian Theology." In *Cross Examinations: Readings on the Meaning of the Cross Today*, edited by Marit Trelstad, 225–39. Minneapolis: Augsburg Fortress, 2006.
Weaver, J. Denny, and Gerald Biesecker-Mast, eds. *Teaching Peace: Nonviolence and the Liberal Arts*. Lanham, MD: Rowman & Littlefield, 2003.
Weaver, J. Denny, and Gerald J. Mast. "Anabaptist Christology, Racial Reconciliation, and Postconservative Evangelical Theology." *Direction* 41 (2012) 125–38.
Wenger, John Christian. *The Doctrines of the Mennonites*. Scottdale, PA: Mennonite Publishing House, 1952.
———. *Glimpses of Mennonite History and Doctrine*. 4th printing, rev. Scottdale, PA: Herald, 1959.
———. *Introduction to Theology: A Brief Introduction to the Doctrinal Content of the Scripture, Written in the Anabaptist-Mennonite Tradition*. Scottdale, PA: Herald, 1966.
———. *Introduction to Theology: An Interpretation of the Doctrinal Content of Scripture, Written to Strengthen a Childlike Faith in Christ*. Scottdale, PA: Herald, 1954.
———. *Separated Unto God: A Plea for Christian Simplicity of Life and for a Scriptural Nonconformity to the World*. Scottdale, PA: Mennonite Publishing House, 1951.
———. "Sought and Found." In *They Met God: A Number of Conversion Accounts and Personal Testimonies of God's Presence and Leading in the Lives of His Children*, edited by J. C. Wenger, 169–75. Scottdale, PA: Herald, 1964.
Williams, Delores S. *Sisters in the Wilderness: The Challenge of Womanist God-Talk*. Maryknoll, NY: Orbis, 1993.
Wink, Walter. *Engaging the Powers: Discernment and Resistance in a World of Domination*. Minneapolis: Fortress, 1992.
———. *Naming the Powers: The Language of Power in the New Testament*. Philadelphia: Fortress, 1984.
———. *Unmasking the Powers: The Invisible Forces that Determine Human Existence*. Philadelphia: Fortress, 1986.
Wolpert, Stanley. *A New History of India*. 8th ed. Oxford: Oxford University Press, 2008.
Wright, N. T. *Jesus and the Victory of God*. Christian Origins and the Question of God 2. Minneapolis: Fortress, 1996.
Yoder, John Howard. *Anabaptism and Reformation in Switzerland: An Historical and Theological Analysis of the Dialogues between Anabaptists and Reformers*. Edited by C. Arnold Snyder. Translated by David Carl Stassen and C. Arnold Snyder. Kitchener, ON: Pandora, 2004.
———. "The Anabaptist Shape of Liberation." In *Why I Am a Mennonite: Essays on Mennonite Identity*, edited by Harry Loewen, 338–48. Scottdale, PA: Herald, 1988.
———. "Armaments and Eschatology." *Studies in Christian Ethics* 1 (1988) 43–61.
———. "The Authority of Tradition." In *The Priestly Kingdom: Social Ethics as Gospel*, 63–79. Notre Dame: University of Notre Dame Press, 1984.
———. *Body Politics: Five Practices of the Christian Community before the Watching World*. Scottdale, PA: Herald, 2001.

———. "The Burden and the Discipline of Evangelical Revisionism." In *Nonviolent America: History Through the Eyes of Peace*, edited by Louise Hawkley and James C. Juhnke. Cornelius H. Wedel Historical Series 5. North Newton, KS: Bethel College, 1993.

———. "'But We Do See Jesus': The Particularity of Incarnation and the Universality of Truth." In *The Foundations of Ethics*, edited by Leroy S. Rouner, 57–75. Boston University Studies in Philosophy and Religion 4. Notre Dame: University of Notre Dame Press, 1983.

———. "'But We Do See Jesus': The Particularity of Incarnation and the Universality of Truth." In *The Priestly Kingdom: Social Ethics as Gospel*, 46–62. Notre Dame: University of Notre Dame Press, 1984.

———. "'But We Do See Jesus': The Particularity of Incarnation and the Universality of Truth." In *A Pacifist Way of Knowing: John Howard Yoder's Nonviolent Epistemology*, edited by Christian E. Early and Ted G. Grimsrud, 22–39. Eugene, OR: Cascade, 2010.

———. "Chapter 5: With and Beyond Girard." http://www3.nd.edu/~theo/jhy/writings/punishment/girard.htm.

———. *Christian Attitudes to War, Peace, and Revolution*. Edited by Theodore J. Koontz and Andy Alexis-Baker. Grand Rapids: Brazos, 2009.

———. *The Christian Witness to the State*. Institute of Mennonite Studies 3. Newton, KS: Faith and Life, 1964.

———. *The Christian Witness to the State*. Scottdale, PA: Herald, 2002.

———. "Confessing Jesus in Mission." In *Christology after* The Politics of Jesus, 1–6. http://www3.nd.edu/~theo/jhy/writings/christology/confessing.htm.

———. "The Constantinian Sources of Western Social Ethics." In *The Priestly Kingdom: Social Ethics as Gospel*, 135–47. Notre Dame: University of Notre Dame Press, 1984.

———. "The Disavowal of Constantine: An Alternative Perspective on Interfaith Dialogue." In *The Royal Priesthood: Essays Ecclesiological and Ecumenical*, edited by Michael G. Cartwright, 242–61. Grand Rapids: Eerdmans, 1994.

———. *The End of Sacrifice: The Capital Punishment Writings of John Howard Yoder*. Edited by John C. Nugent. Harrisonburg, VA: Herald, 2011.

———. *Essential Writings*. Selected with an Introduction by Paul Martens and Jenny Howell. Modern Spiritual Masters Series. Maryknoll, NY: Orbis, 2011.

———. "The Evolution of the Zwinglian Reformation." *Mennonite Quarterly Review* 43 (1969) 95–122.

———. *For the Nations: Essays Public and Evangelical*. Grand Rapids: Eerdmans, 1997.

———. *He Came Preaching Peace*. Scottdale, PA: Herald, 1985.

———. "The Hermeneutics of the Anabaptists." *Mennonite Quarterly Review* 41 (1967) 291–308.

———. "The Hermeneutics of the Anabaptists." In *Essays on Biblical Interpretation: Anabaptist-Mennonite Perspectives*, edited by Willard Swartley, 11–28. Text-Reader Series 1. Elkhart, IN: Institute of Mennonite Studies, 1984.

———. *The Jewish-Christian Schism Revisited*. Edited by Michael G. Cartwright and Peter Ochs. Grand Rapids: Eerdmans, 2003.

———. *Karl Barth and the Problem of War, and Other Essays on Barth*. Edited by Mark Thiessen Nation. Eugene, OR: Cascade, 2003.

---. "Karl Barth: How His Mind Kept Changing." In *How Karl Barth Changed My Mind*, edited by Donald K. McKim, 166–71. 1986. Reprint, Eugene, OR: Wipf and Stock, 1998.

---. "Karl Barth: How His Mind Kept Changing." In *Karl Barth and the Problem of War, and Other Essays on Barth*, edited by Mark Thiessen Nation, 169–74. Eugene, OR: Cascade, 2003.

---, trans. and ed. *The Legacy of Michael Sattler*. Classics of the Radical Reformation 1. Scottdale, PA: Herald, 1973.

---. Letter to Harold Bender, January 12, 1951. Harold S. Bender papers, box 42, Archives of the Mennonite Church, Goshen, Indiana.

---. Letter to Paul Peachey, April 8, 1954. John Howard Yoder papers, box 11, Archives of the Mennonite Church, Goshen, Indiana.

---. Letter to Paul Peachey, June 15, 1954. John Howard Yoder papers, box 11, Archives of the Mennonite Church, Goshen, Indiana.

---. *Nevertheless: Varieties and Shortcomings of Religious Pacifism*. Rev. and expanded. Scottdale, PA: Herald, 1992.

---. "On Christian Unity: The Way from Below." *Pro Ecclesia* 9 (2000) 165–83.

---. "On Not Being Ashamed of the Gospel: Particularity, Pluralism, and Validation." In *A Pacifist Way of Knowing: John Howard Yoder's Nonviolent Epistemology*, edited by Christian E. Early and Ted G. Grimsrud, 40–57. Eugene, OR: Cascade, 2010.

---. *The Original Revolution: Essays on Christian Pacifism*. Scottdale, PA: Herald, 1971.

---. *A Pacifist Way of Knowing: John Howard Yoder's Nonviolent Epistemology*. Edited by Christian E. Early and Ted G. Grimsrud. Eugene, OR: Cascade, 2010.

---. "Peace without Eschatology?" In *The Royal Priesthood: Essays Ecclesiological and Ecumenical*, edited by Michael G. Cartwright, 143–67. Grand Rapids: Eerdmans, 1994.

---. *The Politics of Jesus: Vicit Agnus Noster*. Grand Rapids: Eerdmans, 1972.

---. *The Politics of Jesus: Vicit Agnus Noster*. 2nd ed. Grand Rapids: Eerdmans, 1994.

---. *Preface to Theology: Christology and Theological Method*. Elkhart, IN: Goshen Biblical Seminary; distributed by Co-op Bookstore, 1981.

---. *Preface to Theology: Christology and Theological Method*. Grand Rapids: Brazos, 2002.

---. *The Priestly Kingdom: Social Ethics as Gospel*. Notre Dame: University of Notre Dame Press, 1984.

---. *Radical Christian Discipleship*. Harrisonburg, VA: Herald, 2012.

---. "The Recovery of the Anabaptist Vision." *Concern* 18 (1971) 5–23.

---. *Reinhold Niebuhr and Christian Pacifism*. Scottdale, PA: Herald, 1968.

---. *The Royal Priesthood: Essays Ecclesiological and Ecumenical*. Edited by Michael G. Cartwright. Grand Rapids: Eerdmans, 1994.

---. "Sacrament as Social Process: Christ the Transformer of Culture." In *The Royal Priesthood: Essays Ecclesiological and Ecumenical*, edited by Michael G. Cartwright, 359–73. Grand Rapids: Eerdmans, 1994.

---. "Sacrament as Social Process: Christ the Transformer of Culture." *Theology Today* 48 (1991) 33–44.

---. "A Summary of the Anabaptist Vision." In *An Introduction to Mennonite History: A Popular History of the Anabaptists and Mennonites*, edited by Cornelius J. Dyck, 103–11. Scottdale, PA: Herald, 1967.

———. *Täufertum und Reformation im Gespräch: Dogmengeschictliche Untersuchung der frühen Gespräche zwischen Schweizerischen Täufern und Reformatoren*. Basler Studien zur historischen und systematischen Theologie 13. Zürich: EVZ, 1968.

———. *Täufertum und Reformation in der Schweiz. 1: Die Gesprache Zwischen Taufern und Reformatoren, 1523-1538*. Schriftenreihe des Mennonitischen Geschichtsvereins 6. Karlsruhe: H. Schneider, 1962.

———. "That Household We Are." Keynote address at the sixth Believers Church Conference, "Is There a Believers' Church Christology?" Bluffton College, Bluffton, Ohio, October 23-25, 1980.

———. "The Theological Basis of the Christian Witness to the State." In *On Earth Peace: Discussions on War/Peace Issues between Friends, Mennonites, Brethren and European Churches, 1935-1975*, edited by Donald F. Durnbaugh, 136-43. Elgin, IL: Brethren Press, 1978.

———. *To Hear the Word*. Eugene, OR: Wipf and Stock, 2001.

———. "To Serve Our God and Rule the World." In *The Royal Priesthood: Essays Ecclesiological and Ecumenical*, edited by Michael G. Cartwright, 127-40. Grand Rapids: Eerdmans, 1994.

———. "The Turning Point in the Zwinglian Reformation." *Mennonite Quarterly Review* 32 (1958) 128-40.

———. *The War of the Lamb: The Ethics of Nonviolence and Peacemaking*. Edited by Glen H. Stassen, Mark Thiessen Nation, and Matt Hamsher. Grand Rapids: Brazos, 2009.

———. *When War Is Unjust: Being Honest in Just-War Thinking*. 2nd ed. Maryknoll, NY: Orbis, 1996.

———. "You Have It Coming: Good Punishment." In *The End of Sacrifice: The Capital Punishment Writings of John Howard Yoder*, edited by John C. Nugent, 153-238. Harrisonburg, VA: Herald, 2011.

Zarefsky, David. "Four Senses of Rhetorical History." In *Doing Rhetorical History: Concepts and Cases*, edited by Kathleen J. Turner, 19-32. Tuscaloosa: University of Alabama Press, 1998.

Zehr, Howard. *Changing Lenses: A New Focus for Crime and Justice*. 3rd ed. Christian Peace Shelf Selection. Scottdale, PA: Herald, 2005.

———. *Transcending: Reflections of Crime Victims*. Intercourse, PA: Good Books, 2001.

Zimmerman, Earl. "Church and Empire: Free-Church Ecclesiology in a Global Era." *Political Theology* 10 (2009) 471-95.

———. *Practicing the Politics of Jesus: The Origin and Significance of John Howard Yoder's Social Ethics*. C. Henry Smith Series 8. Telford, PA: Cascadia, 2007.

Žižek, Slavoj. *The Fragile Absolute—or, Why Is the Christian Legacy Worth Fighting For?* London: Verso, 2000.

Index

A

Abraham (biblical), 36, 37, 38, 100, 101, 188, 211, 213, 274, 283, 320
Acosta, José de, 322
Adams, Ron, xvi
Alexander, Michelle, 307
Alexis-Baker, Nekeisha, 312, 369n53
Anselm of Canterbury, 17, 146, 309, 311. *See also* Atonement, satisfaction
Arius, 53, 55, 56n90
Athanasius/Athanasian Creed, 56n90, 270, 281, 286n51, 313, 314
Atonement, 2, 22, 33, 35, 40, 47, 136, 170, 182, 217n32, 251n21, 295, 299–301, 317, 333, 338n7, 366, 383
    Narrative Christus Victor, 299–313
    Satisfaction, 308, 309–12
    Substitutionary, 308, 311
Augustine, 17, 146, 213, 301

B

Baker-Fletcher, Garth Kasimu, 307, 308
Baptism, 66n118, 175n31, 95, 98, 100, 114, 129, 177, 228n7. *See also* Yoder, John Howard, baptism
Baptists, 75, 254
Barbour, Hugh, 256
Barth, Karl, xi, 21, 88, 93n10, 146, 147, 148, 163n54, 167–84, 242, 243, 258, 373
    Church Dogmatics, 168, 170, 171, 172, 175, 177, 179, 184n65
Basil of Caesarea, 54, 326
Bebbington, David, 326
Believers church, 4, 27, 59, 66n118, 67, 78, 101, 119, 174, 175n31, 177, 209, 210n13, 213, 300, 318
Bell, Rob, 331
Bender, Harold S. 17, 21, 88, 92, 93n14, 98, 116, 122–24, 127, 128, 129, 132–37, 141, 143, 208n5, 255, 361, 363
    "Anabaptist Vision," 21, 88, 116, 117, 118, 123024, 132, 136, 143, 184, 361, 362, 363, 368, 369, 370
Berkhof, Hendrik, 88, 148, 166, 192, 196, 197, 215, 216n27, 217, 218, 220n41, 267, 301n10, 347, 354n12
Biesecker-Mast, Gerald. *See* Mast, Gerald J.
Black Theology, 22, 295, 304, 305–8, 318–26, 386. *See also* Baker-Fletcher, Garth Kasimu; Carter, J. Kameron; Cone, James H.; Jennings, Willie James.
Bornkamm, Günther, 18
Boyarin, Daniel, 185, 269–71, 273, 274, 276, 279, 281–84, 289, 291, 292
Brandt, Di, 368
Brethren in Christ, 366
Brueggemann, Walter, 236
Bucer, Martin, 95n17, 96, 97
Burke, Kenneth, 119–21
Burkholder, J. Lawrence, 351n1
Burrus, Virginia, 56n90, 270, 271, 276, 281

C

Cadbury, Henry J., 18

413

Index

Calvin, John. *See* Yoder, John Howard, Calvin John
Capito, Wolfgang, 95n17, 96, 97
Carter, Craig, 7n19, 11, 20n49, 28, 62n108, 78n146, 131n50, 167, 177n43
   The Politics of the Cross, 7n19, 62n108, 78n146, 90n3, 93n11
Carter, J. Kameron, 305, 318–26
Catholicism
   Contemporary, 2, 22, 59, 62, 63, 89, 123, 180, 254, 256, 267, 276, 382
   Historic, 102, 103, 106, 107, 108, 118n4, 132, 133, 134, 138
Chalcedon (other than Yoder), 287n52, 313, 325
Challenge of Peace, 256
Childress, James, 262
Christian Century, 382
Christianity Today, 1, 331
Church of the Brethren, 256, 259, 357, 361
Churches of Christ, 209
Claiborne, Shane, 183
Coakley, Sarah, 231, 232, 233n25
Cold War, 147
Colenso, William, 322
Cone, James H., 304, 305–7, 311, 314, 315, 316, 319
Constantinople, 53, 60, 292, 313
Cosmology, 45, 69, 71n32, 72, 79, 83, 169, 184, 290, 291, 372
Cullmann, Oscar, 88, 145–66, 219, 220nn39 & 41, 258, 373
Culver Military Academy, 263

D

Daly, Mary, 386
David Joris, 356n20
Davies, W. D., 18
Derrida, Jacques, 168, 169, 241
Dintaman, Stephen F., 255, 363, 364n38
Disciples of Christ, 209
Domination System, 217, 219, 301
Drake, H. A., 104n48

Dula, Peter, 10, 13, 89n2, 90n3, 110n73, 219n38
Dunkards. *See* Church of the Brethren
Durnbaugh, Donald, 66n118, 151n18, 357n20

E

Eck, Diane, 268
Equiano, Olaudah, 322
Erasmus, 99n33, 113
Erb, Charletta, 378
Eucharist. *See* Yoder, John Howard, on Lord's Supper

F

Feminist theology, 24, 231, 311, 367, 383, 385, 386, 388, 389, 390
Fisher, Marian, 229, 232, 235
Forgiveness, xiii, 29, 33, 35, 36, 49, 50, 73n138, 214, 240, 241, 242, 251n21, 252, 254, 257, 259, 260, 339, 354, 368, 391
Franciscans, 142, 209
Free church, 89n2, 90, 101, 105n52, 110n63, 116n82, 130, 174–79, 184n65, 207–12, 215, 255
Freire, Paulo, 383
Friesen, Abraham, 99n33
Friesen, Duane, 255, 262

G

Galli, Mark, 331–32
Gandhi, Mahatma, 75, 245, 250, 254, 258, 266, 289, 290, 291, 386
Gelassenheit, 256
Gilligan, 335, 337, 338, 340
Gingerich, Ray, 93n12, 118n4, 310n24
Girard, René, 227n4 383n8
Gnosticism, 46, 47, 48, 49, 78, 319
Goshen School. *See* Bender, Harold S.
Graber, Barbra, 378, 393, 394
Grace, 36, 68, 74, 136, 155, 169, 171, 172, 173, 174, 182, 183, 188, 189, 206, 237, 240, 242, 253, 255–60, 299, 324, 327, 351, 352, 353, 357, 359, 360, 368, 370

paradox of, 299
Grebel, Conrad, 17, 94, 95, 107, 113, 117, 118n6, 125, 134
Gregory of Nazianzus, 54, 326
Gregory of Nyssa, 54, 223n47, 301, 319, 320, 326
Grenzfall, 172, 173
Grimsrud, Ted, xvi, 22, 185, 186, 356nn19-20
The Good War That Wasn't, 336
Gundy, Jeff, 361, 363, 365

H

Hamel, Johannes, 200, 234n27
Harris, Rabia Terri, 287
Hauerwas, Stanley, 4n8, 56n90, 70n129, 77n146, 89n2, 110n63, 175n31, 181, 182, 225n54, 249, 250, 341, 342, 343
Haustafeln, 198, 200, 201
Heggen, Carolyn Holderread, 378
Heinzekehr, Hannah, 378, 383
Hellwig, Monika, 287n52
Henry the Navigator, 322
Herzog, Frederick, 18
Hess, Cynthia, 353
Hinduism, xii, 22, 185, 261, 269, 284, 287, 288-91, 292, 348, 373
Hitler, Adolf, 154, 203, 258, 337
Holland, Scott, 361, 362, 363
Hubmaier, Balthasar, 228n7, 240n37
Huebner, Chris K., 7n16, 10, 11n24, 12, 13, 90n3, 174n29

I

Irenaeus, 301, 319, 320
Islam, xii, 22, 183, 185, 261, 268, 269, 272, 274, 284-87, 288, 289, 291, 292, 348, 373, 387

J

Jenkins, Philip, *Jesus Wars*, 55n89, 56n90, 61n104, 64n114, 116n82, 213n21, 27n9, 277n25
Jennings, Willie James, 305, 318-2
Joris, David. *See* David Joris.

Justin, 270, 272

K

Kabul, Afghanistan, 384
Kindy, Cliff, 183
King, Martin Luther, Jr., 75, 234, 235, 245, 254, 258, 266, 290
Koontz, Ted, 255
Krall, Ruth, 358, 378, 381, 386, 388, 390, 392, 393
Krehbiel, Stephanie, 378, 382
Kreider, Alan, 104n48

L

Lasserre, Jean, 148, 151, 153, 154, 166
Leithart, Peter, 104n48, 110n63, 111n67
Lessing, Gotthold Ephraim, 19, 67, 70, 73
Luther, Martin. *See* Yoder, John Howard, Luther, Martin

M

Mantz, Felix, 17
Martens, Paul, 7n19, 11, 79n150, 177n43, 178nn43 & 47, 220n41, 255
Martyrs Mirror, 15, 305
Mast, Gerald J., xvi, 14-16, 210, 21, 22, 23, 112n71, 139n78, 181n58, 185, 186, 295n2, 317n39, 353n2, 383, 386, 388
Defenseless Christianity, 217n39
Teaching Peace, 181n58
Menno Simons, 125, 209, 352
Miller, Alice, 335, 336, 337, 338, 340
Miller, Richard, 256
Montel, Angela Horn, 229
Murphy, Debra Dean, 210
Murphy, Nancey, 229

N

Narrative Christus Victor. *See* Atonement, narrative Christus Victor

Nation, Mark Thiessen, 5, 7, 11n27, 20, 62n108, 77n146, 93n13, 104n48, 116n82, 118n6
  John Howard Yoder, 7, 20n49, 77n146, 91n7, 116n82, 118n6
Nestorius, 60–61, 276n24
Nicea (other than Yoder), 270, 271, 286n51, 287, 313, 315
Niebuhr, H. Richard, 10, 14, 251
Niebuhr, Reinhold, 10, 100n33, 146, 246–47, 250, 267
Nisly, Weldon, 183
Nonviolence, 107, 148, 150, 234, 280, 289, 291, 309, 310, 367, 383, 384. *See also* Yoder, John Howard, Nonviolence
Nugent, John, 104n48, 239, 366, 383n8
Nyce, Dorothy Yoder, 367
Nyce, Lynda, 367

O

Olson, Roger, 295, 326–29, 331, 332
Oppenheimer, Mark, 380
Origen, 52, 53

P

Pacifism, 10, 379, 380, 383, 385, 386–95. *See also* Yoder, John Howard, Pacifism
Parler, Branson, *Things Hold Together*, 7n19, 11, 20n49, 55n89, 95n58, 62n108, 71n132, 80n151
Peacebuilding, 354n15, 363, 378, 379, 382, 384, 386, 387, 388, 389, 393, 394
Peachey, Linda Gehman, 378
Peachey, Paul, 16, 17, 91, 146
Penn, William, 250
Pentecostals, 258, 259
Peterson, Eugene, 235, 237, 238
Postconservative Evangelicals, 296, 326–32, 333
Price, Tom, 334, 341, 342, 343, 355n19, 356n20
Protestant Reformers, 92, 94, 103, 115, 136

Puidoux Conferences, 149, 151, 153, 154
Puritans, 258, 259

Q

Quakers, 75, 209, 211n13

R

Racism, 295, 302–08, 311, 314, 317, 318, 323, 324, 329, 338, 347
Radner, Ephraim, 354
Ramsey, Paul, 262
Rauschenbusch, Walter, 10, 79n150
Resurrection
  in Theology, 56, 155, 172, 173, 178n43, 217, 227–30, 243, 250, 256, 258, 282, 285, 298–301, 303, 308, 309, 316, 328, 329, 330, 331, 332, 351, 372
  New Testament, 30, 32–36, 38, 41, 43, 44, 68, 78n146, 113, 161, 188, 196, 205, 213, 296
Reimer, A. James, 7n19, 11, 93n11
Rhetorical analysis, 14, 15, 88, 105, 119, 117–44
Rieger, Joerg, 315, 316
Roth, John D., 255

S

Satisfaction atonement. *See* Atonement, satisfaction theory
Sattler, Michael, 94, 95n17, 96, 97, 101n38, 113n76, 118n6, 208n6, 280
Schirch, Lisa, xvi, 24, 362, 376
Schleitheim Articles, 15, 94, 95n17, 96–97, 101, 112n72
Sola scriptura, 105
Seibert, Eric, 366
Sermon on the Mount, 204, 248
Shank, David A., 242–43
Shank, Duane, 255
Sharp, Gene, 250
Shenk, David W., xvi
Shenk, Sara Wenger, 378

Index

Sider, J. Alexander, 4n8, 11n25, 56n90, 70n129, 77n146, 104n48, 147n6, 180, 214n24, 364, 365
Simons, Menno. *See* Menno Simons
Snyder, C. Arnold, 118n4
South Africa, 266, 322, 383
Stassen, Glen Harold, xvi, 18–19, 20, 22, 185, 246n6, 334
  Authentic Transformation, 18, 251, 252
  "Defining Violence," 246n6
Starhawk, 386
Staehelin, Ernst, 91
Stutzman, Ervin, 379
Substitutionary atonement. *See* Atonement, substitutionary theory

T

Tertullian, 52
Theodosius, 271, 273, 282, 292
Tolstoy, Leo, 245, 258, 290
Tran, Jonathan, 295, 318n40, 323n54
Trinity. *See*, Yoder, John Howard, on Trinity.
Trocmé, André, 88, 148, 149, 166
Troeltsch, Ernst, 10, 146, 248

V

Van Hulst, Fulco, xvi
Volf, Miroslav, 241, 242, 286n51

W

Waldensians, 137, 209
Walton, Robert, 131
Walton, Zachary, xvi, 21
Weaver, Alain Epp, 7n19
Weaver, Carol Ann, 386
Weaver, J. Denny, xi, 22, 73n138, 124, 135, 136n71, 139n78, 178n43, 181n58 185, 246n6, 251n21, 269n4, 275, 285, 287n52, 313, 366, 378, 383, 386
  Becoming Anabaptist, 209n9
  Defenseless Christianity, 217n39
  The Nonviolent Atonement, 217n32, 295n2, 302n11, 310n24, 323n54
  The Nonviolent God, 104n48, 251n21, 310n24, 366
  Teaching Peace, 181n58
Wenger, John Christian, 90, 116, 118n3, 124–26, 127, 133, 134, 135, 136, 137, 142, 143, 352
  Glimpses of Mennonite History and Doctrine,136
Westmoreland-White, Michael, 246n6, 334
Williams, Delores, 308, 311
Williams, Roger, 250
Williams, Rowan, 365
Wink, Walter, 192n15, 217, 224, 301n10, 335, 336, 339, 340, 347
Womanist theology, 308, 311, 312, 369n53, 386, 388
World Council of Churches, 9
World War II, 147, 148n6, 165, 218, 345

Y

Yoder, John Howard,
  Abuse, xii, xv, 23, 142, 224n53, 334–35, 339, 340–45, 349, 350, 355–58, 374, 376, 377–83, 385, 389, 391, 392, 393
  and Anabaptism, contemporary, xi, 5n9, 16, 18, 20, 22, 64, 66n118, 88, 110–16, 117, 143–44, 146, 147, 184, 185, 186, 208–10, 213, 215, 232, 258, 259, 276, 277, 278, 300, 330, 332, 344, 346, 350, 351–53, 355, 357–60, 361–70, 386
  and Anabaptism, historical, 13, 14–16, 17, 21, 23, 63, 88, 89–110, 175n30, 213, 228n7, 256, 280, 305, 317, 345, 348, 349, 356n20, 373, 390, 392
  Apostles' Creed, 20n48, 49–50, 53, 63, 138, 278
  and "Anabaptist Vision," 117, 118, 127–32, 137–42. *See also*, Bender, Harold S.

Index

Yoder, John Howard, *(continued)*
  on baptism, 96, 101, 102, 221–22, 303
  Body Politics, 83n156, 106n54, 112n74, 178, 180n55, 181n58, 185, 219–23, 240, 251, 252
  "But We Do See Jesus," 4, 5, 7, 8, 18, 19, 21, 28, 45, 59n101, 65, 66–76, 77n146, 78, 79, 83, 84, 146, 365, 371, 372, 375
  and Calvin, John/Calvinism, 17, 63, 99, 146, 182, 203, 278, 299
  Christian Witness to the State, 12, 78, 112n74, 154, 181n58, 218n34, 251
  on Christology, Chalcedon, 3, 7n19, 8, 11n27, 20, 27, 28, 55n89, 60–65, 76, 79, 81, 82, 83, 84, 116, 214, 275, 276, 277, 279, 281, 286, 318, 372, 374, 375
  on Christology, New Testament, 4, 5, 6, 8, 9, 19, 23, 27–48, 66–76, 83, 84, 87, 112–14, 115, 145–66, 187–206, 215–19, 290, 291–99, 305, 316, 317, 318, 320, 322, 323–25, 328, 330, 371, 372
  On Christology, Nicene, 3, 4, 7n19, 8, 11, 13, 14, 20, 21, 23, 50–59, 60, 61, 62n108, 65, 76, 77n146, 79, 80, 81, 83, 84, 115, 116n82, 147n6, 214, 275, 276, 277, 279, 281, 285, 286, 292, 314, 318, 325, 371, 372, 373, 375, 377
  on Constantine, 6, 13, 53, 59, 78n146, 92, 103, 104n48, 110, 111n67, 147n6, 150, 176, 177, 189, 204, 213, 214, 215, 219n38, 248, 272, 274, 276, 315, 355
  dissertation, 15, 17, 87, 89–116, 118n6, 127, 129, 277, 348
  on ecclesiology, 8, 13, 23, 27, 66, 67, 69, 71n132, 77n146, 78, 79n150, 83, 89n2, 92, 96, 99, 101, 105, 110n63, 119, 131, 137, 139, 142, 144,169, 171, 174–79, 184, 197, 208–12, 216n27, 224, 279, 300, 318, 352, 365

  For the Nations, 12, 13, 223–25, 250, 251, 254, 259, 261
  "grain of the universe," 32n15, 181, 225, 226, 227, 242, 246, 347
  interpretations of, xv, 1, 10–13
  Jewish-Christian Schism Revisited, 12, 22, 205, 211n16, 212n19, 238, 261, 267, 269, 274, 279, 280, 281, 347
  Jewish Jesus, 46, 69, 205, 211–13, 260–61, 270–74, 283, 289, 320, 324, 348, 373, 386
  on just war, xii, 22, 79, 156, 162, 248, 249, 258, 262–63, 266, 267
  Karl Barth and the Problem of War, 168
  on Lord's Supper, 221
  and Luther, Martin/Lutheran, 63, 99, 105, 118n4, 133, 134, 136, 137, 138, 150, 160n42, 209, 263
  methodology, xi, 1, 6, 7nn16 & 19, 8, 9, 13, 14, 15, 16, 21, 22, 23, 24, 27–85, 113, 129, 144, 187, 193, 246, 249, 253, 261n54, 263, 267, 295, 313, 318, 319, 325, 346, 349, 366, 371–75, 377,
  Nevertheless, 256, 258
  Nonviolence, 5, 10, 12, 13, 14, 20, 22, 27, 55n89, 69, 85, 115, 117, 142, 155, 156, 158, 162, 173, 181n58, 182, 185, 187, 197, 206, 216, 225, 227, 230, 235, 244–67, 291, 293, 324, 366, 373, 374
  Original Revolution, 5, 6n14, 12, 55n89, 158=59, 275, 346
  Pacifism, xii, 10, 12, 13, 22, 24, 88, 89n2, 110n63, 144, 148, 170–74, 212, 225, 226–27, 235, 236, 240, 243, 246–49, 251, 256, 257, 259, 261, 262–63, 266, 267, 281, 283, 289, 346, 348, 373, 377, 378, 379, 381, 386
  Politics of Jesus, 1, 2, 5, 6, 7n19, 10, 12, 14, 16, 17, 20, 32n15, 62n108, 93n12, 116n82, 146, 148, 149, 159, 181n59, 183, 187, 188, 189, 192, 205, 227, 228, 233, 234n27,

238, 245, 248, 251, 261, 269, 279, 295, 353, 367n46, 375n58, 386
and the Powers, 46, 88, 148, 189, 192–97, 215–19, 220, 224, 230, 267, 301, 336, 354n12, 367–68
Preface to Theology, 3–9, 12–14, 16, 21, 27–65, 66 67, 70n129, 71, 76, 77n146, 79, 82, 83, 102n42, 116n82, 146, 147n6, 187, 188, 205, 258, 259, 263, 264, 275, 276, 278, 286, 295, 313, 333, 371, 372, 395n58
Priestly Kingdom, 4n7, 6, 12, 13, 14, 15, 16, 71n132, 84, 112n74, 208n3, 218n34, 231, 251, 252, 365n42
as radical theologian, xvii, 9, 10, 13, 16, 18, 20, 21, 23, 27, 88, 92, 113, 142, 146, 147, 159, 166, 184, 264, 292, 317, 333, 344, 345, 349, 355, 357n20, 360, 368, 370, 375, 376, 377, 379, 390, 393, 394
Revolutionary subordination, 163–65, 189, 198–201, 206, 233, 234, 243, 369, 383–85
On Romans 13, 153, 159–63, 164, 189, 200, 201–5

on Trinity, xii, 2, 3, 7n19, 9, 11, 13, 14, 18, 50–59, 60, 63, 65, 76, 93n11, 231, 258, 259, 269–77, 284–87, 291, 292, 294, 313–17, 319, 325, 333, 372, 373, 374
War of the Lamb, 12, 20n48, 22, 73n138, 245, 246, 248–51, 258, 260, 262n55, 265, 267
When War Is Unjust, xii, 263

Z

Zealots, 157, 158, 272
Zehr, Howard, 335, 338, 354n15, 394
Zimmerman, Earl, xvi, 5n9, 16, 20, 21, 22, 82n155, 119, 144, 149n11, 167, 185, 187, 219n38, 277, 287, 288, 291, 345, 386, 392
Practicing the Politics of Jesus, xvi, 5n9, 16, 82n155, 89n1, 141n1, 149n11, 208n5, 345
Žižek, Slavoj, 363
Zurara, Gomes Eanes de, 322
Zwingli, Ulrich, 17, 63, 94–96, 98–101, 1–3, 105–08, 112, 113, 127–32, 133, 134, 137, 138, 141, 203, 280, 392

www.ingramcontent.com/pod-product-compliance
Lightning Source LLC
Chambersburg PA
CBHW021928290426
44108CB00012B/756